The Essential Aldo Leopold

Leopold recording the morning's observations, August 3, 1942. (Photo by Irving Buss. Courtesy Aldo Leopold Foundation)

The Essential
Aldo Leopold

QUOTATIONS AND COMMENTARIES

Edited by
Curt Meine & Richard L. Knight

The University of Wisconsin Press

The University of Wisconsin Press
1930 Monroe Street
Madison, Wisconsin 53711

3 Henrietta Street
London WC2E 8LU, England

www.wisc.edu\wisconsinpress

The quotation on p. xi from *Haroun and the Sea of Stories* by Salman Rushdie, copyright ©
1990 by Salman Rushdie, is used by permission of Viking Penguin, a division of Penguin
Putnam Inc., and the Wylie Agency, Inc. Quotations from *A Sand County Almanac and
Sketches Here and There* by Aldo Leopold, copyright © 1949 by Oxford University Press, Inc.,
are reprinted by permission of Oxford University Press, Inc. Quotations from *Round River:
From the Journals of Aldo Leopold*, edited by Luna B. Leopold, copyright © 1953 by Oxford
University Press, Inc., are reprinted by permission of Oxford University Press, Inc. Quota-
tions from *Auk* (American Ornithologists' Union), *Ecology* (Ecological Society of America),
Journal of American Forestry (Society of American Foresters), *Journal of Wildlife Management*
(The Wildlife Society), *Living Wilderness* (The Wilderness Society), *Missouri Conservationist*
(Missouri Department of Conservation), *North American Wildlife and Natural Resources Con-
ference* (Wildlife Management Institute), *Outdoor America, Outdoor Life, Outdoor Nebraska* (Nebraska Game and Parks Commission), *Passenger Pigeon* (Wisconsin Society of Ornithology),
Sunset Magazine, and *Wisconsin Agriculturist* have been reprinted by permission of their respective editors and publishers.

Library of Congress Cataloging-in-Publication Data

The essential Aldo Leopold : quotations and commentaries/
edited by Curt Meine & Richard L. Knight.
384 pp.   cm.
Includes bibliographical references.
ISBN 0-299-16550-7 (cloth: alk. paper)
ISBN 0-299-16554-X (pbk.: alk. paper)
1. Leopold, Aldo, 1886–1948 Quotations.   2. Naturalists—United States Biography.
I. Meine, Curt. II. Knight, Richard L.
QH31.L618.E77   1999
333.7'2—dc21   99-6424

To the descendants of Aldo Leopold
—familial and intellectual

Contents

Foreword

David Ehrenfeld

Different parts of the Ocean contained different sorts of stories,
and . . . all the stories that had ever been told and many that were
still in the process of being invented could be found here. . . . And
because the stories were held here in fluid form, they retained the
ability to change, to become new versions of themselves, to join up
with other stories and so become yet other stories; so that . . . the
Ocean of the Streams of Story was much more than a storeroom of
yarns. It was not dead but alive.
—Salman Rushdie, *Haroun and the Sea of Stories* (1990)

He who owns a veteran bur oak owns more than a tree. He owns a
historical library, and a reserved seat in the theater of evolution.
—Aldo Leopold, "Bur Oak," in *A Sand County Almanac* (1949)

As I look out the sealed window of the Environmental and Natural Resource Science Building where I work, I can see the middle-aged students who are taking the short course in Global Positioning System
Training and Certification. They are pacing slowly and solemnly about
the grassy circle in front of the building, staring fixedly at the GPS me-
ters in their hands, yellow equipment packs with stout antennas strapped
to their backs. Occasionally they pass the little bur oak that was planted
in the center of the circle last year—one of only five bur oaks on campus—and their antennas brush its leaves, but they don't notice; it has
no message for them. They are too busy, waiting for orbiting satellites to
tell them where they are.

The world has changed in many ways since Aldo Leopold died in 1948,
perhaps most of all in the barriers we have erected between ourselves
and nature. Yet Leopold's words remain as vivid and compelling as ever.
Never mind that increasing numbers of Americans have never seen and
never will see the mists advance "like the white ghost of a glacier . . .
riding over phalanxes of tamarack, sliding across bog-meadows heavy
with dew." Nor are they likely, any more, to experience "a single silence,"
which "hangs from horizon to horizon."[1] Leopold calls to something
deeper within us even than our personal memories, an elemental awareness of nature that resides in our cells and circulates with our blood. He
does this in one of the few ways left that can penetrate the defensive

shell of our unnatural civilization and reconnect us with the world out-side—he does it by telling stories.

Aldo Leopold was a storyteller, and the source of his stories, his master teacher, was nature. He admitted as much toward the end of his life, in "Wherefore Wildlife Ecology?": "I am trying to teach you that this alpha-bet of 'natural objects' (soils and rivers, birds and beasts) spells out a story, which he who runs may read—if he knows how. Once you learn to read the land, I have no fear of what you will do to it, or with it. And I know many pleasant things it will do to you."[2]

Most of the stories that Leopold tells are not long and formal like the history, recorded in *A Sand County Almanac,* of the celebrated lightning-killed oak he and his wife, Estella, sawed for firewood on his Wisconsin farm one crisp February day. That chronology, traced through the eighty annual rings traversed by the singing saw, took twelve pages to tell. More often, Leopold's stories are brief, as concise as poetry: "In the creek-bottom pasture, flood trash is lodged high in the bushes. The creek banks are raw; chunks of Illinois have sloughed off and moved seaward. Patches of giant ragweed mark where freshets have thrown down the silt they could not carry."[3] And some of his stories are shorter still, at least in their essential elements: "just as a deer herd lives in mortal fear of its wolves, so does a mountain live in mortal fear of its deer."[4]

The language that Leopold used is as elegant as it is effective. In our times, when television and networks of electronic communication re-quire a ceaseless outpouring of words to stave off the new devil of si-lence, language often becomes a mere stitching together of stale phrases. Even a Dickens might have trouble maintaining inventiveness in the face of such an unholy demand for utterance. Against this drab background the words of Aldo Leopold stand out like a snow-covered mountain peak rising above a layer of smog. When he writes, "To build a road is so much simpler than to think of what the country really needs," we feel a fresh wind blowing.[5] We are invigorated not only be-cause what he says makes sense, but because these seventeen words and only twenty syllables exercise the full healing power of English at its best.

Why are Leopold's words and stories so perpetually alive, his wisdom so enduring? I am not the first to recognize that there are two interde-pendent elements that mark this kind of great writing. First, we can only state with clarity the things we know well; and then we must find the right words to clothe our thoughts. I do not know where Leopold acquired his exceptional ability to clothe his thoughts in words, but I think I know where he discovered the meaning he conveyed so lastingly. He found it in nature.

Aldo Leopold's genius included the gift of perceiving and untangling the myriad, interwoven, multicolored streams of story in the nature that flowed unceasingly around him. He could read the landscape as easily as we read the words he wrote about it. Leopold first developed this ability in his earliest childhood days on the banks of the Mississippi River in Iowa and later honed his talents in places as widely separated as the wooded hills of central New Jersey and the forests of Germany and New Mexico. He saw and understood nature everywhere, not just in wilderness but along railroad tracks and roadsides, in cemeteries and farmyards. Wherever he was, he was aware of the process and story in the life around him. In these, as in all stories, there is not only a present but a past and a probable future. Leopold wrote: "To see merely what a range is or has is to see nothing. To see *why* it is, how it *became,* and the direction and velocity of its changes—this is the great drama of the land."[6]

Thus the land told its stories to Aldo Leopold; he listened and he passed the stories on. Sometimes they speak in feelings:

> The sadness discernible in some marshes arises, perhaps, from their once having harbored cranes. Now they stand humbled, adrift in history.[7]

Sometimes they speak in music:

> In the German forest—that forest which inspired the *Erlkönig*—one now hears only a dismal fugue out of the timeless reaches of the carboniferous.[8]

Sometimes they speak in the metaphors of art:

> The landscape of any farm is the owner's portrait of himself.[9]

Always they show us nature flowing through time, as stories do.

From stories comes understanding, from understanding, love. Aldo Leopold said it explicitly: "We love (and make intelligent use of) what we have learned to understand."[10] This is the message of his writing and the heart of his conservation philosophy. The land is safe with those who listen to its stories.

Introduction

In the autumn of 1949 a modest collection of essays on natural history and conservation appeared under the unassuming title *A Sand County Almanac and Sketches Here and There*. Its author, Aldo Leopold, was a highly respected figure within conservation circles, having made fundamental contributions to forestry, wildlife ecology and management, wilderness protection, and other fields during a forty-year career as a land manager, scientist, teacher, writer, and advocate. *A Sand County Almanac* would be Leopold's valedictory contribution to conservation. In April 1948, just one week after learning that Oxford University Press had accepted his manuscript for publication, Leopold died while fighting a grass fire on a neighbor's property near his family's "shack" in central Wisconsin.

With publication of *A Sand County Almanac* the ripples from Aldo Leopold's lifework began to move out beyond the core audience of conservation professionals. Leopold's insight into the complex "delights and dilemmas" of conservation allowed readers from all walks of life to fathom the far-reaching implications of our altered relationship with "things natural, wild, and free."[1] Aldo Leopold changed the course of conservation: the way we think about it, the way we do it, the priority we give it on the roster of contemporary concerns, the connections we recognize between it and other domains of our lives. He saw clearly that environmental challenges could not be met through superficial solutions; rather, they require constant self-examination of means and ends, of perceptions and values. Conservation by definition involves the ways in which we shape our hearts and our minds, and the social costs and benefits we assign in what he sometimes called "our land relations."

But keen insight alone cannot account for Leopold's continuing influence. It was the evocative literary voice that gave *A Sand County Almanac* its staying power. As successive generations of readers have come to the *Almanac*, Leopold's ideas have remained vital in no small part because his writing remains vivid and distinct. With a handful of others Leopold stands as one of the twentieth century's preeminent conservation leaders. And as robust (to use Wes Jackson's word from this volume) as Leopold's vision was, his influence is likely to extend well into the next century.

The power of *A Sand County Almanac* reflects the lifetime of dedicated work, thought, and writing that preceded it. Leopold was a prolific writer throughout his career, his publications invariably tracking the leading trends in conservation science, philosophy, policy, and practice. Many of these lesser known writings have been made available to the public through the collections *Round River: From the Journals of Aldo Leopold* (1953), *Aldo Leopold's Wilderness: Selected Early Writings by the Author of "A Sand County Almanac"* (1990; reprinted as *Aldo Leopold's Southwest*, 1995), and *The River of the Mother of God and Other Essays by Aldo Leopold* (1991).[2] However, a substantial amount of Leopold's writing remains inaccessible, buried deep in library and archival sediments. In this volume we have tried to gather up the well-known gems, but also to unearth other enduring nuggets of Leopold's prose.

In the essay "Good Oak" from *A Sand County Almanac*, Leopold described how, in his local Wisconsin landscape, the preponderance of surviving oak seedlings at any given time can indicate the relative scarcity or abundance of seedling-nibbling rabbits. "Some day," he wrote, "some patient botanist will draw a frequency curve of oak birth-years, and show that the curve humps every ten years, each hump originating from a low in the ten-year rabbit cycle."[3] Just so may a patient historian someday trace the record of conservation thought by examining the frequency with which certain passages from Leopold have been invoked.

For example, as the environmental movement gathered momentum in the 1960s and 1970s, the following passage from "The Land Ethic" rose to prominence: "Quit thinking about decent land-use as solely an economic problem. Examine each question in terms of what is ethically and esthetically right, as well as what is economically expedient. A thing is right when it tends to preserve the integrity, stability, and beauty of the biotic community. It is wrong when it tends otherwise."[4] This famous passage, which J. Baird Callicott has characterized as Leopold's "summary moral maxim," reflected the need for guidelines by which reformers of the time could challenge the environmental status quo.[5] Yet it served a less immediate purpose as well. It became one of the cornerstones upon which a more elaborate construction of thought—the burgeoning field of environmental ethics—could be and has been built. It probably remains the "all-time leader" in overall citations of Leopold.

But as ideas and attentions in conservation shift, so do the uses of Leopold's legacy. Since the early 1980s conservationists have focused increasingly on the functions of ecosystems, the value of biodiversity in natural systems, and the magnitude of biodiversity loss locally and globally. Another Leopold passage has accordingly became ascendant: "If the biota, in the course of aeons, has built something we like but do not understand, then who but a fool would discard seemingly useless parts?

To keep every cog and wheel is the first precaution of intelligent tinkering."[6] Leopold deemed this the "first principle of conservation," and his simple metaphor has been widely used in both popular and professional contexts. The passage has been constructively criticized, yet it still manages to convey the essential shift that has taken place in environmental conservation during this period: toward recognition of the basic importance of keeping, and where necessary restoring, biological diversity and ecological processes to maintain ecosystem health.

Our future historian may find other, more subtle trends hidden amid the numbers of the raw citation index. And not all of the trends may be so broad or conceptual. The following sentence seems to have gained ground recently, and not merely in print or conference halls, but in quiet conversations at the end of the day: "One of the penalties of an ecological education is that one lives alone in a world of wounds."[7] Leopold touched a nerve with that one. Every conservationist must develop something of a hardened shell, but every hardened shell has its weak point. The emotional costs of conservation work are not always easy to bear, and many have found comfort in these words from an elder. There may be comfort as well in the fact that, through his writing, Leopold helped to ensure that future conservationists would not feel quite so alone.

The quoting of Leopold, then, offers a fair barometer by which to measure the changing conditions of conservation. This collection is intended to serve as a repository and a reference, but above all as a resource. Aldo Leopold was a creative reader of history, of the landscape, and of the written word. He could draw insight from the scratches on a pine board washed up along a riverbank, from the "clear tenor chant" of a field sparrow at dawn, from a colleague's latest research findings, from an Old Testament passage remembered from his youth. There is no predicting which of the gleanings in this collection may inspire a new thought or enrich a new trend in conservation. All that we may safely say is that such creativity will become even more necessary in conservation's next century.

The quotations we have selected for this collection are drawn from the wide range of Leopold's published works: the two books that appeared during his lifetime; *A Sand County Almanac;* collections published after his death; and the several hundred articles, essays, commentaries, reviews, and other items from his extensive bibliography. We have also drawn upon reports of the many committees on which Leopold served (and for which he almost invariably served as lead writer). Included as well are several key passages from manuscripts and other unpublished documents.

Although we have followed no single formula or standard, several basic criteria guided our selections. These passages are of historic significance; they distill a thought; they provide insight into Leopold's intellectual and emotional growth; they are felicitous of phrase; they are expressions of Leopold's distinctive style. Our choices no doubt reflect our own biases, but we have sought to identify most if not all of the key passages from Leopold's written record. We hasten to add, however, that we have hardly exhausted the possibilities. That record remains a rich source for those who wish to dig even deeper.

In bringing this collection together we faced several basic dilemmas. First, we have had to wrestle with a paradox. Leopold was a model generalist and synthesizer who was also proficient in conservation's many subspecialties. Indeed, the great value of Leopold's legacy rests in its breadth, balance, and integrity. In his own lifetime he both witnessed and bemoaned the balkanization of the conservation movement, and he worked explicitly to counter it. In a review of a 1940 conservation textbook that bore the marks of this segregation of interests, he complained: "No one seems yet to have questioned the sufficiency of this 'compartmental' scheme for describing the behavior of land under human use. I do. It is too much like describing the 'separate' organs of an animal or plant, and then leaving to inference their collective behavior as an organism."[8] We have chosen nonetheless to organize the selected quotations by subject area. The reader should constantly bear in mind, however, that these areas not only overlapped in Leopold's mind and in his experience, but impinged upon one another. The boundaries between these topic areas are (and, in our own view, should be) fuzzy. Many quotations could have been placed within any of a half dozen different topic areas. The discerning reader will in fact detect a progressive integration of Leopold's thought as he matured. Thus these chapters may best be thought of as transects through the wide open range of Leopold's literary estate. They take the measure along a line of thought, and they cross over other transects. The total effort, we hope, gives the reader a feel for the dynamics of Leopold's ecological conscience at work.

Our second dilemma involved the fact that Leopold, far from being born with the wisdom of a sage, came to his insights through long and often difficult experience in the field, office, classroom, and meeting hall. Leopold's views on many key conservation issues—for example, the functions of predators and fire in natural systems, the appropriate role of government in conservation, and the varied values of wilderness— changed over the course of his career. The *essence* of Leopold lay not just in the conclusions he reached but in the process by which he reached them. And so in each chapter we have offered not just his ultimate statements but quotations that show the development of Leopold's thinking in that area.

Finally, the reader should also consider that these quotations are presented *ex situ;* that is, they are taken out of their direct literary context as well as the context of events in Leopold's life. The living sense of a word or sentence or paragraph, like that of a gene or species or habitat, can be fully understood or appreciated only *in situ*—in relation, that is, to its narrative environment. And so we encourage the more adventurous reader to seek out the original sources, to read Leopold in his own time and place.

Aldo Leopold's is a living legacy. The ideas, principles, questions, concerns, and hopes to which he gave voice continue to challenge conservationists and citizens in general. In the varied fields to which Leopold contributed, practitioners have extended and modified—and sometimes contradicted—his thought. This critical examination of accepted thought is in itself a hallmark of Leopold's legacy as an original and provocative thinker. On difficult conservation questions, he once observed, "there is confusion of counsel, and only the most uncritical minds are free from doubt."[9] Conservation grows, often painfully, in response to new demands, new information, new organizing concepts, and new social and political realities.

To help place Leopold's contributions in historical context, but also to connect them to current conditions and future concerns, we have invited leading contemporary voices to offer introductory commentaries for each of the chapters. All of our commentators have found Leopold's work to be a rich source for their own innovations. Collectively they demonstrate the creative influence that Leopold had in his lifetime, and in the decades since, on a wide range of disciplines and callings. We have asked the contributors to review Leopold's words, to orient the reader, and to gauge Leopold's influence within their area of expertise. We have also encouraged them, however, to speak their own hearts and minds, to extend Leopold's legacy according to their own insights. The result, we hope, is a fair snapshot of Leopold's legacy as we embark upon the next millennium.

We are, as N. Scott Momaday has so powerfully remarked, "made of words."[10] We find wonder in the world, and bring order to the world, through our songs and stories, poems and formulas, memories and prayers. Words identify us. Aldo Leopold crafted words with care and respect, using them as sparingly as, during his Wisconsin years, he used exotic woods to craft fine arrows in his basement workshop. He sought to make his words, like his arrows, fly true.

Leopold's words could carry great weight without themselves overburdening the reader. This may have been because, as greatly as he respected words, he respected silence even more, and understood well the background against which he was working. In his essay "Song of the Gavilan," Leopold recalled the ambient music of the wild waters and hills in Mexico's Sierra Madre Occidental: "On a still night, when the campfire is low and the Pleiades have climbed over rimrocks, sit quietly and listen for a wolf to howl, and think hard of everything you have seen and tried to understand. Then you may hear it—a vast pulsing harmony—its score inscribed on a thousand hills, its notes the lives and deaths of plants and animals, its rhythms spanning the seconds and the centuries."[11] Leopold set words to music. He found his muses in many places, and many have found theirs in part through him. The words in this collection are offered in the hope that they may help to conserve both the places and the muses.

Editors' Note

We have arranged the quotations in each chapter of this volume in as close to chronological order as can be determined from the bibliographic and archival records. A list of sources, in the order of their original publication, is at the end of the volume. A comprehensive chronological list of the publications of Aldo Leopold can be found in *The River of the Mother of God and Other Essays by Aldo Leopold* (pp. 349–70).

In most cases the quotations could easily be placed in chronological order. Occasionally, however, choosing among different text versions, and hence providing dates, proved problematic. Aldo Leopold regularly revised his own writings as opportunities for republication of his work arose. A given passage may have appeared in print several times during his lifetime, Leopold fine-tuning his prose at each turn. In addition, many of his writings first appeared in print only posthumously.

To resolve these difficulties, we have adhered to the following method.

- For all quotations, a date of publication or composition is provided.
- For materials first published during Leopold's lifetime, the date and the title of the original publication are provided.
- For materials first published in *A Sand County Almanac,* the date "1949" is used.
- For materials that had been published earlier and that were incorporated into *A Sand County Almanac,* the date and the title of the original publication are given. We have chosen, however, to use the text from the *Almanac,* to accommodate any final adjustments Leopold may have made in language. In most cases, the differences between versions of a given passage are minor. For two essays, however—"Wilderness" and "The Land Ethic"—the distinctions are more important. Both essays were newly synthesized for the *Almanac,* with Leopold extracting, revising, and melding passages from older essays, and supplementing them with new text. In some instances we have provided a cross-reference to the earlier essay; the notation "cf." indicates that the versions differ.
- For materials first published in *Round River,* the date of composition is given.
- Quotations from materials that remain unpublished (or that, in a few cases, have been published only in part) are indicated by the abbrevi-

ation "ms." Most of these works date from the 1940s. Where the exact date of composition is unknown, an approximate date is provided (e.g., "c. 1942").

To assist the reader in referring to the full text from which a quotation has been selected, all materials published or republished posthumously are accompanied by references, with page numbers, to the works in which they have appeared: ASCA, for *A Sand County Almanac and Sketches Here and There* (1949); RR, for *Round River: From the Journals of Aldo Leopold* (1953); RMG, for *The River of the Mother of God and Other Essays by Aldo Leopold* (1991); and ALS, for *Aldo Leopold's Southwest* (1995). Page numbers are also provided for quotations from Leopold's *Report on a Game Survey of the North Central States* (1931) and *Game Management* (1933). We have used the 1949 edition of *A Sand County Almanac* and the 1953 edition of *Round River,* rather than the later combined edition that was first published in 1966. Page numbers refer to these earlier editions, which remain in print.

In reproducing the quotations for this volume we have observed the following practices. We have generally retained the punctuation, spelling, and capitalization of the original text, but in a few cases we have silently corrected obvious misprints. We have used ellipsis dots to indicate an omission and brackets to indicate the alteration or addition of a word or phrase to allow the quotation to flow more easily. The first line of a quotation begins with a paragraph indention if it stood at the beginning of the paragraph in the original text; if it occurred within the paragraph, it is flush left here. If a quotation is drawn from more than one paragraph, material from subsequent paragraphs is indented; ellipsis dots introducing the paragraph indicate the omission of words or sentences preceding the quoted material.

Acknowledgments

This volume has evolved over many years, and many hands have contributed to it. We would especially like to thank Charlie Luthin for his early encouragement and persistence in giving shape to the project. Allen Fitchen, director emeritus of the University of Wisconsin Press, along with Mary Braun, Scott Lenz, Elizabeth Steinberg, and the University Press Committee, offered their constant and much-needed support. Jack Kirshbaum brought to the effort his greatly appreciated editorial skills. Susan L. Flader, Buddy Huffaker, Charlie Luthin, and T. H. Watkins provided valuable advice and suggestions as the manuscript came together. The Aldo Leopold Foundation and the family of Aldo Leopold gave their full blessing and cooperation. We would also like to express our gratitude to Oxford University Press and the other publishers who have graciously granted permission for the use of materials in this volume. Finally, we thank all our colleagues who found time in their schedules to contribute their voices to this volume. You are a swell chorus.

⟫ PART I ⟪
Conservation Science and Practice

Aldo Leopold saw conservation whole. He was keenly aware of the modern tendency to partition knowledge, interests, and landscapes, and understood well the consequences. He, by contrast, was an instinctive synthesizer, seeking out continuities and establishing connections within conservation. In "Conservation Economics" (1934) he wrote, "to be a practitioner of conservation on a piece of land takes more brains, and a wider range of sympathy, forethought, and experience, than to be a specialized forester, game manager, range manager, or erosion expert in a college or a conservation bureau."[1] Leopold exemplified his own maxim. The quotations in this section reflect Leopold's contributions across the broad spectrum of his professional experience.

The arrangement of chapters within this section follows in a rough way Leopold's professional development. He grew through the steady accretion of interests. He began his career as a forester—the one option available to aspiring conservationists as Theodore Roosevelt and Gifford Pinchot led the Progressive conservation crusade in the early 1900s. Graduating from Yale University's Forest School, Leopold was assigned to the Apache National Forest in the Arizona Territory in 1909. Except for a brief stint as secretary of Albuquerque's Chamber of Commerce, he remained with the U.S. Forest Service for the next nineteen years. During this period he carved out new professional niches within forestry, expanding its responsibilities—and his own work—beyond silviculture proper to include range management, recreation, erosion control, game conservation, and the protection of watersheds and wild lands.

Moving to Wisconsin in 1924, he would carry forward all of these interests, supplementing them in the 1930s with more focused attention on the management, first of "game," then of "wildlife" more generally. In the Midwest he inevitably found his view redirected to farm landscapes, though not to the exclusion of forests, rangeland, wilderness, or wildlife. Indeed, much of his writing in these years stressed the need to better integrate wild and domesticated landscapes, and to appreciate the ecological basis of a sound agriculture.

1

Leopold did not live to see the emergence of such integrative fields as sustainable agriculture, restoration ecology, and conservation biology. However, his work and writing in the 1930s and 1940s provided the conceptual foundations for these later innovations. "Land ecology," he wrote in 1942, "is putting the sciences and arts together for the purpose of understanding our environment."[2] He lived just long enough after World War II to see the sciences and arts moving in the opposite direction—and not long enough to see the necessary counterreaction that his own work would help to inspire. Only with time would science and society heed his call for "a reversal of specialization; instead of learning more and more about less and less, we must learn more and more about the whole biotic landscape."[3]

1 FOREST ECOLOGY AND MANAGEMENT

Axe-in-Hand

Susan L. Flader

Aldo Leopold began his career as a forester. He entered Yale University in 1905, intent on a career in the newly established U.S. Forest Service, and upon graduation with his master's degree in forestry in 1909 was assigned to map and cruise timber in the Arizona Territory. From the start he was deeply imbued with the utilitarian conservation philosophy espoused by the service's first chief, Gifford Pinchot. But also from the start he pushed foresters toward a broader definition of their responsibilities and more thoughtful consideration of the objectives of forest management.

Half a century after his death, during which time forestry in America has moved away from rather than toward his vision, Leopold is once again pointing the way to the future for his profession. A band of renegades formed an Association of Forest Service Employees for Environmental Ethics in 1989. Inspired by Leopold's writing, the profession's key arbiter, the Society of American Foresters, in the early 1990s engaged in an exhaustive process of adding a land ethic to their canon. Then in 1992 the chief of the Forest Service, with specific reference to Aldo Leopold, promulgated a new philosophy of ecosystem management to replace Gifford Pinchot's resource conservation philosophy as the service entered the twenty-first century.[1] Since then Leopold's ideas have been at the center of the continuing debate about ecosystem management.

The ebb and flow in the receptivity of foresters and other land managers to Aldo Leopold's message is owing to larger forces in our society, but the fact that Leopold is still regarded as a guiding light reflects the clarity and credibility of his message and the depth of experience in which it was grounded.

At a time when the national forests were devoted by law to conservation of timber and water, Leopold in one of his earliest publications, a 1913 letter to his fellow officers of the Carson National Forest in New Mexico, laid out virtually the entire range of purposes—"Timber, water, forage, farm, recreative, game, fish, and esthetic resources"—that would be enshrined half a century later in the Multiple Use Sustained Yield Act of 1960.[2] All that was missing was wilderness, but Leopold would soon become the leading advocate for wilderness preservation as well. Even more significant in his 1913 essay, however, was his emphasis on measuring successful management by "the effect on the Forest," rather than by mere adherence to official policies and procedures.[3] It was this preoccupation with what actually happened on the ground, with what we now call the forest ecosystem, that marked Leopold as a person of vision.

Leopold's Carson letter was written at a time when he was recuperating from a serious illness that would force him to give up his youthful ambition to be a forest supervisor only two years after having attained it. For the remainder of his career in the Southwest he would serve in a succession of regional office positions in which he would seek to broaden the scope of national forest administration and improve the quality of forest ecosystems. He initiated game management programs modeled on principles of forest management, promoted wilderness hunting grounds as a form of recreational land designation, and even advocated sanitary engineering (of recreation facilities) as a new sideline for foresters.

But perhaps his most far-reaching contributions came in the realm of ecological interpretation as he sought to discern the interactions of grass, brush, timber, and fire on Southwestern watersheds in his capacity as a forest inspector. With an ever open and inquiring mind, Leopold observed the marked increase in soil erosion, the continuing replacement of grass by unpalatable brush, the pattern of fire scars on ancient junipers, and the growth of yellow pine in dense, stunted thickets. In what was rank heresy in an agency dedicated to growing and harvesting trees, committed to absolute fire prevention, and funded largely by grazing fees, he argued that grass was a more effective watershed cover than trees and that fire, which was necessary to maintain grass cover, was less destructive than grazing. And he drove home the point: "15 years of Forest administration were based on an incorrect interpretation of ecological facts and were, therefore, in part misdirected."[4]

The Leopold who so boldly challenged the Forest Service by pointing out the implications of ecological interpretation was then chief of operations, the second highest post in the administration of twenty million acres of national forests in the Southwest. Though some of his colleagues thought of him as highbrow, moving along "with his feet somewhat off the ground," there is no question that he was well respected.[5] Many of his innovations in game management, wilderness designation, and inspection methodology influenced forest policy in his own time, though it would be years before his concern about the integrity of watersheds and the implications of ecology would be understood. The Forest Service in its early years was an enormously creative and vibrant institution, willing to respond to at least some of the prodding of a freethinker like Leopold because there was, in fact, relatively little demand for the timber that was its principal reason for existence.

Leopold left the Southwest in 1924 to become assistant director of the U.S. Forest Products Laboratory in Madison, Wisconsin, then the principal research arm of the Forest Service. Though the chemists, physicists, and engineers on its staff were concerned primarily with research on utilization of wood products after the tree was cut, Leopold wrote a series of essays in an effort to shift the focus of research to the growth of forests, with a decided bent toward natural reproduction, ecologically understood. His frustration in this endeavor led him to resign from the Forest Service in 1928 to devote himself full-time to laying the groundwork for the new profession of game management. The day before he resigned he published a parting shot in the *Service Bulletin,* the house organ of the Forest Service: "Whether we like it or no, National Forest policy is outgrowing the question of boards." Consistent with his approach for nearly two decades, he asserted the claims of "sociology as well as silviculture" and the possibility of social evolution to a higher understanding of the ends as well as the means of forest management.[6]

After he left the Forest Service, Leopold continued to identify himself as a forester. He showed his respect for the craft by modeling the techniques and standards of game management on those of forestry, even as he continued to criticize foresters for their too narrow, too commodity-oriented view. An opportunity in 1935 to observe forestry and wildlife management in Germany profoundly reinforced his conviction of the need for a more naturalistic, less "cubistic" or "wood factory" approach.[7] He was impressed by the *Dauerwald* concept that was even then replacing the "cabbage brand" of silviculture in Germany, and he realized that America, with a population density only one-tenth that of Germany, had a much better chance of preserving ecological and esthetic values in land.

But America was not ready to restrain its appetite for wood in favor of the integrity of its forests. As wartime demands fueled the cutting of the last sizable stand of virgin hardwoods in the Lake States, Leopold bent his pencil to the effort to save Michigan's Porcupine Mountains as a remnant of "decent forest."[8] The violent slashing he inveighed against would only increase in the postwar decades, as the demand for housing surged and as new technologies for pulp and fiber products spurred utilization of second-growth that would regenerate quickly once "over-mature" stands were removed. Clearcutting became the silvicultural technique of choice on the national forests as well as on industry lands, and the annual cut more than quadrupled. Leopold did not live to see the worst of the assault. But as environmentalists rallying around the vision of forester Aldo Leopold sought to stem the tide by promoting congressionally designated wilderness and filing lawsuits, professional foresters in both industry and government, devoted now more than ever to fiber production, began to view him as a flaky idealist or, worse, a threat. It would require nearly half a century before this phase of management would run its course and foresters, in their professional society and in government, would begin to look to Leopold for guidance on ecosystem management and ecological ethics.

That Leopold can still provide such guidance half a century after his death is owing to the force of his spirit, embodied in simple prose grounded in personal experience. The most enduring of his writing, we now know, was in the little book that described his efforts to restore the health of the worn-out, abandoned farm he acquired in 1935 in the sand country of central Wisconsin. "I was made to live on and work on *my own* land," he had written to his family a quarter century earlier, explaining why he was so eager to become a forest supervisor. "Whether it's a 100 acre farm or a 1,700,000 acre Forest doesn't matter—it's all the same principle."[9]

Now, as he planted and thinned his own woods, he became increasingly pensive, humble even, about his use of shovel and axe, and he came with humility to a sense of husbandry, "realized only when some art of management is applied to land by some person of perception."[10] The individual decisions required with every stroke were a constant exercise in ecological reasoning and ethical judgment. So it is little wonder that Leopold put his faith for the future in the slow sensitizing of people to land. "A conservationist," Leopold decided as he stood with axe-in-hand, "is one who is humbly aware that with each stroke he is writing his signature on the face of his land."[11]

A conservationist is one who is humbly aware that with each stroke he is writing his signature on the face of his land.

Leopold planting a sapling at the Shack, 1939. (Photo by Carl Leopold. Courtesy Aldo Leopold Foundation)

We are entrusted with the protection and development, through wise use and constructive study, of the Timber, water, forage, farm, recreative, game, fish, and esthetic resources of the areas under our jurisdiction. I will call these resources, for short, "The Forest." . . .

. . . I here offer a 66 foot chain wherewith to measure our progress. My measure is THE EFFECT ON THE FOREST.

To the Forest Officers of the Carson (1913); RMG 43–44

When the pioneer hewed a path for progress through the American wilderness, there was bred into the American people the idea that civilization and forests were two mutually exclusive propositions. Development and forest destruction went hand in hand; we therefore adopted the fallacy that they were synonymous. A stump was our symbol of progress.

We have since learned, with some pains, that extensive forests are not only compatible with civilization, but absolutely essential to its highest development.

The Popular Wilderness Fallacy: An Idea That Is Fast Exploding (1918); RMG 49

Forest fires and prairie fires incident to the early stages of settlement burned up or starved out a great deal of game. But today these destroyers are on the wane. Under the influence of man they are approaching zero, whereas many fires ravaged the aboriginal wilderness, set by lightning and by the Indians. The time will come when there will be much less destruction by fires than took place before the coming of the white man.

> The Popular Wilderness Fallacy: An Idea That Is Fast Exploding (1918); RMG 51

The technical education of the American forester aims principally to teach him how to raise and use timber. This is obviously proper. Handling timber lands is his major function.

But when the forester begins actual work on a forest he is called upon to solve a much broader problem. He is charged with the duty of putting land to its highest use.

> Forestry and Game Conservation (1918); RMG 53, ALS 75

. . . Foresters have labored under the vague fear that a real crop of game might interfere with both grazing and silviculture, as if grazing and silviculture might not also interfere with each other! The principle of "highest use" has evidently been more talked about than understood.

> Forestry and Game Conservation (1918); RMG 54, ALS 77

"Light-burning" means the deliberate firing of forests at frequent intervals in order to burn up and prevent the accumulation of litter and thus prevent the occurrence of serious conflagrations. . . .

Foresters generally are strenuously opposing the light-burning propaganda because they believe that the practice of this theory would not only fail to prevent serious fires but would ultimately destroy the productiveness of the forests on which western industries depend for their supply of timber.

. . . [This] is the very negation of the fundamental principle of forestry, namely, to make forests productive not only of a vegetative cover to clothe and protect our mountains, but also of the greatest possible amount of lumber, forage, and other forest products. . . .

The Forest Service policy of absolutely preventing forest fires insofar as humanly possible is directly threatened by the light-burning propaganda.

> "Piute Forestry" vs. Forest Fire Prevention (1920); RMG 68–69, ALS 139–41

Isaiah (41–9) seems to have had some knowledge of forest types and the ecological relations of species. He quotes Jehovah in this manner: "I will plant in the wilderness the cedar, the acacia tree, and the myrtle, and the oil tree; I will set in the desert the fir tree, the pine, and the box tree together."

The Forestry of the Prophets (1920); RMG 76–77

[Gifford] Pinchot's promise of [forest] development has been made good. The process must, of course, continue indefinitely. But it has already gone far enough to raise the question of whether the policy of development (construed in the narrower sense of industrial development) should continue to govern in absolutely every instance, or whether the principle of highest use does not itself demand that representative portions of some forests be preserved as wilderness.

The Wilderness and Its Place in Forest Recreational Policy (1921);
RMG 78, ALS 146

It is quite possible that the serious discussion of this [wilderness] question will seem a far cry in some unsettled regions, and rank heresy to some minds. Likewise did timber conservation seem a far cry in some regions, and rank heresy to some minds of a generation ago.

The Wilderness and Its Place in Forest Recreational Policy (1921);
RMG 79, ALS 148

The body of written scientific knowledge in forestry is really limited to trees in their various relations. . . . Yet every day foresters are rendering judgments on fire control, range management, watershed protection, erosion control, game and fish management, and recreation, the effects of which may be felt for centuries. Those effects are as vital to the permanent productivity of the forest and the permanent welfare of the nation as the effects of good or bad judgment in forestry proper. Yet some of these subjects are scarcely yet baptized. . . .

Skill in Forestry ms. (c. 1922)

[Discussing the policy implications of his theory of landscape changes in southern Arizona]

We have learned that during the pre-settlement period of no grazing and severe fires, erosion was not abnormally active. We have learned that during the post-settlement period of no fires and severe grazing, erosion became exceedingly active. Has our administrative policy applied these facts?

It has not. Until very recently we have administered the southern Arizona Forests on the assumption that while overgrazing was bad for erosion, fire was worse, and that therefore we must keep the brush hazard grazed down to the extent necessary to prevent serious fires.

In making this assumption we have accepted the traditional theory as to the place of fire and forests in erosion, and rejected the plain story written on the face of Nature. He who runs may read that it was not until fires ceased and grazing began that abnormal erosion occurred.

> Grass, Brush, Timber, and Fire in Southern Arizona (1924); RMG 118, ALS 185–86

First, 15 years of Forest administration were based on an incorrect interpretation of ecological facts and were, therefore, in part misdirected. Second, this error of interpretation has now been recognized and administrative policy corrected accordingly. Third, while there can be no doubt about the enormous value of European traditions to American forestry, this error illustrates that there can also be no doubt about the great danger of European traditions . . . uncritically accepted and applied, especially in such complex fields as erosion.

> Grass, Brush, Timber, and Fire in Southern Arizona (1924); RMG 119, ALS 186

. . . The watershed work of the future belongs quite as much to the forester as to the hydrographer and engineer.

> Grass, Brush, Timber, and Fire in Southern Arizona (1924); RMG 122, ALS 190

It looks like a very simple thing for an acorn to fall upon the soil, get stepped on by a cow, and forthwith sprout and grow into another oak. As our knowledge develops, however, it becomes more and more apparent that the reproduction of even an individual tree involves the interplay of many variable forces, some of them as yet ill-understood, while the reproduction of a forest (or society of trees) involves the interplay of forces so numerous and complex as to baffle the forester's attempts to analyze the process. He is forced to rely largely on empirical methods, and to apply the history of what has happened in one place as best he can to the question of what will happen in another.

> Natural Reproduction of Forests (1925)

. . . Forest trees can probably not be "Burbanked" without sacrificing their ability for natural reproduction, and natural rather than artificial reproduction will have to be relied upon for the bulk of our forestry operations for at least as far as we can see into the future. Artificial planting is necessary, in fact imperative, for restoring denuded forest lands, but artificial planting as a universal basis for forestry is neither possible nor desirable. In addition to its usually higher costs, it has met with unexpected difficulties in Germany, where in certain regions generation after generation of artificially planted spruce has not only produced a mysterious deterioration of the soil, but has resulted in such uniform stands as to invite the rapid spread of insect pests. The tendency, even in Europe, is to prefer natural reproduction of forests.

Natural Reproduction of Forests (1925)

The acceptance of the idea of wilderness areas entails, I admit, a growth in the original conception of National Forests. The original purposes were timber production and watershed protection, and these are and must always remain the primary purposes. But the whole subsequent history of these Forests has been a history of the appearance and growth of new uses, which, when skillfully adjusted to the primary uses and to each other, were one by one provided for and the net public benefit correspondingly increased. Public recreation was one of these. When the forests were first established, recreation did not exist in the minds of either the foresters or the public as an important use of the public Forests. Today it has been added to timber production and watershed protection as an important additional public service. It has been proven that skillful administration can provide for both in the same system of Forests without material sacrifice of either.

The Last Stand of the Wilderness (1925)

It has been known for years that our processes for converting forest trees into houses, furniture, implements, newspapers and a thousand other necessary wooden products were wasteful, but nobody knew, for the country as a whole, just how wasteful or just why. . . .

Good wood costs good money. Why then should a competitive industry need to be urged to adopt methods of preventing wood waste already found to be feasible and often profitable? Why do they not seize upon these improved methods of their own accord? Every American conservationist should note and ponder well the answer to this question.

The Home Builder Conserves (1928); RMG 143

A public which lives in wooden houses should be careful about throwing stones at lumbermen, even wasteful ones, until it has learned how its own arbitrary demands as to kinds and qualities of lumber help cause the waste which it decries.

The Home Builder Conserves (1928); RMG 144

The long and short of the matter is that forest conservation depends in part on intelligent consumption, as well as intelligent production of lumber.

The Home Builder Conserves (1928); RMG 145

The issue is whether any human undertaking as vast as the National Forests can be run on a single objective idea, executed by an invariable formula. The formula in question is: Land + forestry = boards. We need to use it more than we do. But can we run the National Forests by it alone?

Mr. Thompson's Wilderness (1928)

Whether we like it or no, National Forest policy is outgrowing the question of boards. We are confronted by issues in sociology as well as silviculture—we are asked to show by our deeds whether we think human minorities are worth bothering about; whether we regard the current ideals of the majority as ultimate truth or as a phase of social evolution; whether we weigh the value of any human need (like recreation) wholly by quantitative measurements; whether we too have forgotten that economic prosperity is a means, not an end.

Mr. Thompson's Wilderness (1928)

The slow differentiation of the forest-game relationship may be due in part to the separatist policy of many foresters—their refusal to become coordinate parts of state conservation departments. I do not overlook the dangers involved in such official coordination; I merely call attention to the possibility that failure to hang together is sometimes occasion to ultimately hang separately. There is no dodging the fundamental fact that timber and game, like crops and livestock, are the plant and animal products of the same land. . . .

Environmental Controls for Game through Modified Silviculture (1930)

For a century the whole world sought to emulate the artificially planted spruce forests of Germany. Their absence of competing hardwoods, their astonishing yields, their long black rows of dense, even-aged trees, were held up as a model of "efficiency." Suddenly the soil turned "sick"—of too much spruce. Insect pests swept through the unbroken stands like a forest fire. Today the Germans are seeking the beneficent fertilization of beech trees and other hardwoods; cuttings are made selectively as in nature; natural reproduction instead of artificial planting is becoming the rule. Artificiality failed in the long run.

Game Management (1933), 396

We have here simply one more instance of the crying need for naturalism in conservation—one more proof that the forester with a single eye for sawlogs, or the game manager with a single eye for fur or feathers, is an anachronism. In the long run we shall learn that there is no such thing as forestry, no such thing as game management. The only reality is an intelligent respect for, and adjustment to, the inherent tendency of land to produce life.

Review of *Notes on German Game Management* (1934)

Multiple Use.—Nearly all maladjustments in land have one thing in common: the difficulty of adjusting two or more simultaneous uses for the same soil. Yet land warranting exclusive dedication to a single use is exceptional, especially in forest regions. Diversity of use inheres in diversity of soil, vegetation, and topography.

The rarity of harmonized and balanced uses doubtless harks back to the rarity of harmonized and balanced users.

A part of the remedy seems to lie in the development of a keener ecological perception in foresters and other land technicians. Courses in ecology may or may not impart this perception. Those which do may have become more important to foresters than silviculture.

Preliminary Report on Forestry and Game Management (1935)

Most German forests . . . though laid out over a hundred years ago, would do credit to any cubist. The trees are not only in rows and all of a kind, but often the various age-blocks are parallelograms, which only an early discovery of the ill-effects of wind saved from being rectangles. . . . The Germans are now making a determined effort to get away from cubistic forestry—experience has revealed that in about the third successive crop of conifers in "pure" stands the microscopic flora of the soil becomes upset and the trees quit growing, but it will be another generation before the new policy emerges in landscape form.

Wilderness (1935); RMG 227

Our forestry is still so new that we can select the right kind if we want to, and thus avoid the inevitable collision with land esthetics from which the Germans are now suffering.

Notes on Wild Life Conservation in Germany (1935)

. . . In Germany, over-artificialized forestry is now recognized as having unknowingly inflicted a near-disaster on forest bird-life. We are here accustomed to regard wild-life conservation and forest conservation as parallel and interdependent objectives, and, of course, this is still true. The German experience, however, indicates that it is true *only when the system of forestry is of the right kind.* In other words, we must convert an indiscriminate into a discriminate enthusiasm. . . .

. . . The present point is that the native bird fauna cannot thrive, or even survive, in a forest so utterly unlike the natural forest.

Naturschutz in Germany (1936)

The German experience . . . is a plain warning that forestry willy-nilly involves more public interests than just timber supply, and that those interests may be injured or aided by the forester, depending on the broadmindedness, skill, and foresight he brings to his job.

Naturschutz in Germany (1936)

The observer [in Germany] is soon forced to the conclusion that better silviculture is possible only with a radical reform in game management. Later, as he learns to decipher what silviculture has done to the deer range, he also grasps the converse conclusion that better game management is possibly only with a radical change in silviculture.

Germany, in short, presents a plain case of mutual interference between game and forestry. The situation flatly contradicts the uncritical assumption, dying but not yet dead in America, that the practice of forestry in and of itself, regardless of what kind or how much, promotes the welfare of wildlife.

Deer and Dauerwald in Germany: I. History (1936)

. . . [Plantations of] pure spruce, the precocious child of timber famine and "wood factory" economics, grew up into an unlovely and unproductive maturity.

. . . In general, it is now conceded that mixed forest, naturally reproduced, outyields pure conifers in the long run. Speed of reproduction, decay of litter, self-pruning of trees, rate of stump-rotting, and other indices to ecological health are speeded up to an almost phenomenal extent.

Deer and Dauerwald in Germany: I. History (1936)

What specific amendments of American practice are indicated by the German experience?

First, I would say that a generous proportion of each forest must be devoted entirely to floral and faunal conservation.

Deer and Dauerwald in Germany: II. Ecology and Policy (1936)

[An] obvious lesson [from the German experience] is a deep respect for natural mixtures, and deep suspicion of large pure blocks of any species, especially species not indigenous to the locality.

Deer and Dauerwald in Germany: II. Ecology and Policy (1936)

The last two years . . . have brought increasing confusion of thought to the entire conservation field. An intellectual revolution seems to be in process, the net effect of which is to vastly expand both the importance and the difficulty of the conservation idea. During this process it is difficult to see far ahead. . . .

The Complexity of Multiple Use.—One mistake . . . is the notion that coordination of land uses is easy. In the enthusiasm of trying to get both game management and silviculture started, both professions have adopted the uncritical assumption that they fit beautifully together.

They do fit beautifully, but not always easily. Nor can the fitting be accomplished without mutual concessions.

> Second Report of [the Society of American Foresters] Game Policy Committee (1937)

The Chihuahua Sierras burn over every few years. There are no ill effects, except that the pines are a bit farther apart than ours, reproduction is scarcer, there is less juniper, and there is much less brush, including mountain mahogany—the cream of the browse feed. But the watersheds are intact, whereas our own watersheds, sedulously protected from fire, but mercilessly grazed before the forests were created, and much too hard since, are a wreck.

> Conservationist in Mexico (1937); RMG 240, ALS 203

In Europe, foresters for two centuries tried to clean the woods of every dead, hollow, or defective tree. They succeeded so well that woodpeckers, squirrels, owls, titmice, and other hole-nesting birds have become alarmingly scarce. In Germany, I saw dead oaks laboriously being riddled with auger-holes to encourage woodpeckers. . . .

This does not make sense. A few hollow trees, especially durable live basswoods or oaks, and a few dead and down logs, are essential to a balanced assortment of wildlife on the farm.

> Woodlot Wildlife Aids (1938)

. . . The Germans, who taught the world to plant trees like cabbages, have scrapped their own teachings and gone back to mixed woods of native species, selectively cut and naturally reproduced *(Dauerwald)*. The "cabbage brand" of silviculture, at first seemingly profitable, was found by experience to carry unforeseen biotic penalties: insect epidemics, soil sickness, declining yields, foodless deer, impoverished flora, distorted bird population. In their new Dauerwald the hard-headed Germans are now propagating owls, woodpeckers, titmice, goshawks, and other useless wildlife.

> A Biotic View of Land (1939); RMG 271

Have you ever wondered why a thick crust of corky bark covers the whole tree, even to the smallest twigs? This cork is armor. Bur oaks were the shock troops sent by the invading forest to storm the prairie; fire is what they had to fight. . . .

Engineers didn't discover insulation; they copied it from these old soldiers of the prairie war.

> Bur Oak Is Badge of Wisconsin (1941); ASCA 26–27

Many forest plantations are producing one-log or two-log trees on soil which originally grew three-log and four-log trees. Why? Advanced foresters know that the cause probably lies not in the tree, but in the microflora of the soil, and that it may take more years to restore the soil flora than it took to destroy it.

Wilderness as a Land Laboratory (1941); RMG 288

Sometime in 1943 or 1944 an axe will bite into the snowy sapwood of a giant maple. On the other side of the same tree a crosscut saw will talk softly, spewing sweet sawdust into the snow with each repetitious syllable. Then the giant will lean, groan, and crash to earth: the last merchantable tree of the last merchantable forty of the last virgin hardwood forest of any size in the Lake States.

With this tree will fall the end of an epoch.

There will be an end of cheap, abundant, high-quality sugar maple and yellow birch for floors and furniture. We shall make shift with inferior stuff, or with synthetic substitutes.

There will be an end of cathedral aisles to echo the hermit thrush, or to awe the intruder. There will be an end of hardwood wilderness large enough for a few days' skiing or hiking without crossing a road. The forest primeval, in this region, will henceforward be a figure of speech.

There will be an end of the pious hope that America has learned from her mistakes in private forest exploitation. Each error, it appears, must continue to its bitter end; conservation must wait until there is little or nothing to conserve.

Finally, there will be an end of the best schoolroom for foresters to learn what remains to be learned about hardwood forestry: the mature hardwood forest. We know little, and we understand only part of what we know.

The Last Stand (1942); RMG 290–92

The existence of the term microflora implies, to the layman, that science knows all the citizens of the underground community, and is able to push them around at will. As a matter of fact, science knows little more than that the community exists, and that it is important. In a few simple communities like alfalfa, science knows how to add certain bacteria to make the plants grow. In a complex forest, science knows only that it is best to let well enough alone.

The Last Stand (1942); RMG 293

[Selective logging] differs from slash logging in that the mature trees are cut periodically instead of simultaneously, and the striplings are left to grow instead of to burn in the next fire.

How has industry, with its ear ever cocked for new technology, received this innovation? The answer is written on the face of the hills. Industry, with the notable exception of a half-dozen companies, is slashing as usual. The reason given is that most mills are so nearly cut out anyhow that they cannot await the deferred returns of selective logging; they prefer to die quickly in their accustomed shower of sawdust, rather than to live forever on a reduced annual budget of boards.

The Last Stand (1942); RMG 293

When we abolish the last sample of the Great Uncut, we are, in a sense, burning books. I am convinced that most Americans of the new generation have no idea what a decent forest looks like. The only way to tell them is to show them. To preserve a remnant of decent forest for public education is surely a proper function of government, regardless of one's views on the moot question of large-scale timber production.

The Last Stand (1942); RMG 294

Paul Bunyan was too busy a man to think about posterity, but if he had asked to reserve a spot for posterity to see what the old north woods looked like, he likely would have chosen the Flambeau, for here the cream of the white pine grew on the same acres with the cream of the sugar maple, yellow birch, and hemlock. This rich intermixture of pine and hardwoods was and is uncommon. The Flambeau pines, growing on a hardwood soil richer than pines are ordinarily able to occupy, were so large and valuable, and so close to a good log-driving scheme, that they were cut at an early day, as evidenced by the decayed condition of their giant stumps. Only defective pines were spared, but there are enough of these alive today to punctuate the skyline of the Flambeau with many a green monument to bygone days.

Flambeau: The Story of a Wild River (1943); ASCA 114

Acts of creation are ordinarily reserved for gods and poets, but humbler folk may circumvent this restriction if they know how. To plant a pine, for example, one need be neither god nor poet; one need only own a shovel. By virtue of this curious loophole in the rules, any clodhopper may say: Let there be a tree—and there will be one.

If his back be strong and his shovel sharp, there may eventually be ten thousand. And in the seventh year he may lean upon his shovel, and look upon his trees, and find them good.

Pines above the Snow (1943); ASCA 81

If you are thriftily inclined, you will find pines congenial company, for, unlike the hand-to-mouth hardwoods, they never pay current bills out of current earnings; they live solely on their savings of the year before. In fact every pine carries an open bankbook, in which his cash balance is recorded by 30 June of each year. If, on that date, his completed candle has developed a terminal cluster of ten or twelve buds, it means that he has salted away enough rain and sun for a two-foot or even a three-foot thrust skyward next spring. If there are only four or six buds, his thrust will be a lesser one, but he will nevertheless wear that peculiar air that goes with solvency.

Pines above the Snow (1943); ASCA 82–83

It is in midwinter that I sometimes glean from my pines something more important than woodlot politics, and the news of the wind and weather. This is especially likely to happen on some gloomy evening when the snow has buried all irrelevant detail, and the hush of elemental sadness lies heavy upon every living thing. Nevertheless, my pines, each with his burden of snow, are standing ramrod-straight, rank upon rank, and in the dusk beyond I sense the presence of hundreds more. At such times I feel a curious transfusion of courage.

Pines above the Snow (1943); ASCA 87

What kind of a wood lot or forest fauna can we support if every important tree species has to be sprayed in order to live?

The Outlook for Farm Wildlife (1945); RMG 325

The predatory animals, in proper numbers, including wolves, coyotes, foxes, bobcats, hawks, and owls, are necessary to the future forests of Wisconsin. It would be fatal to the forestry program to allow tree-eating rabbits and deer to increase to unreasonable levels.

Deer, Wolves, Foxes and Pheasants (1945)

I doubt whether anyone but a forester can fully visualize [the] process by which excess deer gradually pull down the quality of a forest. I am certain that it is invisible to most laymen, including most deer hunters.

The Deer Dilemma (1946)

I have read many definitions of what is a conservationist, and written not a few myself, but I suspect that the best one is written not with a pen, but with an axe. It is a matter of what a man thinks about while chopping, or while deciding what to chop. A conservationist is one who is humbly aware that with each stroke he is writing his signature on the face of his land. Signatures of course differ, whether written with axe or pen, and this is as it should be.

I find it disconcerting to analyze, *ex post facto*, the reasons behind my own axe-in-hand decisions. I find, first of all, that not all trees are created free and equal. Where a white pine and a red birch are crowding each other, I have an *a priori* bias; I always cut the birch to favor the pine. Why? . . .

The birch is an abundant tree in my township and becoming more so, whereas pine is scarce and becoming scarcer; perhaps my bias is for the underdog. But what would I do if my farm were further north, where pine is abundant and red birch is scarce? I confess I don't know. My farm is here.

Axe-in-Hand (1949); ASCA 68–69

The only conclusion I have ever reached is that I love all trees, but I am in love with pines.

Axe-in-Hand (1949); ASCA 70

The wielder of an axe has as many biases as there are species of trees on his farm. In the course of the years he imputes to each species, from his responses to their beauty or utility, and their responses to his labors for or against them, a series of attributes that constitute a character. I am amazed to learn what diverse characters different men impute to one and the same tree.

Axe-in-Hand (1949); ASCA 70–71

It is . . . evident that our plant biases reflect not only vocations but avocations, with a delicate allocation of priority as between industry and indolence. The farmer who would rather hunt grouse than milk cows will not dislike hawthorn, no matter if it does invade his pasture. The coon-hunter will not dislike basswood, and I know of quail hunters who bear no grudge against ragweed, despite their annual bout with hayfever. Our biases are indeed a sensitive index to our affections, our tastes, our loyalties, our generosities, and our manner of wasting weekends.

Be that as it may, I am content to waste mine, in November, with axe in hand.

Axe-in-Hand (1949); ASCA 72

In my own field, forestry, group A is quite content to grow trees like cabbages, with cellulose as the basic forest commodity. It feels no inhibition against violence; its ideology is agronomic. Group B, on the other hand, sees forestry as fundamentally different from agronomy because it employs natural species, and manages a natural environment rather than creating an artificial one. Group B prefers natural reproduction on principle. It worries on biotic as well as economic grounds about the loss of species like chestnut, and the threatened loss of the white pines. It worries about a whole series of secondary forest functions: wildlife, recreation, watersheds, wilderness areas. To my mind, Group B feels the stirrings of an ecological conscience.

The Land Ethic (1949); ASCA 221

2 RANGE ECOLOGY AND MANAGEMENT

Open Thinking on the Range

Jack Ward Thomas

In these quotations Aldo Leopold speaks to us from what might seem like a remote past. Yet, decades later, most of his words remain applicable. Little seems to have changed in the intervening years. We can recognize the same political realities, the same socioeconomic concerns, the same cultural conditions—inside and outside the land management agencies—and the same projection of professional hubris. And to this day we cannot bring ourselves to ask if, in the time frame of centuries, it is possible to graze arid and semiarid ecosystems without continued ecological deterioration of those systems.

It is worth reflecting on Leopold's situation when he first confronted the issues he addresses in these passages. He was a Yale-trained forester from the upper Midwest, thrust into a Southwestern landscape where appropriate controls of livestock grazing were urgently needed. He and many other young Forest Service technicians were "fish out of water"— technically and culturally. But for a budding conservation philosopher this was perhaps the most fortunate of circumstances. In the semiarid Southwest the effects of centuries of human exploitation were more immediately obvious than in wetter regions with shorter histories of exploitation by Euro-Americans.

These effects were most evident in the degraded condition of forest watersheds, in the widespread erosion, gullying, and deterioration of stream courses and associated riparian zones, all of which led the budding ecologist-philosopher to think at watershed scales. Having taken that first leap toward more inclusive thinking, he would finally emerge as a man trying to "think like a mountain." In this sense Leopold's experience in the Southwest provided the intellectual foundations for later insights into what we refer to today as "sustainable forestry" and "ecosystem management." At the same time, Leopold's initial unwillingness to consider whether grazing should continue or whether the new Forest Service technocrats could devise appropriate grazing schemes was likely rooted in professional hubris. His view may also have been influenced by the fact that he married into one of the region's most influential Hispanic ranching families.

But these are observations merely on Leopold's starting point. The quotations presented here reflect how he learned, observed, and formulated new concepts. In today's parlance they illustrate clearly the development of his capacity to think "outside the box." Even a cursory review of these quotations reveals a tension involving three general and recurring themes: first, that livestock grazing on semiarid ranges inevitably produced erosion, degradation of bottomlands, overall ecological deterioration, and outbreaks of range rodents; second, that "nobody advocates that we cease grazing";[1] and third, that grazing experts could devise and enforce schemes that would allow grazing to continue in what we would call today a sustainable fashion. In only one quote do we see past this façade when Leopold admits, "I sometimes wonder whether semiarid mountains can be grazed at all without ultimate deterioration."[2]

There are other passages here in which Leopold is not so forthcoming. He suggests, for example, that as late as 1935 the Forest Service grazing programs in the Southwest were "under technical administration free from politics."[3] Really? In the same passage he implies that the inability to deal appropriately with abusive grazing was partially attributable to lack of courage. If the managers were free of politics, why did they need "courage" to deal with the problems? Was it true that Forest Service managers were free of political pressures? Was that the agency line? Or, more likely, was Leopold indulging in a bit of wishful thinking?

If in fact the Forest Service was free from political pressures regarding the grazing program at that time (which I doubt), it has certainly not been true for the past forty-two years of which I have firsthand knowledge. Holders of grazing permits on the National Forests—particularly in the Southwest—have more political "clout" than any other group with which the Forest Service deals on a regular basis. A simple administrative action on a single grazing allotment can and does bring elected and appointed officials to question the district ranger, the forest supervisor, and even the chief of the Forest Service and the secretary of agriculture about the matter. For decades political movements have arisen and abated in response to debates over grazing on public lands. As I write, serious moves are underway in the Congress to dramatically enhance permit holders' "rights" and influence over public land management. There are precious few management decisions regarding the public lands that are free from politics.

Yet what Aldo Leopold observed in 1924 seems eerily prescient. After providing a litany of the problems associated with grazing in semiarid landscapes, he observes that the situation "does not call for a taboo upon grazing, but rather constitutes a challenge to the craftsmanship of our stockmen and the technical skills of grazing experts in devising controls that will work, and to the courage of our administrators in enforcing those controls in a manner fair both to the conflicting interests and to the community."[4] As the wag once put it, "the more things change, the more they stay the same."

I am tempted to close with that comment, but such would be premature. Change is underway and seems to be accelerating. Pertinent to these changes are Leopold's observation that "to keep every cog and wheel is the first precaution of intelligent tinkering" and his full statement of a land ethic.[5] These two expressions have come to fruition in, among other measures, the Endangered Species Act, whose stated purpose is to provide "a means whereby the ecosystems upon which threatened and endangered species depend may be conserved."[6]

Enforcement of the act, which is occurring piecemeal through the mechanism of lawsuits and appeals of land use decisions, has forced, and will continue to force, significant and long overdue changes in grazing practices in the arid Southwest. Attention has focused first and foremost on the protection and recovery of riparian zone habitats for threatened aquatic and terrestrial species. These concerns are rapidly expanding to include upland conditions and the influence of grazing regimes and intensity. Unfortunately, these changes have too rarely reflected courage on the part of the federal land management and regulatory agencies. The will to confront threatened or endangered species issues has been instilled primarily through the insistence of the federal courts that our nation's laws are in fact to be obeyed.

I do believe that our technical experts and stock raisers can do a far better job of managing grazing within the limits of the land. Their failure to do so has been the result more of economic, social, and political factors than the "lack of technical skill or ecological understanding." We can point to an increasing number of creative innovations and success stories in public land grazing. These, I believe, are harbingers of a better future for our rangelands.

Why? It is becoming clear that if the public who owns the public lands does not approve, grazing on those lands will become more difficult, more complex, more expensive, more subject to uncertainty, and over time may even be eliminated. In the end, private use of the public lands will take place only with the sufferance of the owners—the American people as a whole. Full recognition of and the willingness to deal with the realities of politics and public opinion have led many graziers and public land managers to an epiphany of sorts. There is nothing like enlightened self-interest to bring about change.

The politics surrounding these ongoing changes will be fierce in their intensity. Elected officials who consider graziers on the public lands an important constituency will have to supply funding, either from increased grazing fees or from the public purse. Many of those resources will go for the "artificial control works" deemed essential by Leopold[7]— fencing, water developments, stream and riparian zone restoration, road management, and rehabilitation of upland ranges.

Yet for those who seriously ponder such matters, the old unthinkable question will come again and again in the midnight quiet—whether semiarid mountains "can be grazed at all without ultimate deterioration." I find myself, as Leopold reveals himself to be in these quotations, of two minds—schizophrenic if you will—on questions of public land grazing in semiarid areas. The political realities of the moment tell me that such grazing will continue. Professional hubris insists that we can, if allowed the leeway and the resources, conduct grazing operations on those lands in a sustainable fashion. However, experience over the centuries, in arid and semiarid lands around the earth, tells us that long-term grazing under such climatic conditions leads to deterioration. Therein lies the rub, and therein lies the challenge—the very same challenges that Leopold recognized and skirted over a half century ago.

It seems likely that without steady improvements in range management and range conditions this question will be discussed with increasing intensity. As circumstances, demographics, laws, ecological understanding, economics, and public opinion continue to change, it is well to understand what has come before. No such examination will be considered complete if it fails to trace the evolution of Aldo Leopold's views on the ecology of the Southwestern rangelands and the effects there of human exploitation, and of livestock grazing in particular. Perhaps we have finally come to the moment when we can deal appropriately and honestly with these insights—insights that evolved and sharpened as Leopold matured as a conservationist, land manager, and philosopher in the Southwest.

The stockmen must recognize that the privilege of grazing use carries with it the obligation to minimize and control its effects by more skilful and conservative methods.

Leopold shortly after his arrival at the Apache National Forest in 1909. (Photo by Raymond E. Marsh. Courtesy Aldo Leopold Foundation)

When foresters took charge of the National Forests in 1908 they were not slow to see that they were responsible for the regeneration and development of the Forest ranges. The fact that large areas were overgrazed was considered no reason for letting them remain so. The fact that selfish interests stood in the way of reorganization and progress was considered no obstacle against going ahead. The fact that nobody had ever heard of scientific range management was considered no reason for the continuance of an obsolete system.

Forestry and Game Conservation (1918); RMG 53, ALS 75

It is . . . a fact, at least in the Southwest, that in spite of range control, erosion continues on a serious scale. The truth of the matter is that (1) any system of grazing, no matter how conservative, induces erosion, (2) no system of range control, no matter how conservative, can be relied upon to stop erosion already started, and that (3) erosion can be controlled only by a proper system of grazing control, *supplemented by artificial erosion control works.*

> A Plea for Recognition of Artificial Works in Forest Erosion
> Control Policy (1921)

. . . There has been a widespread assumption among foresters that [artificial erosion control] works are unnecessary and impracticable. I have even heard it said, by experts on watershed problems, that *to admit the necessity of artificial control works would be admitting the failure of our range control system.* I take strong exception to any such viewpoint. Our function is not to prove the infallibility of our initial forest policies, but to conserve the Forests.

> A Plea for Recognition of Artificial Works in Forest Erosion
> Control Policy (1921)

Grazing means concentration of stock at ranch headquarters, watering places, salt grounds, driveways, shearing pens, roundup grounds, bed grounds, sunny sheltered spots on south hillsides, and cool breezy spots under shade. All of these concentrations mean some degree of trampling and the starting of trails along drainage lines. It is impossible to graze stock at all without causing these trampled spots and trails, and any trampled spot or trail may start local erosion. Any local erosion may spread, even through the most well preserved ground cover. Thousands of these incipient erosion spots exist on even the best regulated range. The stage is now set for a cloudburst. In the course of years, the cloudburst is bound to come. When it comes, the deeper soils begin to gully and the creek bottoms begin to go out. When the gullying and loss of bottom lands once starts, no system of range control, unaided by artificial works, can possibly check the process.

> A Plea for Recognition of Artificial Works in Forest Erosion
> Control Policy (1921)

We hear of "good grazing men." I never saw one, i.e., a man who possessed really deep penetration in both range and livestock. Many men seem to have an astounding knowledge of stock, and a few are really at home in range management, but I have never seen great capacity in both lines combined in one individual. A common case is the ranger who often possesses an almost uncanny "cow-sense" but knows nothing about range. Such a man can ride past a bunch of cattle and read their complete history for months past as well as their probable future movements and condition. But he can ride a piece of range for ten years without reading anything.

> Skill in Forestry ms. (c. 1922)

The tree rings show ... that about every eleven years we have a drouth. ...

The point is that, if every eleven years we may expect a drouth, why not manage our ranges accordingly? This means either stocking them to only their drouth capacity, or arranging to move the stock or feed it when the drouth appears. But instead, we stock them to their normal capacity, and, when drouth comes, the stock eat up the range, ruin the watershed, ruin the stockman, wreck the banks, get credits from the treasury of the United States, and then die. And the silt of their dying moves on down into our reservoirs to someday dry up the irrigated valleys— the only live thing left!

> Some Fundamentals of Conservation in the Southwest (1923); RMG 90–91

All our existing knowledge in forestry indicates very strongly that overgrazing has done far more damage to the Southwest than fires or cuttings, serious as the latter have been. Even the reproduction of forests has now been found to be impossible under some conditions without the careful regulation of grazing, whereas fire was formerly considered the only enemy.

... A century of fires without grazing did not spoil the Sapello [watershed], but a decade of grazing without fires ruined it, as far as the water courses are concerned.

> Some Fundamentals of Conservation in the Southwest (1923); RMG 92

Attainment of personal skill in the diagnosis of watershed problems and formulation of an effective watershed policy have made slow progress as compared with other lines of conservation work. It is hoped that this brief presentation of what we know about the subject to date may stimulate more widespread and effective thinking and action.

> *Watershed Handbook* (1923)

Brush ranges present a constant temptation to overgraze because the brush keeps the cattle alive long after both the grass and the watershed have been severely injured or destroyed. Stated in another way, the carrying capacity of the soil in brush country is often passed long before the starvation point is reached and the watershed damage checked by "die-offs." In no case is it the policy of the District to tolerate injury to the watershed because enough forage remains to support livestock.

> *Watershed Handbook* (1923)

Grazing is one of our most useful means of fire control, but it is dangerous if not used intelligently. We must avoid attaining reduction of fire hazard at the expense of watershed conservation. Intelligent use of grazing for fire control necessitates weighing the possible benefit to fire against the possible injury to watersheds. There is no blanket rule which will apply generally—it is a case of applying local skill and knowledge to local conditions.

Watershed Handbook (1923)

It is a conspicuous fact that we have many areas which bear evidence of having been burned over for centuries but which did not start to erode abnormally until they began to be grazed.

Watershed Handbook (1923)

Where land along a stream is in the hands of various owners, [erosion] control works must be correlated for the stream as a whole, else there is danger that works installed by one owner will merely pass the trouble down the stream to his neighbor. Securing such correlation is an excellent field for leadership by Forest officers. If there is a Ranger Station on the stream, the Service should of course set a good example by controlling its own stream frontage.

Watershed Handbook (1923)

Never break sod or other natural watershed cover for a road or trail without a definite plan for preventing its forming or causing a new gully, or without considering the opportunities offered for checking existing erosion.

Watershed Handbook (1923)

So far little has been said about remedies, which are, of course, the thing really worth talking about. It has been asserted that erosion is the result of overgrazing, and that some local overgrazing is difficult to avoid, even on ranges that are not overstocked. But nobody advocates that we cease grazing.

The situation does not call for a taboo upon grazing, but rather constitutes a challenge to the craftsmanship of our stockmen and the technical skill of grazing experts in devising controls that will work, and to the courage of our administrators in enforcing those controls in a manner fair both to the conflicting interests and to the community.

The stockmen must recognize that the privilege of grazing use carries with it the obligation to minimize and control its effects by more skilful and conservative methods.

Pioneers and Gullies (1924); RMG 110, ALS 170

A diagnosis of the process of [rangeland] destruction gives the most reliable pointers as to the best process of prevention and cure. First and

foremost, a vigorous growth of grass on the watershed, and more especially on the watercourses, is essential.

> Pioneers and Gullies (1924); RMG 111, ALS 171

In the National forests a genuine and frequently successful effort has
been made to prevent overgrazing by careful regulation, but on the public range outside of the forests no control of any kind is exercised. First
come, first served. This lack of regulation causes each stockman to try
to get as much stock as possible on the range at the earliest possible
moment, resulting in continuous and disastrous overgrazing. Further
procrastination in effecting a public-domain policy is unthinkable.

> Pioneers and Gullies (1924); RMG 111, ALS 171

. . . The acceptance of my theory as to the ecology of these brushfields
carries with it the acceptance of the fact that at least in this region grass
is a much more effective conserver of watersheds than foresters were at
first willing to admit, and that grazing is the prime factor in destroying
watershed values.

> Grass, Brush, Timber, and Fire in Southern Arizona (1924); RMG
> 118, ALS 185

Wholesale exclusion of grazing is neither skill nor administration, and
should be used only as a last resort. The problem which faces us constitutes a challenge to our technical competency as foresters—a challenge we have hardly as yet answered, much less actually attempted to
meet. We are dealing right now with a fraction of a cycle involving centuries. We can not obstruct or reverse the cycle, but we can bend it; in
what degree remains to be shown.

> Grass, Brush, Timber, and Fire in Southern Arizona (1924); RMG
> 119, ALS 187

. . . Most forest and range lands are still used destructively, i.e. the primary "crop" is not yet a crop at all, but results from destructive exploitation of the remnants of a virgin resource. Cropping the game may help
to bring about cropping the wood and grass.

> Report to the American Game Conference on an American Game
> Policy, Appendix (1930)

The Excess Game Issue. Where the available range cannot be expanded
there is nothing more harmful (short of extermination of a species)
than to allow the indefinite continuance of overstocking, especially on
arid lands. It is imperative that the non-scientific protectionist be made
to realize that an overgrazed range may take longer to recover than a

decimated herd of game; that excess population always ends in disease, starvation, or new enemies; and that prompt control is always more humane than delay.

> Report to the American Game Conference on an American Game Policy, Appendix (1930)

The disappearance of brush cover through grazing is so gradual that even conservationists often do not realize it is taking place, nor do they realize that the process must in some way be halted or offset, before other conservation measures can become effective. . . . Its effects on all brush-loving wild life, game and non-game, is the most important single present fact mentioned in this report. All other conservation measures are at best but stop-gaps until this fundamental deterioration of environment is in some way checked.

> *Report on a Game Survey of the North Central States* (1931), 59–61

. . . Overgrazing is more than mere lack of visible forage. It is rather a lack of vigorous roots of desirable forage plants. An area is overgrazed to the extent its palatable plants are thinned out or weakened in growing power. It takes more than a few good rains, or a temporary removal of livestock, to cure this thinning or weakening of palatable plants. In some cases it may take years of skillful range management to effect a cure; in others erosion has so drained and leached the soil that restoration is a matter of decades. . . . In the latter event restoration involves geological periods of time, and thus for human purposes must be dismissed as impossible.

> The Virgin Southwest (1933); RMG 178

Probably nowhere is there to be found a more important example of big-scale manipulation of the factors of productivity [affecting game] than the artificial development of watering places for livestock throughout the semi-arid ranges of the West. . . . This factor was controlled for the benefit of livestock rather than game, yet this very fact emphasizes rather than detracts from its significance. . . .

Water for livestock has been developed on scores of millions of acres of western ranges. Most of that water is available to and used by game, wherever game has not been eliminated by overgrazing or overhunting.

> *Game Management* (1933), 299

The present prevalence of overgrazing and erosion, even on public forests, is a threat not merely to game, but to the whole idea that technical men know how to conserve land. Continued overgrazing of public properties which have been under technical administration free from politics can be ascribed only to two things: lack of courage, or lack of ecological perception (ability to "read country"). Of the two, the latter seems by far the most probable.

Preliminary Report on Forestry and Game Management (1935)

The public domain is in worse condition than any other part of the western range (namely, 67 per cent depleted, 95 per cent still depreciating, 2 per cent improving). It is suggested that other forms of use than livestock grazing must be found for much of it. Some of the most interesting and valuable forms of wildlife are found, in part, on the public domain. . . .

It seems to the Committee that, to save something from the wreck of this vast area, there must be a swift and effective reduction of livestock to a point where the range can begin to improve. This alone would bring about a fundamental benefit to its remaining wildlife. Steady improvement of the range and a considerable quantity of wildlife will go together.

Second Report of [the Society of American Foresters] Game Policy Committee (1937)

I sometimes wonder whether semi-arid mountains can be grazed at all without ultimate deterioration. I know of no arid region which has ever survived grazing through long periods of time, although I have seen individual ranches which seemed to hold out for shorter periods. The trouble is that where water is unevenly distributed and feed varies in quality, grazing usually means overgrazing.

Conservationist in Mexico (1937); RMG 243, ALS 206–7

Today the honey-colored hills that flank the northwestern mountains derive their hue not from the rich and useful bunchgrass and wheatgrass which once covered them, but from the inferior cheat which has replaced these native grasses. The motorist who exclaims about the flowing contours that lead his eye upward to far summits is unaware of this substitution. It does not occur to him that hills, too, cover ruined complexions with ecological face powder.

The cause of the substitution is overgrazing. When the too-great herds and flocks chewed and trampled the hide off the foothills, something had to cover the raw eroding earth. Cheat did.

Cheat Takes Over (1941); ASCA 155–56

While the sportsmen and stockmen wrangle over who should move first in easing the burden on the winter range, cheat grass is leaving less and less winter range to wrangle about.

Cheat Takes Over (1941); ASCA 157

Overgrazing is probably the basic cause of some or most outbreaks of range rodents, the rodents thriving on the weeds which replace the weakened grasses. This relationship is still conjectural, and it is significant that no rodent-control agency has, to my knowledge, started any research to verify or refute it. Still, if it is true, we may poison rodents till doomsday without effecting a cure. The only cure is range-restoration.

> What Is a Weed? (1943); RMG 309

The reader may well ask *why* the encroachment [of mesquite and cedar] has taken place. The authors tactfully avoid any answer, except to say that the invasion is "the direct result of heavy use." This seems to be a polite paraphrase for overgrazing. I prefer plain words for plain facts.

> Review of "Fighting the Mesquite and Cedar Invasion on Texas Ranges" (1944); ALS 214

. . ."Paradise Ranch". . . lay tucked away on the far side of a high peak, as any proper paradise should. Through its verdant meadows meandered a singing trout stream. A horse left for a month on this meadow waxed so fat that rain-water gathered in a pool on his back. After my first visit to Paradise Ranch I remarked to myself: what else *could* you call it?

Despite several opportunities to do so, I have never returned to the White Mountain. I prefer not to see what tourists, roads, sawmills, and logging railroads have done for it, or to it. I hear young people, not yet born when I first rode out "on top," exclaim about it as a wonderful place. To this, with an unspoken mental reservation, I agree.

> On Top (1949); ASCA 128

3   OUTDOOR RECREATION

Leopold and the "Still Unlovely Mind"

Richard L. Knight

Aldo Leopold was a lifelong recreationist. Whether fishing, hunting with gun or bow, birdwatching, canoeing, or exploring wild lands on foot or horseback, Leopold sought out recreational opportunities on open lands. These activities in turn fed his commitment to conservation. Indeed, behind his early efforts to keep roads out of still-unbisected public lands lay the conviction that generations yet to come should have the opportunity to experience places that have been spared the commercializing influences of modern industry, transport, and marketing. He sought to protect these roadless areas from the kinds of recreational activities promoted by chambers of commerce and the automobile-oil conglomerates, activities that tended to bring "modern" technologies to bear on what were once simple human avocations.

Leopold recognized that both private and public lands offered recreational opportunities and pursued his own play on both. He saw outdoor recreation not as the exclusive privilege of the wealthy, but as a basic human need and an inherent desire shared by most people. Leopold's Mr. Babbitt did not need a Ph.D. in ecology to participate in birdwatching, angling, or tramping through a prairie remnant. From Leopold's perspective outdoor recreation allowed individuals to connect with the wild things and places that were part of our history and that helped define our national culture. For Leopold outdoor recreation was the medium through which he could explore and bring together human and natural histories.

Enjoying diverse forms of outdoor recreation, Leopold was nonetheless troubled by the increasing artificiality of outdoor experiences and the power of government and industry to deprive certain recreational activities of their requisite human skills and inherent mysteries. In "Conservation Esthetic," Leopold presaged the increasingly blurred line between ever-higher technology and recreation: "A gadget industry pads the bumps against nature-in-the-raw; woodcraft becomes the art of using gadgets."[1] Today hikers may venture into wilderness with little understanding of map and compass; they simply seek their location by dialing up satellites on their Global Positioning Systems. And the cellular phone is always available in a pinch. Anglers depend less on their understanding of fish ecology and habitat as they captain boats outfitted with instruments and gadgets that locate the fish, and then entice the fish with artificially enhanced baits and lures.

Land management agencies that cater to recreationists have reduced the inherent hazards of recreation by posting and signing any real or perceived dangers: "Stay away from edge," "Bears in area," "Climb in case of flood." Magazines, sporting organizations, and government agencies leave no stone unturned before the advancing recreationist. Rock climbers are provided handhold-by-handhold descriptions of climbing routes. Mountain bikers, hikers, and equestrians are given specific directions to stay on the trail (apparently signs are not enough). The guidebook may tell us, "At the juncture marked by a sign, turn left and proceed 3 tenths of a mile, past a steep cliff on the right side and. . . ." Outdoor adventure magazines exploit the ever-decreasing "undiscovered" sites on this planet with stories and details of destination points that haven't yet been victimized by guidebooks. Seldom, for example, does an issue of a climbing magazine appear without a detailed topographical description of some remote but just-discovered cliff. Where plants and animals unique to the vertical had found refuge for eons, there now appear brightly colored nylon runners; approaching climbers are dazzled by sunlight shining brightly off newly installed bolts; the vegetation is soon "gardened"; the cliff base is littered with waste and human refuse.

Perhaps this is what Leopold feared when he wrote, "This is Outdoor Recreation, Latest Model."[2]

Leopold certainly saw the oncoming deluge of diverse recreationists and sensed the potential effect on our wild places. "Very evidently," he wrote in 1921, "we have here the old conflict between preservation and use, long since an issue with respect to timber, water power, and other purely economic resources, but just now coming to be an issue with respect to recreation."[3] His words have proven true. In a recent review of taxpayer-subsidized uses of public lands, outdoor recreation was second only to water development projects as the culprit behind the decline of federally listed threatened and endangered species. The traditional threats to our natural heritage—forestry, livestock grazing, hardrock mining—affected fewer species.[4]

That Leopold anticipated such effects is clear. He stated in 1934, "The salient geographic character of outdoor recreation, to my mind, is that recreational use is self-destructive."[5] Moreover, recreational use seemed increasingly to defeat its own purpose. Leopold feared that the excitement, adventure, and mystery of being outdoors *seeking something* was being turned into just the latest in a long line of exploitative American industries, "a self-destructive process of seeking but never quite finding, a major frustration of mechanized society."[6]

This trend has not abated. Many in the land management agencies today seek budgetary and political salvation in the increasing public demand for outdoor recreation. And, as in the past, the road to salvation has tended to bisect the wild. The U.S. Forest Service provides one example. Today, thanks to foresters' proclivity to build roads, there are enough formally designated roads on our national forests to encircle the globe fifteen times (there is no guessing how many more trips around the world we could take on the unauthorized roads). In 1999 Chief Forester Michael Dombeck proclaimed a moratorium on road construction in national forest roadless areas. This is an encouraging antidote to road mania and an indication perhaps that the attitude Leopold spoke for is finally gaining credence: "Mechanized recreation already has seized nine-tenths of the woods and mountains; a decent respect for minorities should dedicate the other tenth to wilderness."[7]

Because Leopold saw important value in outdoor recreation, he was never too critical in his appraisals of it. His statements read more like warnings than dire forecasts. He also appreciated that to lump together under a single label all "outdoor recreationists" is to simplify a very complex issue. "Recreation," he wrote, "is a perpetual battlefield because it is a single word denoting as many diverse things as there are diverse people. One can discuss it only in personal terms."[8]

Most significant for the future, Leopold offered an alternative route for those who wish to avoid the well-worn path down which he saw outdoor recreation heading. Although he participated in "mainstream" recreation activities such as hunting and fishing, Leopold also pioneered a form of recreation that brought him closer to the land, deepened his understanding of its complexities, and allowed him to develop more fully his land ethic. He proposed that mystery and adventure could be restored to the outdoors through the honing of one's perception (especially through the lens of the natural sciences) and the use of that knowledge and insight in the service of the wild. "It is the intellectual exploration of land," he wrote, "including aboriginal land or wilderness, that constitutes the frontier of the present century."[9]

This is where Leopold offers his most salient observations regarding outdoor recreation and the American mood. Concerned with the "qualitative bankruptcy of the recreational process," Leopold offered a radical reconception of the very idea: "Recreational development is a job not of building roads into lovely country, but of building receptivity into the still unlovely human mind."[10] Such receptivity, he suggested, might allow us to expand our notion of recreation to include such activities as nature study and research, ecological restoration, and participation in conservation projects. "This sport knows no bag limit, no closed season. It needs teachers, but not wardens. It calls for a new woodcraft of the highest cultural value."[11]

Obviously this type of recreation is not as widely pursued as mountain biking or jet skiing, but it is gaining in popularity. The Nature Conservancy is just one of many nongovernmental organizations that provide opportunities for volunteers to participate in restoring degraded landscapes. City, county, state, and federal agencies concede that they have neither the time nor resources to undo the damage to land health that has occurred over the last century. The response of these agencies has been to mobilize the energy and commitment of legions of citizens who feel that restoring sick land is a valuable and positive way of recreating outdoors.

Just as Leopold forecast the modern state of much outdoor recreation, so also perhaps he anticipated this trend, as more and more Americans take to the outdoors to put right lands that have been abused by past practices. This unprecedented growth in volunteer work on conservation projects would surely have pleased Leopold. Even more pleasing to him, I suspect, would be the underlying significance of the trend: that as a culture we may be growing into a new conception of ourselves, one that views the restoration of our lands and waters as a legitimate form of outdoor recreation.

Recreational development is a job not of building roads into lovely country, but of building receptivity into the still unlovely human mind.

Aldo and Luna Leopold on the Wisconsin River. (Courtesy Aldo Leopold Foundation)

The man who can not enjoy his leisure is ignorant, though his degrees exhaust the alphabet, and the man who does enjoy his leisure is to some extent educated, though he has never seen the inside of a school.

A Man's Leisure Time (1920); RR 3

Sporting magazines are groping toward some logical reconciliation between getting back to nature and preserving a little nature to get back to. Lamentations over this or that favorite vacation ground being "spoiled by tourists" are becoming more and more frequent. Very evidently we have here the old conflict between preservation and use, long since an issue with respect to timber, water power, and other purely economic resources, but just now coming to be an issue with respect to recreation.

The Wilderness and Its Place in Forest Recreational Policy (1921);
RMG 79, ALS 148

The recreational desires and needs of the public, whom the forests must serve, vary greatly with the individual. Heretofore we have been inclined to assume that our recreational development policy must be based on the desires and needs of the majority only. The only new thing about the premise in this case is the proposition that inasmuch as we have plenty of room and plenty of time, it is our duty to vary our recreational development policy, in some places, to meet the needs and desires of the minority also.

> The Wilderness and Its Place in Forest Recreational Policy (1921); RMG 79, ALS 148–49

The booster is intensely provincial. A year ago he demanded a National Park for New Mexico. He did not know where or how, but he knew jolly well why: A National Park would be a tourist-getter of the first water, and tourists are to be desired above all things. They come, they see, they spend, and they are even known to come back.

> A Criticism of the Booster Spirit (1923); RMG 101

Wild places are the rock-bottom foundation of a good many different kinds of outdoor play, including pack and canoe trips in which hunting, fishing, or just exploring may furnish the flavoring matter. By "wild places" I mean wild regions big enough to absorb the average man's two weeks' vacation without getting him tangled up in his own back track. I also mean big areas wild enough to be free from motor roads, summer cottages, launches, or other manifestations of gasoline. Driving a pack train across or along a graded highway is distinctly not a pack trip—it is merely exercise, with about the same flavor as lifting dumbbells. Neither is canoeing in the wake of a motor launch or down a lane of summer cottages a canoe trip. That is paddling—and the supply is unlimited.

> The Last Stand of the Wilderness (1925)

. . . I had better explain that motor roads, cottages, and launches do not necessarily destroy hunting and fishing, but they destroy the wilderness, which to certain tastes is quite as important.

Neither do I imply that motors, cottages, summer resorts, and dude ranches are not in themselves highly valuable recreational assets. Obviously they are. Only they are a different *kind* of recreation. We need to preserve as many different kinds as we possibly can. The civilized kinds tend to preserve themselves through the automatic operation of economic laws. But wilderness travel is a kind that tends to disappear under the automatic operation of economic laws, just as the site for a city park tends to disappear with the growth of a city. Unlike the city park, however, the wilderness can not be re-created when the need for it is determined by hindsight.

> The Last Stand of the Wilderness (1925)

Wilderness is the one kind of playground which mankind can not build to order.

                                        The Last Stand of the Wilderness (1925)

. . . So sacred is our dogma of "development" that there is no effective protest. The inexorable molding of the individual American to a standardized pattern in his economic activities makes all the more undesirable this unnecessary standardization of his recreational tastes.

                              Wilderness as a Form of Land Use (1925); RMG 140

The day is almost upon us when a pack-train must wind its way up a graveled highway and turn out its bell-mare in the pasture of a summer hotel. When that day comes the pack-train will be dead, the diamond hitch will be merely rope, and Kit Carson and Jim Bridger will be names in a history lesson. Rendezvous will be French for "date," and Forty-Nine will be the number preceding fifty. And thenceforth the march of empire will be a matter of gasoline and four-wheel brakes.

                              Wilderness as a Form of Land Use (1925); RMG 141

Wilderness areas are primarily a proposal to conserve at least a sample of a certain kind of recreational environment, of which game and hunting is an essential part, but nevertheless only a part. Who shall say that the diamond hitch and the tumpline are not as much worth conserving as the black-tail buck or the moose? Who shall say that the opportunity to disappear into the trackless wild is not as valuable as the opportunity to hang up a trophy? Who shall say that we have not room enough in this huge country to earn a living without destroying the opportunity to enjoy it after it is earned, each after his own taste?

                       A Plea for Wilderness Hunting Grounds (1925); ALS 160–61

If we accept the principle that human welfare is to be measured in standards of living rather than in millions of population, and that the privilege of taking a vacation in the real wilds is one of those standards, then the wilderness theory is irrefutable.

                              Untitled address on wilderness conservation (1926)

The potential American system [of game management] ought to be just as effective as the European in getting large scale production, and at the same time more desirable from the *ethical, aesthetic,* and social points of view.

                       Report of the Committee on American Wild Life Policy (1929)

. . . The [north-central] region presents the whole gamut of possible opportunities for creating an orderly adjustment between "men who love sport" and the wild life resources which produce it; men who insist on conserving "Outdoor America" but at the same time insist on expanding an already unprecedented population growth and economic prosperity. Can they do both? Can wild game be produced in a motorized and moneyed democracy? Here, if anywhere, is the place to seek the answer.

Report on a Game Survey of the North Central States (1931), 21

The wild-life conservation movement is an attempt to prevent our expanding population from destroying its own opportunities for sport.

Management is a way to maintain a supply of game, and other wild life, in the face of that expansion.

But it is not merely a *supply* of game, in the strictly quantitative sense, that is in question. The conservation movement seeks rather to maintain values in which *quality* and distribution matter quite as much as quantity.

Game Management (1933), 391–92

Recreation is a perpetual battlefield because it is a single word denoting as many diverse things as there are diverse people. One can discuss it only in personal terms. A sawlog can be scaled, and a covey of quail is 15 birds, but there is no unit of either volume or value wherewith diverse persons can impersonally measure or compare recreational use.

Conservation Economics (1934); RMG 196

The salient geographic character of outdoor recreation, to my mind, is that recreational use is self-destructive. The more people are concentrated on a given area, the less is the chance of their finding what they seek. This is not true of the uncritical mob, but I see no more reason for running a national or state park to please the mob than a public art gallery or a public university. A slum is a slum, whether in the Bowery or on the Yellowstone. Dispersion, then, is the first principle of recreational planning.

Conservation Economics (1934); RMG 196

It is obviously impossible to provide the recreation-seeker with all the solitude he needs, but it is certainly bad planning to overlook the fact that the enjoyment of natural beauty is in its essence a solitary occupation. That this principle is overlooked is patent in the yearly outpouring of printed matter measuring the increase of recreational use in terms of man-days. Such statistics tacitly assume that all man-days are of equal value, and there is a linear relationship between recreational service and the number of ciphers on the tally-register at the gate.

Some Thoughts on Recreational Planning (1934)

The mechanization of society is, willy-nilly, increasing the quantity of recreation-seekers at a staggering rate. However fast we may build up the acreage of public recreation-grounds, the automobile bears down on each new accession like a modern Juggernaut.

Some Thoughts on Recreational Planning (1934)

We need a new category of public reservation, the sole specification of which is to be let alone. To such a place your solitary recreationist can repair of a Sunday with his stick and his dog, and make believe in his own small way that he is LaSalle or Kit Carson, giving the new lands the "once-over." That such capacity for illusion persists in only a few, is all the more reason why its remnants should be husbanded with zeal, for it is more precious to our spiritual future than fine gold.

Some Thoughts on Recreational Planning (1934)

. . . It is inconceivable to me that the prospective demand for out-door recreation can be more than partially accommodated on public lands. . . .

The park movement has been so occupied in enlarging the area of public parks that no positive policy for the conservation of recreational values on private lands, or for their orderly use by the public, has been formulated.

Some Thoughts on Recreational Planning (1934)

Barring love and war, few enterprises are undertaken with such abandon, or by such diverse individuals, or with so paradoxical a mixture of appetite and altruism, as that group of avocations known as outdoor recreation. It is, by common consent, a good thing for people to get back to nature. But wherein lies the goodness, and what can be done to encourage its pursuit? On these questions there is confusion of counsel, and only the most uncritical minds are free from doubt.

Recreation became a problem with a name in the days of the elder Roosevelt, when the railroads which had banished the countryside from the city began to carry city-dwellers, *en masse*, to the countryside. It began to be noticed that the greater the exodus, the smaller the per-capita ration of peace, solitude, wildlife, and scenery, and the longer the migration to reach them.

The automobile has spread this once mild and local predicament to the outermost limits of good roads—it has made scarce in the hinterlands something once abundant on the back forty. But that something must nevertheless be found. Like ions shot from the sun, the week-enders radiate from every town, generating heat and friction as they go. A tourist industry purveys bed and board to bait more ions, faster, further. Advertisements on rock and rill confide to all and sundry the whereabouts of new retreats, landscapes, hunting-grounds, and fishing-lakes just beyond those recently overrun. Bureaus build roads into new hinterlands, then buy more hinterlands to absorb the exodus accelerated by the roads. A gadget industry pads the bumps against nature-in-the-raw; woodcraft becomes the art of using gadgets. . . . To him who seeks in the woods and mountains only those things obtainable from travel or golf, the present situation is tolerable. But to him who seeks something more, recreation has become a self-destructive process of seeking but never quite finding, a major frustration of mechanized society.

Conservation Esthetic (1938); ASCA 165–66

The retreat of the wilderness under the barrage of motorized tourists is no local thing; Hudson Bay, Alaska, Mexico, South Africa are giving way, South America and Siberia are next. Drums along the Mohawk are now honks along the rivers of the world. *Homo sapiens* putters no more under his own vine and fig tree; he has poured into his gas tank the stored motivity of countless creatures aspiring through the ages to wiggle their way to pastures new. Ant-like he swarms the continents.

This is Outdoor Recreation, Latest Model.

Conservation Esthetic (1938); ASCA 166

That [the feeling of isolation in nature] is acquiring a scarcity-value that is very high to some persons is attested by the wilderness controversy. . . .

. . . The very scarcity of wild places, reacting with the *mores* of advertising and promotion, tends to defeat any deliberate effort to prevent their growing still more scarce.

It is clear without further discussion that mass-use involves a direct dilution of the opportunity for solitude; that when we speak of roads, campgrounds, trails, and toilets as "development" of recreational resources, we speak falsely in respect of this component. Such accommodations for the crowd are not developing (in the sense of adding or creating) anything. On the contrary, they are merely water poured into the already-thin soup.

Conservation Esthetic (1938); ASCA 171–72

Recreation . . . is not the outdoors, but our reaction to it. Daniel Boone's reaction depended not only on the quality of what he saw, but on the quality of the mental eye with which he saw it. Ecological science has wrought a change in the mental eye. It has disclosed origins and functions for what to Boone were only facts. It has disclosed mechanisms for what to Boone were only attributes. We have no yardstick to measure this change, but we may safely say that, as compared with the competent ecologist of the present day, Boone saw only the surface of things. The incredible intricacies of the plant and animal community—the intrinsic beauty of the organism called America, then in the full bloom of her maidenhood—were as invisible and incomprehensible to Daniel Boone as they are today to Mr. Babbitt. The only true development in American recreational resources is the development of the perceptive faculty in Americans. All of the other acts we grace by that name are, at best, attempts to retard or mask the process of dilution.

Conservation Esthetic (1938); ASCA 173–74

It is the expansion of transport without a corresponding growth of perception that threatens us with qualitative bankruptcy of the recreational process. Recreational development is a job not of building roads into lovely country, but of building receptivity into the still unlovely human mind.

Conservation Esthetic (1938); ASCA 176–77

All wilderness areas, no matter how small or imperfect, have a large value to land-science. The important thing is to realize that recreation is not their only or even their principal utility. In fact, the boundary between recreation and science, like the boundaries between park and forest, animal and plant, tame and wild, exists only in the imperfections of the human mind.

Wilderness as a Land Laboratory (1941); RMG 289

The social value of any experience is determined by the number who participate times the intensity or quality of their participation.

In measuring the value of recreation, we are so obsessed with the numbers who now participate that we have forgotten all about the intensity or quality of their experience. This obsession is especially prevalent in the land-owning bureaus, which justify their mounting costs and expanding domain by their mounting public patronage. What the public gets from the parks and forests is assumed to be sufficient. Is it?

Wilderness Values (1941)

No man is wise enough to say at just what point the loss in quality of recreation outweighs the gain in quantity, but any man with half an eye can see on which side of the scale official leadership should throw its weight. The parkward hegira of the landless needs no prodding; whether we will or no it is upon us, like an army with banners. From now on it is quality, not quantity, which needs the attention of far-seeing administrators.

Wilderness Values (1941)

The recreationist arrives in the wilds draped and festooned with gadgets, each tending to destroy the contrast value of his vacation. I am not such a purist as to disdain all of them, but I do claim that the presence or absence of gadget inhibitions is a delicate test of any man's outdoor education. Most tourists have no gadget inhibitions whatever.

Wilderness Values (1941)

To many sensitive minds the worst fate that could befall a favorite recreation or study area is its incorporation in a park or forest. If this seems too jaundiced an arraignment, let me tell of a "wild" river bluff which until 1935 harbored a falcon's eyrie. Many visitors walked a quarter mile to the river bank to picnic and to watch the falcons. Comes now some alphabetical builder of "country parks," and dynamites a road to the river, all in the name of "recreational planning." The excuse is that the public formerly had no right of access, now it has such a right. Access to what? Not access to the falcons, for they are gone. Just so does the quality of wilderness fade before the juggernaut of mass recreation. If forestry and recreational engineering are entitled to professional status, has not our employer, the public, a right to demand of us some degree of skill and resourcefulness in preserving the quality of wild areas despite mass use?

Wilderness Values (1941)

Then came the gadgeteer, otherwise known as the sporting-goods dealer. He has draped the American outdoorsman with an infinity of contraptions, all offered as aids to self-reliance, hardihood, woodcraft, or marksmanship, but too often functioning as substitutes for them. Gadgets fill the pockets, they dangle from neck and belt. The overflow fills the auto-trunk, and also the trailer. Each item of outdoor equipment grows lighter and often better, but the aggregate poundage becomes tonnage. The traffic in gadgets adds up to astronomical sums, which are soberly published as representing "the economic value of wildlife." But what of cultural values?

Wildlife in American Culture (1943); ASCA 180

I do not pretend to know what is moderation, or where the line is between legitimate and illegitimate gadgets. . . . I use many factory-made gadgets myself. Yet there must be some limit beyond which money-bought aids to sport destroy the cultural value of sport.

Wildlife in American Culture (1943); ASCA 181

The last decade . . . has disclosed a totally new form of sport, which does not destroy wildlife, which uses gadgets without being used by them, which outflanks the problem of posted land, and which greatly increases the human carrying capacity of a unit area. This sport knows no bag limit, no closed season. It needs teachers, but not wardens. It calls for a new woodcraft of the highest cultural value. The sport I refer to is wildlife research.

Wildlife in American Culture (1943); ASCA 184

Wilderness areas are first of all a series of sanctuaries for the primitive arts of wilderness travel, especially canoeing and packing.

I suppose some will wish to debate whether it is important to keep these primitive arts alive. I shall not debate it. Either you know it in your bones, or you are very, very old.

Wilderness (1949); ASCA 193

There are those who decry wilderness sports as "undemocratic" because the recreational carrying capacity of a wilderness is small, as compared with a golf links or a tourist camp. The basic error in such argument is that it applies the philosophy of mass-production to what is intended to counteract mass-production. The value of recreation is not a matter of ciphers. Recreation is valuable in proportion to the intensity of its experiences, and to the degree to which it *differs from* and *contrasts with* workaday life. By these criteria, mechanized outings are at best a milk-and-water affair.

Mechanized recreation already has seized nine-tenths of the woods and mountains; a decent respect for minorities should dedicate the other tenth to wilderness.

Wilderness (1949); ASCA 193–94

4 WILDLIFE ECOLOGY
AND MANAGEMENT

᪣

Building the Foundations of Wildlife Conservation

Stanley A. Temple

Aldo Leopold's life and writings span the era when both ecology and wildlife management were establishing themselves as legitimate scientific undertakings. The fledgling discipline of ecology was struggling to convince the rest of the scientific world that it was more than just a new name for descriptive studies of natural history, and deserved to be fully recognized for new and unique contributions within the family of natural sciences. Somewhat similarly, the emerging field of wildlife management was struggling to identify and formulate a set of general guiding principles so that it could provide more than case-by-case solutions to conservation problems involving wildlife species.

Both ecology and wildlife management became organized professional activities during Leopold's life. The Ecological Society of America was formed in 1915, when Leopold was a young forester, and the Wildlife Society in 1937, by which time Leopold was already a recognized leader in the new field. Although his professional attentions and contributions focused more on wildlife management, Leopold was well respected by ecologists for his application of ecological principles to conservation challenges. Reflecting the high regard in which both ecologists and wildlife managers held his achievements, Aldo Leopold remains the only individual who has served as president of both professional organizations.

Among Leopold's most important contributions to these young disciplines was, in fact, his recognition of the enormous potential of their partnership. He saw the relevance of the science of ecology and the practice of wildlife management to each other, and he was concerned that this partnership was not being forged as quickly as he thought it should be. In its earliest days wildlife management was regarded as "a sort of stepchild in that austere family known as The Sciences."[1] Leopold saw, as many scientists and conservationists could not, that ecological principles could provide the conceptual framework that had previously been missing from wildlife conservation and management. And so, in a time (the 1930s) when both financial resources and basic knowledge were scarce,

Leopold became a strong advocate of wildlife research, lamenting that "half a dozen New Deal bureaus are spending a score of millions on wildlife work, but not a red penny for research."[2] He was likewise convinced that wildlife research had much to contribute to basic science even as it provided guidance to management. He recognized that research in the new field had quickly shifted "to the job of plugging the holes in this foundational knowledge. Practical techniques will have to come later. For the moment we are, for the most part, ecologists rather than managers."[3]

The series of intellectual insights through which Leopold reached these conclusions are well documented in this chapter's selection of quotations. Essentially, Leopold's approach was to adapt principles he had learned as a forester. And that approach followed from a basic premise: wildlife conservation requires the deliberate manipulation of wildlife and the environment, aimed at achieving specific goals. He realized that, given the historical and ecological circumstances in which wildlife species found themselves in the twentieth century, a passive approach was doomed to failure. "We have learned," he wrote in 1925, "that game, to be successfully conserved, must be positively produced, rather than merely negatively protected."[4]

These fundamental insights set the stage for what we might today call the "strategic plan" of wildlife conservation: the establishment of goals; the collection of information to define obstacles and opportunities; the development of management techniques to overcome obstacles and take advantage of opportunities; the prescription of where, when, and to what those methods would be applied; and the establishment of a vision of what success might look like. Leopold's contributions, as revealed in these quotations, fundamentally shaped the emerging field in all these ways.

The Goals of Wildlife Management. Leopold understood that wildlife management worked toward several goals. Today we generally recognize four basic objectives of wildlife management: (1) to produce sustainable yields of exploited wildlife populations; (2) to control overabundant wildlife populations; (3) to recover rare and declining wildlife populations; and (4) to maintain intact wildlife communities as essential components of healthy ecosystems. As the field was taking shape in the 1920s and early 1930s, Leopold was clearly preoccupied with the goal of producing sustained harvests of game. In his 1933 text *Game Management* he defined game management as "the art of making land produce sustained annual crops of wild game for recreational use."[5] However, he also recognized and embraced each of these other goals as well. "Songbirds and other non-game animals," he noted, were in the 1930s "not yet thought of as subject to management."[6] He nevertheless recognized "the fact that the objective is something to look at, rather than something to shoot, catch, or trap is, from the scientific point of view, irrelevant. It remains true that population levels are determined by environment, and the environment of non-game species is subject to manipulation or management just as in game or fish."[7]

I suspect Leopold would have been disappointed that wildlife management remained overwhelmingly preoccupied with game management for much of the twentieth century. I am also sure, however, that he would have championed the expanded role that wildlife management now plays in conserving biological diversity and managing ecosystems. He wrote in 1939 that "the basic skill of the wildlife manager is to diagnose the landscape, to discern and predict trends in its biotic community, and to modify them where necessary in the interest of conservation." This notably prescient view helped to define the difference between "the static natural history of yesterday and the dynamic ecology of tomorrow."[8]

Ecological Insights Needed to Guide Wildlife Management. Leopold relied heavily on insights from ecological research to guide management practices. He saw such research as fundamental and indispensable, and in the role of professor he helped to shape the field's early research agenda. The influence of his friend Charles Elton, a leading theoretical animal ecologist, on Leopold, the practical wildlife manager, was significant. Through the 1930s Elton's ecological ideas provided the scientific underpinnings for many of the conservation principles Leopold was developing. Chief among these key principles was the basic importance of habitat quality, carrying capacity, and "limiting factors" in determining wildlife populations ("Every species in every locality has a limiting factor. It may be winter feed, or spring cover, or unlawful hunting, or overstocking, or a certain kind of vermin, or shortage of water, salt, dust, grit, or what-not. Whatever it is, a skilled man can isolate and identify it").[9]

Leopold also understood the fundamental importance of predator-prey relationships, and how they had been widely misconstrued by wildlife managers (including himself at a younger age) intent on increasing game populations. After observing firsthand, in Mexico's Sierra Madre, "an abundant game population thriving in the midst of its natural enemies," he encouraged "those who habitually ascribe all game scarcity to predators or who prescribe predator control as the first and inevitable step in all game management" to reexamine their premises.[10] Reflecting the rapidly changing state of ecological knowledge during his lifetime, Leopold hoped to see changes in the profession's views as more information became available on predator-prey relationships.

That same openness to new information shaped his views on other aspects of applied ecology, in ways that today seem remarkably current. He cautioned, for example, against reliance on traditional notions of "the so-called 'balance of nature.' . . . The growth of biological knowl-edge trends strongly to show that while population curves may oscillate about a horizontal median, a single curve seldom or never stays hori-zontal from year to year even in virgin territory. Fluctuation in numbers is nearly universal."[11] Similarly, he shifted his own views on Frederic Clement's paradigm of the ecological community as a "super-organism" (coming to prefer, in his own parlance, the term "land").

At all stages of his career Leopold remained open to new ideas and advocated a healthy measure of skepticism and critical thinking among his professional colleagues, lest they become too set in their ways. In the mid-1930s, just as wildlife management was gaining definition, he warned his peers that "no researcher can keep a sharp edge on his own faculty for self-criticism unless his contemporaries nail down such loose thinking as may escape his own vigilance."[12]

Wildlife Management Techniques. Leopold "wrote the book" on wildlife management, and *Game Management* remains the century's most influ-ential book on the subject. In its pages Leopold discussed many specific techniques of wildlife management, but also offered broader thoughts on where and what managers should manage. Among his first premises was the belief that wildlife conservation had to be practiced on all lands, not just refuges. He held that wildlife should be "one of the normal products of every farm, and the enjoyment of it a part of the normal environment."[13] As noted above, he also led the profession in expanding its scope to embrace not only game species but the entire biota. Al-though he promoted what we may now recognize as ecosystem manage-ment to achieve specific goals, he advocated applying as little manage-ment as necessary, seeking *"a happy medium* between the evident necessity of *some* management, and the aesthetic desideratum of *not too much."*[14] Further, he railed against certain types of management activities (espe-cially the stocking of exotic game) that threatened to transform the nat-ural character of the plant-animal community. He recognized that the proper and effective application of techniques depended upon the landscape in which they were to be applied, and he appreciated that wilderness areas required far less management attention than human-dominated landscapes.

Obstacles That Stand in the Way of Conservation. Leopold was not an ivory tower idealist. He understood that, in the real world, formidable ob-stacles stood in the way of achieving conservation goals. He identified clearly the social and economic factors that prevented people from adopting some of his ideas about wildlife conservation. He recognized, for example, that cultural prejudices had influenced his own early atti-tude toward predators. He subsequently changed his view and urged the public, especially sportsmen, to tolerate predators. He did so most fa-mously in his essay "Thinking Like a Mountain" in *A Sand County Alma-nac,* but as several quotations included in this chapter illustrate, he also did so in many a professional publication and conference hall address.

Leopold was keenly interested in overcoming the social and economic momentum that resulted in the destruction of wildlife habitat, especially on farms. Soon after shifting his own professional focus to game man-agement in the late 1920s, he wrote that "conservation is short of doers. We need plants and birds and trees restored to ten thousand farms, not merely to a few paltry reservations."[15] Ultimately, his approach to these difficult issues would involve not only a deeper examination of the poli-tics of social and economic reform, but a call for fundamental changes in society's moral stance. "The Land Ethic" stands as Leopold's most complete and eloquent statement on the moral dimensions of our rela-tionship with nature, but there are many indications that it was rooted in his previous writings on wildlife ecology and conservation. In a key passage from *Game Management,* for example, he offered a retort to those who might yearn for a world in which such a field was not needed. "The hope of the future," he wrote, "lies not in curbing the influence of hu-man occupancy—it is already too late for that—but in creating a better understanding of the extent of that influence and a new ethic for its governance."[16]

The Contributions of Wildlife Ecology and Management. Other sections of this volume explore Leopold's vision of a world in which human beings might coexist more harmoniously with nature. But what did Leopold see as the fundamental contributions of wildlife ecology and management, the pillars of his professional career, toward achieving that ideal? He suggests, and I agree, that one major contribution has been the convic-tion that active management of the environment, guided by ecological principles, tempered by humility, can preserve, conserve, and restore nature. In an increasingly human-dominated world, the old laissez-faire dicta—"nature knows best" and "let nature take its course"—are simply inadequate, and Leopold's style of responsible, ecologically informed intervention will remain the byword for conservation in the twenty-first century. What began in Leopold's mind as a crusade to conserve and restore game populations has yielded prescriptions for far-reaching ef-forts to conserve life on earth. As we embark on the new millennium those prescriptions have not, as Leopold feared, lost "the hurly-burly vigor of [that] youthful idea" he gave us.[17]

There seem to be few fields of research where the means are so largely of the brain, but the ends so largely of the heart.

Leopold weighing and measuring a woodcock after a hunt in the autumn of 1946. (Photo by Robert A. McCabe. Courtesy University of Wisconsin–Madison Memorial Library, Department of Special Collections)

No wilderness seems vast enough to protect wild life, no countryside thickly populated enough to exclude it.

It seems safe to call a fallacy the idea that civilization excludes wild life. It is time for the American public to realize this. Progress is no longer an excuse for the destruction of our native animals and birds, but on the contrary implies not only an obligation, but an opportunity for their perpetuation.

> The Popular Wilderness Fallacy: An Idea That Is Fast Exploding (1918); RMG 52

. . . The American people have already answered, in a vigorous affirmative, the question of *whether* our game shall be conserved. Game conservation is ready to enter its second stage, and even the layman is beginning to ask *how* it shall be accomplished. . . . The time has come for *science* to take the floor, *prepared to cope with the situation.*

> Forestry and Game Conservation (1918); RMG 55, ALS 78

. . . The writer is sensible of the fact that in arraigning the profession of forestry for a passive attitude toward the game problem, he speaks from the standpoint of a game conservation enthusiast. But why, indeed, should not more foresters likewise be enthusiasts on this question? They should—in fact, they must be, if they are to act as leaders in launching the new science of game management. Enthusiasm for forest conservation was a conspicuous attribute of foresters until long after the propaganda stage of forestry—and a very necessary one. Without it the tremendous first obstacles to launching the new science of forestry would not have been overcome. Without it we shall not overcome the first obstacles to making American game a major forest product.

> Forestry and Game Conservation (1918); RMG 59, ALS 83–84

. . . The time is ripe for aggressive thought and action on the game question, lest we be overwhelmed by a demand for which we are unprepared. The development and perpetuation of the nation's last free hunting grounds—is that not an opportunity for service which should stir the imagination of more than a mere handful of "cranks"?

> The National Forests: The Last Free Hunting Grounds of the Nation (1919)

What are the Game Farmers? . . . In general, the Game Farmers propose to supplement wild game with, or substitute for it, a supply produced under artificially regulated conditions. . . .

What are the Wild Lifers? They are the advocates of restrictive game laws; the scarcer the game the more restrictions. . . .

A first and fundamental distinction between the two is that the Game Farmer seeks to produce merely something to shoot, while the Wild Lifer seeks to perpetuate, at least, a sample of all wild life, game and non-game. The one caters to the gunner, the other to the whole outdoors-loving public. . . .

Secondly, the Game Farmer, so far, at least, is purely materialistic as to what his "something to shoot" consists of. If Chinese pheasant is cheaper and easier to raise than the American heath hen, and is equally good game, then, he says, let the heath hen go hang! . . . On the other hand, the Wild Lifer regards the perpetuation of native species as an end in itself, equal if not greater in importance than the perpetuation of "something to shoot."

> Wild Lifers vs. Game Farmers: A Plea for Democracy in Sport (1919); RMG 63–64, ALS 56–57

The advisability of controlling vermin is plain common sense, which nobody will seriously question.

> Wild Lifers vs. Game Farmers: A Plea for Democracy in Sport (1919); RMG 65, ALS 57

There is no question about the ability of the deer to increase and multiply if we can maintain an adequate breeding stock. How is a breeding stock to be kept up? As long as the whole country is open to hunting it cannot be done. The bung is in the bottom of the barrel, and we need blame only ourselves if the barrel drains dry. But why not put the bung in the side of the barrel? Why not close about twenty or thirty per cent of our territory to hunting, and thus insure the maintenance of an irreducible minimum of breeding animals, and thus automatically restock the surrounding territory?

> A Turkey Hunt in the Datil National Forest (1919); ALS 49–50

To try and raise game in a refuge infested with mountain lions, wolves, coyotes, and bobcats, would, of course, be even more futile than to try and run a profitable stock ranch under similar conditions. Predatory animals are the common enemy of both the stockman and the conservationist, and the establishment of game refuges will further strengthen the alliance between sportsmen and stockmen and give new incentive against these pests.

> Wanted—National Forest Game Refuges (1920)

... The first step toward efficient management of big game on the National Forests must consist of a quantitative regulation of the annual kill. In other words, the kill must be limited to the productive capacity of the herd.

> Determining the Kill Factor for Blacktail Deer in the Southwest (1920); ALS 88

... The methods [of estimating game populations] are merely an adaptation of methods known to every scientific man, while the principle of sustained production, toward the practice of which the whole proposed system of game management is aimed, is borrowed directly from forestry.

> Determining the Kill Factor for Blacktail Deer in the Southwest (1920); ALS 91

I wish deliberately and emphatically to state that the settlement of the West is improving rather than destroying the possibilities for successful game production. ...

... These artificial improvements involve an adjustment in the economy of nature. Some species, like the elk and buffalo, are damaged and must be relegated to areas offering exceptional conditions. Other species are benefited or damaged in varying degrees. And, of course, there are certain things we must do to aid in the adjustment. But the net result can be made a benefit, not a loss. The march of empire, therefore, is no excuse for lying down on this job.

The Game Situation in the Southwest (1920)

It takes four things to raise public game: land, breeding stock, good administration and good sportsmanship.

The Game Situation in the Southwest (1920)

It is going to take patience and money to catch the last wolf or lion in New Mexico. But the last one must be caught before the job can be called fully successful.

The Game Situation in the Southwest (1920)

First of all, a refuge is not a refuge unless it is surrounded by hunting grounds. The purpose of a refuge is to overflow. . . .

Secondly, a refuge is not a refuge unless the closed area is freed from vermin and provided with the necessary food-plants, water, fences, salt, etc., to make the breeding stock as productive as possible. . . .

Thirdly, a refuge is not a refuge unless it is enforced. . . .

Fourthly, the boundaries must be marked. . . .

Fifthly, the boundaries must be permanent. . . .

The Essentials of a Game Refuge (1921)

Every species in every locality has a limiting factor. It may be winter feed, or spring cover, or unlawful hunting, or overstocking, or a certain kind of vermin, or shortage of water, salt, dust, grit, or what-not. Whatever it is, a skilled man can isolate and identify it. A problem correctly stated is often a problem solved. If we can intensify the limiting factor by carelessness (as when somebody burned the deer yards), why can we not mitigate it by skill and care? We can. Artificial control of limiting factors is the essence of practical game management.

Wild Followers of the Forest (1923)

The most important single development which the last ten years have brought forth is implied in the word "management." We have learned that game, to be successfully conserved, must be positively produced, rather than merely negatively protected. The growing use of the terms "game management" and "game administration" reflects this change of viewpoint. In short, we have learned that game is a crop, which Nature will grow and grow abundantly, provided only we furnish the seed and a suitable environment.

Ten New Developments in Game Management (1925); ALS 113

Game management problems are absolutely parallel to forest management problems, and the underlying principles are not merely parallel—they are identical. All the Forester has to do is to learn a few facts about game species and the people that are interested in them, and he is in a position to render effective technical services in a field that sorely needs them and so far, at least, has developed practically no technicians of its own.

Forestry and Game Management (1925)

A goose is like a grizzly, his mere presence can add a sort of flavor to a whole county.

The Way of the Waterfowl (1926)

. . . Let me state with all of the emphasis at my command that *game management research is a job of continental proportions.* It involves every acre of rural and forest land in the country. This job is not going to be done, or even scratched, in the spare time of a few enthusiasts, or by a dribbling appropriation here and there.

Science and Game Conservation ms. (1928)

The game survey is an effort to determine the condition of American game resources, and to find out what is being done, and what needs to be done, to stabilize and increase the game crop.

The Game Survey and Its Work (1928)

What determines the game crop? The game crop is the resultant of:
1. The breeding habits of the species.
2. The environment in which it lives.
Breeding habits are biologically fixed and cannot be changed.
While they differ as between species, all species breed at a rate which would soon over-populate any favorable environment, were it not for natural or artificial checks.
If there is any breeding stock at all, *the one and only thing we can do to raise a crop of game is to make the environment more favorable.* This is a mathematical axiom, and holds true for all classes of game at all times and places. It is the fundamental truth which the conservation movement must learn if it is to attain its objective.

Report of the Committee on American Wild Life Policy (1929)

What kinds and numbers of predatory species can be allowed to inhabit [a quail range]?

Environmental Controls: The Forester's Contribution to Game
Conservation (1929)

The thought I am trying to express is that all the laws in the world will not save our game unless the farmer sees fit to leave his land in a habitable condition for game.

> Wild Game as a Farm Crop (1930)

... Future predator control must be localized and discriminate.... There should probably, in most localities, be more control of small and perhaps less of large predators.

> Game Management in the National Forests (1930); ALS 128

Game conservation is at this moment in a particularly difficult stage of its development. The set of ideas which served to string out the remnants of the virgin game supply, and to which many of us feel an intense personal loyalty, seem to have reached the limit of their effectiveness. Something new must be done.

> The American Game Policy in a Nutshell (1930)

No game program can command the good-will or funds necessary to success, without harmonious cooperation between sportsmen and other conservationists.

To this end sportsmen must recognize conservation as one integral whole, of which game restoration is only a part.

> Report to the American Game Conference on an American Game Policy (1930); RMG 154

[From a list of "standards" that would promote "greater harmony among conservationists"]

No predatory species should be exterminated over large areas....

Rare predatory species, or species of narrow distribution and exceptional biological interest or aesthetic value should not be subjected to control.

> Report to the American Game Conference on an American Game Policy, Appendix (1930)

That native species should be given preference in management is a self-evident principle of game esthetics.

> Report to the American Game Conference on an American Game Policy, Appendix (1930)

A game policy should seek a happy medium between the evident necessity of *some* management, and the aesthetic desideratum of *not too much.*

> Game Methods: The American Way (1931); RMG 159

One thorn has festered in the heart of European naturalists and nature-lovers for years: the ruthless suppression of predators which goes
with game management in most European countries. . . .

. . . European predator-policy is empirical, not scientific. Its standards
were set before biological science was born. Our standards can be better.
This is not Europe's fault, but our own good luck, in that our biology
preceded our management.

> Game Methods: The American Way (1931); RMG 161–62

The maximum population [of game animals] of any given piece of land
depends not only on the environmental types or composition, but also
on the *interspersion* of these types in relation to the cruising radius of the
species. Composition and interspersion are the two principal determinants of potential abundance on game range.

> Game Range (1931)

Management of game range is largely a matter of determining the environmental requirements and cruising radius of the possible species of
game, and then manipulating the composition and interspersion of
types on the land so as to increase the density of the game population.

> Game Range (1931)

The purpose of this survey is to appraise the chance for the practice
of game management as a means to game restoration in the north central region. It attempts to describe game conditions as they exist, the
opportunities which those conditions offer, the human machinery available for acting on them, and the probable consequences of their further neglect.

> *Report on a Game Survey of the North Central States* (1931), 5

. . . Game environments, and hence game abundance, are the result of
dynamic and fluctuating, not static or stationary, forces. Many of these
forces can be controlled.

> *Report on a Game Survey of the North Central States* (1931), 15

It is important . . . to start out with the conception that the status of any
species of game is not a static condition nor a uniform trend, but rather
the constantly changing result of the interplay of many forces, some of
which are visible and others invisible, but all dynamic. Nothing is more
fatal to straight thinking in conservation than to assume that we see everything that happens, or that causes are simple, separate, or constant.

> *Report on a Game Survey of the North Central States* (1931), 24

Here is one of the most astonishing incidents observed during the
[game] survey: I was introduced to a highly educated dirt-farmer, who

was so keen for game conservation that he drove 20 miles to town each week to attend a meeting of his local chapter of the Izaak Walton League. I asked him how the game fared on his farm. He replied that he had hardly any, in spite of the fact that he allowed no shooting. I asked him about the cover, and learned he had recently cleared off the only remaining cover on his place—a strip of brushy timber along a creek bank. It was apparently a revelation to him that this had anything to do with his game crop.

Report on a Game Survey of the North Central States (1931), 253

Any appraisal of game research and education at this particular moment must inevitably consist in part of a mere sketch of things hoped for, as distinguished from a recital of things accomplished. Research aimed deliberately toward the production of game crops is barely in its swaddling clothes, much less out of them.

Report on a Game Survey of the North Central States (1931), 259

The idea of controlling environment is the fundamental thing for game management to contribute to the conservation movement. Shooting and all other aspects of game utilization are simply things which become possible when environments are kept favorable.

Report on a Game Survey of the North Central States (1931), 262

. . . Does anyone still believe that restrictive game laws alone will halt the wave of destruction which sweeps majestically across the continent, regardless of closed seasons, paper refuges, bird-books-for-school-children, game farms, Izaak Walton Leagues, Audubon Societies, or the other feeble palliatives which we protectionists and sportsmen, jointly or separately, have so far erected as barriers in its path? . . .

I have tried to build a mechanism whereby the sportsmen and the Ammunition Industry could contribute financially to the solution of this problem, without dictating the answer themselves. . . .

These things I have done, and I make no apology for them.

Game and Wild Life Conservation (1932); RMG 166

The [game] protectionists will . . . remind me of the possibilities of inviolate sanctuaries, publicly owned, in which habitable environments are perpetuated at public expense. Let us by all means have as many as possible. But will Mr. Babbitt vote the necessary funds for the huge expansion in sanctuaries which we need? He hasn't so far. It is "blood money" which has bought a large part of what we have. Moreover, sanctuaries propose to salvage only a few samples of wild life. I, for one, demand more. I demand . . . that game and wild life be one of the normal products of every farm, and the enjoyment of it a part of the normal environment of every boy, whether he live next door to a public sanctuary or elsewhere.

> Game and Wild Life Conservation (1932); RMG 167

Game management lubricates the engine we call "Nature," rather than building a substitute engine in the form of a propagating plant. The motive power is that natural force implied in the biblical injunction, "Go forth and replenish the earth," and which professors define impersonally as "the tendency of any species to increase to the capacity of its environment."

> Grand-Opera Game (1932); RMG 169

We have dug up the life histories of corn, cattle, quail, grass, and oaks, but where is the experiment to find how to grow all of them on the same farm? We have studied ducks, fish, and fur, but where is the experiment to show how to grow them in the same pond? In addition to digging deeper into specialized researches, is it not time to tie some of them together?

> Weatherproofing Conservation (1933)

Given . . . the knowledge and the desire, this idea of controlled wild culture or "management" can be applied not only to quail and trout, but to *any living thing* from bloodroots to Bell's vireos. Within the limits imposed by the plant succession, the soil, the size of the property, and the gamut of the seasons, the landholder can "raise" any wild plant, fish, bird, or mammal he wants to. A rare bird or flower need remain no rarer than the people willing to venture their skill in *building it a habitat*. Nor need we visualize this as a new diversion for the idle rich. The average dolled-up estate merely proves what we will some day learn to acknowledge: that bread and beauty grow best together. Their harmonious integration can make farming not only a business but an art; the land not only a food-factory but an instrument for self-expression, on which each can play music of his own choosing.

> The Conservation Ethic (1933); RMG 190–91

The subject matter of this volume has been hung upon a framework of "factors," rather than of species or land units, because the object is to portray the mechanism which produces *all* species on *all* lands, rather than to prescribe the procedures for producing particular species or managing particular lands.

> *Game Management* (1933), xxxii

Game management is the art of making land produce sustained annual crops of wild game for recreational use.

> *Game Management* (1933), 3

Game management and forestry grow natural species in an environment not greatly altered for the purpose in hand, relying on partial control of a few factors to enhance the yield above what unguided nature would produce. . . .

There are all degrees of control. What degree represents the best compromise between quantity and quality is a perplexing problem in esthetics and social engineering. It seems reasonable to accept some moderate degree of control, rather than to lose species, or to suffer the restriction of sport to those financially able to follow the wholly wild game of the shrinking frontier into other lands.

Game Management (1933), 3–4

Game management is merely an attempt to deal with the . . . question: How shall we conserve wild life without evicting ourselves?

Game Management (1933), 19

The early attempts to apply biology to the management of game as a wild crop soon disclosed the fact that science had accumulated more knowledge of how to distinguish one species from another than of the habits, requirements, and inter-relationships of living populations. . . . It is now become more realistic. Scientists see that before the factors of productivity can be economically manipulated, they must first be discovered and understood; that it is the task of science not only to furnish biological facts, but also to build on them a new technique by which the altruistic idea of conservation can be made a practical reality.

Game Management (1933), 20

There are still those who shy at this prospect of a man-made game crop as at something artificial and therefore repugnant. This attitude shows good taste but poor insight. Every head of wild life still alive in this country is already artificialized, in that its existence is conditioned by economic forces. Game management merely proposes that their impact shall not remain wholly fortuitous. The hope of the future lies not in curbing the influence of human occupancy—it is already too late for that—but in creating a better understanding of the extent of that influence and a new ethic for its governance.

Game Management (1933), 21

The so-called "balance of nature" is simply a name for the assumed tendency of the population curves of various species in an undisturbed plant and animal community to keep each other horizontal. The growth of biological knowledge trends strongly to show that while population curves may oscillate about a horizontal median, a single curve seldom or never stays horizontal from year to year even in virgin territory. Fluctuation in numbers is nearly universal.

Game Management (1933), 26

The extent [to which limiting factors affect a species' breeding potential] is exceedingly variable. It is determined by that whole vast and unstable gamut of circumstance which we call environment, and its interplay with the properties and also the numbers of a given species at a given time and place. This jig-saw puzzle is the province of the science of ecology. . . . Game management, like every other form of land-cropping, is applied ecology.

Game Management (1933), 38–39

. . . The mobility of the species determines the minimum unit of management. . . .

Mobility varies greatly as between species. The yearly mobility may be almost zero in quail, but almost half the circumference of the earth in certain migratory birds like the golden plover or the arctic tern. . . .

In any comparison of mobility as between species, the unit of time must be taken into account. The daily radius, the radius as between seasons, and the lifetime radius may each be an entirely different thing.

Game Management (1933), 73–74

Susceptibility to artificial rearing is of importance to game management mainly as a source of seed for restocking ranges on which the species in question is exterminated, or for planting new or restocking shot-out range. It happens, however, to be a property easily dramatized to and visualized by the lay mind, and hence has received such a large share of public attention as to become, to the rank and file, almost synonymous with conservation.

Game Management (1933), 94–95

The game manager who observes, appraises, and manipulates these half-known properties of mobility, tolerance, and sex habits of wild creatures, is playing a game of chess with nature. He but dimly sees the board, the men, or the rules. He can be sure of only two things: for intricacy and interest, any other game pales into insignificance; he must win if wild life is to be restored. If any braver challenge inheres in any human vocation, it takes something more than a sportsman to see it.

Game Management (1933), 123

. . . Game is a phenomenon of *edges*. It occurs where the types of food and cover which it needs come together, *i.e.,* where their edges meet. . . .

It will also be observed that edge-effects are most numerous in game of low mobility and high [environmental] type requirements. . . .

. . . Abundance of non-mobile wild life requiring two or more types appears, in short, to depend on the degree of interspersion of those types, because this determines the length of the edges of those types, and this in turn their vegetative richness and simultaneous availability.

The same thing may be stated mathematically as a law of dispersion: *The potential density of game of low mobility requiring two or more types is, within ordinary limits, proportional to the sum of the type peripheries.*

Game Management (1933), 131–32

Counting the invisible hosts of migratory waterfowl over a whole continent by means of such an ingenious device as Lincoln's banding ratio is a feat which has excited either incredulity or admiration, depending on the mental capacity of the onlooker. Even those able to grasp the method, however, have often not yet grasped the fact that "finding out how many there are left" is the least of the purposes of game census. Measuring the response of game populations to changes—deliberate or accidental—in their environment is the big purpose. Continuous census is the yardstick of success or failure in conservation.

Game Management (1933), 169–70

The objective of the game management program is to retain for the average citizen an opportunity to hunt. . . . This implies much more than the annual production of a shootable surplus of live birds to serve as targets. It implies a kind and quality of wild game living in such surroundings and available under such conditions to make hunting a stimulus to the esthetic development, physical welfare, and mental balance of the hunter.

Game Management (1933), 403

A pair of wood thrushes is more valuable to a village than a Saturday evening band concert, and costs less. What does it cost? A piece of woodland with undergrowth. What kind and size of trees? How many acres? What undergrowth? Does it matter what surrounds the woodland? Can it be grazed? Must it contain water? What other species help, or hinder, its occupancy? Research in applied ornithology is just as capable of answering these questions, not only for wood thrushes but for a hundred other species, as the equivalent questions for quail or pheasants.

Game Management (1933), 404

I think it is time for somebody to point out that game management is still a sort of stepchild in that austere family known as The Sciences. Nay, we are perhaps a sort of foundling left on the doorstep by unauthorized enthusiasts.

Necessity for Game Research (1934)

There are 12,000,000 acres of farmland in southern Wisconsin, capable of carrying at least 6,000,000 game birds, of which 2,000,000 to 3,000,000 could safely be shot annually, if and when they are brought into existence. There are possibly 100,000 shooters on this area, which means that each could shoot 20 to 30 birds per year, if and when the farmers and sportsmen will get together, under shooting-preserve licenses or otherwise, and provide food and cover so that the birds can multiply. The state cannot provide food and cover. Farmers can. The Lord helps those who help themselves.

Helping Ourselves (1934); RMG 208

[In Germany] the culling function of predators seems to be universally recognized as a biotic necessity. Will this happy day come to America before, or after, our magnificent predators are gone?

Review of *Notes on German Game Management* (1934)

Any review of American wildlife conservation today must begin with the waterfowl problem. The ducks desperately need two things: more marsh and less killing. They need not the one *or* the other, but *both*, and right away.

Whither 1935?—A Review of the American Game Policy (1935)

The technical literature of game management is growing apace, and is welcomed by the scientific journals. I think we may be proud of its quality. There is just one thing lacking: *criticism*. No researcher can keep a sharp edge on his own faculty for self-criticism unless his contemporaries nail down such loose thinking as may escape his own vigilance.

Whither 1935?—A Review of the American Game Policy (1935)

The zoophile has exactly the same affection for his hawks and owls as we have for our quail, partridge, or woodcock. I ask you to picture your own feeling if some group, such as farmers, set about to quietly exterminate your game birds in the alleged interest of corn, apples, or earthworms, meanwhile voting for pious policies of tolerance.

Whither 1935?—A Review of the American Game Policy (1935)

By killing off all species having predatory tendencies we may have been doing a greater damage to our game species than ever did the predators.

Wildlife Research Rapidly Growing (1935)

The era of geographical exploration of the earth is about over, but the era of ecological exploration of our own dooryards has just begun. Wild life research is one of many virgin fields of inquiry in which any persis-

tent investigator may contribute not only to science, but to the permanence of the organic resources on which civilization is dependent.
Wild Life Research in Wisconsin (1935)

Few would question the assertion that to perpetuate the grizzly as a part of our national fauna is a prime duty of the conservation movement. . . . Yet no one has made a list of the specific needs of the grizzly, in each and every spot where he survives, and in each and every spot where he might be reintroduced, so that conservation projects in or near that spot may be judged in the light of whether they *help or hinder* the perpetuation of the noblest of American mammals.
Threatened Species (1936); RMG 230–31, ALS 193–95

Most species of shootable non-migratory game have at least a fighting chance of being saved through the process of purposeful manipulation of laws and environment called management. . . .

The same cannot be said, however, of those species of wilderness game which do not adapt themselves to economic land-use, or of migratory birds which are owned in common, or of non-game forms classed as predators, or of rare plant associations which must compete with economic plants and livestock, or in general of all wild native forms which fly at large or have only an esthetic and scientific value to man. . . . Like game, these forms depend for their perpetuation on protection and a favorable environment. They need "management"—the perpetuation of good habitat—just as game does, but the ordinary motives for providing it are lacking. They are the threatened element in outdoor America— the crux of conservation policy. The new organizations which have now assumed the name "wildlife" instead of "game," and which aspire to implement the wildlife movement, are I think obligated to focus a substantial part of their effort on these threatened forms.
Threatened Species (1936); RMG 231–32, ALS 195–96

It was explicitly charged [at the 1936 North American Wildlife Conference] that the grizzly, the mountain sheep, the sage hen, the trumpeter swan, and the caribou were, if anything, in worse rather than better status since the initiation of the combined labor, land purchase, and road building program. It was recommended that an interbureau committee undertake an inventory of rare and threatened species to the end that management and land acquisition programs might be directly focused upon their needs.
Wildlife Conference (1936)

. . . I plead for a generous policy in building carrying capacity [for deer], and a stingy one in building up stock. Lucky is he who has a comfortable margin of safety between the two.

Deer and Dauerwald in Germany: II. Ecology and Policy (1936)

. . . I will claim no importance for the new profession of wild-life management save only this: that its services are vital to those atavistic few for whom a world without wild things would be no world at all—even though every citizen in it were given a Ford airplane, a Wright house, and a Townsend pension.

Means and Ends in Wild Life Management (1936); RMG 235

In edible game there is an incidental meat value, but its triviality is conveyed by the reflection that a single inedible Carolina Parakeet today may be worth more than a million edible pheasants. . . .

In any event, there is no standard scale wherein the wildlife manager may weigh his output. Consequently there is the widest conceivable range of opinion as to what is worth trying and as to which of two conflicting ends is the more important. There seem to be few fields of research where the means are so largely of the brain, but the ends so largely of the heart. In this sense the wild life manager is perforce a dual personality. Whether he achieves any degree of consistency as between his tools and his objectives, we must leave for others to judge.

Means and Ends in Wild Life Management (1936); RMG 236

Agriculture has assumed that by the indefinite pyramiding of new "controls," an artificial plant-animal community can be substituted for the natural one. There are omens that this assumption may be false. Pests and troubles in need of control seem to be piling up even faster than new science and new dollars for control work. . . .

Wild life management, however, has already admitted its inability to replace natural equilibria with artificial ones, and its unwillingness to do so even if it could.

Means and Ends in Wild Life Management (1936); RMG 237

[This] booklet is technically unsound mainly in its assumption that predator control must accompany any and all efforts to manage game. Nowhere does it admit the proved fact that game can often be restored to satisfactory population levels without any predator control. Nor does it recognize the growing conviction, universal among non-shooting conservationists, and not unknown even among sportsmen, that predatory species have an esthetic value equal to that of game, which value the sportsmen is in decency bound to respect and in no case to destroy. That the [sporting arms] industry is still oblivious of this conviction is

indicated by the inclusion of the fast-disappearing duckhawk in its pro-
scription list.

Review of Upland Game Restoration (1936)

[Summarizing lessons from wildlife conservation]
1. It does little good for the wildlife conservationist to cry over spilled
   milk.
2. The spillage cannot be gathered up by legislative fiat, and only to a
   limited extent by legislative appropriation.
3. Much more milk was spilled than was necessary, and the spilling is
   still in process.
4. One fundamental remedy, as yet barely tried, is to find out how to
   minimize the spillage—that is, how to dovetail wildlife conservation
   with economic land-use. *This is research.*
5. Another fundamental remedy is to give more people the desire and
   the skill to avoid spillage. *This is education.*

The University and Conservation of Wisconsin Wildlife (1937)

Songbirds and other non-game animals are not yet thought of as subject to management. The fact that the objective is something to look at,
rather than something to shoot, catch, or trap is, from the scientific
point of view, irrelevant. It remains true that population levels are determined by environment, and the environment of non-game species is subject to manipulation or management just as in game or fish.

The University and Conservation of Wisconsin Wildlife (1937)

To hold a species down or to build it up requires the same research.
Both operations require the same detailed knowledge of life history and
relation to environment. . . . Research, in short, is an indispensable insurance against losses arising either from too much wildlife, or too little.

The University and Conservation of Wisconsin Wildlife (1937)

Half a dozen New Deal bureaus are spending a score of millions on
wildlife work, but not a red penny for research. They come to some research unit whose total budget would not pay their office boys and say:
"Please give us the facts on which to build our program." Naturally we
can't. Nor could we if we stood with them under the financial cloudburst. Facts, like pine trees, take not only rain, but time.

The Research Program (1937)

. . . Would not our rougher mountains be better off and might we not
have more normalcy in our deer herds, if we let the wolves and lions
come back in reasonable numbers?

At the very least, [Mexico's] Sierras present to us an example of an abundant game population thriving in the midst of its natural enemies. Let those who habitually ascribe all game scarcity to predators or who prescribe predator control as the first and inevitable step in all game management, take that to heart.

Conservationist in Mexico (1937); RMG 241–42, ALS 205

Sportsmen, as well as rabbits, have their cycles of disease. Tularemia discolors the rabbit's liver, but Chukaremia distorts the sportsman's point of view.

A rabbit recovering from tularemia becomes immune to reinfection, but few sportsmen ever become immune to the idea that foreign game birds are the answer to the "more game" problem.

Tularemia may kill the rabbit, but Chukaremia never kills the sportsman. It never even makes him sick. The only damage which can, up to this date, be charged to Chukaremia is that it has depleted the game funds of 48 states for half a century, and has served as a perfect alibi for postponing the practice of game management.

Chukaremia (1938); RMG 245

In most states a dollar invested in game management will produce more long-time results and less public applause than a dollar invested in Chukars. Must we conclude then, that the average administrator is more interested in applause than in results? I think not. I think he is entirely unconscious of the distinction. By keeping himself uninformed about wildlife history and about wildlife ecology, the average administrator is able to entertain the same genuine enthusiasm for nostrums as exists in the public mind.

A profession is a body of men who voluntarily measure their work by a higher standard than their clients demand. To be professionally acceptable, a policy must be sound as well as salable. Wildlife administration, in this respect, is not yet a profession.

Chukaremia (1938); RMG 246

Fifteen years ago we started out to discover, by research, how wildlife can be increased by means of management. Have we succeeded? My answer is "No, except in a few species." That is to say, the hoped-for discoveries, leading promptly and directly to successful management, have not, in most cases, been forthcoming.

What has happened is this: The search for technique has usually disclosed an insufficient knowledge of the mechanism by which each species maintains its population. Most research enterprises have been sidetracked to the job of plugging the holes in this foundational knowledge.

Practical techniques will have to come later. For the moment we are, for the most part, ecologists rather than managers.

Wildlife Research—Is It a Practical and Necessary Basis for Management? (1938)

It was admitted by all, a decade ago, that any bird taken by a predator was a bird subtracted from the game bag, or from the residual breeding population. The new concept of carrying capacity has changed all this (although the average sportsman doesn't know it yet). It has explained—however imperfectly—the age-old paradox of the lion and the lamb not only lying down together, but being (as a race) dependent on each other for mutual thrift and welfare. It has explained, in at least a preliminary fashion, what every pioneer sees but persistently refuses to believe, namely the simultaneous abundance, on a good range, of both hunting and hunted things.

Wildlife Research—Is It a Practical and Necessary Basis for Management? (1938)

During the past decade a profession of wildlife management has sprung into existence. A score of universities teach its techniques, conduct research for bigger and better wild animal crops. However, when carried too far, this stepping-up of yields is subject to a law of diminishing returns. Very intensive management of game or fish lowers the unit value of the trophy by artificializing it.

Conservation Esthetic (1938); ASCA 169

The former one-credit course, "Survey of Game Management," will be discontinued this year. In its place will be offered a new three-credit course to be called "Wildlife Ecology."

Game Research News Letter 16 (1938)

The wildlife conservation movement is divided over several basic issues, one of which is control of predatory species.

Many (but no means all) sportsmen set a higher value on game than on other forms of wildlife, and are willing to sacrifice non-game to game species on a large scale in the form of "vermin control."

On the other hand, some sportsmen and nearly all ornithologists, mammalogists, botanists, etc., refuse to set a preferential value on game. They challenge the efficiency of "vermin control" as a means to increase game. They assert that improving food and cover is a better way to accomplish game increase, and that the way to improve food and cover may be found by scientific investigation.

I adhere to the latter school, but by reason of a lifetime of hunting and fishing am sympathetic toward the ends (if not the means) of the former.

Report on Huron Mountain Club (1938)

The objective of deer management is to preserve a safe margin between carrying capacity and population.

Report on Huron Mountain Club (1938)

Let me venture a prediction: the highest value of wildlife research
will lie not in enhanced game crops, but in enhanced understanding of
natural mechanisms. More game, after all, will benefit only a few; more
comprehension will raise the cultural level of all.

Farmer-Sportsman, A Partnership for Wildlife Restoration (1939)

The greatest single gain since 1930 lies, I think, in the growth of detail
in the idea that resources are interdependent. We knew then that you
can't have healthy fish in sick waters. We knew something of the interdependence of animals and forests. But the idea of sick soils undermining
the health of the whole organic structure had not been born. We had a
vague notion that game and predators might be interdependent, but we
lacked details as to why and how. We do not yet have many details, but
we have a few.

The clearest is the idea that browsing mammals, unlike birds, are in
constant danger of destroying their own range, and that hunting alone
is seldom a sufficiently delicate control to keep the herds in balance. We
need predators as well.

Farmer-Sportsman, A Partnership for Wildlife Restoration (1939)

It is clear by now that *there is no short cut* to wildlife conservation. Neither
laws, nor appropriations, nor bureaus, nor the training of technical
men, nor popular agitation of the subject is going to accomplish much
until there exists:

  (a) A critical judgment in the average citizen as to what wildlife
        conservation is, what methods are sound or unsound, what
        worthwhile or trivial.
  (b) A personal enthusiasm for and enjoyment of wildlife in a high
        proportion of citizens, especially landowners.
  (c) A much deeper knowledge of natural mechanisms, and a corre-
        spondingly sounder technique.

To bring these three things into existence is a job requiring generations rather than years.

[Report of the] Chair of Wildlife Management ms. (1939)

The basic skill of the wildlife manager is to diagnose the landscape, to
discern and predict trends in its biotic community, and to modify them
where necessary in the interest of conservation. . . .

To appraise the landscape the student must know its component parts
and something of their interrelationships. That is to say, he must know
its plants and animals, its soils and waters, and something of their inter-

dependence, successions, and competitions. He must know the industries dependent on that landscape, their effect upon it, and its effect upon them. He must know and habitually use visible "indicators" of those slow landscape changes that are invisible but nonetheless real. . . .

In viewing the landscape, he should habitually infer its past and foresee its future; that is to say, he should think in terms, not of plant and animal species alone, but of communities; not of types alone, but of successions. In this lies the difference between the static natural history of yesterday and the dynamic ecology of tomorrow. . . .

Last and most important, he should have developed in some degree that imponderable combination of curiosity, skepticism, and objectivity known as the "scientific attitude."

Academic and Professional Training in Wildlife Work (1939)

. . . The fight over predator control is no mere conflict of interest between field-glass hunters and gun-hunters. It is a fight between those who see utility and beauty in the biota as a whole, and those who see utility and beauty only in pheasants or trout.

A Biotic View of Land (1939); RMG 271

Some fear that we are getting too much research and not enough management into our journals and (by implication) into our programs. I do not share in this view; in fact, I think the shoe is on the other foot. We know how to manage only a few easy species like deer and pheasants. In other species we know a few fragmentary treatments which are *probably* beneficial, but this is not enough. Until we know more it is proper that a high proportion of our professional effort should go into research.

The State of the Profession (1940); RMG 278

I take pen in hand to review this latest publication of the Senate Wildlife Committee because I am struck by a double meaning, doubtless unintentional, in its title. It does describe the status of wildlife, but it describes even more faithfully the status of the wildlife field. Both are a jungle of information, rich, exuberant, boundless, and nearly pathless.

. . . Like a new gusher, a pressure of creative energy in the substrata of a newly tapped intellectual field is emitting a stream of facts faster than the surface crew can handle them. There are shoutings and confusion and hasty attempts to connect tanks and pipelines. . . .

When some methodical scholar in the year 2000 writes the history of conservation in America, his first chapter will draw heavily on Senate Report 1203. Perhaps conservation by that time will be a card-indexed affair, but perhaps it will lack the hurly-burly vigor of a youthful idea.

Review of *The Status of Wildlife in the United States* (1940)

How long shall we apply the name "conservation" to a system which attempts to replenish game and fish by stripping the landscape of owls, hawks, kingfishers, and herons? How long will those who want *all* kinds of wildlife turn the other cheek also to those who want only *one* kind? How soon will the sportsman find out that the reason for gameless coverts and fishless streams is not owls and herons, but rather overgrazing, overcutting, erosion, and drainage? That the remedy lies not in pest-hunts, but in a system of agriculture which is tolerant and friendly toward wild as well as tame plants and animals?

Pest-hunts (1941)

All of the errors listed below I have made, but some I am now cured of. Others I am still making, but hope some day to learn better. . . .

3. *MISCELLANEOUS.* The following miscellaneous errors are frequent enough to deserve listing:

    (a) Failing to digest the literature until field work is well along. One never finds all of it, but to search the literature *ex post facto* is to find too little of it too late.

    (b) Ignoring statistical cautions. Most "old-timers" lack statistical training, but we are not for that reason excused from developing at least home-made rules of statistical safety.

    (c) Failing to "translate" research for the layman. There is no research job so complex that it cannot be described in non-technical terms. Searching for these terms is part of the job.

    (d) Leaving a field worker "out in the sticks" for protracted periods without a break.

Mistakes I Have Made in Wildlife Research ms. (1943)

Predators originally performed for deer and elk the function of dispersal which most other species perform for themselves. When we elect to remove deer and elk predators, we automatically assume responsibility for performing their job. We have failed to do this because we have failed to realize that they had a job.

The Excess Deer Problem (1943)

Science knows little about home range: how big it is at various seasons, what food and cover it must include, when and how it is defended against trespass, and whether ownership is an individual, family, or group affair. These are the fundamentals of animal economics, or ecology. Every farm is a textbook on animal ecology; woodsmanship is the translation of the book.

Home Range (1943); ASCA 81

. . . Wildlife is never destroyed except as the soil itself is destroyed; it is simply converted from one form to another. You cannot prevent soil from growing plants, nor can you prevent plants from feeding animals. The only question is: What kind of plants? What kind of animals? How many?

> The Outlook for Farm Wildlife (1945); RMG 324

. . . A deer irruption cannot be understood at all except in terms of plant ecology. The public does not know the plants, much less how they react as a community to excess deer or other browsers.

> Adventures of a Conservation Commissioner (1946); RMG 334

It cannot be right, in the ecological sense, for the deer hunter to maintain his sport by browsing out the forest, or for the bird-hunter to maintain his by decimating the hawks and owls, or for the fisherman to maintain his by decimating the herons, kingfishers, terns, and otters. Such tactics seek to achieve one kind of conservation by destroying another, and thus they subvert the integrity and stability of the community.

> The Ecological Conscience (1947); RMG 345

. . . Two decades of game research have exhausted the easy pickings. What do we do now?

The thing for us to do now is what science always does in the same predicament—start over and dig deeper.

> Why and How Research? (1948)

. . . I have lived to see state after state extirpate its wolves. I have watched the face of many a newly wolfless mountain, and seen the south-facing slopes wrinkle with a maze of new deer trails. I have seen every edible bush and seedling browsed, first to anaemic desuetude, and then to death. I have seen every edible tree defoliated to the height of a saddlehorn. Such a mountain looks as if someone had given God a new pruning shears, and forbidden Him all other exercise. In the end the starved bones of the hoped-for deer herd, dead of its own too-much, bleach with the bones of the dead sage, or molder under the high-lined junipers.

I now suspect that just as a deer herd lives in mortal fear of its wolves, so does a mountain live in mortal fear of its deer. And perhaps with better cause, for while a buck pulled down by wolves can be replaced in two or three years, a range pulled down by too many deer may fail of replacement in as many decades.

> Thinking Like a Mountain (1949); ASCA 130–32

5 SOIL AND WATER CONSERVATION

≋

Traveling in the Right Direction
Paul W. Johnson

The need to conserve soil and water seems obvious today. It was not always so. When Aldo Leopold began his conservation career with the U.S. Forest Service, our nation was on a destructive rampage. Forests and croplands were thought to exist in limitless supply. Rangelands were considered useful only to the extent that they could support livestock grazing; range health was not an issue. Wetlands were considered wastelands. Surface waters were treated as sewers. Meandering streams were deemed too slow and inefficient, and wild rivers needed to be harnessed "for the good of mankind."

Aldo Leopold was not the first to see that all was not well with our national attitude toward land. In 1864 George Perkins Marsh warned that the process of settlement should not "derange or destroy what . . . it is beyond the power of man to rectify or restore."[1] In the 1870s John Wesley Powell argued for a watershed-based approach to development in the West, even as federal surveyors were laying the range-and-township grid across it. As the 1900s began, Theodore Roosevelt and Gifford Pinchot ushered in the Progressive conservation movement and the forestry revolution. John Muir waged many a campaign for wild parklands before losing the epic battle against construction of the Hetch-Hetchy dam at Yosemite.

In Aldo Leopold's day Hugh Hammond Bennett was warning of the "national menace" that soil erosion posed. Leopold was not a soil scientist, but he was an early proponent of soil conservation, and his contributions continue to guide our efforts today. Leopold's interest in this aspect of conservation dates to his early days in the Forest Service. In 1920, while on assignment in Arizona's Prescott National Forest, Leopold wrote offhandedly to his mother, "I have a new hobby. I am seriously thinking of specializing in erosion control. The problem is perfectly tremendous here in the Southwest, and I seem to be the only one who has any faith in the possibilities of tackling it successfully."[2] Leopold went on to prepare in 1923 the Forest Service's first manual on erosion control.

Many of his conservation essays from this period—and over the rest of his life—focused on the effects of poor land use on soil and water.

In the United States the first concerted national effort to address the problem of soil erosion on private lands came in 1933 with establishment of the Soil Erosion Service. Among the service's first acts was the establishment of watershed demonstration projects at twenty sites across the country. The very first of these was at Coon Valley in southwestern Wisconsin. Aldo Leopold was immediately enlisted as a technical advisor. He saw at Coon Valley the opportunity—and the need—to conserve all the area's natural values; not only the agricultural soils and waters, but the forests, fish, wildlife, and scenery as well. In a 1935 essay on Coon Valley he stated, "The crux of the land problem is to show that integrated use is possible on private farms, and that such integration is mutually advantageous to both the owner and the public."[3] This comprehensive approach to conservation set a powerful precedent for the fledgling agency.

Soon after the watershed projects began, Secretary of Interior Harold Ickes stripped the projects of their wildlife conservation component (a result, probably, of interagency squabbling). Aldo Leopold swung into action, encouraging other conservation leaders to voice their support for the more comprehensive approach to conservation. Secretary Ickes backtracked. Thus did the Soil Erosion Service—and its successor, the Soil Conservation Service—assume from the beginning a comprehensive mission. They were to assist landowners in conserving land in Leopold's full sense of the word: the "soil, water, plants, animals, and people."[4]

Leopold's ideas about land and our relationship to it developed over his entire lifetime. He came to recognize that conservation involved far more than acquisition and preservation of public lands. As he worked toward definition of his land ethic, he focused increasingly on the role of the individual landowner. In an early version of his 1939 essay "The Farmer as a Conservationist" he defined conservation as a state of harmony between people and land. "When the land does well for its owner, and the owner does well by his land—when both end up better by reason of their partnership—then we have conservation. When one or the other grows poorer, either in substance, or in character, or in responsiveness to sun, wind and rain, then we have something else, and it is something we do not like."[5]

Unfortunately, as Leopold's concept of land broadened, our nation's soil and water conservation efforts did not. In the decades following his death we became enamored of engineering fixes. Conservation in the private sector focused on protecting and maximizing the land's capacity to produce food and fiber commodities. We came to view soil and water merely as basic production inputs, to be shoved around and shaped to achieve short-term individual economic goals. Efforts to integrate human land use activities into the larger community of life were marginal at best.

This is not to say that our soil and water conservation actions since Coon Valley have been undertaken in vain. Quite the contrary. Our landscapes are much healthier today than they would have been otherwise. Erosion rates have been significantly reduced. Farms that stood on the brink of abandonment in the 1930s are once again producing bumper crops. But it is now time to take the next step in soil and water conservation. It is time to catch up with the thinking of Leopold and his colleagues from fifty years ago. This, I think, is beginning. We are seeing the first stirrings, perhaps, of a new conservation era.

In 1994 our nation took an important step toward formal recognition of land in Leopold's sense when the Soil Conservation Service was rechristened the Natural Resources Conservation Service. The 1996 Farm Bill provided a host of new resources to advance private land conservation, including support for whole-farm planning, enhanced programs for agricultural wetlands restoration, farmland protection easements, wildlife habitat restoration incentives, payments for vegetative buffers (with an emphasis on native species) and assistance for more holistic management of grazing lands. The Soil Conservation Service has not gone away. Its name may have changed, but it will always focus strongly on soils. And meanwhile, thanks in part to Aldo Leopold, it has found its roots again and is returning to a more comprehensive approach to land conservation.

Where will the legacy of Leopold and Bennett lead us in the future? First, our concept of soil and soil conservation must continue to mature. Soil is more than just sands, silts, and clays. It is a living system. It serves multiple functions. It is a filter and a buffer; it partitions water; it stores and releases carbon; it processes nitrogen and a host of other nutrients; it serves as home for a great diversity of life. As Wendell Berry has reminded us, soil is the place where death becomes life again. Leopold called it our "basic natural resource."[6]

Despite the fundamental importance of soil, we still show little respect for it. Our nation has adopted all manner of resource protection acts— a Clean Water Act, a Safe Drinking Water Act, a Clean Air Act, an Endangered Species Act. Yet we as citizens have assumed almost no responsibility for the protection of our soils. Is it time to develop a national soil quality act that would initiate an effort to define soil health and our responsibility to protect and enhance it? I think so—if our political leaders can somehow develop the will to address our individual and collective responsibilities for soil quality. Were Leopold here today, he would no doubt contribute to the national debate. At the very least he would see in the process a much-needed educational effort.

We are making more rapid progress in water conservation through our state and national laws, and through the dialogue that accompanies such legislative efforts. We have developed in the last generation a greater respect for rivers and streams, and are taking our first steps toward working with them rather than forcing them into concrete chutes. We have begun to recognize the value of wetlands, both for the important role they play in hydrologic processes and as places rich in life. Although drainage will no doubt continue on our best agricultural lands, there is no excuse for wiping the landscape dry. Natural wetlands should be part of our agricultural landscapes as well as wilderness landscapes.

Perhaps we are finally coming to see water, if not yet soil, as part of Leopold's comprehensive conservation vision. "Conservation is a state of health in the land," Leopold wrote in his essay "Conservation: In Whole or in Part." "The land consists of soil, water, plants, and animals, but health is more than a sufficiency of these components. It is a state of vigorous self-renewal in each of them, and in all collectively."[7]

In the autumn of 1995, while serving as chief of the Natural Resources Conservation Service, I slipped out of Washington with a handful of my agency leadership for a weekend at the Leopold family's "shack" in Wisconsin. There we walked the land, read from *A Sand County Almanac,* and reflected on the previous sixty years of land conservation in America. The air that weekend was crisp, the silence broken periodically by the sound of Canada geese overhead and in the nearby marsh. At one point as we walked, we all stopped at a sandy opening in an oak savannah. Using a stick we sketched out a vision for private land conservation that we eventually brought forward in the 1996 NRCS publication *America's Private Land: A Geography of Hope.*

America's Private Land calls upon us to rededicate our efforts to conserve the land. We ended that publication with a challenge for our nation to "achieve an added measure of that state of harmony between people and land" that Leopold called conservation. "We can no longer be satisfied with slowing erosion, water pollution, and other forms of land degradation. Harmony will demand that we set our sights higher— to improve the land upon which our destiny rests by restoring those places that are damaged, by enhancing those places whose condition is merely adequate, and by protecting those areas that remain pristine."[8]

It is fashionable to be discouraged about conservation these days. We shouldn't be. The Soil Erosion Service . . . the Soil Conservation Service . . . the Natural Resources Conservation Service. We have quite a legacy to build upon. As Leopold wrote in his 1947 essay "The Ecological Conscience," "I have no illusions about the speed or accuracy with which an ecological conscience can become functional. . . . In such matters we should not worry too much about anything except the direction in which we travel."[9] We are traveling in the right direction.

Soil is the fundamental resource, and its loss the most serious of all losses.

Leopold's student Joseph Hickey points out the original surface soil horizon in an eroded valley of Wisconsin's driftless region, 1942. (Photo by Aldo Leopold. Courtesy University of Wisconsin–Madison Memorial Library, Department of Special Collections)

All civilization is basically dependent upon natural resources. All natural resources, except only subterranean minerals, are soil or derivatives of soil. Farms, ranges, crops and livestock, forests, irrigation water, and even water power resolve themselves into questions of soil. Soil is therefore the basic natural resource.

It follows that the destruction of soil is the most fundamental kind of economic loss which the human race can suffer. With enough time and money, a neglected farm can be put back on its feet—if the soil is still there. With enough patience and scientific knowledge, an overgrazed range can be restored—if the soil is still there. By expensive replanting and with a generation or two of waiting, a ruined forest can again be made productive—if the soil is still there. With infinitely expensive

works, a ruined watershed may again fill our ditches or turn our mills—
if the soil is still there. But if the soil is gone, the loss is absolute and irrev-
ocable.

Erosion and Prosperity ms. (1921)

. . . We generally make the fatal mistake of assuming that floods are
the real cause of erosion loss. We can not cause the floods to cease; therefore we throw up our hands and say "nothing can be done!" But I maintain that it is not floods, but weakened resistance to floods, that is the
real root of the trouble, and that by *artificial erosion control works* we can
build up this resistance.

Erosion and Prosperity ms. (1921)

Nature held these creek valleys, before we settled them, in spite of innumerable floods; could not nature be aided to hold them now?

Erosion and Prosperity ms. (1921)

Every year we are losing thousands of acres of good land. Every year
makes control more difficult. And every acre that goes down the creek
seems to me a loss that is preventable, needless, and beyond recall.

Erosion and Prosperity ms. (1921)

Some study has . . . been given to the differentiation of normal and abnormal erosion. This seems a question of academic rather than practical
interest. If erosion is taking away land heretofore untouched, at a rate
which will destroy that land within a generation, and if that erosion looks
in any degree preventable, the first step is to prevent, not classify.

A Plea for Recognition of Artificial Works in Forest Erosion
Control Policy (1921)

. . . We the community have "developed" Blue River by overgrazing
the range, washing out half-a-million in land, taking the profits out of
the livestock industry, cutting the ranch homes by two-thirds, destroying
conditions necessary for keeping families in the other third, leaving the
timber without an outlet to the place where it is needed, and now we are
spending half-a-million to build a road around this place of desolation
which we have created. And to replace this smiling valley which nature
gave us free, we are spending another half-a-million to reclaim an equal
acreage of desert in some place where we do not need it nearly as badly
nor can use it nearly so well. This, fellow-citizens, is Nordic genius for
reducing to possession the wilderness.

Erosion as a Menace to the Social and Economic Future of the
Southwest (1922/1946)

Half-way measures [to conserve land and water resources in the Southwest] will be of doubtful efficacy. It will be better to take radical action and obtain real relief. I would advocate that either the state or the national government put all land under inspection as to the adequacy of erosion control and force all owners, whether private or public, to conserve their lands or pass title to some owner that will.

> Erosion as a Menace to the Social and Economic Future of the Southwest (1922/1946)

By artificially impounding water we are steadily adding to our irrigated area, but these gains are being offset by erosion losses in the smaller valleys, where water was easily available simply through diversion. Broadly speaking, no net gain is resulting. We are losing the easily irrigable land and "replacing" it by land reclaimed at great expense. The significant fact that is not understood is that this "replacement" is no replacement at all, but rather slicing at one end of our loaf while the other end sloughs away in waste. Some day the slicing and sloughing will meet. Then we shall realize that we needed the whole loaf.

> Some Fundamentals of Conservation in the Southwest (1923);
> RMG 87

Erosion eats into our hills like a contagion, and floods bring down the loosened soil upon our valleys like a scourge. Water, soil, animals, and plants—the very fabric of prosperity—react to destroy each other and us. Science can and must unravel those reactions, and government must enforce the findings of science. This is the economic bearing of conservation on the future of the Southwest.

> Some Fundamentals of Conservation in the Southwest (1923);
> RMG 93

Whenever, through a long period of time (say a generation) [the forces of resistance and disintegration] approximately balance, and no material change in the configuration of the country occurs, the country may be said to be in equilibrium, and the state of erosion may be called normal.

Whenever, through a similar period of time, a material change occurs in the configuration of the country (such as the disappearance of creek bottoms or gullying of slopes) the state of erosion may be called abnormal. . . .

For practical purposes, no distinction need be made between normal and abnormal. Any erosion that is doing damage and that can be controlled should be controlled. There is no danger of our control work being so successful as to interfere with normal or beneficial erosion.

> *Watershed Handbook* (1923)

Engineers have so far discovered no practicable method for removing silt from reservoirs, and accordingly siltage limits the life of every reservoir in the Southwest. Slowing up siltage by watershed conservation is therefore vital to the future of reclamation, and constitutes one of the most important functions of the Forest Service.

Watershed Handbook (1923)

[Artificial or engineering measures] are merely supplementary to conservation of vegetative cover through proper forest and range management. As foresters we naturally approach the erosion problem from the vegetative viewpoint, and use engineering works only to aid rather than take the place of forest and range conservation.

Watershed Handbook (1923)

[Under "Check List of Erosion Problems and Remedies: Farms and Ranches"]
1. To prevent gullying of plowland
    (a) Plow on contours, rather than up and down slopes.
    (b) Terrace steep slopes with rock walls, logs, or embankments.
    (c) Do not remove natural brush or sod from watercourses.
    (d) Be especially watchful while land lies fallow.
    (e) While irrigating see that water does not spill off in such a way as to start gullies.

Watershed Handbook (1923)

. . . If we saw a Nordic settler perspiring profusely to put a new field under irrigation while a flood was eating away his older field for lack of a few protective works, we should call that settler an inefficient pioneer. Yet that is exactly what we seem to be doing in trying to develop the Southwest. The only difference is that while one individual is putting the new field under irrigation, another individual is losing the older field from floods, and a third is causing the floods through misuse of his range. This scattering of cause and effect and of loss and gain among different owners or industries may give the individual his alibi, but it changes not one whit the inefficiency of our joint enterprise in "developing" the country. We, the community, are saving at the spigot and wasting at the bunghole, and it is time we realized it and mended our ways.

Pioneers and Gullies (1924); RMG 106, ALS 164

. . . In the Southwest it is doubtful whether we are creating more useful land with the labor of our hands than we are unintentionally destroying with the trampling of our feet.

Pioneers and Gullies (1924); RMG 109, ALS 168

Every region seems to have a different resistance to every kind of use or abuse by man. The degree and nature of this resistance seem to be determined by climate. The more arid the climate, the less the resistance of the region to abuse.

Pioneers and Gullies (1924); RMG 109, ALS 168

Vanished forests can be replaced by huge expenditures, but no country has ever replaced lost agricultural land on a big scale. The Incas came the nearest to it in the terraces which they built with soil packed in on their backs. We will not have the patience to do that. We have no way to restore the soil to lands that have washed away. Soil is the fundamental resource, and its loss the most serious of all losses.

Pioneers and Gullies (1924); RMG 109, ALS 169

A part of the erosion which is undermining the fertility of farm lands and choking rivers and harbors with silt is due to the same devegetation of gullies, creek banks, and drainage channels which is undermining the game crop.

What is the remedy? Obviously we are dealing with an economic trend in the direction of more intensive farming, and this trend has behind it not only the tremendous force of economic law, but also the entire machinery for agricultural research and extension represented by the system of agricultural colleges.

Progress of the Game Survey (1929)

The most important and least supported of all the fields of conservation activity is that dealing with the control of soil erosion. Deterioration or removal of the soil inevitably reduces the farm, forest, or game crops which can be produced upon it. Deficient land crops can be improved within relatively short periods, but deteriorated land may require centuries for its rehabilitation.

The north central States are just beginning to realize the fundamental importance of protecting land against deterioration through abnormal erosion.

Report on a Game Survey of the North Central States (1931), 247

There is something almost absurd in the expenditure of hundreds of millions for navigation and flood control in the large rivers which drain from the north central region, without even an attempt to influence agricultural practices on their watersheds. The engineering personnel in charge of navigation and flood control seem either oblivious to the biological mechanisms which help determine the behavior of rivers, or else take the attitude that because unsound claims have in times past been advanced as to their effects, that therefore they have no effects.

Report on a Game Survey of the North Central States (1931), 249–50

The rivers on which we have built storage reservoirs or power dams deposit their deltas not only in the sea, but behind the dams. We build these to store water, and mortgage our irrigated valleys and our industries to pay for them, but every year they store a little less water and a little more mud. Reclamation, which should be for all time, thus becomes in part the source of a merely temporary prosperity.

The Virgin Southwest (1933); RMG 179

. . . We think of reclamation as a net addition to the wealth of the arid west. In the Southwest it is more accurate to regard it, in part, as a mere offset to our own clumsy destruction of the natural bottoms which required no expensive dams and reservoirs, and which the Indians cultivated before irrigation bonds had a name and before the voice of the booster was heard in the land.

The Virgin Southwest (1933); RMG 179

Public acquisition of sub-marginal soils is being urged as a remedy for their misuse. It has been applied to some extent, but it often comes too late to check erosion, and can hardly hope more than to ameliorate a phenomenon involving in some degree *every square foot* on the continent. Legislative compulsion might work on the best soils, where it is least needed, but it seems hopeless on poor soils where the existing economic set-up hardly permits even uncontrolled private enterprise to make a profit. We must face the fact that, by and large, no defensible relationship between man and the soil of his nativity is as yet in sight.

The Conservation Ethic (1933); RMG 186

With the exception of the grouse of the north, which by reason of their bud-eating habit are partially independent of a rich variety of seed-bearing flora, there is a remarkable correlation between game supply and soil fertility throughout North America.

Game Management (1933), 307

This disease of erosion is a leprosy of the land, hardly to be cured by slapping a mustard plaster on the first sore. The only cure is the universal reformation of land-use, and the longer we dabble with palliatives, the more gigantic grows the job of restoration.

Conservation Economics (1934); RMG 196

. . . In 1933 there appeared upon the stage of public affairs a new federal bureau, the United States Soil Erosion Service. Erosion-control is one of those new professions whose personnel has been recruited by the fortuitous interplay of events. Previous to 1933 its work had been to define and propagate an idea, rather than to execute a task. Public responsibility had never laid its crushing weight on their collective shoulders. Hence the sudden creation of a bureau, with large sums of easy money at its disposal, presented the probability that some one group would prescribe its particular control technique as the panacea for all the ills of the soil. There was, for example, a group that would save land by building concrete check-dams in gullies, another by terracing fields, another by planting alfalfa or clover, another by planting slopes in alternating strips following the contour, another by curbing cows and sheep, another by planting trees.

It is to the lasting credit of the new bureau that it immediately decided to use not one, but all, of these remedial methods. It also perceived from the outset that sound soil conservation implied not merely erosion control, but also the integration of all land crops. Hence, after selecting certain demonstration areas on which to concentrate its work, it offered to each farmer on each area the cooperation of the government in installing on his farm a reorganized system of land-use, in which not only soil conservation and agriculture, but also forestry, game, fish, fur, flood-control, scenery, songbirds, or any other pertinent interest were to be duly integrated. It will probably take another decade before the public appreciates either the novelty of such an attitude by a bureau, or the courage needed to undertake so complex and difficult a task.

> Coon Valley: An Adventure in Cooperative Conservation (1935);
> RMG 219

To those who know the speech of hills and rivers, straightening a stream is like shipping vagrants—a very successful method of passing trouble from one place to the next. It solves nothing in any collective sense.

> Coon Valley: An Adventure in Cooperative Conservation (1935);
> RMG 223

... The wholesale straightening of small rivers and creeks ... is done to hasten the runoff of local flood waters, and of course aggravates the piling up of flood peaks in major streams. It is, on its face, a process of pushing trouble downstream, of seeking benefit for the locality at the expense of the community. In justice the stream-straightener should indemnify the public for damage; in practice I fear the public may at times subsidize him with relief labor.

> Engineering and Conservation (1938); RMG 252

... In the drouths of the thirties, when the wells went dry, everybody learned that water, like roads and schools, is community property. You can't hurry water down the creek without hurting the creek, the neighbors, and yourself.

> The Farmer as a Conservationist (1939); RMG 264

Land . . . is not merely soil; it is a fountain of energy flowing through a circuit of soils, plants, and animals. Food chains are the living channels which conduct energy upward; death and decay return it to the soil. The circuit is not closed; some energy is dissipated in decay, some is added by absorption from the air, some is stored in soils, peats, and long-lived forests; but it is a sustained circuit, like a slowly augmented revolving fund of life.

A Biotic View of Land (1939); ASCA 216; cf. RMG 268–69

Recent discoveries in mineral and vitamin nutrition reveal unsuspected dependencies in the [energy] up-circuit; incredibly minute quantities of certain substances determine the value of soils to plants, of plants to animals. What of the down-circuit? What of the vanishing species, the preservation of which we now regard as an esthetic luxury? They helped build the soil; in what unsuspected ways may they be essential to its maintenance?

A Biotic View of Land (1939); ASCA 220, RMG 271

. . . When a soil loses fertility we pour on fertilizer, or at best alter its tame flora and fauna, without considering the fact that its wild flora and fauna, which built the soil to begin with, may likewise be important to its maintenance.

Wilderness as a Land Laboratory (1941); RMG 288

As is true of the carp, the starling, and the Russian thistle, the cheat-afflicted regions make a virtue of necessity and find the invader useful. Newly sprouted cheat is a good forage while it lasts; like as not the lamb chop you ate for lunch was nurtured on cheat during the tender days of spring. Cheat reduces the erosion that would otherwise follow the overgrazing that admitted cheat. (This ecological ring-around-the-rosy merits long thought.)

Cheat Takes Over (1941); ASCA 157–58

Mechanized man, having rebuilt the landscape, is now rebuilding the waters. The sober citizen who would never submit his watch or his motor to amateur tamperings freely submits his lakes to drainings, fillings, dredgings, pollutions, stabilizations, mosquito control, algae control, swimmer's itch control, and the planting of any fish able to swim. So also with rivers. We constrict them with levees and dams, and then flush them with dredgings, channelizations, and the floods and silt of bad farming. . . .

Thus men too wise to tolerate hasty tinkerings with our political constitution accept without a qualm the most radical amendments to our biotic constitution.

Lakes in Relation to Terrestrial Life Patterns (1941)

Soil health and water health are not two problems, but one. There is a circulatory system of food substances common to both, as well as a circulatory system within each. The downhill flow is carried by gravity, the uphill flow by animals.

There is a deficit in uphill transport, which is met by the decomposition of rocks. Long food chains, by retarding downhill flow, reduce this deficit. It is further reduced by storage in soils and lakes. The continuity and stability of inland communities probably depend on this retardation and storage.

Lakes in Relation to Terrestrial Life Patterns (1941)

The recent history of biology is largely a disclosure of the importance of qualitative nutrition within plants and animals, and within land and water communities. Is it also important as between land and water? Does the wild goose, reconnoitering the farmer's cornfield, bring something more than wild music from the lake, take something more than waste corn from his field?

Such questions are, for the moment, beyond the boundaries of precise knowledge, but not beyond the boundaries of intelligent speculation. We can at least foresee that the prevalent mutilations of soil and water systems, and wholesale simplification of native faunas and floras, may have unpredictable repercussions. Neither agriculturists nor aquiculturists have so far shown any consciousness of this possibility. A prudent technology should alter the natural order as little as possible.

Lakes in Relation to Terrestrial Life Patterns (1941)

Conservation is usually thought of as dealing with the *supply* of resources. This "famine concept" is inadequate, for a deficit in the supply in any given resource does not necessarily denote lack of health, while a failure of function always does, no matter how ample the supply. Thus erosion, a malfunction of soil and water, is more serious than "timber famine," because it deteriorates the entire land community permanently, rather than one resource temporarily.

Conservation: In Whole or in Part? (1944); RMG 311

A veritable epidemic of violence prevails at the present moment in the field of water management. Flood control dams, hydro electric dams, channelization and dyking of rivers, watershed authorities, drainages, lake outlet controls, and impoundments are running riot, all in the name of development and conservation. I am not wise enough to know which of these conversions are ecologically sound, but the most superficial observer can see that:

(1) Most of them deal with symptoms, not with organic causes.

(2) Their promoters are innocent of (or oblivious to) the principle that violence is risky.

(3) Many of them involve irreversible changes in the organization of the biota.

(4) Collectively, their use of economic arguments is naive. In one case, economic advantage is held to supercede all opposing considerations; in the next, "intangible" benefit is held to supercede all economics.

(5) In all of them, control of nature by concrete and steel is held to be inherently superior to natural or biotic controls.

(6) In all of them, the economic products of violence are held to be more valuable than natural products.

The Land-Health Concept and Conservation ms. (1946)

It cannot be right, in the ecological sense, for a farmer to channelize his creek or pasture his steep slopes, because in so doing he passes flood trouble to his neighbors below, just as his neighbors above have passed it to him. In cities we do not get rid of nuisances by throwing them across the fence onto the neighbor's lawn, but in water-management we still do just that.

The Ecological Conscience (1947); RMG 345

The sign says, "You are entering the Green River Soil Conservation District." In smaller type is a list of who is cooperating: the letters are too small to be read from a moving bus. It must be a roster of who's who in conservation.

The sign is neatly painted. It stands in a creek-bottom pasture so short you could play golf on it. Near by is the graceful loop of an old dry creek bed. The new creek bed is ditched straight as a ruler; it has been "uncurled" by the county engineer to hurry the run-off. On the hill in the background are contoured strip-crops; they have been "curled" by the erosion engineer to retard the run-off. The water must be confused by so much advice.

Everything on this farm spells money in the bank. The farmstead abounds in fresh paint, steel, and concrete. A date on the barn com-memorates the founding fathers. The roof bristles with lightning rods, the weathercock is proud with new gilt. Even the pigs look solvent.

The old oaks in the woodlot are without issue. There are no hedges, brush patches, fencerows, or other signs of shiftless husbandry. The cornfield has fat steers, but probably no quail. The fences stand on nar-row ribbons of sod; whoever plowed that close to barbed wires must have been saying, "Waste not, want not."

In the creek-bottom pasture, flood trash is lodged high in the bushes. The creek banks are raw; chunks of Illinois have sloughed off and moved seaward. Patches of giant ragweed mark where freshets have thrown down the silt they could not carry. Just who is solvent? For how long?

Illinois Bus Ride (1949); ASCA 118–19

6 AGRICULTURE

 ⿻

Preparing for a Sustainable Agriculture

Wes Jackson

More times than I can count, and for more years than I can remember, I have (with countless others I'm sure) had to handle with forced composure the question: "Who is this man Aldo Leopold you keep talking about?" The question comes in various forms, of course, but parsed out it is the same. And over the years I've tried various answers: author of *A Sand County Almanac;* preeminent leader in the conservation movement; composer of a brilliant and comprehensive statement he called "The Land Ethic." My answers have always been feeble, partly because the man's thought was so comprehensive, partly because his life was comprehensive as well. A typical follow-up question has been: "What does he have to do with sustainable agriculture?" Again, my answers have always seemed incomplete, partly because of the completeness of the man.

In all of my halting answers to these legitimate questions about Leopold's relevance to agriculture, I have wanted to use a term now enjoying increased popularity. That term is "robust." Not in the sense of a robust athlete, but in the more formal sense of something like a law that holds across a wide range of observed phenomena, bridging such disciplines as ecology, economics, and physics.

Leopold's insights were "robust" because he kept himself abreast of both older principles and emerging developments in ecology. He was also a student of history, society, and culture. Such a field naturalist is more than a student of predator-prey or host-parasite relationships, more than a student of trophic levels. His was an integrated life, one in which the insights of his expansive scholarship made him a prominent member of a select ecological academy. He recognized the *problem of agriculture* as a dilemma. It came from his appreciation of a reality inherent in all of nature's ecosystems, a reality at work since the earliest days of life on this planet. Through this special lens of his own fashioning he examined our history and fate as tillers of the soil.

A bit about that lens and what it brings into focus. Yes, everywhere nature features nutrient cycling and energy flow; but disrupt those components of the land responsible for orderly cycling and flowing, and the ecosystem will decline—meaning the harvest of contemporary sunlight will decline over the long haul. The attempts by early agriculturists to meet specific dietary requirements on a broad scale expanded the Neolithic garden to the scale we call fields. Over time we continued to ratchet up the scale of fields even as we expanded into more of nature's lands. Leopold understood that agriculture is a recent phenomenon, a departure from the way nature has worked through hundreds of millions of years of evolutionary change.

Beyond Leopold's ecological awareness was a deep sense that the human, as a sociopolitical creature, is either ignorant of or cares little about the discontinuity between nature's way and the way of the agricultural human. His frustration on this point is thinly veiled. His essay "The Land Ethic" is at once a philosophical discourse and, at minimum, a prototype for a moral code. Anticipating the changes still to come, he wrote, "We can bolster poundage from depleted soils by pouring on imported fertility, but we are not necessarily bolstering food-value. The possible ultimate ramifications of this idea are so immense that I must leave their exposition to abler pens."[1]

After "The Land Ethic," my favorite of all his essays is "Odyssey." Here he follows an atom through the world of the Native American and then follows another atom through the world of the immigrant settler-farmer. The greatly accelerated speed of the latter tells the story of land exhaustion through agriculture: "So the engineers built pools like gigantic beaver ponds, and [atom] Y landed in one of these, his trip from rock to river completed in one short century."[2]

Aldo Leopold's ecological savvy turned him into a first-rate philosopher of sorts. We don't know whether it was witting or unwitting, but his ecological insights *de facto* caused him to challenge basic assumptions of modern science itself. More than any notable ecologist since Darwin, Leopold's mind ran against the tide of Baconian-Cartesian thinking. Bacon advocated that nature be tortured to learn her truths. Descartes insisted that priority be placed on the part over the whole. Bacon and Descartes had a 250-year running start on Darwin, a head start that has made the consequences of their thinking hard to overcome.

In 1887, when Leopold was born, Darwin's ideas were not three decades old. Leopold died in 1948, eighty-nine years after the publication of *The Origin of Species*. In that short time no one in the conservation movement, perhaps no one anywhere, had internalized the Darwinian evolutionary ecological worldview more completely than Aldo Leopold, and no one had moved ecology more toward becoming the discipline that would eventually challenge the worldview spawned by Bacon and Descartes. Of course, agriculture had arisen long before Bacon and Descartes, but their scientific worldview drove (and still drives) the modern trend toward the industrialization of agriculture.

Finally, a word on the intellectual climate among ecologists at the height of Leopold's career is in order. Ecologists had flirted with the idea that much was to be gained if physics-envy could be overcome. Starting in the mid-1930s, ecology began increasingly to emphasize the breaking up of problems into their parts so as to put ecology back on a proper track. This is understandable. Soft thinking during the mechanism-versus-vitalism era had yielded a hard-won victory for the antivitalist forces. Ecologists, however, continued to shrink before the possibility of creeping vitalism. I doubt that Leopold was a vitalist, at least not of the dewy-eyed mystical stripe. But as numerous ecologists caved in, neither Leopold nor his friend Charles Elton was so easily seduced by the trend. A good thing, too, for in the thirteen years that followed, Leopold provided much of the intellectual framework leading toward the eventual marriage of ecology and agriculture.

No person in the twentieth century was more responsible for the intellectual underpinnings of sustainable agriculture than Aldo Leopold, just as no one in the previous century offered more fundamental insights than Charles Darwin. They are an important part of the company we keep at the Land Institute and an important part of the conversations we have. But we have other kinds of conversation as well, for it is clear to us that a future agriculture will require the diversity of the wild as its informant. The conversation must go both ways: if we don't save agriculture, we won't save wilderness. Who would have led that conversation better than Aldo Leopold?

The landscape of any farm is the owner's portrait of himself.

Leopold at the Faville Grove Farms near Lake Mills, Wisconsin, c. 1938. (Photo by Douglas E. Wade. Courtesy Aldo Leopold Foundation)

The typical booster is entirely out of contact with the most fundamental of his boasted resources, the soil. Ask the average one how many bushels an acre of corn produces in our valley and he doesn't know, but he will quote you yards of statistics on what the tourist spends in our town. Ask him what is wrong with the livestock industry and he will answer drouth, or foreign competition, or other accessories-after-the-fact. He doesn't know that the fundamental reason is lack of a stable land tenure to produce grass, and that his own unintelligent and irresponsible politics is in turn responsible for this.

A Criticism of the Booster Spirit (1923); RMG 103

Growing away from the soil has spiritual as well as economic consequences which sometimes lead one to doubt whether the booster's hundred per cent Americanism attaches itself to the country, or only to the living which we by hook or by crook extract from it.

A Criticism of the Booster Spirit (1923); RMG 103

While our Government and our capitalists are laboring to bring new land under irrigation by the construction of huge and expensive works, floods are tearing away, in small parcels, here and there, an aggregate of old land, much of it already irrigated, which is comparable to the new land in area and value. The opening of these great reclamation projects we celebrate by oratory and monuments, but the loss of our existing farms we dismiss as an act of God—like the storm or the earthquake, inevitable. But it is not an act of God; on the contrary, it is the direct result of our own misuse of the country we are trying to improve.

Pioneers and Gullies (1924); RMG 106–7, ALS 165

One evening I was talking to a settler in one of those irrigated valleys that stretch like a green ribbon across the colorful wastes of southern Arizona. He was showing me his farm, and he was proud of it. Broad acres of alfalfa bloom, fields of ripening grain, and a dip and a sweep of laden orchards redolent of milk and honey, all created with the labor of his own hands. Over in one corner I noticed a little patch of the original desert, an island of sandy hillocks, sprawling mesquite trees, with a giant cactus stark against the sky, and musical with the sunset whistle of quail. "Why don't you clear and level that too, and complete your farm?" I asked, secretly fearing he intended to do so.

"Oh, that's for my boys—a sample of what I made the farm out of," he replied quietly. There was no further explanation. I might comprehend his idea, or think him a fool, as I chose.

Conserving the Covered Wagon (1925); RMG 128

I insist that many farmers, once shown how to modify their agriculture to provide food and cover for game, would do so voluntarily. If all farmers were actuated solely by the profit-motive, few would continue to be farmers.

Game Cropping in Southern Wisconsin (1927)

. . . All the laws in the world will not save our game unless the farmer sees fit to leave his land in a habitable condition for game.

Wild Game as a Farm Crop (1930)

When . . . we allow the economic order to devegetate the agricultural countryside, we should realize that we are trading something valuable for a mess of pottage. And when we imagine that laws restricting killing (plus here and there a compacted state refuge or park) constitute a remedy, we are imagining an absurdity. The average farm must be kept habitable for wild life, or our laws become a mere gesture of laudable intent, and our conservation a sure-fire failure.

Vegetation and Birds (1931)

. . . Entomologists are beginning to suspect that the advocacy of "slick and clean" farming by agricultural authorities has been too indiscriminate. . . . The advocates of "slick and clean" farming have generalized too much, and the same error should not now be repeated by conservationists. The present need is for investigations which discriminate— which measure the effects of particular covert plants with a particular distribution on particular species of birds, insects, and crops, under specified conditions. Only thus can a rational adjustment between agriculture and conservation be ultimately worked out.

Report on a Game Survey of the North Central States (1931), 63

A city consisting of endless restaurants and dining rooms, with no bedrooms or living-rooms nearby, would support about as many people as Iowa supports upland game birds. Birds cannot rest, breed, or dodge their enemies in one continuous soup-kitchen, nor will a rising flood of tears from their sympathetic friends, nor increasingly rigid laws against shooting, help them to do so. Until the other elements of a habitable range are provided, tears and laws are simply beside the point. Protection has helped a few birds to persist in spite of this unbalanced range, but it will hardly restore the conditions necessary for increase. Iowa's problem is to induce the farmer to let some grass and brush grow.

Report of the Iowa Game Survey, Chapter One: The Fall of the Iowa Game Range (1932)

Agriculture, by the introduction of dozens of grains, forage plants and weeds, and by alteration of the native flora and fauna, has completely rebuilt the game food map of the continent. . . . Agriculture always changes and usually improves the game food supply, although the change may be so great as to necessitate the substitution of one species of game for another. . . .

In considering the effect of any industry on game food supply, one must take into account not only the primary operations which are purposeful and controlled, but also the tools and forces used to accomplish them which are commonly accidental and uncontrolled. Thus marsh fires are an uncontrolled tool of agriculture, and forest fires the unwelcome aftermath of lumbering.

Game Management (1933), 274

The idea of rewarding the farmer for game cropping has made some headway. I am not convinced, however, that shooting revenue alone is a sufficiently powerful incentive to bring thousands of farms under management. I now incline to believe that the full development of game cropping on farms, as well as most other kinds of conservation, must await some rather fundamental changes in rural culture and in land economics.

... Conservation, in short, is at direct variance with the moral and esthetic standards of our generation, and until those standards change, we can have only such fragments as happen to "come easy."

Whither 1935?—A Review of the American Game Policy (1935)

Ecologists like [John E.] Weaver are discovering that on the plains the physical structure and moisture regimen of the soil deteriorate under even the best agriculture. Granulation and moisture equilibrium can be restored, he thinks, by restoring the native vegetation. Perhaps a periodic reversion to prairie is to be the price of farming the inland empire.

Means and Ends in Wildlife Management (1936); RMG 237

Those who think it is impossible to interest any considerable number of farmers in wildflower management simply display the fact that they have never entered into the life and thought of a farm community. There exists in many farm communities not merely a receptivity to but an actual demand for such ideas.

Wildlife Crops: Finding Out How to Grow Them (1936)

The farmer takes pride in his gadgets, that is, his radio, car, icebox, tractor, milker, etc. This is as it should be. He takes pride in his tame crops, and this is as it should be.

But how often do we find a farmer who takes pride in his wild crops, his woodlot, his stand of quail, his coon dens, the fish in his creek or pond? Until a majority of our farmers are as proud of having a flock of prairie chickens as of owning a new car, we shall not have the chickens. . . .

Farmers do not yet have this attitude, neither do we who are not farmers.

Whither Missouri? (1938)

The fertile productive farm is regarded as a success, even though it has lost most of its native plants and animals. Conservation protests such a biased accounting.

The Farmer as a Conservationist (1939); RMG 255

Can a farmer afford to devote land to woods, marsh, pond, windbreaks? These are semi-economic land uses—that is, they have utility but they also yield non-economic benefits.

Can a farmer afford to devote land to fencerows for the birds, to snag-trees for the coons and flying squirrels? Here the utility shrinks to what the chemist calls a "trace."

Can a farmer afford to devote land to fencerows for a patch of ladyslippers, a remnant of prairie, or just scenery? Here the utility shrinks to zero.

Yet conservation is any or all of these things.

The Farmer as a Conservationist (1939); RMG 258

It is the individual farmer who must weave the greater part of the rug on which America stands. Shall he weave into it only the sober yarns which warm the feet, or also some of the colors which warm the eye and the heart? Granted that there may be a question which returns him the most profit as an individual, can there be *any* question which is best for his community? This raises the question: is the individual farmer capable of dedicating private land to uses which profit the community, even though they may not so clearly profit him? We may be over-hasty in assuming that he is not.

The Farmer as a Conservationist (1939); RMG 260

The landscape of any farm is the owner's portrait of himself.

Conservation implies self-expression in that landscape, rather than blind compliance with economic dogma.

The Farmer as a Conservationist (1939); RMG 263

Fertility is the ability of soil to receive, store, and release energy. Agriculture, by overdrafts on the soil, or by too radical a substitution of domestic for native species in the superstructure, may derange the channels of flow or deplete storage. Soils depleted of their storage, or of the organic matter which anchors it, wash away faster than they form. This is erosion.

A Biotic View of Land (1939); ASCA 217; cf. RMG 269

Biotic farming (if I may coin such a term) would . . . employ all native wild species not actually incompatible with tame ones. These species would include not merely game, but rather the largest possible diversity of flora and fauna.

Biotic farming, in short, would include wild plants and animals with tame ones as expressions of fertility. To accomplish such a revolution in the landscape, there must of course be a corresponding revolution in the landholder. The farmer who now seeks merely to preserve the soil must take account of the superstructure as well; a good farm must be one where the wild fauna and flora has lost acreage without losing its existence.

A Biotic View of Land (1939); RMG 272

Perhaps we are due for a change of attitude toward fence rows. They use up land and sometimes harbor insects, but if we abolish them we lose our birds and increase our wind.

Windbreaks Aid Wildlife (1940)

One-half of one per cent of the corn raised on an average southern Wisconsin farm will winter a good stand of wildlife. Does wildlife add one-half of one per cent to the satisfaction of rural living?

Birds Earn Their Keep on Wisconsin Farms (1940)

... To accomplish ... "wildlife management" ... the farmer must be moved by something more than a vague liking for wild things. He must be moved by a positive affection for the fauna and flora as a whole, and he must take pride in the skill and knowledge exercised in their management. In short, each farmer must build up, and cherish, his social "rating" as a producer of wild as well as tame animals and plants.

Planning for Wildlife ms. (1941)

The present ideal of agriculture is clean farming; clean farming means a food chain aimed solely at economic profit and purged of all non-conforming links, a sort of *Pax Germanica* of the agricultural world. Diversity, on the other hand, means a food chain aimed to harmonize the wild and the tame in the joint interest of stability, productivity, and beauty.

Clean farming, to be sure, aspires to rebuild the soil, but it employs to this end only imported plants, animals, and fertilizers. It sees no need for the native flora and fauna that built the soil in the first place. Can stability be synthesized out of imported plants and animals? Is fertility that comes in sacks sufficient? These are the questions at issue.

The Round River—A Parable (c. 1941); RR 164

Fires thinned [the prairie's] grasses, but they thickened its stand of leguminous herbs: prairie clover, bush clover, wild bean, vetch, lead-plant, trefoil, and Baptisia, each carrying its own bacteria housed in nodules on its rootlets. Each nodule pumped nitrogen out of the air into the plant, and then ultimately into the soil. Thus the prairie savings bank took in more nitrogen from its legumes than it paid out to its fires. That the prairie is rich is known to the humblest deermouse; why the prairie is rich is a question seldom asked in all the still lapse of ages.

Odyssey (1942); ASCA 105–6

The old prairie lived by the diversity of its plants and animals, all of which were useful because the sum total of their co-operations and competitions achieved continuity. But the wheat farmer was a builder of categories; to him only wheat and oxen were useful. He saw the useless pigeons settle in clouds upon his wheat, and shortly cleared the skies of them. He saw the chinch bugs take over the stealing job, and fumed because here was a useless thing too small to kill. He failed to see the downward wash of over-wheated loam, laid bare in spring against the pelting rains. When soil-wash and chinch bugs finally put an end to wheat farming, [atom] Y and his like had already traveled far down the watershed.

Odyssey (1942); ASCA 107

To live in harmony with plants is, or should be, the ideal of good agriculture. To call every plant a weed which cannot be fed to livestock or people is, I fear, the actual practice of agricultural colleges.

What Is a Weed? (1943); RMG 306

It seems to me that both agriculture and conservation are in the process of inner conflict. Each has an ecological school of land-use, and what I may call an "iron-heel" school. If it be a fact that the former is the truer, then both have a common problem of constructing an ecological land-practice. Thus, and not otherwise, will one cease to contradict the other. Thus, and not otherwise, will either prosper in the long-run.

What Is a Weed? (1943); RMG 309

In my view the most encouraging [omen] is the recent discovery that the fertility of the soil determines the nutritional value of the plants grown on it. We have heretofore assumed that it determined only the size of the crop.

At first glance this may seem irrelevant to conservation. Actually, it may prove to be revolutionary. It means that hereafter every plant, including every agricultural product grown for food, will have a qualitative as well as a quantitative value. "A bushel of wheat" will no longer define anything. It must also be specified what vitamins, minerals and other determiners of nutritive value that particular bushel offers. Wheat grown on healthy soil carries the potentiality of healthy animals and healthy people: wheat grown on abused soil is something less than wheat. . . .

[This] places on the landowner a new obligation to conserve the soil, and one less easily evaded than the old and familiar obligation to posterity. He who erodes his field now erodes the health of his children and his neighbors. It is ironical that chemistry, the most materialistic of sciences, has thus unwittingly synthesized a conscience for land-use.

Post-war Prospects (1944)

. . . On the fertile soils of southern Wisconsin, the strongholds of our remaining wildlife are the wood lot, the fencerow, the marsh, the creek, and the cornshock. The wood lot is in process of conversion to pasture;

the fencerow is in process of abolition; the remaining marsh is in process of drainage; the creeks are getting so flashy that there is a tendency to channelize them. The cornshock has long been en route to the silo, and the corn borer is speeding up the move.

The Outlook for Farm Wildlife (1945); RMG 324

Behind [contemporary] trends in the physical status of the landscape lies an unresolved contest between two opposing philosophies of farm life. I suppose these have to be labeled for handy reference, although I distrust labels:
1. *The farm is a food-factory,* and the criterion of its success is salable products.
2. *The farm is a place to live.* The criterion of success is a harmonious balance between plants, animals, and people; between the domestic and the wild; between utility and beauty.

Wildlife has no place in the food-factory farm, except as the accidental relic of pioneer days. The trend of the landscape is toward a monotype, in which only the least exacting wildlife species can exist.

On the other hand, wildlife is an integral part of the farm-as-a-place-to-live. While it must be subordinated to economic needs, there is a deliberate effort to keep as rich a flora and fauna as possible, because it is "nice to have around."

It was inevitable and no doubt desirable that the tremendous momentum of industrialization should have spread to farm life. It is clear to me, however, that it has overshot the mark, in the sense that it is generating new insecurities, economic and ecological, in place of those it was meant to abolish. In its extreme form, it is humanly desolate and economically unstable. These extremes will some day die of their own too-much, not because they are bad for wildlife, but because they are bad for farmers.

When that day comes, the farmer will be asking us how to enrich the wildlife of his community. Stranger things have happened. Meanwhile we must do the best we can on the ecological leavings.

The Outlook for Farm Wildlife (1945); RMG 326

The true problem of agriculture, and all other land-use, is to achieve both utility and beauty, and thus permanence. A farmer has the same obligation to help, within reason, to preserve the biotic integrity of his community as he has, within reason, to preserve the culture which rests on it. As a member of the community, he is the ultimate beneficiary of both.

The Land-Health Concept and Conservation ms. (1946)

Girdling the old oak to squeeze one last crop out of the barnyard has the same finality as burning the furniture to keep warm.

Deadening (c. 1946); RR 129

Scientific agriculture was actively developing before ecology was born, hence a slower penetration of ecological concepts might be expected. Moreover the farmer, by the very nature of his techniques, must modify the biota more radically than the forester or the wildlife manager. Nevertheless, there are many discontents in agriculture which seem to add up to a new vision of "biotic farming."

Perhaps the most important of these is the new evidence that poundage or tonnage is no measure of the food-value of farm crops; the products of fertile soil may be qualitatively as well as quantitatively superior. We can bolster poundage from depleted soils by pouring on imported fertility, but we are not necessarily bolstering food-value. The possible ultimate ramifications of this idea are so immense that I must leave their exposition to abler pens.

The discontent that labels itself "organic farming," while bearing some of the earmarks of a cult, is nevertheless biotic in its direction, particularly in its insistence on the importance of soil flora and fauna.

The ecological fundamentals of agriculture are just as poorly known to the public as in other fields of land-use. For example, few educated people realize that the marvelous advances in technique made during recent decades are improvements in the pump, rather than the well. Acre for acre, they have barely sufficed to offset the sinking level of fertility.

> The Land Ethic (1949); ASCA 222–23; cf. A Biotic View of Land
> (1939); RMG 272

7 WILDERNESS

❦

A Place of Humility

Terry Tempest Williams

A Sand County Almanac changed my life. It is the only book that I can remember where and when I read it for the first time: Dinosaur National Monument, June 1974. My mother and grandmother were talking comfortably in their lawn chairs, my brothers were playing on the banks of the Green River, and I was sitting beneath the shade of a generous cottonwood tree.

Aldo Leopold spoke to me.

With a yellow marker in hand, I underlined the words: "Wilderness is the raw material out of which man has hammered the artifact called civilization. . . . The rich diversity of the world's cultures reflects a corresponding diversity in the wilds that gave them birth."[1]

And a few pages later: "Ability to see the cultural value of wilderness boils down, in the last analysis, to a question of intellectual humility."[2]

I closed the book having finished the last two chapters, "Wilderness" and "The Land Ethic." I wanted desperately to talk to someone about these ideas, but I kept quiet and tucked Leopold into my small denim pack, not realizing what the personal effect of that paperback copy, with its flaming orange sunset over wetlands, would be.

I was eighteen years old.

Twenty-five years later, I can honestly say it is Aldo Leopold's voice I continue to hear whenever I put pen to paper in the name of wildness.

The essays of *A Sand County Almanac* were published in 1949. They were revolutionary then and they are revolutionary now. His words have helped to create the spine of the American wilderness movement.

The vision of Aldo Leopold manifested itself on the land in 1924, when he persuaded the United States Forest Service to designate 1,200 square miles within the Gila National Forest as a wilderness area. That was forty years before the Wilderness Act of 1964 was signed into law.

Aldo Leopold perceived the value of wilderness to society long before it was part of the public discourse. He has inspired us to see the richness in biological systems and to hear all heartbeats as one unified pulse in a diversified world. He understood this as a scientist and land manager, and he understood it as a natural philosopher.

When Leopold writes about "the community concept" and states that "the individual is a member of a community of interdependent parts,"[3] he instinctively elevates the discussion above what one typically hears in wilderness debates—that the land is meant for our use at our discretion, that profit must dictate public lands policy.

And when he takes this notion of interdependent parts one step further and proposes that we "[enlarge] the boundaries of the community to include soils, waters, plants, and animals, or collectively: the land," he challenges us.[4] In a politically conservative and theocratic state like mine (Utah), this kind of thinking may be regarded as grounds for heresy, evidence of paganism, the preemptive strike before black helicopters fueled by the United Nations move in to defend public lands against the people who live there.

But what I love most about Aldo Leopold is that he keeps moving through his lines of natural logic with eloquent rigor and persistence. Finally, he ruptures our complacency and asks simply, "Do we not already sing our love for and obligation to the land of the free and the home of the brave? Yes, but just what and whom do we love?"[5]

Wilderness.

In the American West, there may not be a more explosive, divisive, and threatening word.

Wilderness.

The place of a mind, where slickrock canyons hold a state of grace for eons whether or not human beings make an appearance.

Wilderness.

The mind of a place, where perfection is found through the evolutionary path of a mountain lion slinking down the remote ridges of the Kaiparowitz Plateau like melted butter.

Roadless.

Ruthless.

Wilderness.

"A resource which can shrink but not grow."[6] . . . Shrink but not grow . . . Aldo Leopold's words echo throughout the wildlands of North America.

Why is this so difficult for us to understand? Why as we enter the twenty-first century do we continue to find the notion of wilderness so controversial?

Perhaps Leopold would say wilderness is becoming more difficult to understand because there is less and less wilderness to be found.

Wilderness is threatening as a word because it is now threatened as a place.

How can we begin to understand what wilderness is if we have never experienced a place that is unaltered and unagitated by our own species? How are we to believe in the perfect mind of the natural world if we have not seen it, touched it, felt it, and found our own sense of proportion in the presence of wildness. If there is a greatness to the American spirit, a spirit aligned with freedom and faith, surely its origin is to be found in the expanse of landscapes that have nurtured us: coastlines, woodlands, wetlands, prairies, mountains, and deserts.

"Shall we now exterminate this thing that made us American?" writes Leopold.[7] The extinction of places we love may not come as a result of global warming or a meteor heading in our direction, but as a result of our lack of imagination. We have forgotten what wildness means, that it exists, here, now. If we continue to cut, whittle, and wager it away, stone by stone, tree by tree, we will have turned our backs on bears, wolves, cougars, mountain goats and mountain sheep, martins, fishers, wolverines, caribou, musk oxen, otters, sea lions, manatees, alligators, gila monsters, blue-collared lizards, roadrunners, song sparrows, milkweeds and monarchs, spring peepers and fireflies and the myriad other creatures with whom we share this continent.

Call their names. Remember their names. When Leopold speaks of silphium, sedge, leatherleaf, tamarack, buffalo, bluebirds, cranes, geese, deer, and wolves, one recognizes them as family. His language of landscape evokes an intimacy born of experience. And his experience in nature, on the land, allowed him to test his ideas, change, grow, alter his opinions, and form new ones. We are the beneficiaries of his philosophical evolution.

In 1925, Aldo Leopold wrote in "A Plea for Wilderness Hunting Grounds," "There are some of us who challenge the prevalent assumption that Christian civility is to be measured wholly by the roar of industry, and the assumption that the destruction of the wild places is the objective of civilization, rather than merely a means providing it with a livelihood. Our remnants of wilderness will yield bigger values to the nation's character and health than they will to its pocketbook, and to destroy them will be to admit that the latter are the only values that interest us."[8]

Brave words in an America on the verge of the Dust Bowl, the Depression, and the postwar build-up. Leopold held the long view in a country that was spoiled by its abundance of natural resources and whose native gifts were seen as infinite. He took his stand in and for the wilderness.

We continue to learn from Leopold—that wilderness is not simply an idea, an abstraction, a cultural construct devised to mirror our own broken nature. It is home to all that is wild, "a blank place on the map" that illustrates human restraint.

There are those within the academy who have recently criticized "the wilderness idea" as a holdover from our colonial past, a remnant of Calvinist tradition that separates human beings from the natural world and ignores concerns of indigenous people. They suggest that wilderness advocates are deceiving themselves, that they are merely holding on to a piece of American nostalgia, that they are devoted to an illusory and static past, that they are apt to "adopt too high a standard for what counts as 'natural.'"[9] These scholars see themselves as ones who "have inherited the wilderness idea" and are responding as "Euro-American men" within a "cultural legacy . . . patriarchal Western civilization in its current postcolonial, globally hegemonic form."[10]

I hardly know what that means.

If wilderness is a "human construct," how do we take it out of the abstract, and into the real? How do we begin to extend our notion of community to include all life forms so that these political boundaries will no longer be necessary? And whom do we trust in matters of compassion and reverence for life?

I believe that considerations of wilderness as an idea and wilderness as a place must begin with conscience.

I come back to Leopold's notion of "intellectual humility." We are not alone on this planet, even though our behavior at times suggests otherwise. Our minds are meaningless in the face of one perfect avalanche or flash flood or forest fire. Our desires are put to rest when we surrender to a grizzly bear, a rattlesnake, or a goshawk defending its nest. To step aside is an act of submission; to turn back is an act of admission that other beings can and will take precedence when we meet them on their own wild terms. Our manic pace as modern human beings can be brought into balance by simply giving in to the silence of the desert, the pounding of a Pacific surf, the darkness and brilliance of a night sky far away from a city.

Wilderness is a place of humility.

Humility is a place of wilderness.

Aldo Leopold understood these things. He stepped aside for other wild hearts beating in the Gila National Forest, in the Boundary Waters, in the wetlands of the sand counties, and in the fields of his own home lands where he must have puffed his pipe in admiration as the sandhill cranes circled over him at the Shack.

When contemplating Aldo Leopold and wilderness, I believe we will need in the days ahead both intellectual humility and political courage. We will need humility to say we may not know enough to intrude on these wildlands with our desire for more timber, more coal, more housing and development. We may have to bow our heads and admit that our intellectual ceiling may be too low to accommodate the vast expanse above and inside the Grand Canyon. We will need political courage to say: we need to honor and protect all the wilderness that is left on this continent to balance all the wilderness we have destroyed; we need wilderness for the health of our communities and for the health of the communities we acknowledge to exist beyond our own species. We will need both intellectual humility and political courage to say, for example, we made a mistake when we dammed Hetch-Hetchy and Glen Canyon; let us take down with humility what we once built with pride. Political courage means caring enough to explain what is perceived at the time as madness and staying with an idea long enough, being rooted in a place deep enough, and telling the story widely enough to those who will listen, until it is recognized as wisdom—wisdom reflected back to society through the rejuvenation and well-being of the next generation who may still find wild country to walk in.

This is wilderness—the tenacious grip of beauty.

In 1974, as a self-absorbed teenager, I was unaware of the efforts made twenty years earlier on my behalf by people like Howard Zahniser, Margaret and Olaus Murie, David Brower, and Wallace Stegner. They kept the Green River free-flowing through Split Mountain in Dinosaur National Monument. Nor did I realize as I sat by the river that summer day that it had been threatened by the Bureau of Reclamation's efforts to dam Dinosaur as part of the Colorado River Basin Storage Project. It was a history no one told us in Utah's public schools. All I knew was that I felt safe enough there to continue dreaming about wildness. Aldo Leopold was tutoring me sentence by sentence, showing how ecological principles are intrinsically woven into an ethical framework of being.

Historians have said the defeat of the dam on the Green River in Dinosaur National Monument marked the coming of age of the conservation movement. Conservationists of my generation were born under this covenant. The preservation and protection of wilderness became part of our sacred responsibility, a responsibility that each generation will carry.

In order to protect that which is original in the land and in ourselves, we can draw on the intellectual humility, the political courage, the wisdom and strength of character of Aldo Leopold. His lifelong respect for wilderness, revealed so compellingly in these words, inspires us not to compromise out of expediency and social pressure, not to consider lifestyles over lifezones. Rather, as Leopold states in "The River of the Mother of God," "In this headlong stampede for speed and ciphers we are crushing the last remnants of something that ought to be preserved for the spiritual and physical welfare of future Americans, even at the cost of acquiring a few less millions of wealth or population in the long run. Something that has helped build the race for such innumerable centuries that we may logically suppose it will help preserve it in the centuries to come."[11]

To those devoid of imagination, a blank place on the map is a useless waste; to others, the most valuable part.

Camp along the Rio Gavilan, 1938. (Courtesy Aldo Leopold Foundation)

By "wilderness" I mean a continuous stretch of country preserved in its natural state, open to lawful hunting and fishing, big enough to absorb a two weeks' pack trip, and kept devoid of roads, artificial trails, cottages, or other works of man.

> The Wilderness and Its Place in Forest Recreational Policy (1921);
> RMG 79, ALS 148

The argument for such wilderness areas is premised wholly on highest recreational use.

> The Wilderness and Its Place in Forest Recreational Policy (1921);
> RMG 79, ALS 148

It will be much easier to keep wilderness areas than to create them. In fact, the latter alternative may be dismissed as impossible.

> The Wilderness and Its Place in Forest Recreational Policy (1921);
> RMG 80, ALS 149

Under the policy advocated in this paper, a good big sample of [the Southwest] should be preserved. This could easily be done by selecting such an area as the headwaters of the Gila River on the Gila National Forest. . . . It is the last typical wilderness in the southwestern mountains. Highest use demands its preservation.

> The Wilderness and Its Place in Forest Recreational Policy (1921); RMG 81, ALS 150–51

. . . When I read that MacMillan has planted the Radio among the Eskimos of the furthest polar seas, and that Everest is all but climbed, and that Russia is founding fisheries in Wrangel Land, I know the time is not far off when there will no more be a short line on the map, without beginning and without end, no mighty river to fall from far Andean heights into the Amazonian wilderness, and disappear. Motor boats will sputter through those trackless forests, the clank of steam hoists will be heard in the Mountain of the Sun, and there will be phonographs and chewing gum upon the River of the Mother of God.

> The River of the Mother of God (1924); RMG 124

If the wilderness is to be perpetuated at all, it must be in areas exclusively dedicated to that purpose. . . .

Like parks and playgrounds and other "useless" things, any system of wilderness areas would have to be owned and held for public use by the Government. The fortunate thing is that the Government already owns enough of them, scattered here and there in the poorer and rougher parts of the National Forests and National Parks, to make a very good start. The one thing needful is for the Government to draw a line around each one and say: "This is wilderness, and wilderness it shall remain." . . .

Such a policy would not subtract even a fraction of one per cent from our economic wealth, but would preserve a fraction of what has, since first the flight of years began, been wealth to the human spirit.

> The River of the Mother of God (1924); RMG 125

The thing that is choking out the wilderness is not true economics at all, but rather that Frankenstein which our boosters have builded, the "Good Roads Movement."

This movement, entirely sound and beneficial in its inception, has been boosted until it resembles a gold-rush, with about the same regard for ethics and good craftsmanship. . . .

And of all the foolish roads, the most pleasing [to the Motor Tourist] is the one that "opens up" some last little vestige of virgin wilderness. With the unholy zeal of fanatics we hunt them out and pile them upon his altar, while from the throats of a thousand luncheon clubs and Chambers of Commerce and Greater Gopher Prairie Associations rises the solemn chant "There is no God but Gasoline and Motor is his Prophet!"

The more benignant aspects of the Great God Motor and the really sound elements of the Good Roads Movement need no defense from me. They are cried from every housetop, and we all know them. What I am trying to picture is the tragic absurdity of trying to whip the March of Empire into a gallop.

. . . In this headlong stampede for speed and ciphers we are crushing the last remnants of something that ought to be preserved for the spiritual and physical welfare of future Americans, even at the cost of acquiring a few less millions of wealth or population in the long run. Something that has helped build the race for such innumerable centuries that we may logically suppose it will help preserve it in the centuries to come.

The River of the Mother of God (1924); RMG 126–27

To my mind the Good Roads Movement has become a Good Roads Mania; it has grown into a pleurisy. We are building good roads to give the rancher access to the city, which is good, and to give the city dweller access to recreation in the forests and mountains, which is good, but we now, out of sheer momentum, are thrusting more and ever more roads into every little remaining patch of wilderness, which in many cases is sheer stupidity.

Conserving the Covered Wagon (1925); RMG 130

It is the opportunity, not the desire, on which the well-to-do are coming to have a monopoly. And the reason is the gradually increasing destruction of the nearby wilderness by good roads. The American of moderate means can not go to Alaska, or Africa, or British Columbia. He must seek his big adventure in the nearby wilderness, or go without it.

Conserving the Covered Wagon (1925); RMG 130

Ten years ago . . . there were five big regions in the National Forests of Arizona and New Mexico where . . . a man could pack up a mule and disappear into the tall uncut for a month without ever crossing his back track. Today there is just one of the five left. The Forest Service, the largest custodian of land in either State, has naturally and rightly joined with the good roads movement, and today has built or is helping to build good roads right through the vitals of four of these five big regions. As wilderness, they are gone, and gone forever. So far so good. But shall the Forest Service now do the same with the fifth and the last?

Conserving the Covered Wagon (1925); RMG 130

. . . The wilderness area idea is assumed to be an anti-road idea. The assumption is incorrect. . . .

Roads and wilderness are merely a case of the pig in the parlor. We now recognize that the pig is all right—for bacon, which we all eat. But there no doubt was a time, soon after the discovery that many pigs meant much bacon, when our ancestors assumed that because the pig was so useful an institution he should be welcomed at all times and places. And I suppose that the first "enthusiast" who raised the question of limiting his distribution was construed to be uneconomic, visionary, and anti-pig.

The Pig in the Parlor (1925); RMG 133

In all the category of outdoor vocations and outdoor sports there is not one, save only the tilling of the soil, that bends and molds the human character like wilderness travel. Shall this fundamental instrument for building citizens be allowed to disappear from America, simply because we lack the vision to see its value? Would we rather have the few paltry dollars that could be extracted from our remaining wild places than the human values they can render in their wild condition?

The Last Stand of the Wilderness (1925)

An incredible number of complications and obstacles . . . arise from the fact that the wilderness idea was born after, rather than before, the normal course of commercial development had begun. The existence of these complications is nobody's fault. But it will be everybody's fault if they do not serve as a warning against delaying the immediate inauguration of a comprehensive system of wilderness areas in the West, where there is still a relatively unimpeded field for action.

The Last Stand of the Wilderness (1925)

Our system of land use is full of phenomena which are sound as tendencies but become unsound as ultimates. . . . The question, in brief, is whether the benefits of wilderness-conquest will extend to ultimate wilderness-elimination.

Wilderness as a Form of Land Use (1925); RMG 134

. . . Wilderness is a resource, not only in the physical sense of the raw materials it contains, but also in the sense of a distinctive environment which may, if rightly used, yield certain social values.

Wilderness as a Form of Land Use (1925); RMG 135

Shall we now exterminate this thing that made us American?

Wilderness as a Form of Land Use (1925); RMG 137

[In Arizona and New Mexico] our six big wilderness areas of a decade ago have been, for good and sufficient reasons, reduced to one. Are those reasons good and sufficient to "develop" that one also? I say no reason is good enough to justify opening up the Gila. I say that to open up the Gila wilderness is not development, but blindness. The very fact that it is the last wilderness is in itself proof that its highest use is to remain so.

What I am trying to make clear is that if in a city we had six vacant lots available to the youngsters of a certain neighborhood for playing ball, it might be "development" to build houses on the first, and the second, and the third, and the fourth, and even the fifth, but when we build houses on the last one, we forget what houses are for. The sixth house would not be development at all, but rather it would be mere short-sighted stupidity.

A Plea for Wilderness Hunting Grounds (1925); ALS 158–59

Some centuries ago that conqueror of the wilderness, Sir Humphrey Gilbert, naively remarked: *"The countries lying North of Florida God hath reserved to be reduced into Christian civility by the English Nation."* But even old Sir Humphrey might turn uneasily in his grave if he could know at what rate they have been "reduced," and with what profligate waste of their beauty and their resources. The question now is not whether they will be "reduced," but what constitutes that "Christian Civility" for which "God hath reserved" them. There are some of us who challenge the prevalent assumption that Christian civility is to be measured wholly by the roar of industry, and the assumption that the destruction of the wild places is the objective of civilization, rather than merely a means providing it with a livelihood. Our remnants of wilderness will yield bigger values to the nation's character and health than they will to its pocketbook, and to destroy them will be to admit that the latter are the only values that interest us.

A Plea for Wilderness Hunting Grounds (1925); ALS 161

. . . It is often assumed that only mountain lands are suitable for wilderness areas. Why not swamps, lakelands, river routes, and deserts also? Surely our sons are entitled to see a few such samples of primeval America, and surely the few nickels which exploitation would put into their pockets are less important than the fundamental human experience which would be taken out of their lives.

Untitled address on wilderness conservation (1926)

The wilderness idea is a small but significant outgrowth of the idea of National Forests. Its importance is that of a test case. The decision, in my opinion, will indicate whether the U.S. Forest Service is tending to become a federal bureau which executes the laws, or a national enterprise which makes history.

Mr. Thompson's Wilderness (1928)

A few wilderness areas have been officially established in National Forests and Parks, and these should be rapidly extended.

There is an inevitable tendency for such wilderness areas to shrink,
even after they are officially set aside. They can never expand, hence the
system should be large and well-distributed, and should look to the future as well as the present need.

Report of the Committee on American Wild Life Policy (1929)

Minnesota, and to some extent Wisconsin, Michigan, and Missouri,
have a fast-fading opportunity to acquire wilderness game lands. No action is as yet visible except in Minnesota.

Report on a Game Survey of the North Central States (1931), 267

Wilderness game consists of species harmful to or harmed by economic land uses, and therefore suitable for preservation only in special
public game reservations, or in public wilderness areas. Elk and buffalo
are in this class because they damage farms and compete with livestock;
grizzly bear, moose, caribou, and mountain sheep because they usually
fail to thrive in contact with settlement; mountain goats because they
require a topography so rough as to be automatically wilderness.

Game Management (1933), 134

. . . The wilderness idea is also applicable to state, county, municipal, and
even institutional lands. We as yet recognize no such thing as a roadless
state park or forest, or a roadless spot in such areas, but we should.

Some Thoughts on Recreational Planning (1934)

Perhaps it is a truth, one day to be recognized, that no idea is significant except in the presence of its opposite.

This country has been swinging the hammer of development so long
and so hard that it has forgotten the anvil of wilderness which gave value
and significance to its labors. The momentum of our blows is so unprecedented that the remaining remnant of wilderness will be pounded into
road-dust long before we find out its values.

Why the Wilderness Society? (1935)

Wilderness remnants are tempting fodder for those administrators who
possess an infinite labor supply but a very finite ability to picture the real
needs of [this] country.

Why the Wilderness Society? (1935)

The Wilderness Society is, philosophically, a disclaimer of the biotic
arrogance of *homo americanus*. It is one of the focal points of a new attitude—an intelligent humility toward man's place in nature.

Why the Wilderness Society? (1935)

To an American conservationist, one of the most insistent impressions received from travel in Germany is the lack of wildness in the German landscape.

Wilderness (1935); RMG 226

[Mexico's] Sierra Madre offers us the chance to describe, and define, in actual ecological measurements, the lineaments and physiology of an unspoiled mountain landscape. What is the mechanism of a natural forest? A natural watershed? A natural deer herd? A natural turkey range? On our side of the line we have few or no natural samples left to measure. I can see here the opportunity for a great international research enterprise which will explain our own history and enlighten the joint task of profiting by its mistakes.

Conservationist in Mexico (1937); RMG 244, ALS 208

To build a road is so much simpler than to think of what the country really needs.

Marshland Elegy (1937); ASCA 101

Solitude, the one natural resource still undowered of alphabets, is so far recognized as valuable only by ornithologists and cranes.

Thus always does history, whether of marsh or market place, end in paradox. The ultimate value in these marshes is wildness, and the crane is wildness incarnate. But all conservation of wildness is self-defeating, for to cherish we must see and fondle, and when enough have seen and fondled, there is no wilderness left to cherish.

Marshland Elegy (1937); ASCA 101

To those devoid of imagination, a blank place on the map is a useless waste; to others, the most valuable part.

Conservation Esthetic (1938); ASCA 176

There are four jobs for the future now in sight.

The first is to make the system of wild areas mean something in terms of particular rare plants and animals (like the grizzly).

The second is to guard against the disruption of the areas still wild. Disruption may come from unexpected quarters. A deer herd deprived of wolves and lions is more dangerous to wilderness areas than the most piratical senator or the go-gettingest Chamber of Commerce.

The third is to secure the recognition, as wilderness areas, of the low-altitude desert tracts heretofore regarded as without value for "recreation" because they offer no pines, lakes, or other conventional scenery.

The fourth is to induce Mexico to save some samples of what we no longer have on our side of the border. Great scientific as well as recreational values are here at stake. It will some day be of the utmost importance to be able to study, just across the line, samples of unspoiled mountain country, to compare them with samples on our own side which have been subjected to the classical exploitation-conservation process. We have, in Arizona and New Mexico, hardly a stream still in normal condition; in the Mexican mountains such streams are still found. We have no faunas or floras which have not been abused, modified, or "improved"; in the Mexican mountains the whole biota is intact with the single exception of the Apache Indian, who is, I fear, extinct.

Origin and Ideals of Wilderness Areas (1940)

The recreational value of wilderness has been often and ably presented, but its scientific value is as yet but dimly understood.

Wilderness as a Land Laboratory (1941); RMG 287

A science of land health needs, first of all, a base datum of normality, a picture of how healthy land maintains itself as an organism.

We have two available norms. One is found where land physiology remains largely normal despite centuries of human occupation. I know of only one such place: northeastern Europe. It is not likely that we shall fail to study it.

The other and most perfect norm is wilderness. Paleontology offers abundant evidence that wilderness maintained itself for immensely long periods; that its component species were rarely lost, neither did they get out of hand; that weather and water built soil as fast or faster than it was carried away. Wilderness, then, assumes unexpected importance as a laboratory for the study of land-health.

Wilderness as a Land Laboratory (1941); ASCA 196; cf. RMG 288–89

Completely wild lands have one function which is important, but as yet ill-understood. Every region should retain representative samples of its original or wilderness condition, to serve science as a sample of normality. Just as doctors must study healthy people to understand disease, so must the land sciences study the wilderness to understand disorders of the land-mechanism.

Planning for Wildlife ms. (1941)

One of the symptoms of immaturity in our concept of recreational values is the assumption, frequent among administrators, that a small park or forest has no place for wilderness. No tract of land is too small for the wilderness idea. It can, and perhaps should, flavor the recreational scheme for any woodlot or backyard. Of course such small wild places lack the scarcity value of large ones, and should not constitute an excuse for sacrifice of large ones. Small areas are not wild in any strict ecological sense, but they may nevertheless add much to the quality of recreation.

Wilderness Values (1941)

[Describing the effect of wilderness adventure on two young men]

The elemental simplicities of wilderness travel were thrills not only because of their novelty, but because they represented complete freedom to make mistakes. The wilderness gave them their first taste of those rewards and penalties for wise and foolish acts which every woodsman faces daily, but against which civilization has built a thousand buffers. . . .

Perhaps every youth needs an occasional wilderness trip, in order to learn the meaning of this particular freedom.

Flambeau: The Story of a Wild River (1943); ASCA 113

When the sun peeped over the Sierra Madre, it slanted across a hundred miles of lovely desolation, a vast flat bowl of wilderness rimmed by jagged peaks. On the map the Delta was bisected by the river, but in fact the river was nowhere and everywhere, for he could not decide which of a hundred green lagoons offered the most pleasant and least speedy path to the Gulf. So he traveled them all, and so did we. He divided and rejoined, he twisted and turned, he meandered in awesome jungles, he all but ran in circles, he dallied with lovely groves, he got lost and was glad of it, and so were we. For the last word in procrastination, go travel with a river reluctant to lose his freedom in the sea.

The Green Lagoons (1945); ASCA 141–42

Man always kills the thing he loves, and so we the pioneers have killed our wilderness. Some say we had to. Be that as it may, I am glad I shall never be young without wild country to be young in. Of what avail are forty freedoms without a blank spot on the map?

The Green Lagoons (1945); ASCA 148–49

. . . The Arctic Institute now foreshadows the industrialization of the Arctic seas and islands, as well as the tundra and the land of little sticks. A mining railroad into the Labrador is in the offing. Need I dwell on the probable fate of the caribou, the musk ox, the barren ground grizzly, and perhaps even the walrus and polar bear?

One cannot blame the Canadians for this; it is the logical consequence of our American dogma that nothing is as important as more industrialization. (I, for one, can think of many things much more important to me, and the survival of the wilderness is one of them.)

Summarization of the Twelfth North American Wildlife Conference (1947)

A wilderness area more or less, a salmon fishery more or less, a mountain valley more or less, an Indian reservation more or less—such things are peanuts to the elephant.

A decade ago we considered sky-line drives and fire roads quite a danger to wilderness. They seem like minor irritations now. . . .

Viewing the whole wilderness field, one cannot escape the impression that conservation of wilderness and wilderness species is by way of becoming merely a pious wish.

> Summarization of the Twelfth North American Wildlife
> Conference (1947)

It was [in Chihuahua's Sierra Madre] that I first clearly realized that land is an organism, that all my life I had seen only sick land, whereas here was a biota still in perfect aboriginal health. The term "unspoiled wilderness" took on a new meaning.

> Draft foreword to *A Sand County Almanac* (1947)

There are degrees and kinds of solitude. An island in a lake has one kind; but lakes have boats, and there is always the chance that one might land to pay you a visit. A peak in the clouds has another kind; but most peaks have trails, and trails have tourists. I know of no solitude so secure as one guarded by a spring flood; nor do the geese, who have seen more kinds and degrees of aloneness than I have.

So we sit on our hill beside a new-blown pasque, and watch the geese go by. I see our road dipping gently into the waters, and I conclude (with inner glee but exterior detachment) that the question of traffic, in or out, is for this day at least, debatable only among carp.

> Come High Water (1949); ASCA 25

We all strive for safety, prosperity, comfort, long life, and dullness. The deer strives with his supple legs, the cowman with trap and poison, the statesman with pen, the most of us with machines, votes, and dollars, but it all comes to the same thing: peace in our time. A measure of success in this is all well enough, and perhaps is a requisite to objective thinking, but too much safety seems to yield only danger in the long run. Perhaps this is behind Thoreau's dictum: In wildness is the salvation of the world. Perhaps this is the hidden meaning in the howl of the wolf, long known among mountains, but seldom perceived among men.

> Thinking Like a Mountain (1949); ASCA 133

Wilderness is the raw material out of which man has hammered the artifact called civilization.

Wilderness was never a homogeneous raw material. It was very diverse, and the resulting artifacts are very diverse. These differences in the end-product are known as cultures. The rich diversity of the world's cultures reflects a corresponding diversity in the wilds that gave them birth.

For the first time in the history of the human species, two changes are now impending. One is the exhaustion of wilderness in the more habitable portions of the globe. The other is the world-wide hybridization of cultures through modern transport and industrialization. Neither can be prevented, and perhaps should not be, but the question arises whether, by some slight amelioration of the impending changes, certain values can be preserved that would otherwise be lost.

> Wilderness (1949); ASCA 188

One of the fastest-shrinking categories of wilderness is coastlines. Cottages and tourist roads have all but annihilated wild coasts on both oceans, and Lake Superior is now losing the last large remnant of wild shoreline on the Great Lakes. No single kind of wilderness is more intimately interwoven with history, and none nearer the point of complete disappearance.

> Wilderness (1949); ASCA 190

One of the most insidious invasions of wilderness is via predator control. It works thus: wolves and lions are cleaned out of a wilderness area in the interest of big-game management. The big-game herds (usually deer or elk) then increase to the point of overbrowsing the range. Hunters must then be encouraged to harvest the surplus, but modern hunters refuse to operate far from a car; hence a road must be built to provide access to the surplus game. Again and again, wilderness areas have been split by this process, but it still continues.

> Wilderness (1949); ASCA 191

In many cases we literally do not know how good a performance to expect of healthy land unless we have a wild area for comparison with sick ones. . . .

. . . All available wild areas, large or small, are likely to have value as norms for land science. Recreation is not their only, or even their principal, utility.

> Wilderness (1949); ASCA 197–98; cf. Wilderness as a Land
> Laboratory (1941); RMG 289

Wilderness is a resource which can shrink but not grow. Invasions can be arrested or modified in a manner to keep an area usable either for recreation, or for science, or for wildlife, but the creation of new wilderness in the full sense of the word is impossible.

> Wilderness (1949); ASCA 199–200

Unless there be wilderness-minded men scattered through all the conservation bureaus, the society may never learn of new invasions until the time for action has passed. Furthermore a militant minority of wilderness-minded citizens must be on watch throughout the nation, and available for action in a pinch.

Wilderness (1949); ASCA 200

Ability to see the cultural value of wilderness boils down, in the last analysis, to a question of intellectual humility. The shallow-minded modern who has lost his rootage in the land assumes that he has already discovered what is important; it is such who prate of empires, political or economic, that will last a thousand years. It is only the scholar who appreciates that all history consists of successive excursions from a single starting-point, to which man returns again and again to organize yet another search for a durable scale of values. It is only the scholar who understands why the raw wilderness gives definition and meaning to the human enterprise.

Wilderness (1949); ASCA 200–201

8   ECOLOGICAL RESTORATION

The Continuing Challenge of Restoration

Joy B. Zedler

Aldo Leopold was practicing ecological restoration long before the term was invented.

He spoke in his day of "reconstruction," "restocking," and "rebuilding," of "doctoring sick land." He wielded simple tools: an educated eye and a shovel. He and his family, his friends, and colleagues formed the field crew. More formally, Leopold, in his capacity as the first director of research at the University of Wisconsin Arboretum, helped guide some of the earliest restoration work undertaken anywhere. In so doing, he broadened the boundaries of conservation.

When we look at photographs from the 1930s and see the erosion and gullying that decades of unwise cultivation had produced, we can appreciate the aptness of the "doctoring" metaphor—and the foresight Leopold demonstrated in trying to heal wounded landscapes.

He did not employ detailed plans, experimental designs, or systematic treatments. He did not have at hand a restoration guidebook, for (as he noted) "the science of land health [was] yet to be born."[1] What he accomplished at the family's "shack" and what he helped to begin at the University of Wisconsin Arboretum rested upon firsthand knowledge and insight, and was marked by a personal and lifelong commitment to the task.

Since Leopold's day the context and the status of ecological restoration have evolved dramatically. "Land doctors" now have access to vast stores of information, both anecdotal and scientific; multitudes of articles, books, and conference proceedings; and a wealth of advice from experts and practitioners. Many of the fundamental principles upon which contemporary ideas in restoration ecology rest can be found in Leopold's works and writings. For example:

- Habitat restoration is both desirable and feasible. This is the most obvious part of the Leopold legacy, as demonstrated at his sand county farm and elsewhere.
- Restoration programs should be based on sound science. Although

116

restoration ecology had yet to be born, Leopold drew upon a broad knowledge of botany, forestry, wildlife management, and ecology to restore biological diversity and productivity to degraded lands at his farm and elsewhere.

- Vegetation restoration begins with the soil. Leopold witnessed the ecological havoc of the Dust Bowl years and understood that the earth's wounds could only be healed if soil erosion was reduced and soil fertility restored.
- Local genotypes should be used. In the accompanying quotations, for example, we find Leopold arguing that desert wolves would not be appropriate for restocking Yellowstone and that more northern populations would be preferable.
- The task of restoration will be more difficult where degradation is more severe. Restoration at Leopold's sand county farm was no easy challenge; it took more than a few weekends of work, and more than a few years of plant growth, to rebuild there a healthier and more productive ecosystem.
- Cause-effect relationships within natural systems may be indirect and complex. Leopold suggested an analogy with medicine, recognizing that "as in the human body, the symptoms may lie in one organ and the cause in another."[2]
- The recovery of native species enhances esthetic value. As attested again and again in his writings, Leopold had an immense appreciation of the native flora and fauna of waters, wetlands, deserts, grasslands, and forests.
- People benefit from hands-on involvement in restoration. Leopold's regular reference to such concepts as "husbandry" and "land health," and his very definition of conservation as "a state of harmony" between people and land, convey the sense of personal value and reward that may be found through restoration efforts.

Leopold's restoration legacy remains very much alive for modern practitioners of "land doctoring." His influence is evident, for example, in the rapidly expanding efforts to restore rangelands and prairies that have been degraded through intensive grazing and plowing. Across the continent, volunteers help to collect and sow seeds, land managers employ prescribed fires to encourage native plants and animals, and landowners experiment with new approaches to grazing in the effort to restore health to savannahs and grasslands. The scale of the restoration enterprise is impressive, with many native plant nurseries, consultants, and landscape architects active in business, in agencies, in training programs, or in conservation organizations. In Wisconsin alone, some thirty-five schoolyards each have a 1,000-square-foot prairie planted by students for combined educational and restoration purposes. The experience that Leopold provided for his own children is now being propagated throughout the state where he worked!

Although one as astute as Leopold might have anticipated the diversification of restoration into a broad field, a resulting dilemma would have been more difficult to predict. The growing enthusiasm for restoration is now being used to rationalize further destruction of natural habitats. In recent years some decision makers have embraced the idea that disturbed ecosystems can be restored or new ecosystems constructed to offset the impacts of development (for example, the unavoidable filling of wetlands). This practice is termed "mitigation" and comes into play under the Clean Water Act (for wetlands) and the Endangered Species Act (for all habitats with endangered species jeopardized by development). The presumption is that damage to a natural wetland or other community can be compensated through restoration or creation of a similar habitat nearby.

The concept is attractive but may also be seductive. Consider, for example, building a road over one half of a typical Wisconsin fen—a wetland that might harbor one hundred plant species, many of them rare. Could the loss be compensated by building a new fen? Can the layers of centuries-old peat be salvaged, moved, or replicated? Will the plants and seed banks survive? Does groundwater of the appropriate chemistry and flow rate exist in the mitigation site? Can the values that a fen has secured over many millennia be reconstructed nearby within a decade? Not likely.

Vandalism of a treasured work of art cannot be "mitigated" by repainting the damaged part on a separate canvas. And imagine how difficult the task would be if all we had were vague recollections of the painting's prior state. Such is the case with most damaged habitats, whether they are filled wetlands, channelized streams, dammed rivers, converted prairies, or fragmented forests. We know little about the processes by which the former plant and animal communities came to acquire their present composition and configuration. And even if we could recover all the species, the newly created ecosystem would have lost something of its full esthetic value—just as a painting doctored by a skilled forger is not the same as the original.

How would Leopold view mitigation? How might he respond to the assumption that natural habitats can be bartered in the hope that lost values can be replaced through restoration or construction efforts? Today, in the urbanized portions of our landscape, wetland restoration is regularly undertaken with mitigation funding. Often it is extremely costly, based on poor planning, unlikely to be implemented even as planned, heavy on engineering, limited in biological understanding, and destined to provide disappointing outcomes. This does not mean that habitats cannot be created or re-created to conduct useful functions, but we should not hold unrealistic expectations that full compensation can be achieved through the mitigation process.

Mitigation has also been undertaken in terrestrial habitats, especially where endangered species populations are jeopardized by proposed developments. It is no simpler to create a prairie or savannah for rare butterflies than it is to construct a fen. One still needs to understand which plant species must be established, how they should be propagated and introduced, where and when they should be planted, and what disturbance regimes will keep them viable within the system. Furthermore, the reestablishment of vegetation does not ensure the restoration of animal populations. Animals may not be able to find mitigation sites or may be sensitive to habitat qualities that are not obvious to researchers or practitioners.

These two scenarios—restoration as conservation and restoration as mitigation—offer many contrasts. Efforts at the former are to be applauded, especially when volunteers become involved in the long-term care of a restored ecosystem. Such restoration work demands long-term commitment. During the dry years of the 1930s the Leopold family had to plant their pines and prairie plants many times over before they took hold. The modern equivalent might be the repeated attempts required to reintroduce a species that formerly occupied the ecosystem or to hold off the spread of an invasive exotic.

Efforts at mitigation, by contrast, are misguided when critical habitats are allowed to be destroyed based upon a promise of compensation that is rarely fulfilled. Mitigation has emerged as a policy only recently—too late for a penetrating critique by Leopold. But the restoration lessons he taught us, through his example and his words, can be readily appreciated and applied:

- Do not confuse the practice of restoration with mitigation. Mitigation projects, for example, rarely involve long-term study and maintenance.
- Do not allow further destruction of critical habitat until the mitigation project is in place and shown to function as a replacement.
- Ensure that there is no net loss or degradation of habitat area and function.
- Use restoration to produce a net gain in habitat that will support the region's native plants and animals.
- Do not use the successes of dedicated land stewards to justify mitigation.

Leopold's work at the University of Wisconsin Arboretum and at the Shack property helped to lay the foundations for ecological restoration. The origins were humble but the most significant attributes were present: appreciation of scientific knowledge, persistent effort, and long-term commitment to an improved landscape. The importance of these qualities cannot be overstated as we attempt to fix inherited problems of past habitat abuse, and as we increasingly find mitigation invoked as an adequate response to future habitat alteration. We must insist that scientific knowledge, persistence, and dedication be central to mitigation projects, just as they are with restoration projects undertaken for conservation purposes. The science of land doctoring may have been born since Leopold's day, but it has yet to reach its maturity. Only with opportunities to combine science with land stewardship and public commitment can restoration come to play the role it must in achieving and sustaining healthy landscapes.

On this sand farm in Wisconsin, first worn out and then abandoned by our bigger-and-better society, we try to rebuild, with shovel and axe, what we are losing elsewhere.

Estella and Aldo Leopold planting white pines at the Shack, 1939. (Photo by Carl Leopold. Courtesy Aldo Leopold Foundation)

The American elk is a splendid animal, and an asset in any forest. On the other hand, the elk is endowed with an inborn appetite for alfalfa hay, four long legs, and a fine scorn for haystack fences. The Forests need elk, but the settler needs hay. This is the sum and substance of the problem of reintroducing elk on the National Forest ranges. The work is obviously of the kind which should be pushed with zeal but conducted with discretion.

> Restocking the National Forests with Elk: Where and How It May Be Done (1918); ALS 37

I am a thorough believer in the necessity of public acquisition of marshlands to prevent drainage. I even believe that in some regions we shall have to create new marshlands artificially on a large scale if we want a really adequate duck supply. But first of all we should put all our existing marshlands to work by restoring, by means of refuges, the usefulness of burned-out parts now idle.

> The Way of the Waterfowl (1926)

The job of restoring marshlands is bigger than either the states or the Federal Government can handle alone, and bigger than the two combined are likely to handle adequately. . . .

. . . There are two kinds of marshland restoration projects crying for action.

The first kind is interstate. Buying the Upper Mississippi bottoms is an example. Putting the water back into Klamath Lake is another. . . .

The second kind is intrastate. Restoring [Wisconsin's] Horicon marsh is an example.

> The Next Move: A Size-Up of the Migratory Bird Situation (1926)

It takes all kinds of motives to make a world. If all of us were capable of beholding the burning bush, there would be none left to grow bushes to burn. Doers and dreamers are the reciprocal parts of the body politic: each gives meaning and significance to the other. So also in conservation. Just now, conservation is short of doers. We need plants and birds and trees restored to ten thousand farms, not merely to a few paltry reservations. I would rather see a few feathers flying in the well-stocked fencerows of the future, than to see the paths of young men lead forever through these phantom coverts, grassless, foodless, birdless, inviolate and desolate.

> Game Cropping in Southern Wisconsin (1927)

Too much emphasis is placed on replanting game, and not enough on creating environments where constant replanting is unnecessary. We have still to learn the fundamental fact that in a favorable environment any wild species raises itself.

> Report of the Committee on American Wild Life Policy (1929)

[Recommendation #22 for consideration in Iowa's game survey]

Consider the purchase and reversion to original conditions of a "Virgin Prairie Park," to be dedicated to the perpetuation of the original flora and prairie animals such as pinnated grouse, upland plover, etc.

Outline for Game Survey of Iowa ms. (1931)

The deliberate and purposeful restoration of important waterfowl areas unwisely drained in the past has been talked about for many years. It is therefore gratifying that at least a few such projects are actually being executed. . . .

These projects [in Wisconsin, Minnesota, and Indiana] collectively do not as yet counterbalance to any appreciable degree the decline in the waterfowl resources, but if they are greatly multiplied they hold out the hope that such may soon be the case. A dozen or two projects of this kind, duly completed within the region, would constitute a material gain against the inroads of drainage and depletion.

Report on a Game Survey of the North Central States (1931), 202

[The] processes of devegetation have been accomplished by grazing as well as by cutting, and have accompanied the intensification of agriculture on practically all of the richer lands of the [north-central] region. . . . The necessity of restoring at least part of this vegetation has been pointed out as necessary for the production of game crops. It must here be emphasized that its restoration is equally necessary for the conservation of the land. Game conservation, conservation of soil fertility, and conservation of watersheds are jointly threatened by devegetation, and have a common interest in the reversal of the present trend. It may be said without exaggeration that if the cover needed for watershed conservation were restored to the drainage channels and hillsides of the north central region, the upland game problem would be half solved.

Report on a Game Survey of the North Central States (1931), 249

The central thesis of game management is this: game can be restored by the *creative use* of the same tools which have heretofore destroyed it— axe, plow, cow, fire, and gun. . . .

The conservation movement has sought to restore wild life by the control of guns alone, with little visible success. Management seeks the same end, but by more versatile means.

Game Management (1933), xxxi

Prohibition followed long after by restoration appears to be a fixed sequence of human thought and action on conservation affairs.

Game Management (1933), 12

If civilization consists of coöperation with plants, animals, soil, and men, then a university which attempts to define that cooperation must have, for the use of its faculty and students, places which show what the land was, what it is, and what it ought to be. . . . It is with this dim vision of its future destiny that we have dedicated the greater part of the [University of Wisconsin] Arboretum to a reconstruction of original Wisconsin, rather than to a "collection" of imported trees.

The Arboretum and the University (1934); RMG 210

The time has come for science to busy itself with the earth itself. The first step is to reconstruct a sample of what we had to start with.

The Arboretum and the University (1934); RMG 211

This, in a nutshell, is the function of the Arboretum: a reconstructed sample of old Wisconsin, to serve as a bench mark, a starting point, in the long and laborious job of building a permanent and mutually beneficial relationship between civilized men and a civilized landscape.

What Is the University of Wisconsin Arboretum? ms. (c. 1934)

Taken collectively, the Berlin system of public areas, however praiseworthy in other respects, signally fails, in so far as I have seen it, to answer the question which we hope to answer at Madison, namely: *What did this country look like originally?*

The original native landscape is the starting point. To reconstruct it has exactly the same importance to science and education as to reconstruct the Neanderthal man who first began its subjugation.

Notes on Wild Life Conservation in Germany (1935)

. . . [John E. Weaver] at Nebraska finds that prairie soils lose their granulation and their water-equilibrium when too long occupied by exotic crops. Apparently native prairie plants are necessary to restore that biotic stability which we call conservation. . . .

Here then is a new discovery which may illuminate basic questions of national policy. On it may hinge the future habitability of a third of the continent. But how shall it be followed up if there be no prairie flora left to compare with cultivated flora? And who cares a hang about preserving prairie flora except those who see the values of wilderness?

Why the Wilderness Society? (1935)

. . . The sense of husbandry . . . is unknown to the outdoorsman who works for conservation with his vote rather than with his hands. It is realized only when some art of management is applied to land by some person of perception.

Conservation Esthetic (1938); ASCA 175

Conservation . . . is keeping the resource in working order, as well as preventing over-use. Resources may get out of order before they are exhausted, sometimes while they are still abundant. Conservation, therefore, is a positive exercise of skill and insight, not merely a negative exercise of abstinence or caution.

The Farmer as a Conservationist (1939); RMG 257

In a surprising number of men there burns a curiosity about machines and a loving care in their construction, maintenance, and use. This bent for mechanisms, even though clothed in greasy overalls, is often the pure fire of intellect. It is the earmark of our times.

Everyone knows this, but what few realize is that an equal bent for the mechanisms of nature is a possible earmark of some future generation.

The Farmer as a Conservationist (1939); RMG 257

Professor [John E.] Weaver proposes that we use prairie flowers to reflocculate the wasting soils of the dust bowl; who knows for what purpose cranes and condors, otters and grizzlies may some day be used?

A Biotic View of Land (1939); ASCA 220, RMG 271

The effort to control the health of land has not been very successful. It is now generally understood that when soil loses fertility, or washes away faster than it forms, and when water systems exhibit abnormal floods and shortages, the land is sick.

Other derangements are known as facts, but are not yet thought of as symptoms of land sickness. The disappearance of plants and animal species without visible cause, despite efforts to protect them, and the irruption of others as pests despite efforts to control them, must, in the absence of simpler explanations, be regarded as symptoms of sickness in the land organism. Both are occurring too frequently to be dismissed as normal evolutionary events.

Wilderness as a Land Laboratory (1941); ASCA 194; cf. RMG 287

Many conservation treatments are obviously superficial. Flood-control dams have no relation to the cause of floods. Check dams and terraces do not touch the cause of erosion. Refuges and hatcheries to maintain the supply of game and fish do not explain why the supply fails to maintain itself.

In general, the trend of the evidence indicates that in land, just as in the human body, the symptoms may lie in one organ and the cause in another. The practices we now call conservation are, to a large extent, local alleviations of biotic pain. They are necessary, but they must not be confused with cures. The art of land doctoring is being practiced with vigor, but the science of land health is yet to be born.

> Wilderness as a Land Laboratory (1941); ASCA 195–96; cf. RMG 288

Just as there is honor among thieves, so there is solidarity and co-operation among plant and animal pests. Where one pest is stopped by natural barriers, another arrives to breach the same wall by a new approach. In the end every region and every resource get their quota of uninvited ecological guests.

> Cheat Takes Over (1941); ASCA 154

There is, as yet, no sense of pride in the husbandry of wild plants and animals, no sense of shame in the proprietorship of a sick landscape. We tilt windmills in behalf of conservation in convention halls and editorial offices, but on the back forty we disclaim even owning a lance.

> Cheat Takes Over (1941); ASCA 158

The Yellowstone wolves were extirpated in 1916, and the area has been wolfless ever since. Why, in the necessary process of extirpating wolves from the livestock ranges of Wyoming and Montana, were not some of the uninjured animals used to restock the Yellowstone? How can it be done now, when the only available stocks are the desert wolf of Arizona, and the subarctic form of the Canadian Rockies?

> Review of *The Wolves of North America* (1945); RMG 322, ALS 226

I speak from personal knowledge when I say that we duck hunters are curious animals. In our business or professional life we are glad enough to get 6 per cent on our investments, and we feel a lofty disdain for the financial wildcatter. But in the "never-never land" of outdoor sports we insist on bonanzas. We have scant enthusiasm for any wildlife restoration scheme which recognizes difficulties, disappointments and mistakes, or which admits ignorance of wildlife management, or which calls for deferred profits and the curtailment of shooting privileges. We turn a deaf ear to the obvious fact that a century of destruction cannot be undone by wishful check-writing alone. When we went on our economic drunk, we destroyed not only the life of the land, but also something in ourselves. We have yet to learn that this can be restored only by contrition and sacrifice.

> Review of *The Ducks Came Back* (1946); RMG 328

On this sand farm in Wisconsin, first worn out and then abandoned by our bigger-and-better society, we try to rebuild, with shovel and axe, what

we are losing elsewhere. It is here that we seek—and still find—our meat
from God.

Foreword to *A Sand County Almanac* (1949); ASCA viii

The outstanding conservator of the prairie flora, ironically enough,
knows little and cares less about . . . frivolities: it is the railroad with its
fenced right-of-way. Many of these railroad fences were erected before
the prairie had been plowed. Within these linear reservations, oblivious
of cinders, soot, and annual clean-up fires, the prairie flora still splashes
its calendar of colors, from pink shooting-star in May to blue aster in
October. I have long wished to confront some hard-boiled railway president with the physical evidence of his soft-heartedness. I have not done
so because I haven't met one.

Prairie Birthday (1949); ASCA 48

The Lord giveth and the Lord taketh away, but He is no longer the
only one to do so. When some remote ancestor of ours invented the
shovel, he became a giver: he could plant a tree. And when the axe was
invented, he became a taker: he could chop it down. Whoever owns land
has thus assumed, whether he knows it or not, the divine functions of
creating and destroying plants.

Axe-in-Hand (1949); ASCA 67

9 BIODIVERSITY AND CONSERVATION BIOLOGY

≉

Standing on Solid Shoulders

Gary K. Meffe

Only recently has the discipline of conservation biology come forward as a new and challenging force in conservation. It emerged in the closing decades of the twentieth century, largely through the efforts of a growing number of ecologists, population geneticists, and others who realized that their work, and their world, were at risk. Their field sites were disappearing, their study populations were being fragmented, and their academic isolation from the rapidly deteriorating world around them was not a promising long-term strategy for professional success. They had to change directions, see their world in a larger context, venture beyond their field sites, and apply their collective knowledge to a world in crisis. Key texts, including Raymond Dasmann's *Environmental Conservation* (1959) and David Ehrenfeld's *Biological Conservation* (1970), laid the foundation for the eventual formation, in 1985, of the Society for Conservation Biology.[1] The society and its journal *Conservation Biology* have given voice to a gathering intellectual force whose overriding goals are to understand patterns of biological diversity and ultimately to conserve it in the interests of a more functional and sustainable world.

In the thrill of such intellectual explosions—and indeed we are still in the early stages of a period of tremendous change and excitement— it is easy to fall victim to hubris and to forget those who have brought us to this place and time. I would argue that modern conservation biology—a broadly integrative approach to the protection and management of biodiversity, drawing upon many primary fields and disciplines from the sciences and humanities—developed formally only in the late 1970s and early 1980s. I would argue just as strongly, however, that it has deep roots, going back to a time long before many of its contemporary practitioners were born. One of the major roots can be traced back to Aldo Leopold—forester, wildlife biologist, land manager, philosopher, recreationist, restorationist, wilderness proponent, and, yes, conservation biologist. Half a century after his death, modern conservation biology continues to grow and prosper on the strength of his vision and his deep and prescient insights into nature and the human condition.

As an unabashed follower of Leopold, I had felt that I knew his writings reasonably well. I had read his biography, twice read *A Sand County Almanac,* encountered various of his other writings, and repeatedly used his prose to teach, inspire, and guide conservation efforts. I now realize, however, that I still knew only the surface of Leopold's legacy, only the easily observed aspects, and had not yet explored the real depths of his work. Collected for the first time in one place, the quotations in this section constitute a powerful and evocative medley, revealing the definition and development of his thinking.

Three impressions immediately arise in reading these selections: the foresight in Leopold's thinking and writing over the first half of this century, the relevance of his work to the second half and beyond, and the rather depressing inability of human beings to absorb and understand the lessons Leopold offered.

The discernment of Leopold's thought regarding biodiversity and conservation is astounding. Decades before the term "biodiversity" was coined, he was stating that "the biota as a whole is useful," and calling upon his fellow professionals to put their techniques to work "in the interest of nongame, rare, or threatened species."[2] Long before ecosystem science was much of a science, he recognized the importance of the "interdependence between the complex structure of the land and its smooth functioning."[3] In a time (not yet past) when conservationist efforts focused disproportionately on large species that attracted public attention, he urged his colleagues to look beyond the "show pieces" and "to think in terms of small cogs and wheels."[4] Long before the U.S. Endangered Species Act was passed, and well before broad recognition of impending global mass extinction was gained, he noted that species losses were "occurring too frequently to be dismissed as normal evolutionary events."[5] Reading such words, I frequently found myself checking the dates of their publication, thinking that surely they must represent more contemporary thoughts; but no, 1925 . . . 1935 . . . 1947 were correct.

Equally impressive is Leopold's breadth of understanding. He addressed a remarkable variety of themes that remain central to conservation biology today: environmental ethics and the moral dilemma of human-caused extinction; landscape-level diversity; endangered species; loss of predators and consequent changes in ecosystems; the need for core protected areas with buffers and the importance of the "matrix"; ecological health and integrity; the effect of human arrogance upon the landscape; the importance of genetic diversity; the role of natural disturbance and the nature of nonequilibrium systems; the relationship between complexity and diversity; the problems associated with exotic species; the need to protect large wilderness areas; and process and function in ecosystems. So many of the themes that we think of as new and emerging Leopold in fact confronted time and again over the first half of the twentieth century. This suggests, of course, that we are inventing little that is new; but it also suggests that we can benefit from knowing that we stand on solid shoulders.

Is Leopold right for our times? Does he still inform us? I submit an unequivocal "yes" and suggest that we are still coming to understand the many riches that Leopold left us. In a life consumed by so many demands, pulled in so many directions, and ultimately cut shorter than seems fair, he did not have time to develop fully many of his germinating ideas in conservation biology. Consequently, it remains for us to further develop the ethical, ecological, and human foundations that undergird Leopold's ideas, and to apply them in a complex and fragmented world crying out for unifying themes and visions. I submit that Leopold's work is even more relevant today than in his own day, as evidenced by the growing awareness of his contributions since his death in 1948.

There is a depressing side to the Leopold legacy as well: most of the world has utterly ignored the perspectives of Leopold and other conservation visionaries, and failed to heed their lessons. Fifty years later humanity is still not, by and large, putting into practice their wisdom and guidance. Leopold's words fall largely on the deafened ears of those who much prefer positive economic forecasts and seek perpetual growth; who dwell in human-dominated, artificial landscapes, and can imagine no other; who ignore the lessons, inherent in nature, that are readily available to anyone who cares to pause, look, listen, smell, taste, observe, and simply be quiet and humble.

As we enter not only a new century but also a new millennium, the lessons that Leopold left for us have never been more necessary. They provide the basis for a long-term, healthy, and enspiriting human-land relationship, and they serve as a guide to decency and civility. The quotations in this chapter offer a road map to an improved existence for ourselves and for our fellow creatures. It is up to us to read that map, understand its meanings and nuances, and follow it into the future. For we are, in the end, "all interlocked in one humming community of cooperations and competitions, one biota."[6] We yet have much to learn, much to do, and much to appreciate.

If the biota, in the course of aeons, has built something we like but do not understand, then who but a fool would discard seemingly useless parts? To keep every cog and wheel is the first precaution of intelligent tinkering.

Canyon of the Rio Gavilan, 1938. (Photo by Aldo Leopold. Courtesy Robert A. McCabe family)

Forestry may prescribe for a certain area either a mixed stand or a pure one. But game management should always prescribe a mixed stand—that is, the perpetuation of every indigenous species. Variety in game is quite as valuable as quantity. . . . The perpetuation of interesting species is good business, and their extermination, in the mind of the conservationists, would be a sin against future generations.

                    Forestry and Game Conservation (1918); RMG 58–59, ALS 83

   . . . The Forest Service has arrived at and is now adhering to the following rules of practice in stocking trout waters in the National Forests of Arizona and New Mexico. . . .

. . . Stocked waters will not be further mixed. Restock with the best adapted species, the native species always preferred.

> Mixing Trout in Western Waters (1918)

It hardly seems necessary to say that the wiping out of a species is wanton barbarism, especially species of such high value, from both the sporting and esthetic points of view, as mountain sheep and antelope. It should also be remembered that both mountain sheep and antelope are exceedingly difficult, if not impossible, to replace by artificial restocking.

The necessary conclusion is that the ranges of nearly exterminated species should be closed to hunting altogether.

> Wanted—National Forest Game Refuges (1920)

. . . The privilege of possessing the earth entails the responsibility of passing it on, the better for our use, not only to immediate posterity, but to the Unknown Future, the nature of which is not given us to know.

> Some Fundamentals of Conservation in the Southwest (1923);
> RMG 94

There is a great diversity of evidence and opinion as to whether the ultimate effect of fire on [game] food plants is good or bad. After years of observation on this subject, I have come to the belief that it is nearly always bad. . . .

It must be admitted, however, that in some regions forest fires cause an increase in food plants useful for game. A good example is in the north woods, where berries occur in great abundance after fires and are, of course, valuable food for bear and grouse. For this exception to an otherwise black record, let the fire devil have his due.

> Wild Followers of the Forest (1923)

A big part of practical forestry consists in the deliberate and skillful manipulation of disturbances to secure the kind and amount of reproduction desired and the environment favorable to its protection and thrifty growth.

> Natural Reproduction of Forests (1925)

[From Leopold's recommendations after inspecting the Wichita National Forest]
It is amazing how little is known about the life histories of game.

About the role of wild life in the ecology of the forest, we know even less. Yet we cannot manage either game, forest, or forage without such knowledge.

The Wichita obviously presents exceptional opportunities for such studies, and can contribute enormously valuable facts to forestry, game management, and science in general if these opportunities are utilized.

The proposed ecological studies need not, in fact cannot, be confined to game. They must cover the flora and fauna as a whole, as well as all the factors affecting them, such as fire and grazing.

To facilitate ecological studies, the introduction of exotics should be carefully avoided, except insofar as may be necessary to cultivate exotic food plants for . . . game management studies. . . .

For the same reason it is important to avoid the extermination of predators, but there is no danger of this as yet.

> Memorandum for District Forester Kelly ms. (1925)

We have two groups of men writing the destiny of America's wild life.

One group is the thinking sportsmen. Their job is to decide whether game conservation is worth while.

The other group is the scientists. Their job is to find out the facts of nature which game conservation needs to use to assure success in raising game crops.

The problem is this: These two groups are not yet working as a team. They do not yet speak a mutual language. How can they be brought together?

> Science and Game Conservation ms. (1928)

This is a plan for stimulating the growing of wild game crops for recreational use.

While this plan deals with game only, the actions necessary to produce a crop of game are in large part those which will also conserve other valuable forms of wild life.

> Report of the Committee on American Wild Life Policy (1929)

The public is (and the sportsman ought to be) just as much interested in conserving non-game species, forests, fish, and other wild life as in conserving game.

> Report to the American Game Conference on an American Game Policy (1930); RMG 153–54

. . . Research zoölogists have seldom synthesized, from their vast accumulation of zoölogical knowledge, any concrete technique for use in game management, except in those rare cases where research and application went hand-in-hand.

. . . Game management . . . is a specialized branch of applied ecology and deals with forestry, agronomy, animal husbandry, and all other land-cropping activities, quite as much as with birds and mammals.

> The Forester's Role in Game Management (1931)

If there be any question of "superiority" [in attitude] involved at all, it is whether we will prove capable of regulating our own future human population density by some qualitative standard, or whether, like the grouse, we will automatically fill up the large biological niche which Columbus found for us, and which Mr. Edison and Mr. Ford, through "management" of our human environment, are constantly making larger. I fear we will. The boosters fear we will not, or else they fear there will be some needless delay about it.

Game Methods: The American Way (1931); RMG 159

Wild species have not been tested, but the laws of inheritance as now understood would indicate less, rather than more, damage from inbreeding in wild species than in domestic, because they represent purer strains from which the tendency toward undesirable variations has been weeded out by competition. . . .

The belief in damage from inbreeding is so widely entertained, however, and management policies throughout the world are so often premised upon it, that its validity should be subjected to scientific test. This will require dividing a homogeneous sample into two halves, and inbreeding one while outbreeding the other in the same environment, for many generations. Some well-to-do sportsman could build a lasting monument to himself by financing such a test in a competent university.

Report on a Game Survey of the North Central States (1931), 54–55

There is a crying need of controlled experimentation to measure the population density of brush-loving insectivorous birds and their effect on insect pests, first on a "modern" farm and then on the same farm deliberately re-vegetated for the purpose of increasing birds. . . . Such an experiment would have great educational, as well as economic and scientific value. For one thing, it might teach sportsmen and "protectionists" that they are wasting their time fighting each other, instead of making common cause to preserve wild life environments, without which neither can attain its ends.

Report on a Game Survey of the North Central States (1931), 63

There is a puzzling absence of [ruffed] grouse from many islands in the Great Lakes which are said [to] have the appearance of being excellent range. . . . It would appear that the smaller the island and the further from shore, the less the probability of ruffed grouse. It should be noted, however, that even the small islands contain units of seemingly suitable range very much larger than the woodlots in which the species successfully persists, in apparent isolation, further south.

Report on a Game Survey of the North Central States (1931), 155

The distribution and abundance of ruffed grouse in southern Wisconsin is in inverse ratio to the development of the dairy industry, and the woodlot grazing which accompanies it. Where the woodlots are small, few, and grazed, there are no grouse. Where the woodlots are large, frequent, and ungrazed, grouse occur.

Report on a Game Survey of the North Central States (1931), 156

[Describing the role of "sanctuaries" in Michigan's proposed system of state refuges]

These will have little or no relation to game and guns. Their function will be to provide typical areas of each important type of country or cover or habitat or of wild-life associations which may be kept "forever" in status naturae—"plumb wild" and uncontaminated to the extent this may prove practicable. Ripe timber may rot under its moss, arbutus wither unpulled . . . Units of this type will be "refuges" in a special sense, but their prime function will be aesthetic and scientific, rather than game management.

Report on a Game Survey of the North Central States (1931), 244

Many volumes would not suffice to describe the scientific researches which repose on the shelves of our university libraries, and which are potentially valuable to game conservation in this region, but which cannot be used until the hiatus between the library and the land is filled in. We have collected, largely at public expense, a million bricks for our conservation structure, but there they lie in idle piles, all for lack of a little mortar and the will to build. The "pure" scientist is too absorbed in more bricks to tell the public what they are for. The "practical" sportsman and the crusading protectionist have been alike oblivious to any need for bricks.

Report on a Game Survey of the North Central States (1931), 264

Quail and pheasants, like tall corn and clean-boled oaks, are at bottom an expression of soil-health, of exuberant activity in that little-known universe which lies beneath the sod. We of the prairie states are doing our best to kill our soil, but it was stronger than [New England's] to begin with, and we have had less time than you to finish the job.

There is no such thing as conserving life without conserving soil and water also.

How Research and Game Surveys Help the Sportsman and Farmer (1933)

Why do species become extinct? Because they first become rare. Why do they become rare? Because of shrinkage in the particular environments which their particular adaptations enable them to inhabit. Can such shrinkage be controlled? Yes, once the specifications are known. How known? Through ecological research. How controlled? By modifying the environment with those same tools and skills already used in agriculture and forestry.

The Conservation Ethic (1933); RMG 190

The early naturalists of the two centuries preceding the birth of "Conservation" regarded a species as one of the phenomena of nature which needed to be discovered, catalogued, and described. . . .

"Gentlemen, look at this wonder," they said, as they held up a new discovery. Then they set about to catalogue it, comfortably assuming that only the same blind forces which had caused it to be there, could, in the fullness of time, cause it to perish from the earth.

But it soon became evident that a species did not continue or discontinue its existence, like a planet or a geological stratum or a sunset, regardless of what the scientist thought or did about it.

This "civilization" which at one moment held it up, saying, "Gentlemen, look at this wonder," might next throw it down and destroy it with all the nonchalance of a glacial epoch.

The naturalist's first response to the realization of this anomaly was to heave a sigh and hasten the completion of his cataloguing, lest by chance some other species disappear before receiving the baptism of a Latin name. . . .

With the Rooseveltian era, however, came the Crusader for conservation, a new kind of naturalist who refused to stomach this anomaly. He insisted that our conquest of nature carried with it a moral responsibility for the perpetuation of the threatened forms of wild life. This avowal was a forward step of inestimable importance. In fact, to any one for whom wild things are something more than a pleasant diversion, it constitutes one of the milestones in moral evolution.

Game Management (1933), 19

[Comment on game population cycles]

That man is unimaginative indeed who can regard these mighty pulsations in the wild life of whole continents without seeing that the myriads of living things which constitute the biological community are a living organism with an entity of its own, as interdependent and co-operative in its parts as his own body.

Game Management (1933), 71–72

. . . There appears in some species to be a minimum population unit, or minimum density of population, below which the species fails to thrive. To account for this failure, the older writers on game conservation hypothecated a "point of resistance" or minimum population, below which the species, for reasons unknown, fails to respond to "protection."

The frequent failure of antelope to "come back," even under completely closed seasons, is a case in point. Such failures have been attributed to the species having fallen below its "point of resistance." . . .

While this is simply a theory based on observation, it has the ring of
probability, and may have many counterparts awaiting discovery and ver-
ification through research.

Game Management (1933), 85–86

Local and temporary exterminations occur on every game range. Where
there is no surrounding population to restock by influx, the extermination is permanent. Low mobility of course decreases the probability of
restocking; high mobility increases it. Thus mountain lions and wolves
have been "exterminated" almost annually from many western regions,
but as long as there are any left in neighboring regions, the blanks
promptly restock.

Game Management (1933), 86

The objective of a conservation program for non-game wild life
should be exactly parallel [to that of game management]: to retain for
the average citizen the opportunity to see, admire and enjoy, and the
challenge to understand, the varied forms of birds and mammals indigenous to his state. It implies not only that these forms be kept in existence, *but that the greatest possible variety of them exist in each community.*

Game Management (1933), 403

. . . Non-game wild life is year by year being decimated in numbers and
restricted in distribution by the identical economic trends—such as
clean farming, close grazing, and drainage—which are decimating and
restricting game. The fact that game is legally shot while other wild life
is only illegally shot in no wise alters the deadly truth of the principle
that it cannot nest in a cornstalk.

Game Management (1933), 404

It has always been admitted that the several kinds of conservation
should be integrated with each other, and with other economic land
uses. The theory is that one and the same oak will grow sawlogs, bind
soil against erosion, retard floods, drop acorns to game, furnish shelter
for song birds, and cast shade for picnics; that one and the same acre
can and should serve forestry, watersheds, wild life, and recreation simultaneously. . . .

. . . The plain lesson is that to be a practitioner of conservation on a
piece of land takes more brains, and a wider range of sympathy, fore-
thought, and experience, than to be a specialized forester, game manager, range manager, or erosion expert in a college or a conservation

bureau. Integration is easy on paper, but a lot more important and more difficult in the field than any of us foresaw.

Conservation Economics (1934); RMG 197

For two centuries science has been so busy pasting labels on species that it has forgotten to study the animal itself. Science has written tons of learned volumes telling us the color, size, and shape of every feather and every bone in each of a thousand species, and recording the distribution of each and whether it is abundant or scarce, but we have not even begun to ponder why any particular species is abundant or scarce. How a species maintains its population level is certainly not the least vital question in the great enigma of evolution, but it has received the least attention from science.

The Game Cycle—A Challenge to Science (1934)

The long and short of the matter is that all land-use technologies— agriculture, forestry, watersheds, erosion, game, and range management—are encountering unexpected and baffling obstacles which show clearly that despite the superficial advances in technique, *we do not yet understand and cannot yet control* the long-time interrelations of animals, plants, and mother earth.

Why the Wilderness Society? (1935)

. . . We have [in Germany] the unfortunate result of what might be called a too purely economic determinism as applied to land use. Germany strove for maximum yields of both timber and game, and got neither. She is now, at infinite pains, coming back to an attitude of respectful guidance (as distinguished from domination) of the intricate ecological processes of nature, and may end up by getting both.

Notes on Wild Life Conservation in Germany (1935)

Look up the "outdoor" literature of the 1870's, or even the 1880's, and you will find that every writer on natural history, no matter how many tears he shed about the disappearance of wild life, was *ready to accept that disappearance* as the inevitable consequence of advancing civilization. Conservation, in short, was (in those days) whipped before it was fairly born.

Today the attitude of even the most ill-informed lover of wild life is one of protest over an *unnecessary* loss.

Forerunners of Game Management (1935)

. . . It admits of no doubt that the immediate needs of threatened members of our fauna and flora must be defined now or not at all.

Threatened Species (1936); RMG 231, ALS 195

This is a proposal, not only for an inventory of threatened forms [of wildlife] in each of their respective places of survival, but an inventory of the information, techniques, and devices applicable to each species in each place, and of local human agencies capable of applying them. Much information exists, but it is scattered in many minds and documents. Many agencies are or would be willing to use it, if it were laid under their noses. If for a given problem no information exists, or no agency exists, that in itself is useful inventory.

Threatened Species (1936); RMG 232, ALS 196

In addition to [plants and animals] which are rare everywhere, there is the equally important problem of preserving the attenuated edges of species common at their respective centres. The turkey in Colorado, or the ruffed grouse in Missouri, or the antelope in Nebraska, are rare species within the meaning of this document. That there are grizzlies in Alaska is no excuse for letting the species disappear from New Mexico.

Threatened Species (1936); RMG 233, ALS 197

We Americans, in most states at least, have not yet experienced a bear-less, wolfless, Eagleless, catless woods. We yearn for more deer and more pines, and we shall probably get them. But do we realize that to get them, as the Germans have, at the expense of their wild environment and their wild enemies, is to get very little indeed?

Naturschutz in Germany (1936)

The most pressing job in both Germany and America is to prevent the extermination of rare species.

Naturschutz in Germany (1936)

The German marshes are gone. The German heaths are fast going. And the German rivers—confined in their strait-jackets of masonry—will bear for centuries the scars of that epidemic of geometry which blighted the German mind in the 1800's. Some of these distortions of nature were necessary, but not many.

. Naturschutz in Germany (1936)

If . . . by artificial winter feeding and predator control and fencing, an abnormal density of deer be maintained in such a nearly foodless woods, it is easily seen how *an intolerable pressure is brought to bear against all palatable plants,* and how, in the course of time, they have been eradicated from the deer ranges. It is also clear that such eradication is the result not of deer alone, nor of silviculture alone, but of an active and mutually destructive interaction between the two.

Deer and Dauerwald in Germany: II. Ecology and Policy (1936)

Silting and warming of streams has pushed the southern boundary of the trout belt steadily northward in the same manner as slick-and-clean farming has pushed the native game birds out of their original range. To this shrinkage in fish habitat has been added the destruction of reproductive capacity, or even the direct poisoning of adult fish, by various forms of pollution. Artificial restocking has masked but in no wise reversed this fundamental deterioration in the fish resource. None of these basic changes has as yet been adequately measured and analyzed. Until this is done the whole fish restoration program must be a mere dabbling with superficialities.

Wildlife Crops: Finding Out How to Grow Them (1936)

In every state in the Union, plants of great esthetic and scientific value are becoming rare by reason of the same accidental changes in environment as are responsible for the depletion of animal wildlife.

. . . No species can persist whose environment is no longer habitable. The next move is to examine each threatened species, to analyze its requirements for reproduction and survival, to build out of this knowledge a technique of conservation, and to bring this technique to the attention of landowners who can apply it. Wildflower conservation can . . . be spread so that it covers more than a few microscopic public reservations. It can be made to become a normal accompaniment of civilized agriculture.

Wildlife Crops: Finding Out How to Grow Them (1936)

Despite the imposing array of subject matter in this book, there are some large gaps. No one mentions the deliberate management of wild flowers or song birds, yet these are intrinsically just as important as the management of forests or game. They are infant conservation fields as yet unbaptized. No bureau stands as their godfather, no "movement" as their guardian and public relations counsel. Even the planners and recreation engineers have neglected to map the destiny of these healthy but unobtrusive waifs.

Review of Our Natural Resources and Their Conservation (1937)

Game versus Wildlife.—Foresters have usually avoided, in thought and word, the sportsman's error of assigning to nongame wildlife a lesser value than to the killable species. In action, however, non-killable wildlife has been consistently neglected by all. It is hard to find instances in which the new and powerful tools now available have been deliberately employed in the interest of nongame, rare, or threatened species, either by foresters or by anyone else.

Second Report of [the Society of American Foresters] Game Policy Committee (1937)

The sandhill crane is the epitome of wilderness. The presence of one in a region, like the presence of the grizzly bear, flavors the whole countryside. To hear the bugling of a sky-bound flock is an outstanding experience. It is a sound which converts a monotonous peat-marsh into a place of ineffable distinction.

The Wisconsin and Michigan peat-marshes contain the largest breeding crane remnants in the United States—a few score pairs in all. Until 1934 no specific action was ever taken, in this or in any other state, for the perpetuation of any particular habitat for cranes. Yet this is a job calling for very definite treatment of very definite spots.

This fact is diagnostic of the whole history of our native animals—they have been evicted by the blind action of economic forces, and the rescue expedition got lost in the fogs of wishful generalization.

The University and Conservation of Wisconsin Wildlife (1937)

Songbird and wildflower [management] techniques do not yet have names. No bureau, school, chair or fellowship is dedicated to their study; no technician avows their care as his profession. Is it any less important to find out the specifications of a favorable environment for the prairie flowers than for the prairie game birds which ride with them on the toboggan?

The Research Program (1937)

This is an expression of discontent, by a conservationist, with the landscape of the world's leading exemplar of conservation: Germany. . . .

This discontent arises mainly from the lack of unity of idea between the German islands or reservations devoted to conservation of the naturalistic type, and the surrounding matrix dominated by conservation of the engineering type. How much greater the disparity between our American islands (forest and parks), and the surrounding matrix dominated by exploitation!

Review of "Forstlicher Naturschutz und Naturschutz im nationalen Lebensraume Deutschlands" (1937)

The high priests of progress knew nothing of cranes, and cared less. What is a species more or less among engineers? What good is an undrained marsh anyhow?

Marshland Elegy (1937); ASCA 100

The elaborate chains of interdependence among species and processes were, a decade ago, largely unknown. The woodchuck who digs holes for the cottontail, the muskrat who builds nests for the trumpeter swan, the deer who digs acorns for the quail—these are simple mechanical dependencies which this era of engineers can understand. More important but less obvious are the chemical and physiological dependencies between animals, plants, and soil now in process of discovery. There are fish in this sea larger than any yet caught.

> Wildlife Research—Is It a Practical and Necessary Basis for Management? (1938)

[The ecologist] feels an engineer's admiration for this [biotic] complexity which defies science, and an engineer's aversion for discarding any of its parts. The real difference lies in the ecologist's conviction that to govern the animate world it must be led rather than coerced. To me this is engineering wisdom; the reason the engineer does not display it is unawareness of the animate world.

> Engineering and Conservation (1938); RMG 253

Need we always await the willy-nilly pressure of wrecked resources before professional cooperation begins?

> Engineering and Conservation (1938); RMG 253

All earth-sciences must, in the long run, learn how to use land by referring to unused land as a base-datum or starting point.

> *Report on Huron Mountain Club* (1938)

The best method of handling the Huron Mountain timber is believed to be the reservation of an interior protected area, and the establishment of a buffer zone of selectively logged areas.

> *Report on Huron Mountain Club* (1938)

The size-scale of a wilderness area for scientific study greatly affects its value. A small area may be "natural" in respect of its plants, but wholly unnatural in respect of its mobile animals or water. However, mobile animals greatly affect plant life, so that a small virgin forest may *appear* to be natural when actually it has been profoundly affected by forces applied to animals, waters, or climate at points far distant.

> *Report on Huron Mountain Club* (1938)

The outstanding scientific discovery of the twentieth century is not television, or radio, but rather the complexity of the land organism. Only those who know the most about it can appreciate how little we know about it. The last word in ignorance is the man who says of an animal or plant: "What good is it?" If the land mechanism as a whole is good, then every part is good, whether we understand it or not. If the biota, in the course of aeons, has built something we like but do not understand, then

who but a fool would discard seemingly useless parts? To keep every cog
and wheel is the first precaution of intelligent tinkering.

Conservation (c. 1938); RR 146–47

American conservation is, I fear, still concerned for the most part with
show pieces. We have not yet learned to think in terms of small cogs and
wheels. Look at our own back yard: at the prairies of Iowa and southern
Wisconsin. What is the most valuable part of the prairie? The fat black
soil, the chernozem. Who built the chernozem? The black prairie was
built by the prairie plants, a hundred distinctive species of grasses, herbs,
and shrubs; by the prairie fungi, insects, and bacteria; by the prairie
mammals and birds, all interlocked in one humming community of co-
operations and competitions, one biota.

Conservation (c. 1938); RR 147–48

In our attempts to save the bigger cogs and wheels, we are still pretty
naive. A little repentance just before a species goes over the brink is
enough to make us feel virtuous. When the species is gone we have a
good cry and repeat the performance.

The recent extermination of the grizzly from most of the western
stock-raising states is a case in point. Yes, we still have grizzlies in the
Yellowstone. But the species is ridden by imported parasites; the rifles
wait on every refuge boundary; new dude ranches and new roads constantly shrink the remaining range; every year sees fewer grizzlies on
fewer ranges in fewer states. We console ourselves with the comfortable
fallacy that a single museum-piece will do, ignoring the clear dictum of
history that a species must be saved *in many places* if it is to be saved at all.

Conservation (c. 1938); RR 148–49

... The average American township has lost a score of plants and animals through indifference for every one it has lost through necessity.

The Farmer as a Conservationist (1939); RMG 255

When [Charles] Van Hise said "Conservation is wise use," he meant, I
think, restrained use.

Certainly conservation means restraint, but there is something else
that needs to be said. It seems to me that many land resources, when
they are used, get out of order and disappear or deteriorate before anyone has a chance to exhaust them.

The Farmer as a Conservationist (1939); RMG 256

Ecology is a new fusion point for all the natural sciences.... The
emergence of ecology has placed the economic biologist in a peculiar
dilemma: with one hand he points out the accumulated findings of his

search for utility, or lack of utility, in this or that species; with the other he lifts the veil from a biota so complex, so conditioned by interwoven cooperations and competitions, that no man can say where utility begins or ends. No species can be "rated" without the tongue in the cheek; the old categories of "useful" and "harmful" have validity only as conditioned by time, place, and circumstance. The only sure conclusion is that the biota as a whole is useful, and biota includes not only plants and animals, but soils and waters as well.

A Biotic View of Land (1939); RMG 266–67

Each species, including ourselves, is a link in many chains. The deer eats a hundred plants other than oak, and the cow a hundred plants other than corn. Both, then, are links in a hundred chains. The pyramid is a tangle of chains so complex as to seem disorderly, yet the stability of the system proves it to be a highly organized structure. Its functioning depends on the co-operation and competition of its diverse parts.

In the beginning, the pyramid of life was low and squat; the food chains short and simple. Evolution has added layer after layer, link after link. Man is one of thousands of accretions to the height and complexity of the pyramid. Science has given us many doubts, but it has given us at least one certainty: the trend of evolution is to elaborate and diversify the biota.

A Biotic View of Land (1939); ASCA 215–16; cf. RMG 268

[The] interdependence between the complex structure of the land and its smooth functioning as an energy unit is one of its basic attributes.

A Biotic View of Land (1939); ASCA 216; cf. RMG 269

Some Sunday in January when the tracking is good, I like to stroll over my acres and make mental note of the birds and mammals whose sign ought to be there, but isn't. One appreciates what is left only after realizing how much has already disappeared.

New Year's Inventory Checks Missing Game (1940); RMG 274

No one seems yet to have questioned the sufficiency of [the] "compartmental" scheme for describing the behavior of land under human use. I do. It is too much like describing the "separate" organs of an animal or plant, and then leaving to inference their collective behavior as an organism.

Review of *Conservation in the United States* (1940)

. . . The shrinkage in *continental* status of rare species is only one part of the problem of conserving the American fauna. The other part is the shrinkage in *local* status of species that may be common elsewhere. Local extirpations make a species almost as inaccessible to the local human population as if the species had disappeared altogether. Moreover, continental extirpations are invariably the cumulative result of many local shrinkages. . . .

The total shortening of local faunal lists by these local shrinkages is probably more important, socially speaking, than the total shortening of continental lists. Under our existing patterns of thought, people do not become alarmed about local faunal losses. "The species still persists elsewhere." This, however, is the same kind of logic as led to the extermination of the Passenger Pigeon. There is littler danger, of course, that many species will repeat the pigeon tragedy, but there is perhaps cause for alarm in the fact that people still think in terms of the same ecological fallacies as prevailed in 1870.

> Report of the [American Ornithologists' Union] Committee on Bird Protection, 1939 (1940)

A good wildlife program reduces itself, in essence, to the deliberate perpetuation of a *diverse* landscape, and to its integration with economic and cultural land-use.

> Improving the Wildlife Program of the Soil Conservation Service ms. (1940)

Our job is to harmonize the increasing kit of scientific tools and the increasing recklessness in using them with the shrinking biotas to which they are applied. In the nature of things we are mediators and moderators, and unless we can help rewrite the objectives of science our job is predestined to failure.

> The State of the Profession (1940); RMG 276–77

The research program is out of balance in that certain kinds of wildlife are omitted altogether; for example, wildflowers and other non-economic vegetation.

> The State of the Profession (1940); RMG 279

Our option in wildlife is a question of quality, not quantity. Shall the wild growths of the soil retain a large part of their original diversity, beauty, and utility? Or shall they consist largely of simple plant and animal weeds? Conservation is the intelligent exercise of this option.

> Wisconsin Wildlife Chronology (1940)

What, in the evolutionary history of this flowering earth, is most closely associated with stability? The answer to my mind is clear: diversity of fauna and flora.

It seems improbable that science can ever analyze stability and write an exact formula for it. The best we can do, at least at present, is to recognize and cultivate the general conditions which seem to be conducive to it. Stability and diversity are associated. Both are the end-result of evolution to date. To what extent are they interdependent? Can we retain stability in used land without retaining diversity also?

Biotic Land Use ms. (c. 1940)

Would the deliberate retention of both fertility and diversity reduce instability? I think it would. But I admit in the same breath that I can't prove it, nor disprove it. If the trouble is in the plant and animal pipelines, I think it would help to keep them more nearly intact. It is a probability based on evolution. It is the only probability in sight. . . .

. . . Do we ourselves, as a group, believe what we cannot prove: that retaining the diversity of our fauna and flora is conducive to stable land?

Biotic Land Use ms. (c. 1940)

Pests cannot read signs; the grizzlies of the inviolate Yellowstone are entertaining the Russian tapeworm, the bighorns are a sanctuary for imported sheep scab and lungworm.

Untitled notes on biotic diversity ms. (c. 1941)

We must not lose our bearings in [the] welter of pests. No one can say what part of the trouble is chargeable to world commerce and development as such, and what part to unnecessary tampering and wrong attitudes. We can say that pests must have been rare in the original biotas, else the biotas would not have been preserved. We can say that pests have emerged as the biotas have been simplified by "clean farming" and its philosophy of land use.

Untitled notes on biotic diversity ms. (c. 1941)

My belief that diverse landscapes tend to be stable is without proof. It is an "act of faith," with only a historical correlation behind it. But the converse theorem, that over-tinkered landscapes are unstable, is written large in recent history. Worldwide commerce has brought a worldwide pooling of floras and faunas, partly by deliberate importation, partly by accidental dispersion as "stowaways." This biotic cocktail has been shaking at the same time that the axe of progress came down on the native food chains. The two cannot be disassociated as causes, but their joint effects are clear; many species have melted away, while others have gotten out of bounds as pests and diseases. The biota has not only run down its storage battery, the soil, but its working parts are flying about the shop at random.

Untitled notes on biotic diversity ms. (c. 1941)

Pests and diseases are economic, even to an economist, but the men who know about them are so narrowly specialized, each to his own bird, bug, or bacillus, that no one has described the general trend of pests. · "Beside, why worry? DuPont will invent something." Will he?

> Untitled notes on biotic diversity ms. (c. 1941)

Each substitution of a tame plant or animal for a wild one, or an artificial waterway for a natural one, is accompanied by a readjustment in the circulating system of the land. We do not understand or foresee these readjustments; we are unconscious of them unless the end effect is bad.

> The Round River—A Parable (c. 1941); RR 163

There is no need to persuade the student of land ecology that machines to dominate the land are useful only while there is a healthy land to use them on, and that land-health is possibly dependent on land-membership, that is, that a flora and fauna too severely simplified or modified may not tick as well as the original. He can see for himself that there is no such thing as good or bad species; a species may get out of hand, but to terminate its membership in the land by human fiat is the last word in anthropomorphic arrogance.

> The Role of Wildlife in a Liberal Education (1942); RMG 303

In 1909, when I first saw the West, there were grizzlies in every major mountain mass, but you could travel for months without meeting a conservation officer. Today there is some kind of conservation officer "behind every bush," yet as wildlife bureaus grow, our most magnificent mammal retreats steadily toward the Canadian border. Of the 6000 grizzlies officially reported as remaining in areas owned by the United States, 5000 are in Alaska. Only five states have any at all. There seems to be a tacit assumption that if grizzlies survive in Canada and Alaska, that is good enough. It is not good enough for me. The Alaskan bears are a distinct species. Relegating grizzlies to Alaska is about like relegating happiness to heaven; one may never get there.

> The Grizzly—A Problem in Land Planning (1942); ASCA 198–99

The old prairie lived by the diversity of its plants and animals, all of which were useful because the sum total of their co-operations and competitions achieved continuity.

> Odyssey (1942); ASCA 107

The whole original ecology of the Mississippi was built upon *unstable* water levels. Waterfowl once congregated there because summer droughts produced vast areas of smartweed and millet on drying mud flats. Sometimes in fall, and always in spring, floods made a duck paradise of these weed fields. The army dams, by their sustained levels, have destroyed them, as well as the mast-bearing timber.

Review of Wildlife Refuges (1943)

. . . No species is inherently a pest, and any species may become one.

What Is a Weed? (1943); RMG 309

The impending industrialization of the world, now foreseen by everyone, means that many conservation problems heretofore local will shortly become global.

No one has yet asked whether the industrial communities which we intend to plant in the new and naked lands are more valuable, or less valuable, than the indigenous fauna and flora which they, to a large extent, displace and disrupt. Such a question requires a degree of objectivity not yet achieved, either by mice or by men.

We have, though, gone half way. The conservation movement is asking whether the impact of industry on the biota cannot be made more gentle, more intelligent, less wasteful.

One defect in conservation is that it is so far an *ex post facto* effort. When we have nearly finished disrupting a fauna and flora, we develop a nostalgic regret about it, and a wish to save the remnants. Why not do the regretting and saving in advance?

Post-war Prospects (1944)

Siberia is being industrialized with dramatic speed. No one knows the details, for the Russians hold their cards close to their chests. If planwise conservation is possible anywhere in the world, it should be possible in Siberia among the pioneers of planning. Siberia has a rich resident fauna, and in addition has long been a reservoir for replenishing the migratory wildlife of Europe, especially waterfowl. What the Siberians do with their newly acquired guns, plows, cows, drainage machinery and roads will be felt from the Arctic Circle to the Nile.

Post-war Prospects (1944)

Our internal problems were heretofore problems of scarcity. The last decade has now added new problems of excess. Excess deer and elk are eating up many national forests, national parks and other forest and range lands. There is little evidence that the public is learning to foresee and *prevent* these outbreaks, as distinguished from attempting to cure them. When the time for cure arrives, the damage to the habitat is already completed.

Post-war Prospects (1944)

Conservation is a state of health in the land.

The land consists of soil, water, plants, and animals, but health is more than a sufficiency of these components. It is a state of vigorous self-renewal in each of them, and in all collectively. Such collective functioning of interdependent parts for the maintenance of the whole is characteristic of an organism. In this sense land is an organism, and conservation deals with its functional integrity, or health.

Conservation: In Whole or in Part? (1944); RMG 310

... Throughout geological time up to 1840, the extinction of one species by another occurred more rarely than the creation of new species by evolution, and that occurred very rarely indeed, for we have little evidence of new species appearing during the period of recorded history. The net trend of the original community was thus toward more and more diversity of native forms, and more and more complex relations between them. Stability or health was associated with, and perhaps caused by, this diversity and complexity.

Conservation: In Whole or in Part? (1944); RMG 312

The conservationist who is interested in land as a whole is compelled to view ... symptoms [of land-illness] collectively, and as probable maladjustments of the land community. Some of them are understood superficially, but hardly any are understood deeply enough to warrant the assertion that they are separate phenomena, unrelated to each other and to the whole. ...

To assert a causal relation would imply that we understand the mechanism. As a matter of fact, the land mechanism is too complex to be understood, and probably always will be.

Conservation: In Whole or in Part? (1944); RMG 315

There are reasons for gentle land-use over and above the presumed risk to the health of the land. [Carl O.] Sauer has pointed out that the domesticated plants and animals which we use now are not necessarily those which we will need a century hence. To the extent that the native community is extinguished, the genetical source of new domesticated plants and animals is destroyed.

Conservation: In Whole or in Part? (1944); RMG 315

Land-health is the capacity for self-renewal in the soils, waters, plants, and animals that collectively comprise the land.

Conservation: In Whole or in Part? (1944); RMG 318

Viewed as conservation, *The Wolves of North America* is, to me, intensely disappointing. The next to the last sentence in the book asserts: "*There still remain, even in the United States, some areas of considerable size in which we feel that both the red and gray [wolves] may be allowed to continue their existence with little molestation.*" Yes, so also thinks every right-minded ecologist, but has the United States Fish and Wildlife Service no responsibility for implementing this thought before it completes its job of extirpation? Where are these areas? Probably every reasonable ecologist will agree that some of them should lie in the larger national parks and wilderness areas; for instance, the Yellowstone and its adjacent national forests.

Review of *The Wolves of North America* (1945); RMG 322, ALS 225–26

Up to the time of the chestnut blight, [biological] runaways did not threaten wildlife directly on any serious scale, but they now do, and it is now clear that the pest problem is developing several new and dangerous angles:

1. World-wide transport is carrying new "stowaways" to new habitats on an ascending scale. (Example: Anopheles gambiae to Brazil, bubonic plague to western states.)
2. Modern chemistry is developing controls which may be as dangerous as the pests themselves. (Example: DDT.)
3. Additional native species, heretofore law-abiding citizens of the flora and fauna, are exhibiting pest behavior. (Example: excess deer and elk.)

The Outlook for Farm Wildlife (1945); RMG 324–25

. . . We face not only an unfavorable balance between loss and gain in habitat, but an accelerating disorganization of those unknown controls which stabilize the flora and fauna, and which, in conjunction with stable soil and a normal regimen of water, constitute land-health.

The Outlook for Farm Wildlife (1945); RMG 326

I now favor restoring the [wolf] bounty because the increase in coyotes makes it necessary, there is a probability that timber wolves have increased, and it is impracticable to distinguish between the two species in paying bounties. I shall fight for again discontinuing the bounty whenever extermination again threatens. We have no right to exterminate any species or wildlife. I stand on this as a fundamental principle.

Deer, Wolves, Foxes and Pheasants (1945)

I myself have cooperated in the extermination of the wolf from the greater part of two states, because I then believed it was a benefit. I do not propose to repeat my error.

Deer, Wolves, Foxes and Pheasants (1945)

All these issues are, or should be, a matter of reasonable give-and-take. It would be unreasonable for foresters to demand wiping out the deer herd because deer eat trees. It is equally unreasonable for deer hunters to demand wiping out wolves because they eat the deer. Foxes and rabbits we couldn't wipe out if we tried.

The aim in all wildlife conservation should be reasonable levels for all members of the native wildlife community.

Deer, Wolves, Foxes and Pheasants (1945)

. . . What are the probable conditions requisite for the perpetuation of the biotic self-renewal of land-health? This would define a goal for conservationists to strive toward. They now have no basic goal bracketing all component groups. Each group has its own goal, and it is common knowledge that these conflict and nullify each other to a large degree.

I will record my own guess first as a figure of speech. The biotic clock may continue ticking if we:

1. Cease throwing away its parts.
2. Handle it gently.
3. Recognize that its importance transcends economics.
4. Don't let too many people tinker with it.

The Land-Health Concept and Conservation ms. (1946)

There will always be pigeons in books and in museums, but these are effigies and images, dead to all hardships and to all delights. Book-pigeons cannot dive out of a cloud to make the deer run for cover, or clap their wings in thunderous applause of mast-laden woods. Book-pigeons cannot breakfast on new-mown wheat in Minnesota, and dine on blueberries in Canada. They know no urge of seasons; they feel no kiss of sun, no lash of wind and weather. They live forever by not living at all.

On a Monument to the Passenger Pigeon (1947); ASCA 109

The shrinkage in the [prairie] flora is due to a combination of clean-farming, woodlot grazing, and good roads. Each of these necessary changes of course requires a larger reduction in the acreage available for wild plants, but none of them requires, or benefits by, the erasure of species from whole farms, townships, or counties. There are idle spots on every farm, and every highway is bordered by an idle strip as long as it is; keep cow, plow, and mower out of these idle spots, and the full native flora, plus dozens of interesting stowaways from foreign parts, could be part of the normal environment of every citizen.

Prairie Birthday (1949); ASCA 47–48

A representative series of these [wilderness] areas can, and should, be kept. Many are of negligible or negative value for economic use. It will be contended, of course, that no deliberate planning to this end is necessary; that adequate areas will survive anyhow. All recent history belies so comforting an assumption. Even if wild spots do survive, what of their fauna? The woodland caribou, the several races of mountain sheep, the pure form of woods buffalo, the barren ground grizzly, the freshwater seals, and the whales are even now threatened. Of what use are wild areas destitute of their distinctive faunas?

Wilderness (1949); ASCA 191–92

The National Parks do not suffice as a means of perpetuating the larger carnivores; witness the precarious status of the grizzly bear, and the fact that the park system is already wolfless. Neither do they suffice for mountain sheep; most sheep herds are shrinking.

The reasons for this are clear in some cases and obscure in others. The parks are certainly too small for such a far-ranging species as the wolf. Many animal species, for reasons unknown, do not seem to thrive as detached islands of population.

The most feasible way to enlarge the area available for wilderness fauna is for the wilder parts of the National Forests, which usually surround the Parks, to function as parks in respect of threatened species. That they have not so functioned is tragically illustrated in the case of the grizzly bear.

Wilderness (1949); ASCA 198

✤ PART II ✤
Conservation Policy

Conservation, as Aldo Leopold understood it, was a matter not just of technical skill, but of social development, which in turn was a matter of changing mores, customs, laws, incentives, and community standards. Unlike many biologists and conservationists, Leopold was not reluctant to cross the threshold separating science and policy, and to enter the sociopolitical fray. As a forester of Progressive Era vintage, he began his career with the instincts of a reformer. Stubbornly independent in his politics, however, he accepted no easy shortcuts or half-hearted solutions. Compromise, however inevitable in conservation battles, did not obviate the need to examine continually the deeper social implications of conservation issues. The quotations in this section illustrate this life-long effort.

The American conservation movement, over the course of its development, has fluctuated in the relative degree of attention it has given to matters affecting private lands and public lands. Leopold concerned himself with both. He was a lifelong employee of public agencies; he was also a private landowner as deeply committed to conservation on "the back forty" as on the nation's public lands. The rights and responsibilities of communities and individuals lay for Leopold along a continuum; they were not polarized according to competing ideologies. Chapters 10 and 11 illustrate the dynamic interrelationship in Leopold's thinking between public and private interests, and public and private lands.

Aldo Leopold was an effective conservation advocate, as well as an insightful observer of the currents of advocacy within the conservation movement. The quotations in Chapter 12 reflect both of Leopold's roles—as an insider in various conservation causes, and as a detached critic of the politics of conservation. Leopold's activity within the political realm did not blind him to the broader economic forces shaping conservation issues. The quotations in Chapter 13 trace Leopold's thoughts on the economic causes and ramifications of the issues of his day. They cover topics ranging from nonsustainable resource extraction to the failure of incentive programs, from recognition of nature's non-market goods and services to the very definition and foundations of economic health. Leopold was personally involved in the formulation of public policy on a broad range of conservation issues. The quotations in Chapter 14 touch on many of these specific issues, as well as broader questions of the appropriate approach to conservation dilemmas within a democracy.

All of the quotations in this section show Leopold as a lifelong citizen of the political as well as the natural landscape. All demonstrate his commitment to work toward better reconciliation of these spheres. As a practical realist he sought to make conservation programs work better for people and for land. As a conservation philosopher he sought to do so in a way that was "capable of expanding with time into that new social concept toward which conservation is groping."[1]

10 PRIVATE LAND

౹౹

Aldo Leopold on Private Land
Eric T. Freyfogle

In the world Aldo Leopold grew up in—Burlington, Iowa, at the turn of the twentieth century—private land ownership held an honored place, right alongside free enterprise, individualism, personal honor, and the family. Leopold shaped his being around these values and institutions and he held fast to them throughout his life, however far he evolved in his thoughts about the land. Planting pines at the Shack, Leopold wore the mantle of private property owner. And as he submitted his land ethic to the public, he spoke to no audience more directly than the dispersed and powerful owners of private land.

Private property, though, quickly became a problem for Leopold the conservationist, and it was a problem that would not abate. Too many owners abused land, he realized, and it was property law that enabled them to do so. Governments might practice conservation on public lands, but wildlife couldn't thrive, nor could soil remain intact and fertile, on public lands alone. For the entire land community to become healthy, private owners everywhere had to practice conservation as a way of life. Encouraging them to do so, Leopold believed, was the central challenge of his day.

But how could this be done in a way consistent with the broad rights that landowners possessed? How could it happen while respecting the independence and economic needs of individual owners? Leopold's initial answer was to offer economic incentives for owners to act more wisely. So long as people viewed land as an economic asset, conservation merely needed to make financial sense. Public money could reward owners who set land aside for wildlife, Leopold proposed. Tax abatements could reduce the need to drain wetlands. Hunting fees could be turned over to owners who took down their "No Hunting" signs.

By the early 1930s, however, incentive programs had been tried long enough for Leopold to realize that a better answer was needed. Incentives worked so long as money flowed, but old habits returned as soon as it stopped. Furthermore, government programs were too blunt an instrument to bring about ecologically sensitive practices. Wise land use required measures attentively tailored to the circumstances of particular parcels. It required the "positive exercise of skill and insight" by individual owners.[1] Incentive programs could never be specific enough to promote that type of behavior, nor could they impart skill to an uncaring owner.

As the limitations of incentive programs became clear, Leopold's thoughts and writings took a turn. Economic incentives were helpful, he observed in 1935, but real conservation required "rather fundamental changes in rural culture and in land economics."[2] Conservation was not something a nation could buy; it was something it had to learn, slowly and painfully. By the end of his life economic incentives played only a minor role in Leopold's thought. "A system of conservation based solely on economic self-interest," he would write in *A Sand County Almanac,* "is hopelessly lopsided."[3] The answer was not greater incentives, nor increased public land ownership, nor new government programs, although all of this could help. The basic need was a new "ethical obligation on the part of the private owner."[4]

Leopold's growing focus on the ecological community—on the whole of nature rather than its parts—gradually pushed him to redefine his ingrained individualism. For a landowner simply to pursue narrow self-interest, he wrote in 1937, was a kind of "bogus individualism."[5] True individualism, the durable and responsible kind, built upon a moral foundation and took community needs into account. An ethical individual thought first of the community, and pursued self-interest only within constraints understood and defined at the community level.

What Leopold did not realize was that the ideas he derived as an ecologist contained strong challenges to the individualism of twentieth-century America. They also challenged the institution of private property as then understood—the ownership-as-domination view that Leopold would portray at the opening of "The Land Ethic" through his recollection of Odysseus' disobedient slaves. Leopold could see well enough how sportsmen's ethics evolved. What he could not quite perceive was how the institution of private property might similarly evolve. He could not see how ownership norms, like ethical norms, could gradually become more sensitive to the land. Lacking this insight, he instinctively viewed private property as an immovable object on the path to land health. Unable to displace it, he could only exhort readers to steer clear of it. Stop thinking about land merely as private property, he urged. Stop dominating land as Odysseus dominated his slaves.

Yet as Leopold progressed along his pilgrimage, he offered observations that in time would stimulate others to rethink the bundle of rights a landowner possessed. Writing in 1922, for instance, he noted the need to view soil erosion as a new type of nuisance or land-use harm. By 1930 he understood that private land use was very much a matter of legitimate public concern, and not just when pollution entered a public stream. The community had a stake in what an owner did within the borders of his land to the soil, the water flows, and the wildlife habitat. By then Leopold was referring regularly to the landowner's duties to the community as such. And in perhaps his most prescient comment he identified the need for a new "concept of land." Where that concept might come from, he admitted humbly, he was not quite sure. But ecology "seems to me the place to look."[6] Leopold remained willing to compensate landowners for their out-of-pocket conservation expenses and for shouldering disproportionate burdens. But each landowner was a public steward and, as such, owed a duty to promote the land's integrity and health.

Not being a student of property, Leopold was unaware how far ownership norms had evolved in preceding generations and how flexible they really were. He did not realize how property norms inherently reflected the values of a human community and needed to evolve as changes occurred in those underlying values. The institution of property as he knew it, the institution that he assumed was timeless, reflected the values and ecological ignorance of the late nineteenth century. But those values and that ignorance were not static, and Leopold's own ideas in time would rise up to challenge them.

By describing land as a community, Leopold has stimulated property scholars to rethink what it means to own a small piece of an integrated, organic whole. He has encouraged them to question the law's tendency toward abstraction—its tendency, that is, to prescribe ownership rights without regard for natural variations in the land itself. And he has stimulated them to ask whether ownership should still include the right to go beyond legitimate use of the land to degrade it and consume it.

Inspired by Leopold, scholars have begun asking whether the law ought to recognize harm to the natural community. They have begun asking, too, whether membership in the land community might properly entail a duty to shoulder a fair share of landscape-scale burdens, such as leaving room for native plants and animals or tailoring drainage practices to minimize flooding and bank erosion.

Ownership norms alone, as Leopold knew, can never prescribe truly sound land use, and so a land ethic will always remain essential. But property law can do far more than it has done. It can halt the most egregious activities. It can protect the most ecologically sensitive lands. And it can stimulate landowners, individually and collectively, to study the land more than they have, pushing them to think seriously, as Leopold himself did, about its somber plight and its rich possibilities.

When land does well for its owner, and the owner does well by his land; when both end up better by reason of their partnership, we have conservation.

Leopold measuring red pines at the Shack, 1946. (Photo by Robert A. McCabe. Courtesy University of Wisconsin–Madison Archives)

The day will come when the ownership of land will carry with it the obligation to so use and protect it with respect to erosion that it is not a menace to other landowners and the public. Just as it is illegal for one landowner to menace the public peace or health by maintaining disorderly or unsanitary conditions on his land, so will it become illegal for him to menace the public streams, reservoirs, irrigation projects, or the lands of his neighbors, by allowing erosion to take place. But it is cheaper to prevent erosion than to cure it, and the cost of such prevention must some day be passed on uniformly by all landowners to all consumers of their products.

Pioneers and Gullies (1924); RMG 110–11, ALS 170

Often it is necessary for landowners along a creek to work out a unified plan, else there is danger that the diligence of one owner will result merely in passing the trouble down the creek to his neighbors.

Pioneers and Gullies (1924); RMG 112, ALS 172

There is no conceivable way by which the general public can legislate crabapples, or grape tangles, or plum thickets to grow up on these barren fencerows, roadsides, and slopes, nor will the resolutions or prayer of the city change the depth of next winter's snow nor cause cornshocks to be left in the fields to feed the birds. All the non-farming public can do is to provide information and build incentives on which farmers may act.

Game Cropping in Southern Wisconsin (1927)

. . . The crux of the game problem is on the farm. Our legislatures decree game conservation; our sportsmen and nature-lovers resolve we shall have it, but our landowners do not practice it, nor are they yet offered any inducement or motive, other than altruism, for doing so. At the same time the public expects the free run of their lands, and of such game as may accidentally persist thereon. Such is our present impasse. Some more tenable relationship between the landowner, the game, and the public is obviously needed.

Report on a Game Survey of the North Central States (1931), 5

The only fundamental remedy [to the cumulative loss of waterfowl breeding habitat] is to recognize the fact that undrained ungrazed private marshlands perform a public service in producing migratory birds, and to give the owner an incentive for keeping, continuing, or restoring that service by according them a preferential tax status, such as is now accorded in some States to private forests, on the same principle of public service. The public can never acquire enough of the small marshes to offset the ones which are being taxed out of existence, nor can science show how to grow ducklings in a cornfield. The steam-roller of economic self-interest must somehow be steered so that it will work with, not against, the feeble palliatives so far employed to avert that spiritual calamity—a duckless America.

Report on a Game Survey of the North Central States (1931), 205

Forestry exhibits another tragedy—or comedy—of *Homo sapiens,* astride the runaway Juggernaut of his own building, trying to be decent to his own environment. A new profession was trained in the confident expectation that the shrinkage in virgin timber would, as a matter of self-interest, bring an expansion of timber-cropping. Foresters are cropping timber on certain parcels of poor land which happen to be public, but on the great bulk of private holdings they have accomplished little. Economics won't let them.

The Conservation Ethic (1933); RMG 186

The recent trend in wild life conservation shows the direction in which ideas are evolving. At the inception of the movement fifty years ago, its underlying thesis was to save species from extermination. The means to this end were a series of restrictive enactments. The duty of the individual was to cherish and extend these enactments, and to see that his neighbor obeyed them. The whole structure was negative and prohibitory. It assumed land to be a constant in the ecological equation. Gun-powder and blood-lust were the variables needing control.

There is now being superimposed on this a positive and affirmatory ideology, the thesis of which is to prevent the deterioration of environment. The means to this end is research. The duty of the individual is to apply its findings to land, and to encourage his neighbor to do likewise.

The Conservation Ethic (1933); RMG 190

If trained technicians on public lands find it no small task to integrate the diverse public interests in land-use, what shall we say of the private landowner, scrambling for a hard-earned living, who has not even been told what these public interests are?

Conservation Economics (1934); RMG 198

Let me . . . plead for what may be called the "suppressed minorities" of conservation. The landowner whose boundaries happen to include an eagle's nest, or a heron rookery, or a patch of ladyslippers, or a remnant of native prairie sod, or an historical oak, or a string of Indian mounds—such a landowner is the custodian of a public interest, to an equal or sometimes greater degree than one growing a forest, or one fighting a gully. We already have such a welter of single-track statutes that new or separate prohibitions or subsidies for each of these "minority interests" would be hard to enact, and still harder to enforce or administer. Perhaps this impasse offers a clue to the whole broad problem of conservation policy. It suggests the need for some comprehensive fusion of interests, some sweeping simplification of conservation law, which sets up for each parcel of land a single criterion of land-use: "Has the public interest in *all* its resources been protected?" which motivates that criterion by a single incentive, such as the differential tax, and which delegates the function of judging compliance to some single and highly trained administrative field-inspector, subject to review by the courts.

Conservation Economics (1934); RMG 201

The crux of the problem is that every landowner is the custodian of two interests, not always identical, the public interest and his own. What we need is a positive inducement or reward for the landowner who respects both interests in his actual land-practice. All conservation problems—erosion, forestry, game, wild flowers, landscapes, or what not—ultimately boil down to this. What should this reward or inducement be? What is a practical vehicle for it? These are the two basic questions in

American conservation. An answer seems to require the collaboration of economists, jurists, regional planners, ecologists and esthetes.

Some Thoughts on Recreational Planning (1934)

I plead . . . for positive and substantial public encouragement, economic and moral, for the landowner who conserves the public values—economic or esthetic—of which he is the custodian. The search for practicable vehicles to carry that encouragement is a research problem, and I think a soluble one. . . .

I might say, defensively, that such a vehicle would not necessarily imply regimentation of private land-use. The private owner would still decide what to use his land for; the public would decide merely whether the net result is good or bad for its stake in his holdings.

Those charged with the search for such a vehicle must first seek to intellectually encompass the whole situation. It may mean something far more profound than I have foreseen.

Land Pathology (1935); RMG 216–17

There are two ways to apply conservation to land.

One is to superimpose some particular practice upon the pre-existing system of land-use, without regard to how it fits or what it does to or for other interests involved.

The other is to reorganize and gear up the farming, forestry, game cropping, erosion control, scenery, or whatever values may be involved so that they collectively comprise a harmonious balanced system of land-use.

Coon Valley: An Adventure in Cooperative Conservation (1935);
RMG 218

The stage . . . is all set for somebody to show that each of the various public interests in land is better off when all cooperate than when all compete with each another. This principle of integration of land uses has already been carried out to some extent on public properties like the National Forests. But only a fraction of the land, and the poorest fraction at that, is or can ever become public property. The crux of the land problem is to show that integrated use is possible on private farms, and that such integration is mutually advantageous to both the owner and the public.

Coon Valley: An Adventure in Cooperative Conservation (1935);
RMG 219

. . . The government cannot buy "everywhere." The private landowner *must* enter the picture. It is easy to side-step the issue of getting lumbermen to practice forestry, or the farmer to crop game or conserve soil, and to pass these functions to government. *But it won't work.* I assert this, not as a political opinion, but as a geographical fact. The basic problem is to *induce the private landowner to conserve on his own land,* and no conceivable millions or billions for public land purchase can alter that fact, nor the fact that so far he hasn't done it.

Untitled ms. (c. 1935)

Relegating conservation to government is like relegating virtue to the Sabbath. Turns over to professionals what should be daily work of *amateurs.*

Lecture notes ms. (c. 1935)

Exclusively governmental conservation is undemocratic in [the] sense that it declines to credit the private citizen with brains, enthusiasm, or public spirit. It says: it's easier to tap his pocket than to teach him his duty.

Lecture notes ms. (c. 1935)

No rounded program for wildlife is possible unless it is applied on private as well as on public lands. . . .

. . . There is danger of using the present scramble for public dollars as a way to forget our zero score in private conservation to date. I say zero because if all the private undertakings in North America were plotted to scale on a map, you would need a microscope to find one, and even then you would have to know where to look.

Remarks on Wildlife Management by Private Agencies (1936)

. . . The greater part of the present public conservation program is a public palliative for the doctrine that the private landowner has no community responsibilities over and above taxes and personal conduct. I now raise the question: Is land-abuse anything but a tax on the neighbors? Is there any form of personal conduct more vital to society than land-conduct?

The Farm Wildlife Program: A Self-Scrutiny ms. (c. 1937)

. . . I conclude that the current doctrine of private-profit and public-subsidy is defective in these respects: It expects subsidies to do more—and the private owner to do less—for the community than they are capable of doing. We rationalize these defects as individualism, but they imply no real respect for the landowner as an individual. They merely condone the ecological ignorance which contrasts so strongly with his precocity in mechanical things. But the final proof that it is bogus individualism lies in the fact that it leads us straight into government ownership. An orator could decry it as radical paternalism, as abject dependence upon government tolerated by the landowners of a free country. I do not decry it, but I hate to see us lean on it as a solution.

The Farm Wildlife Program: A Self-Scrutiny ms. (c. 1937)

I would call it an optimistic guess to say . . . [that] the combined area of national forests, state forests, parks, refuges, etc., can hardly, even in the remote future, exceed a fifth of the area of the state [of Missouri]. We can't produce outdoor facilities for five-fifths of our people on one-fifth of our area. Let's buy land by all means, but let's not delude ourselves with the thought that buying land is a comprehensive solution. There can be no solution until conservation practices are habitual on the private farms of the state.

Whither Missouri? (1938)

. . . The Club should never lose sight of the fact that as an owner of otter range, it is the custodian of a rare and irreplaceable natural resource.

As in the case of wolves and deer, the otter is a *mobile resource* ranging over many ownerships. No one owner can effectively act alone. All these neighborhood responsibilities clearly dictate the need for eventual *group action* in the Huron Mountain region.

Report on Huron Mountain Club (1938)

I had a bird dog named Gus. When Gus couldn't find pheasants he worked up an enthusiasm for Sora rails and meadowlarks. This whipped-up zeal for unsatisfactory substitutes masked his failure to find the real thing. It assuaged his inner frustration.

We conservationists are like that. We set out a generation ago to convince the American landowner to control fire, to grow forests, to manage wildlife. He did not respond very well. We have virtually no forestry, and mighty little range management, game management, wildflower management, pollution control, or erosion control being practiced voluntarily by private landowners. In many instances the abuse of private land is worse than it was before we started. If you don't believe that, watch the strawstacks burn on the Canadian prairies; watch the fertile mud flowing down the Rio Grande; watch the gullies climb the hillsides in the Palouse, in the Ozarks, in the riverbreaks of southern Iowa and western Wisconsin.

To assuage our inner frustration over this failure, we have found us a meadowlark. I don't know which dog first caught the scent; I do know that every dog on the field whipped into an enthusiastic backing-point. I did myself. The meadowlark was the idea that if the private landowner won't practice conservation, let's build a bureau to do it for him.

Like the meadowlark, this substitute has its good points. It smells like success. It is satisfactory on poor land which bureaus can buy. The trouble is that it contains no device for preventing good private land from becoming poor public land. There is danger in the assuagement of honest frustration; it helps us forget we have not yet found a pheasant.

I'm afraid the meadowlark is not going to remind us. He is flattered by his sudden importance.

Conservation (c. 1938); RR 152–53

. . . I no longer believe that a little "bait" for the farmer, either in cash, service, or protection, is going to move him to active custodianship of wildlife. If the wildlife cropping tradition is not in his bones, then no external force, either of my kind or any other kind, is going to put it there. It must grow from the inside, and slowly.

Farmer-Sportsman, A Partnership for Wildlife Restoration (1939)

Conservation means harmony between men and land.

When land does well for its owner, and the owner does well by his land; when both end up better by reason of their partnership, we have conservation. When one or the other grows poorer, we do not.

The Farmer as a Conservationist (1939); RMG 255

. . . We had to amputate many marshes, ponds and woods to make the land habitable, but to remove any natural feature from representation in the rural landscape seems to me a defacement which the calm verdict of history will not approve, either as good conservation, good taste, or good farming.

The Farmer as a Conservationist (1939); RMG 259

It is easy, of course, to wish for better kinds of conservation, but what good does it do when on private lands we have very little of any kind? This is the basic puzzle for which I have no solution.

It seems possible, though, that [the] prevailing failure of economic self-interest as a motive for better land use has some connection with the failure of the social and natural sciences to agree with each other, and with the landholder, on a common concept of land. This may not be it, but ecology, as the fusion point of sciences and all the land uses, seems to me the place to look.

A Biotic View of Land (1939); RMG 272–73

In my opinion no individual blame attaches to the owner of the Faville Grove prairie for converting it to pasture. The public taxes him on the land. It is not his obligation to provide the public with free botanical reservations, especially when all public institutions, from the public school to the federal land bank, urge him to squeeze every possible penny out of every possible acre. No public institution ever told him, or any other farmer, that natural resources not convertible into cash have any value to it or to him. The white-fringed orchis is as irrelevant to the cultural and economic system into which he was born as the Taj Mahal or the Mona Lisa.

Exit Orchis (1940)

[Planning for wildlife] is not primarily a matter of laws, appropriations, or administrative devices, but rather of modifying land-use so as to provide the habitat needed by each species. Hence the execution of a plan rests with farmers and landowners, rather than with government. The function of government is to teach, lead, and encourage.

Planning for Wildlife ms. (1941)

There is lacking . . . a simple formula by which we, and posterity, may act to make America a permanent institution instead of a trial balloon. The formula is: learn how to tell good land-use from bad. Use your own land accordingly, and refuse aid and comfort to those who do not.

Isn't this more to the point than merely voting, petitioning, and writing checks for bigger and better bureaus, in order that our responsibilities may be laid in bigger and better laps?

Land-Use and Democracy (1942); RMG 296

. . . Soil Conservation Districts are perhaps a start toward self-scrutiny in farming, but they dare not use their powers for lack of voter-support. These districts are self-governing farm communities which have set themselves up as legal entities. In many states the district is authorized to write land-use regulations with the force of law. So far they dare not. But if farmers once asked: "Why don't we tackle our own erosion-control? I'll pull my cows off the hill if you will," the machinery for action is at hand.

Farmers do not yet ask such rash questions. Why? Probably because they have been led to believe that CCC camps, AAA checks, 4-H clubs, extension, meetings, speeches, and other subsidies and uplifts will do the trick. Those who really know land know this is not true; these milk-and-water measures have indeed retarded the rate of soil-loss, but they have not reversed it. Thus we see that the painless path not only fails to lead us to conservation, but sometimes actually retards the growth of critical intelligence on the whereabouts of alternative routes.

Land-Use and Democracy (1942); RMG 299–300

. . . The farmer should know the original as well as the introduced components of his land, and take a pride in retaining at least a sample of all of them. In addition to healthy soil, crops, and livestock, he should know and feel a pride in a healthy sample of marsh, woodlot, pond, stream, bog, or roadside prairie. In addition to being a conscious citizen of his political, social, and economic community, he should be a conscious citizen of his watershed, his migratory bird flyway, his biotic zone. Wild crops as well as tame crops should be a part of his scheme of farm management. He should hate no native animal or plant, but only excess or extinction in any one of them.

Cash outlays for unprofitable components of land are of course not to be expected, but outlays of thought, and to a reasonable extent of spare time, should be given with pride, just as they are now given to equivalent enterprises in human health and civic welfare.

Conservation: In Whole or in Part? (1944); RMG 318

. . . The average citizen, especially the landowner, has an obligation to manage his land in the interest of the community, as well as in his own interest. The fallacious doctrine that the government must subsidize all conservation not immediately profitable for the private landowner will ultimately bankrupt either the treasury, or the land, or both. The nation needs, and has a right to expect, the private landowner to use his land with foresight, skill, and regard for the future.

Conservation ms. (c. 1946)

By all the accepted rules of forestry, my neighbor was justified in slashing the [pine] grove. The stand was even-aged; mature, and invaded by heart-rot. Yet any schoolboy would know, in his heart, that there is something wrong about erasing the last remnant of pine timber from a county. When a farmer owns a rarity he should feel some obligation as its custodian, and a community should feel some obligation to help him carry the economic cost of custodianship. Yet our present land-use conscience is silent on such questions.

The Ecological Conscience (1947); RMG 343

The aspirations to better land-use, collectively called conservation, have had little effect on actual private land-practice. They have succeeded only when bolstered by public subsidies, or by public ownership and operation. The reasons for this partial failure are of the utmost national importance, for it is clear that public subsidies or ownership can cover only a fraction of what needs to be done, and this only awkwardly, expensively, and with frequent clashes of interest. Conservation can accomplish its objectives only when it springs from an impelling conviction on the part of private land owners.

Notes on Proposed Centennial Symposium on Ecological Conservation ms. (c. 1947)

Lack of economic value is sometimes a character not only of species or groups, but of entire biotic communities: marshes, bogs, dunes, and "deserts" are examples. Our formula in such cases is to relegate their conservation to government as refuges, monuments, or parks. The difficulty is that these communities are usually interspersed with more valuable private lands; the government cannot possibly own or control such scattered parcels. The net effect is that we have relegated some of them to ultimate extinction over large areas. If the private owner were ecologically minded, he would be proud to be the custodian of a reasonable proportion of such areas, which add diversity and beauty to his farm and to his community.

The Land Ethic (1949); ASCA 212

There is a clear tendency in American conservation to relegate to government all necessary jobs that private landowners fail to perform. Government ownership, operation, subsidy, or regulation is now widely prevalent in forestry, range management, soil and watershed management, park and wilderness conservation, fisheries management, and migratory bird management, with more to come. Most of this growth in governmental conservation is proper and logical, some of it is inevitable. That I imply no disapproval of it is implicit in the fact that I have spent most of my life working for it. Nevertheless the question arises: What is the ultimate magnitude of the enterprise? Will the tax base carry its eventual ramifications? At what point will governmental conservation, like the mastodon, become handicapped by its own dimensions? The answer, if there is any, seems to be in a land ethic, or some other force which assigns more obligation to the private landowner.

Industrial landowners and users, especially lumbermen and stockmen, are inclined to wail long and loudly about the extension of government ownership and regulation to land, but (with notable exceptions) they show little disposition to develop the only visible alternative: the voluntary practice of conservation on their own lands.

The Land Ethic (1949); ASCA 213

11 PUBLIC LAND

❧

Aldo Leopold on Public Land

Charles Wilkinson

The federal public lands have been the crucible for American conservation policy ever since the creation of Yellowstone as the world's first national park in 1872. At the beginning of the twentieth century Teddy Roosevelt and Gifford Pinchot took natural resources issues to center stage in a way that no one else has ever done before or since. The bright light they cast on the American people's vast land estate caught the eye, mind, and soul of Aldo Leopold, just then entering his teenage years. He headed off to the Yale Forest School, endowed by the Pinchot family just a few years before.

During Leopold's time at Yale—1905 through 1909—TR and Pinchot were all the talk. The daring proclamation of the Midnight Reserves in 1907, when the president designated more than sixteen million new acres of national forest land in the teeth of bitter opposition from Western congressmen, was as bold a stroke as American conservation has ever seen. By graduation time Leopold knew that he wanted to work for the Forest Service in the distant Southwest, where Arizona and New Mexico were still in territorial status: "That is where I want to go."[1]

His first assignment as a forest assistant was in the Apache National Forest, in the White Mountains of eastern Arizona Territory, where the headwaters of the Salt River gathered amid a wonderland of pine forests, plateaus, rocky canyons, and cienegas. What he experienced there changed him—and the world. In deep backcountry he encountered a thunderhead and witnessed its fearsome bolt: "It must be poor life that achieves freedom from fear."[2] He met an old wolf, and watched her green fire die. He met "far blue" Escudilla, who was a mountain and thought like one—until they killed off the last grizzly.[3]

In 1911 Leopold was assigned to the Carson National Forest in northern New Mexico Territory. Whereas the Apache had been pristine country, the open range of the Carson had been badly overgrazed by large cattle, and especially sheep, outfits. Leopold quickly saw the connection between soil depletion and wildlife scarcity. "Two elk," the hunter commented sardonically, "were seen here two years ago."[4] The deer, turkey, and bear also had mostly left. Later Leopold would call soil erosion "a leprosy of the land," which required "universal reformation of land-use."[5] In 1912 Leopold became forest supervisor. Under his guidance the Carson forest rangers implemented a permit system to regulate the numbers and ranges of domestic stock. Grazing and its effects were unavoidable issues on the Carson. He also published the *Pine Cone,* a newsletter that allowed the widely dispersed rangers to communicate.

Leopold believed strongly in on-the-ground management and treasured the fieldwork of his Forest Service years. (I have a friend who owns a ranch high on the Vallecitos River and on an autumn, ponderosa hike we agreed that "Leopold must have come through here." Hadn't he and his horse, Polly, visited nearly every ranch in and around the Carson?) But if freedom from fear makes for poor life, the corollary is that wild country can hit us, and hit us hard. In April 1913 Leopold set out to resolve a dispute with recalcitrant sheep ranchers. As was his custom, he slept out at night. One evening a major storm came in. Wet and cold, he tried to make his way home on horseback. Stricken with acute nephritis, he watched helplessly as his lower body swelled up. Recovery from the near-death experience came slowly, and the illness brought an end to his beloved fieldwork.

Leopold was then transferred to the Forest Service's regional office in Albuquerque. This may not have been his preferred location, but he was enormously productive there. He began his career as a writer, addressing issues of game protection, national forest management, grazing policy, and soil erosion. And wilderness. Because of his efforts the Gila Wilderness Area was carved out of national forest lands in western New Mexico in 1924, the first land area set aside by any government solely to preserve its wildness.

After Albuquerque, Leopold followed his star to the Forest Products Laboratory in Madison, Wisconsin, to the University of Wisconsin, and ultimately to his sand county farm. He continued to work on public land conservation through his writing, teaching, and research, focusing on wildlife management, wilderness, and range policy. In *Game Management* he noted the effect of "unstable livestock operations on hundreds of millions of acres in the West, especially on the unregulated public domain. The damage done to game by overgrazing is little appreciated."[6] Several of the most powerful essays in *A Sand County Almanac* drew upon his years as a public land manager in the Southwest.

The public lands continued to hold a central place in Leopold's maturing philosophy. He saw them, constituting nearly one-third of the American land, as playing an essential role in providing wildlife habitat, recreation, wilderness, and watershed protection, as well as timber and forage. Yet Leopold's holistic philosophy requires that these uses be subsumed under a new conservation ethic, shared by all the people, covering all lands and all individual activities. Yes, the public lands are critical to conservation in America. But Leopold, our Dutch uncle, reminds us that we need something larger and broader; that without private land conservation, a strong public lands policy will be "exactly as effective as buying half an umbrella."[7]

Leopold was so precise, so learned—such an intellectual—that we may sometimes forget that he was also a fighter and that his actions, as well as his written words, changed the world. In 1935, building on his advocacy that led to the first wilderness area, he cofounded the Wilderness Society. This event embodied Leopold's approach to conservation, marking as it did the combination of philosophy (the wilderness ideal), government policy (the official designation program), and private mobilization (an activist citizen organization). Three generations later the United States has dedicated more than 100 million acres of public lands to wilderness, and nations around the world have adopted wilderness conservation programs.

Leopold remained actively involved in public lands issues until the end of this life. Another outspoken advocate, Bernard De Voto, a native Utahan, dedicated many of his "Easy Chair" columns in *Harper's* magazine to Western issues. In January 1947 De Voto wrote angrily about one of the periodic land grabs—precursor to the later Sagebrush Rebellion and Wise Use Movement—that have tried to eviscerate the public estate. A month after De Voto's article, the Twelfth North American Wildlife Conference convened in San Antonio. Leopold, well aware that the confiscation proposal and De Voto's call to arms were matters of keen interest to those assembled there, directed his remarks to the issue. His message, delivered now by the nation's leading conservation figure, was straight to the point. The attempt to wrest away Bureau of Land Management lands, he warned, was a national issue, not just a Western one, and its effects "would be felt by every state."[8] The assault, he warned, would directly implicate the national forests and parks. Hold firm. These are the lands of all the people.

When Robert Marshall wrote his famous letter inviting a small group, including Leopold, to found the Wilderness Society, he cautioned that "we want no straddlers." Let us remember that Leopold was no straddler, that for all of his intellectual might he was passionate and fiery in defense of the public lands as a critical element in his larger land ethic. Conservation requires careful analysis and disciplined work, but it needs white-hot emotion, too. One measure of Aldo Leopold was his capacity for possessing these qualities and blending them in his life's work.

Life in Arizona was bounded underfoot by grama grass, overhead by sky, and on the horizon by Escudilla.

The road to Springerville, Arizona, with Escudilla Mountain and the Apache National Forest in the background, c. 1910. (Courtesy University of Wisconsin–Madison Archives)

The Ranger is the man on the ground. He lives there. He is in the position to see the effects of our work at all seasons and under all circumstances, and it is those effects and nothing else, that count.

> To the Forest Officers of the Carson (1913); RMG 46

Regardless of cost, there is an ingrained repugnance in the heart of many sportsmen to having their sport served to them in a spoon. There is a certain rugged independence—I suspect inherited from generations of self-respecting yeomen—poachers of the feudal ages—which eschews "boughten" sport. These estimable throwbacks, regardless of financial ability, will choose to test their skill, not on posted preserves, but on the public hunting grounds of the National Forests, beholden to no man or his dollar, but only to the law of the land.

> The National Forests: The Last Free Hunting Grounds of the Nation (1919)

The writer here and now pays his respects to the man who wrote into the Forest [Service] Manual the absolute prohibition of private game preserves [within national forests]. The larger part of the United States will be a private game preserve in 1940, and to extend this form of mo-

nopoly, inevitable on private lands, to the National Forests would be little
short of a crime against democratic society.

> The National Forests: The Last Free Hunting Grounds of the
> Nation (1919)

. . . The general spread of Game Farming would soon result in the general spread of commercialized shooting privileges, and the poor man
would be left with a few navigable rivers, and the freedom of the seas for
his hunting. . . .
      . . . A wholesale commercialization of shooting privileges . . . would
soon leave nothing open but public lands.

> Wild Lifers vs. Game Farmers: A Plea for Democracy in Sport
> (1919); RMG 66, ALS 58–59

Cannot the public see that a pond which furnishes inspiration, rest, and
health to a score of tired workers has a higher social value than a patch
of corn which furnishes feed for an equal number of hogs or steers? Of
course not, if only millionaires can enjoy the pond! When we take away
the democracy of sport we take away the only chance for fair public consideration of the sportsmen's interests.

> A Plea for State-Owned Ducking Grounds (1919); ALS 65

A network of State-owned ducking grounds, from ocean to ocean and
from Canada to the border, would be a fine thing for the average citizen,
a fine thing for the birds, a wholesome influence of restraint on private
clubs, a business asset to the local community, and a measure of permanent insurance against the undemocratic tendencies now manifest at
every hand.

> A Plea for State-Owned Ducking Grounds (1919); ALS 66

I . . . maintain, (1) that . . . extensions of our road systems into the wilderness are seldom yielding a return sufficient to amortize the public
investment; (2) that even where they do yield such a return, their construction is not necessarily in the public interest, any more than ob-
taining an economic return from the last vacant lot in a parkless city
would be in the public interest.

> Wilderness as a Form of Land Use (1925); RMG 139–40

It is just as unwise to devote 100% of the recreational resources of our
public parks and forests to motorists as it would be to devote 100% of
our city parks to merry-go-rounds.

> Wilderness as a Form of Land Use (1925); RMG 140

Now, if our remaining frontier consisted of $200 corn land there would not be much except theory to argue about. The point is that it consists mostly of the national forests—rough mountain lands embracing here and there particular areas of such crumpled topography and high altitude as to make the customary development of roads, Fords, and summer boarders of very questionable practicability. One would think that the ordinary laws of economics would automatically tend to exclude roads from such areas. But mark this well: the laws of economics are the last thing the roads booster is thinking about. Roads are going to continue to be built into such areas, unless the public at large thinks it is best not to, and unless the public says what it thinks.

A Plea for Wilderness Hunting Grounds (1925); ALS 156

Mere public acquiescence in [a national system of wilderness areas] will never get anywhere because of the normal pressure of economic development and the above-normal pressure of recreational wildcatting. An aggressive public movement in favor of such a system is necessary to its successful establishment.

The Conservation of Wilderness Recreation Areas ms. (1927)

There are already many localities in the National Forests where the hunters are thick enough to destroy the recreational value of the hunting ground, quite regardless of their effect on the game. This is true even on some of the "wilderness areas" set aside for wilderness recreation. Unfortunately many hunters are too thick-skinned to be annoyed. Nevertheless it is unthinkable that the public-service value of the national property should be allowed to progressively deteriorate from overcrowding.

Game Management in the National Forests (1930); ALS 129

. . . Fifty years from now the acquisition of public game lands may be recognized as a milestone in the evolution of democratic government.

The Forester's Role in Game Management (1931)

Doubtless we need [more public ownership of forests]—we are getting it whether we need it or not—but how far can it go? We cannot dodge the fact that the forest problem, like the soil problem, *is coextensive with the map of the United States.*

The Conservation Ethic (1933); RMG 187

I can see clearly only two things:
First, that the economic cards are stacked against some of the most important reforms in land-use.
Second, that the scheme to circumvent this obstacle by public owner-

ship, while highly desirable and good as far as it goes, can never go far enough. Many will take issue on this, but the issue is between two conflicting conceptions of the end towards which we are working. . . .

. . . The real end [of conservation] is a *universal symbiosis with land,* economic and esthetic, public and private. To this school of thought public ownership is a patch but not a program.

The Conservation Ethic (1933); RMG 187–88

One of the most important determinants of game food, water, and coverts is the livestock industry. Here again we must deal not only with legitimate, stabilized animal husbandry, but also with the overgrazing which has accompanied unstable livestock operations on hundreds of millions of acres in the West, especially on the unregulated public domain. The damage done to game by overgrazing is little appreciated by the public. . . . Especially in semi-arid climates, overgrazing eliminates the palatable food plants without apparent reduction in the amount of plant cover. Worthless plants promptly fill in the gaps left by the valuable ones, and the layman sees no difference. To him the ruined countryside is still "beautiful." He suffers no pain over the invisible but fundamental deterioration which his own industries have inflicted.

Game Management (1933), 274–75

Large-scale public ownership of marshlands . . . is feasible. It is also necessary, because the interstate movements of waterfowl render the incentive for their private production partially inoperative.

Conservation Economics (1934); RMG 195

. . . The inherent dispersion of the phenomena dealt with in game management makes public game production a mere supplement to production on private lands.

Conservation Economics (1934); RMG 195

. . . I do not challenge the purchase of public lands for conservation. For the first time in history we are buying on a scale commensurate with the size of the problem. I do challenge the growing assumption that bigger buying is a substitute for private conservation practice. Bigger buying, I fear, is serving as an escape-mechanism—it masks our failure to solve the harder problem. The geographic cards are stacked against its ultimate success. In the long run it is exactly as effective as buying half an umbrella.

Conservation Economics (1934); RMG 196–97

One of the symptoms of inadequacy in our now existing [legal and economic] structure is the perennial stalemate over the public domain.

How can we keep it without a huge expansion of federal machinery? How can we give it away without the certainty of misuse? There is indeed scant choice between the horns of this dilemma. But would there be a dilemma if there were such a thing as *contingent* possession, or else a differential tax exerting a constant positive pressure in favor of good use?

Conservation Economics (1934); RMG 202

The rare species are often vitally affected by misplaced private land. Take the grizzly: Why have the Federal conservation bureaus extirpated the grizzly from all but a few of his last stands in the national forests? Usually because some isolated private rancher lost some sheep or cows. Why didn't they remove the ranch rather than the bear? Because, until recently, no appropriation was available for moving ranches. It is now about last call for evacuating a suitable grizzly range in each of the western national forest regions, and restocking it if need be. No conceivable success in multiplying ordinary game, or in building bear refuges in Alaska, would extenuate our failure to save the "white bear" of Lewis and Clark. One key is the removal of misplaced private lands.

Remarks on Wildlife Management by Private Agencies (1936)

Life in Arizona was bounded under foot by grama grass, overhead by sky, and on the horizon by Escudilla. . . .

To the west billowed the outliers of the Apache National Forest. We cruised timber there, converting the tall pines, forty by forty, into notebook figures representing hypothetical lumber piles. Panting up a canyon, the cruiser felt a curious incongruity between the remoteness of the notebook symbols and the immediacy of sweaty fingers, locust thorns, deer-fly bites, and scolding squirrels. But on the next ridge a cold wind, roaring across a green sea of pines, blew his doubts away. On the far shore hung Escudilla.

Escudilla (1940); ASCA 133–34

An administrator of public lands containing remnants of wilderness should be aware of the fact that the richest values of wilderness lie not in the days of Daniel Boone, nor even in the present, but rather in the future. The administrator has a double responsibility; to keep some wilderness in existence, and to cultivate its qualitative enjoyment.

Wilderness Values (1941)

. . . While many administrators have acquiesced in the establishment of wilderness areas, few have exerted ingenuity in making them serve as many purposes as possible, nor have the landowning bureaus cooperated to such ends. For evidence I cite the precarious status of the grizzly bear, who has no sure citadel for the future, despite the millions of acres of forests and parks dedicated to wildlife conservation. What wildlife? Is it too much to ask that the bureaus get their heads together and map out some really adequate wilderness ranges for threatened species like the grizzly? Or to spend a few dollars to consolidate such ranges and clear them of alienations? Why not substitute some interbureau planning for the present interbureau wars?

Wilderness Values (1941)

Saving the grizzly requires a series of large areas from which roads and livestock are excluded, or in which livestock damage is compensated. Buying out scattered livestock ranches is the only way to create such areas, but despite large authority to buy and exchange lands, the conservation bureaus have accomplished virtually nothing toward this end. The Forest Service has, I am told, established one grizzly range in Montana, but I know of a mountain range in Utah in which the Forest Service actually promoted a sheep industry, despite the fact that it harbored the sole remnant of grizzlies in that state.

Permanent grizzly ranges and permanent wilderness areas are of course two names for one problem. Enthusiasm about either requires a long view of conservation, and a historical perspective. Only those able to see the pageant of evolution can be expected to value its theater, the wilderness, or its outstanding achievement, the grizzly. But if education really educates, there will, in time, be more and more citizens who understand that relics of the old West add meaning and value to the new. Youth yet unborn will pole up the Missouri with Lewis and Clark, or climb the Sierras with James Capen Adams, and each generation in turn will ask: Where is the big white bear? It will be a sorry answer to say he went under while conservationists weren't looking.

The Grizzly—A Problem in Land Planning (1942); ASCA 199

I doubt whether public acquisition, as a means of assuring the national timber supply, is a satisfactory substitute for forestry practice by private owners. The job is too big. When government takes over a small area for decent use, it aims to educate by example, but I fear it also generates a false assurance that things are on the mend.

The Last Stand (1942); RMG 294

. . . Sanctuaries are one of the things government can do, but the growth of private ethics and naturalistic management needed to go with them is beyond the powers of government.

It seems to me that sanctuaries are akin to monasticism in the dark ages. The world was so wicked it was better to have islands of decency than none at all. Hence decent citizens retired to monasteries and convents. Once established, these islands became an alibi for lack of private reform. People said: "We pay the bills for all this virtue. Let goodness stay where it belongs, and not pester practical folks who have to run the world." The present attitude of some duck-hunters offers a close parallel. The more monasteries or sanctuaries, the grimmer the incongruity between inside and outside.

We need more sanctuaries, but some of them will boomerang until they serve a better public.

Land-Use and Democracy (1942); RMG 299

Our program here has given scant recognition to the "Battle for the Public Lands." Perhaps it couldn't, for the opening gun was fired only a month ago. I have this to say:

1. It is perhaps the biggest conservation battle since the Ballinger Controversy.

2. Let no man think that the issue is a western affair of no consequence to other states. The defeat of public land conservation in the West would be felt by every state.

3. Let no man think that this is a grazing district fight. Disrupt the public domain, and the national forests will follow; disrupt the national forests, and the national parks will follow.

4. It is pure evasion to say that the states, or the private owner, could practice conservation on these lands. Neither, by and large, had demonstrated either the capacity or the wish to do so. To organize the practice of conservation on large areas takes decades of hard work.

5. Now is the time for a critical self-examination by all federal land bureaus.

Summarization of the Twelfth North American Wildlife Conference (1947)

A deep chesty bawl echoes from rimrock to rimrock, rolls down the mountain, and fades into the far blackness of the night. It is an outburst of wild defiant sorrow, and of contempt for all the adversities of the world.

Every living thing (and perhaps many a dead one as well) pays heed to that call. To the deer it is a reminder of the way of all flesh, to the pine a forecast of midnight scuffles and of blood upon the snow, to the coyote a promise of gleanings to come, to the cowman a threat of red ink at the bank, to the hunter a challenge of fang against bullet. Yet behind these obvious and immediate hopes and fears there lies a deeper meaning, known only to the mountain itself. Only the mountain has lived long enough to listen objectively to the howl of a wolf.

Thinking Like a Mountain (1949); ASCA 129

12   ADVOCACY

❦

Throwing Your Weight Around

Edwin P. Pister

If not for Aldo Leopold, I likely would not have become a conservation advocate. After reading "The Land Ethic," first as a student in A. Starker Leopold's Wildlife Conservation class at the University of California at Berkeley, then again at a critical stage of my career several years later, it was difficult for me to avoid that fate. Aldo Leopold's summary precept—"A thing is right when it tends to preserve the integrity, stability, and beauty of the biotic community. It is wrong when it tends otherwise"[1]—caused me to examine critically not only my own programs, but also those of my agency (the California Department of Fish and Game). There is probably no stronger call toward advocacy anywhere in the literature of conservation.

Bolstered by Leopold's precept, I found it a simple matter to separate the "good" from the "bad." Yet the "bad" programs (for example, the indiscriminate stocking of non-native game fish in yet unstudied waters), those which tended to diminish the integrity, stability, and beauty of the biotic community, were often the most popular among the public—and, therefore, among higher echelons of resource management agencies. They were politically expedient but often biologically flawed and indefensible.

Even with essentially benign programs (for example, planting put-and-take trout in waters containing no threatened species), there was reason for concern. These programs were depleting financial and personnel resources that should have been devoted to more enduring and meaningful efforts, such as species inventories and habitat evaluation and protection. Leopold's words strengthened the commitment of those who saw flaws in the status quo. We gained resolve from his admonition: "In such matters we should not worry too much about anything except the direction in which we travel. The direction is clear, and the first step is to *throw your weight around* on matters of right and wrong in land-use."[2] This clarion call, along with the observation that "nonconformity is the highest evolutionary attainment of social animals," provided us with all the courage we needed to move in a new and better direction.[3] As a pio-

178

neer in the role of advocate during a crucial period of the American conservation movement, Leopold prepared the way for those who would follow.

There are risks involved in becoming an advocate within an agency not yet ready to accept what one is advocating. On a September afternoon in 1972 I was called on the carpet by my department's top leadership and admonished for my work involving the conservation of California's rare and unique desert fishes. "What you are doing," I was told, "is embarrassing to us and to our colleagues" (meaning the agency directorships of other Western states). In a career that now stretches over fifty years, I have never encountered a more blatant effort to suppress advocacy or employee initiative.

At that point I had to move underground. I continued on as before but simply failed to report my activities. Fortunately, my immediate boss was sympathetic (and headquartered more than three hundred miles away). No one other than my closest associates knew that, on my own time and expense, I was providing testimony—on a Nevada fish in Las Vegas—for the Department of the Interior. Those who were aware of my actions expressed gratitude but were firmly convinced that I was out of my mind. In *Round River* Leopold wrote that "one of the penalties of an ecological education is that one lives alone in a world of wounds."[4] This statement rings profoundly true under such circumstances. The "penalties" seem especially severe when agency policy-makers do not possess an ecological education or refuse to acknowledge or practice it for political reasons. Mercifully, this may be less of a problem today than it was in 1972!

The recent burgeoning of conservation nongovernmental organizations (NGOs) has made it easier for advocates within government to make their voices heard. NGOs played a vital role in the case of the desert fishes. In the early 1970s legal action was contemplated as the only feasible means of saving from extinction the Devils Hole pupfish. The actions of the newly formed Desert Fishes Council and the threat of a mandamus action by the Sierra Club provided the necessary stimulus. The Department of the Interior began a series of three court actions that ended in a favorable decision by the U.S. Supreme Court (*Cappaert vs. United States*, 426 U.S. 128 [1976]). As we enter into the era of ecosystem management, NGOs may be expected to play an even greater role in conservation programs.

Aldo Leopold did not avoid conservation politics, and he served during his life with dozens of organizations, agencies, and professional groups, from the New Mexico Game Protective Association to the Albuquerque Chamber of Commerce, from the Sporting Arms and Ammunition Manufacturers' Institute to the Wilderness Society. He learned early in his career that to be a successful conservation advocate one must possess a good working knowledge (even a mastery) of the political process. This, it goes without saying, remains true.

Leopold also devoted a great deal of thought and energy to comprehending the political tensions within the conservation movement. In "The Land Ethic" he described what he called the "A/B cleavage," which defines dissensions and differences within conservation: "One group (A) regards the land as soil, and its function as commodity-production; another group (B) regards the land as a biota, and its function as something broader."[5] Throughout his career Leopold sought to build bridges between conservation factions. In his classic work *Game Management,* for example, he observed that there is "a fundamental unity of purpose and method between bird-lovers and sportsmen. Their common task of teaching the public how to modify economic activities for conservation purposes is of infinitely greater importance, and difficulty, than their current differences of opinion over details of legislative and administrative policy."[6] This was a constant theme for Leopold in these years: the advocacy of both types of conservationists, bird-lovers and sportsmen alike, must properly be directed toward a common goal of habitat acquisition and protection.

Read thoughtfully the quotations that follow. They may open doors and instigate major changes in your own careers, as they have in mine. My hope is that the idealism of those blessed with open minds may nurture the principles that must guide the nation's conservation programs. Biologically sound programs are inevitably ethically sound programs. Aldo Leopold was among the first to recognize the concordance of what initially appear to be two very different disciplines, ecology and ethics. He blended the two with unmatched eloquence and insight, adding his vision and wisdom as an advocate for what he knew, as an ecologist, to be right. He arrived, finally, at his summary precept of right and wrong, and much of the conservation world followed.

In the final analysis, the resolve of the conservation community to follow its ecological conscience, and to become tireless advocates on behalf of the wild, will determine the character of our world in the future. Only our commitment will allow future generations to inherit the biologically diverse planet we enjoy at the end of the twentieth century—and that much of society naively takes for granted. Such naivete and complacency will likely persist unless we are successful in advocating alternative courses of action.

Conservation, without a keen realization of its vital conflicts, fails to rate as authentic human drama; it falls to the level of a mere Utopian dream.

Leopold explaining his position on the need to check Wisconsin's deer population, 1942. (Photo by Staber W. Reese. Courtesy University of Wisconsin–Madison Archives)

❧

A bill to establish game refuges is now before congress. . . . Everybody wants refuges, especially the stockmen. Unless something is done to establish them, however, and that quickly, the only alternative will be to close up the present open season on deer and turkey absolutely.

> Game Conservation—A Warning, Also an Opportunity (1916);
> ALS 21

The most encouraging sign of the times is the recent organization of four game protective associations, at Flagstaff, Springerville, Tucson, and Payson respectively. These are voluntary organizations of public spirited citizens formed to push all available measures for bringing back Arizona's wild life. Their potentialities for good work are enormous. Nature is with us—only man and predatory animals are against us. These associations have the evident opportunity of persuading men to get on the other side of the fence—in persuading the average citizen that it is his privilege and duty to assume a constructive instead of destructive attitude toward beneficial wild things.

> Game Conservation—A Warning, Also an Opportunity (1916);
> ALS 21–22

We have been working for nearly three years in an endeavor to have Stinking Lake made a game refuge. This body of water is located on the Jicarilla-Apache Indian Reservation in Northern New Mexico. . . .

We are now confronted with the fact that the Jicarilla Sanctuary Association, composed of twenty wealthy Colorado sportsmen, has applied to the Commissioner of Indian Affairs for a long lease of this lake in order to establish a shooting club.

. . . We do contend that the approval of this lease involves two principles: first, the monopolization of our principal source of raw material in the shape of ducks, and second, the monopolization of the greatest natural wonder in the state.

> Make Stinking Lake a Game Refuge (1918); ALS 27–28

Why is the big game of the West disappearing today? Principally for the reason that the game laws are not enforced. And why are they not enforced? *Politics.* Paper game laws and political game wardens are one and inseparable. . . .

. . . Man really prizes only those things which he has earned by the sweat of his brow. Sportsmen do not *really support* a game warden until they have had to *roll up their sleeves* in some common disinterested effort to get a good one. With the vast territory which a western game warden has to handle, this active aid of the whole body of sportsmen is the *sine qua non* of success.

Putting the "AM" in Game Warden (1918)

A new day has dawned in wild life conservation in New Mexico. . . .

Is the reform a permanent one? That remains to be seen. The writer predicts, however, that before the next gubernatorial campaign, the new plan will have so firmly established its success that it will be *bad politics* to attempt the re-establishment of the old order.

Putting the "AM" in Game Warden (1918)

I cannot imagine a worse jumble than to have the whole body politic suddenly "adopt" all the foolish ideas that smolder in happy discontent beneath the conventional surface of society. There is no such danger. Nonconformity is the highest evolutionary attainment of social animals. . . .

A Man's Leisure Time (1920); RR 8

. . . Is it possible to preserve the element of Unknown Places in our national life? Is it practicable to do so, without undue loss in economic values? I say "yes" to both questions. But we must act vigorously and quickly, before the remaining bits of wilderness have disappeared.

The River of the Mother of God (1924); RMG 125

. . . The good roads mania, and all forms of unthinking Boostcrism that go with it, constitute a steam roller the like of which has seldom been seen in the history of mankind. No steam roller can overwhelm a good idea or a righteous policy, but it might very readily flatten out, one by one, the remaining opportunities for applying this particular policy. . . .

. . . Unless the wilderness idea represents the mandate of an organized, fighting and voting body of far-seeing Americans, the steam roller will win.

. . . If the spirit of the Covered Wagon really persists, as I firmly believe it does, its devotees must speak now, or forever hold their peace.

Conserving the Covered Wagon (1925); RMG 131–32

If we are unable to steer the Juggernaut of our own prosperity, then surely there is an impotence in our vaunted Americanism that augurs ill for our future. The self-directed evolution of rational beings does not apply to us until we become collectively, as well as individually, rational and self-directing.

Wilderness as a Form of Land Use (1925); RMG 142

. . . I am asserting that those who love the wilderness should not be wholly deprived of it, that while the reduction of the wilderness has been a good thing, its extermination would be a very bad one, and that the conservation of wilderness is the most urgent and difficult of all the tasks that confront us, because there are no economic laws to help and many to hinder its accomplishment.

Untitled address on wilderness conservation (1926)

Even the thinking citizen is too apt to assume that his only power as a conservationist lies in his vote. Such an assumption is wrong. At least an equal power lies in his daily thought, speech, and action, and especially in his habits as a buyer and user of wood.

I admit that the effective exercise of his power as a purchaser and user of forest products depends on his being well posted. But most problems of good citizenship in these days seem to resolve themselves into just that. Good citizenship is the only effective patriotism, and patriotism requires less and less of making the eagle scream, but more and more of making him think.

The Home Builder Conserves (1928); RMG 147

Is there any human aspiration which ever scored a victory without losing to some extent its capacity for self-criticism? The worthiness of any cause is not measured by its clean record, but by its readiness to see the blots when they are pointed out, and to change its mind. Is there not some way in which our . . . factions can point out each other's sophistries and blunders without losing sight of our common love for what Mr. Babbitt is trampling under foot? Must the past mistakes of each group automatically condemn every future effort of either to correct them?

Game and Wild Life Conservation (1932); RMG 168

The advent of a common danger ought to reveal the loss, delay, and risk inherent in many of these clashes [among conservation groups], and the crying need for replacing or offsetting them insofar as humanly possible, by an attitude of habitual self-criticism and mutual consultation— by some joint concept of a common cause. . . .

. . . Mutual danger may bring the realization that the other side cannot do all the conceding, that cooperation does not necessarily involve moral compromise, that it is possible for a sportsman to be respectable or a bird-lover tolerant, and above all that *technique is lacking* and must often be developed before cooperative agreement on paper can result in cooperative action on actual land, animals, or plants.

Weatherproofing Conservation (1933)

Must we view forever the irony of educating our sons with paper, the offal of which pollutes the rivers which they need quite as badly as books? Would not many people pay an extra penny for a "clean" newspaper? Government may someday busy itself with the legitimacy of labels used by land-industries to distinguish conservation products, rather than with the attempt to operate their lands for them.

The Conservation Ethic (1933); RMG 192

[Regarding the future of the conservation movement]

There are two ways to interpret the present evidence. One is to consider the movement as merely the dying gesture of an obsolete ideal, the regretful sigh of an outdated minority as they hand over to chemists and engineers their proxy for dominion over the earth. The small proportion of young conservationists, and possibly the incessant bickering of old ones, lend color to this view.

The other view is to consider the conservation idea as the beginning of a new conviction that machines alone do not truly liberate mankind; that leisure and security are of little value if, in the process of getting them, the objects on which they could be profitably expended will have disappeared; that the task of the future is to learn how to live with our inventions.

Game Management (1933), 420

Conservationists are sharply divided into groups, interested respectively in soil fertility, soil erosion, forests, parks, ranges, water flows, game, fish, fur, non-game animals, landscape, wild flowers, etc.

These divergent foci of interest clearly arise from individual limitations of taste, knowledge, and experience. They also reflect the age-old conflict between utility and beauty. Some believe the two can be integrated, on the same land, to mutual advantage. Others believe their opposing claims must be fought out and settled by exclusive dedication of each parcel of land to either the one use or the other.

This paper proceeds on two assumptions. The first is that there is only one soil, one flora, one fauna, one people, and hence only one conservation problem. Each acre should produce what it is good for and no two are alike. Hence a certain acre may serve one, or several, or all of the conservation groups.

The second is that economic and esthetic land uses can and must be integrated, usually on the same acre. To segregate them wastes land, and is unsound social philosophy. The ultimate issue is whether good taste and technical skill can both exist in the same landowner.

Land Pathology (1935); RMG 212–13

Every remnant [of threatened wildlife] should be definitely entrusted to a custodian—ranger, warden, game manager, chapter, ornithologist, farmer, stockman, lumberjack. Every conservation meeting—national, state, or local—should occupy itself with hearing their annual reports. Every field inspector should contact their custodians—he might often learn as well as teach. I am satisfied that thousands of enthusiastic conservationists would be proud of such a public trust, and many would execute it with fidelity and intelligence.

I can see in this set-up more conservation than could be bought with millions of new dollars, more coordination of bureaus than Congress can get by new organization charts, more genuine contacts between factions than will ever occur in the war of the inkpots, more research than would accrue from many gifts, and more public education than would accrue from an army of orators and organizers.

Threatened Species (1936); RMG 233–34, ALS 198

Our political parties espouse "conservation" in general terms, but they carefully avoid commitment on its internal contradictions. Hence when occasion arises to split a wilderness with a road, or sacrifice a salmon stream to power dams, they may do so without embarrassment.

Naturschutz in Germany (1936)

Conservation, without a keen realization of its vital conflicts, fails to rate as authentic human drama; it falls to the level of a mere Utopian dream.

Review of *Our Natural Resources and Their Conservation* (1937)

. . .The objective [of university instruction] should be to create a body of public opinion capable of *critical* support of conservation policies. The principal present defect in the conservation movement is that public enthusiasm has outstripped public discrimination.

The University and Conservation of Wisconsin Wildlife (1937)

We face a future marked by a growing public zeal for conservation, but a zeal so uncritical—so devoid of discrimination—that any nostrum is likely to be gulped with a shout. No program is too amateurish for public support if it bears the proper label and is backed by ballyhoo.

Under these conditions is it wise for our universities to focus their teaching on overstocking the market with professionals? Should they instead stock their farms and offices with citizens who know what it is all about?

The Research Program (1937)

Every professional man must, within limits, execute the jobs people are willing to pay for. But every profession in the long run writes its own ticket. It does so through the emergence of leaders who can afford to be skeptical out loud and in public—professors, for example. What I here decry is not so much the prevalence of public error in the use of engineering tools as the scarcity of engineering criticism of such misuse.

Engineering and Conservation (1938); RMG 252

Conservation is a house divided. Few of us realize the extent to which this is true.

The first job . . . is to bring the [conservation] factions together and insist that they thresh out their differences.

It would be Utopian to suppose that they can all agree. But the more threshing, the less disagreement. The more threshing, the better the understanding of the other fellow's interests. Mutual respect is often just as good as mutual agreement. What conservationists need is education, and our opponent is often our best teacher.

The Conservation League ms. (c. 1940)

To John Main, ornithology was a cause as well as a scientific field sport. Such problems as the protection of raptors and the preservation of rare species lay close to his heart. Every farmer who nailed a Redtail to his barn door drove a thorn into John Main's social conscience. He was the self-appointed custodian and trustee of every Sandhill Crane marsh and every Duck Hawk eyrie in the Madison region. Of such stuff, and of such only, can true conservation be built.

John S. Main [obituary] (1941)

If we don't like the way landowner X is using the natural resources of which he is the owner, why do we buy his products? Why do we invest in his securities? Why do we accord him the same social standing as landowner Y, who makes an honest attempt to use his land as if he were its trustee? Why do we tell our government to reform Mr. X, instead of doing it ourselves? The answer must be either that we do not know the limits of what government can do, or that we don't care deeply enough to risk personal action or danger.

Land-Use and Democracy (1942); RMG 295–96

I have no illusion that all of the products of land-abuse are as easy to identify, or as easy to do without, as a wild bird-skin on a hat. I do assert that many products of land-abuse can be identified as such, and can be discriminated against, given the conviction that it is worth the trouble. Conversely, the products of good land-use can often be singled out and favored.

Land-Use and Democracy (1942); RMG 296

No new device in human affairs is ever an unmixed blessing. The idea here proposed: hitching conservation directly to the producer-consumer relation instead of to the government, entails some serious risks. It would present the professional advertiser with an opportunity for euphemized deception and equivocation vastly larger than cigarettes. The more complex the product or process, the wider the field for the trained hoodwinker.

Land-Use and Democracy (1942); RMG 300

There are two kinds of conservationists, and two systems of thought on the subject.

One kind feels a primary interest in some one aspect of land (such as soil, forestry, game, or fish) with an incidental interest in the land as a whole.

The other feels a primary interest in the land as a whole, with incidental interest in its component resources.

The two approaches lead to quite different conclusions as to what constitutes conservative land-use, and how such use is to be achieved.

Conservation: In Whole or in Part? (1944); RMG 310

Fortunately for the human race, pressure groups are never quite unanimous.

Review of The Ducks Came Back (1946); RMG 329

Intelligent management of the deer herd depends, in the last analysis, on public understanding of the deer problem. Does enough understanding exist at this time to make intelligent management possible?

. . . I, of course, do not know. The only way to find out is to try. Many citizen groups have threatened to abolish the [Wisconsin Conservation] commission if it proceeds to reduce the herd. In my view, this might be the best way to test the status of public intelligence. If the public will not tolerate intelligent deer management by its commission, then it does not need a commission. The old system of political conservation football would do just as well.

The Deer Dilemma (1946)

An issue may be so clear in outline, so inevitable in logic, so imperative in need, and so universal in importance as to command immediate support from any reasonable person. Yet that collective person, the public, may take a decade to see the argument, and another to acquiesce in an effective program. . . .

This public we are talking about consists of three groups. Group 1 is the largest; it is indifferent to conservation questions. Group 2 is the smallest; it thinks with its head, but is silent. Group 3 is of intermediate size, and does all its thinking with mouth or pen. Perhaps a Conservation

Commission would do better not to try to convert Group 3, but to convince Group 2 that there is an issue, and that it should say or do something about it.

Adventures of a Conservation Commissioner (1946); RMG 331

In politics, a few advanced thinkers in a few advanced countries have developed a respect for minorities. A rare viewpoint, creed, or culture is perhaps not wholly unlike a rare kind of country, bird, or mammal in its possible contribution to the good life. Certainly both have the common denominator of possible extinguishment.

Just why do we respect political minorities, and accord them a value worth preserving? Perhaps the answer would shed light on the value of ecological "minorities" such as wild country or threatened species of wildlife.

Scarcity Values in Conservation ms. (c. 1946)

I am interested in the thing called "conservation." For this I have two reasons: (1) without it, our economy will ultimately fall apart; (2) without it many plants, animals, and places of entrancing interest to me as an explorer will cease to exist. I do not like to think of economic bankruptcy, nor do I see much object in continuing the human enterprise in a habitat stripped of what interests me most.

Wherefore Wildlife Ecology? (1947); RMG 336–37

I have no illusions about the speed or accuracy with which an ecological conscience can become functional. It has required 19 centuries to define decent man-to-man conduct and the process is only half done; it may take as long to evolve a code of decency for man-to-land conduct. In such matters we should not worry too much about anything except the direction in which we travel. The direction is clear, and the first step is to *throw your weight around* on matters of right and wrong in land-use. Cease being intimidated by the argument that a right action is impossible because it does not yield maximum profits, or that a wrong action is to be condoned because it pays. That philosophy is dead in human relations, and its funeral in land-relations is overdue.

The Ecological Conscience (1947); RMG 345–46

Conservationists are notorious for their dissensions. Superficially these seem to add up to mere confusion, but a more careful scrutiny reveals a single plane of cleavage common to many specialized fields. In each field one group (A) regards the land as soil, and its function as commodity-production; another group (B) regards the land as a biota, and its function as something broader. How much broader is admittedly in a state of doubt and confusion.

The Land Ethic (1949); ASCA 221

13 ECONOMICS

卐

Do Economists Know About Lupines?

Donald Snow

The Thoreauvian philosopher who dwelt within the breast of Aldo Leopold composed these lines in the early summer of 1946: "Sometimes in
June, when I see unearned dividends of dew hung on every lupine, I
have doubts about the real poverty of the sands. On solvent farmlands
lupines do not even grow, much less collect a daily rainbow of jewels. If
they did, the weed-control officer, who seldom sees a dewy dawn, would
doubtless insist that they be cut. Do economists know about lupines?"[1]
It might as well have been Henry David himself speaking of the impoverished vision of the men who tend toward riches. Only a refined impertinence would ask such a question of economists, of anyone, really, who
viewed nature only in terms of what can be extracted from her.

By the time Leopold wrote those lines at age 59, he had made his views
on economics clear enough. Economics may or may not have been a
science, but to him it was surely dismal. The pecuniary motive had
wrecked the great white pine forests of Michigan and the upper Mississippi Valley when the Iowa-born Leopold was still in diapers. And though
he knew of that legacy, and issued from a family that supported early
conservation measures, Leopold himself had once embraced what he
later called "economic biology."[2]

As a young forester he eagerly absorbed the utilitarian ideals of Gifford Pinchot, first chief of the U.S. Forest Service—and that meant intensified timber management on every national forest and making room
for grazing and mining, too. It is well known that in his early career
with the Forest Service, Leopold eagerly organized a coalition of agency
colleagues, stockmen, and sportsmen to eradicate predators. "The last
one must be caught before the job can be called fully successful," he
declared.[3]

He understood that Americans' unthinking embrace of economic
growth had created a juggernaut, and because of that, arguments for
the conservation of nature would have to be couched in terms favorable
to commerce. Leopold's concise way of saying it: "one must speak in the

language of compound interest to get a hearing."⁴ Yet all along in his essays and public addresses, he wrote lines that displayed a profound mistrust of what he called "economic determinism" and revealed his contempt for the fact that it could never fully take into account the value of "things natural, wild, and free."⁵ Dewdrops on the lupines.

His views prefigured an era of ecological economics when some economists and a great many environmental advocacy groups, following the juggernaut, would adopt the lexicon of commerce for the sake of protecting nature. When the Army Corps of Engineers came up with a plan to dam the Flambeau River for flood control, Leopold pointed out the hypocrisy in "the semi-honest doctrine that conservation is only good economics." He went on: "The defenders of the Flambeau tried to prove that the river in its wild state would produce more fish and tourists than the impounded river would produce butterfat, but this is not true."⁶ The quantity argument is a trap set by obedience to convention, Leopold seemed to be saying. What we should be articulating instead is a defense of nature based on principles of quality: the world is simply better, and we are better off in the long run, with wildness left intact.

Had Leopold lived to be a hundred, he might have been pleased to see a rising corps of economists, business leaders, and economic philosophers making precisely the same point. Like the science of ecology, the science of economics has migrated in directions that could not have been predicted in the post-Depression era. It is now clear that when Leopold said "economics" he meant mainly "commerce," and it is equally clear that many contemporary economists would agree with him right down the line—but perhaps with a few substitutions of terms.

Commercial determinism is narrow and foolish and fails to take other values into account. The finest things in life—love, honor, spirituality, a sense of belonging, wildness, music—simply cannot be given price tags. Trying to hang numbers on them violates the very essence we seek to protect. Leopold wrote that "one basic weakness in a conservation system based wholly on economic motives is that most members of the land community have no economic value."⁷ Many economists would now agree, but might substitute the term *monetary* for *economic*. It is an important distinction to one who understands the value of scarcity, and few good economists today would doubt that the things Leopold most valued in nature are fast becoming the scarcest things on the planet.

In his musings on economics Leopold may have been on the brink of a great discovery, one preempted by his untimely death. He may have come to understand fully that conservation usually *is* good economics, and that, in fact, the practices and mindset he decried represent, simply, *bad* economics—the powerful, short-term demands of commercial interests trumping all others.

It was little wonder that Leopold often used the term "economic" as if it were an obscenity. All he ever saw of economics, it seems, was a narrow vision of nature based on a simple-minded model, resource extraction theory, which would eventually be used to justify numerous subsidies for commercial interests to remove minerals and timber from public lands, and for the government to dam the nation's major river basins in the name of progress. Leopold sought instead an economics that would somehow help to protect soil fertility, clean water and air, biodiversity, and ecological processes.

In his final years Leopold seemed to stand on the verge of a new understanding of the mischief wrought by the collaboration of commercial and governmental powers. "Government ownership, operation, subsidy, or regulation is now widely prevalent in forestry, range management, soil and watershed management, park and wilderness conservation . . . ," he wrote. "Most of this growth . . . is proper and logical. . . . Nevertheless the question arises: What is the ultimate magnitude of the enterprise?"[8] As Leopold was beginning to understand, interference in the marketplace is a two-edged sword. The same powerful national government that could cordon off natural areas, create national parks, and perform necessary tasks of regulation could also become a superpower over nature in its willingness to gerrymander natural resource allocations to favor commercial interests. Or, in the case of a monstrosity like the Grand Coulee Dam, it could perform its own massive-scale machinations in the name of something called "conservation."

As his mind turned toward questioning "the ultimate magnitude of the enterprise," Leopold began to see into a deeper pool of economic wisdom. As bad as commerce may be, government, with its nearly limitless powers, is potentially a greater destroyer of nature. For when there is a common pool of capital to plunder, and ringing declarations of "national security" or national cause, fiscal promiscuity runs unchecked. When commercial and governmental interests work hand-in-hand, whole natural systems can be destroyed for the sake of any number of "economic" enterprises that the market process, undisturbed by political favor, never could have afforded.

Leopold did not live long enough to encounter the quasi-scientific vision of what Paul Hawken calls "an ecology of commerce," and Michael Rothschild refers to as "bionomics."[9] These envision a healthy economy that is not antibiological and predatory in its orientation toward nature but rather mimics and seeks to learn from ecological processes. Perhaps the pragmatic Leopold would have approved, or at least bit harder on his pipe and pondered. The empiricist in him was terribly fond, after all, of a proclamation made by Arthur Twining Hadley, a political economist who served as president of Yale when Leopold attended its Forest School. "The criterion which shows whether a thing is right or wrong," wrote Hadley, "is its permanence. Survival is not merely a characteristic of the right; it is a test of the right."[10]

And so must an ecology of economics prove itself. Can it survive the test of the right? And there is another question left for us to ponder: Is there still time to find out?

We fancy that industry supports us, forgetting what supports industry.

Leopold hauling loaded wood sled at the Shack, c. 1940. (Photo by Carl Leopold. Courtesy Aldo Leopold Foundation)

The Game Farmer wants [markets] opened—to his products. . . . The Wild Lifer, on the other hand, regards with apprehension the opening of markets, even to artificially raised game, while the idea of a wide-open market fills him with horror.

Is it possible to reconcile these two points of view? Yes and no. It is conceivable that limited markets—that is, markets for tagged meat raised on licensed game farms—might be indefinitely maintained and even largely expanded, without resulting in serious violation of the laws prohibiting the sale of wild or public game. . . . It seems almost axiomatic, however, that a return to wide-open markets would spell the certain doom of wild game, and even edible non-game. The radical game breeder's hints for a wide-open market, therefore, are a wide-open challenge to choose between Game Farming and public game. With a wide-open market, public game could not exist, and game laws would become useless and unnecessary.

> Wild Lifers vs. Game Farmers: A Plea for Democracy in Sport (1919); RMG 65, ALS 57–58

It is the present duty of American sportsmen to wisely guide the inevitable commercialization of wild game and shooting privileges. Not the least of the problems involved is to prevent monopoly, and to arrive at an ultimate solution compatible with our democratic institutions.

> A Plea for State-Owned Ducking Grounds (1919); ALS 64

Thus far we have considered the problem of conservation of land purely as an economic issue. A false front of exclusively economic determinism is so habitual to Americans in discussing public questions that one must speak in the language of compound interest to get a hearing.

> Some Fundamentals of Conservation in the Southwest (1923); RMG 94

Wilderness as a form of land-use is, of course, premised on a qualitative conception of progress. It is premised on the assumption that enlarging the range of individual experience is as important as enlarging the number of individuals; that the expansion of commerce is a means, not an end; that the environment of the American pioneers had values of its own, and was not merely a punishment which they endured in order that we might ride in motors. It is premised on the assumption that the rocks and rills and templed hills of this America are something more than economic materials, and should not be dedicated exclusively to economic use.

> Wilderness as a Form of Land Use (1925); RMG 142

Some day somebody will promote a railroad into the Gila timber, and the tangible benefits of exploiting it will have to be weighed against the intangible benefits of keeping it. For unnumbered centuries of human history the wilderness has given way. The priority of industry has become dogma. Are we as yet sufficiently enlightened to realize that we must now challenge that dogma, or do without our wilderness? Do we realize that industry, which has been our good servant, might make a poor master? Let no man expect that one lone government bureau is able—even tho it be willing—to thrash out this question alone.

> A Plea for Wilderness Hunting Grounds (1925); ALS 160

There is opposition to the idea of a wilderness policy, but the real danger of failure lies not in opposition but in delay. Those who do not travel continuously in the hinterlands can have no idea of how rapidly the larger wild places are shrinking into nonexistence, and it will do no good to act after they are gone. As to opposition, the signs are multiplying daily that this country is losing confidence in the purely quantitative conception of growth and progress. That conception is the only one on which opposition can logically be based.

Untitled address on wilderness conservation (1926)

The only really comprehensive check against the further shrinkage of marshes would be to accord undrained marshes a special tax status in view of their public service to migratory birds, just as ungrazed farm woodlots and managed forests are beginning to be accorded a special tax status in view of their public value to watersheds and timber supply.

The Decline of the Jacksnipe in Southern Wisconsin (1930)

. . . America consists largely of business men, farmers, and "Rotarians," busily playing the national game of economic expansion. Most of them admit that birds, trees, and flowers are nice to have around, but few of them would admit that the present "depression" in waterfowl is more important than the one in banks, or that the status of the blue goose has more bearing on the cultural future of America than the price of U.S. Steel.

Game and Wild Life Conservation (1932); RMG 165

The conservation movement is, at the very least, an assertion that [ecological] interactions between man and land are too important to be left to chance, even that sacred variety of chance known as economic law.

The Conservation Ethic (1933); RMG 185

Granted a community in which the combined beauty and utility of land determines the social status of its owner, and we will see a speedy dissolution of the economic obstacles which now beset conservation. Economic laws may be permanent, but their impact reflects what people want, which in turn reflects what they know and what they are. The economic set-up at any one moment is in some measure the result, as well as the cause, of the then prevailing standard of living. Such standards change.

The Conservation Ethic (1933); RMG 191

The ultimate issue, in conservation as in other social problems, is whether the mass-mind *wants to* extend its powers of comprehending the world in which it lives, or, granted the desire, *has the capacity to do so.* . . . I do not know the answer to either. I simply affirm that a sufficiently enlightened society, by changing its wants and tolerances, can change the economic factors bearing on land. It can be said of nations, as of individuals: "as a man thinketh, so is he."

The Conservation Ethic (1933); RMG 192

The wholesale public expenditures for 1933 indicate that from now on, whenever a private landowner so uses his land as to injure the public interest, *the public will eventually pay the bill,* either by buying him out, or by donating the repairs, or both. Hence the prevention of damage to the soil, or to the living things upon it, has become a first principle of public finance. Abuse is no longer merely a question of depleting a capital asset, *but of actually creating a cash liability against the taxpayer.*

Conservation Economics (1934); RMG 200

The thing to be prevented is destructive private land-use of any and all kinds. The thing to be encouraged is the use of private land in such a way as to combine the public and the private interest to the greatest possible degree. If we are going to spend large sums of public money anyhow, why not use it to subsidize desirable combinations in land use, instead of to cure, by purchase, prohibition, or repair, the headache arising from bad ones?

I realize fully that such a question qualifies me for the asylum for political and economic dreamers. Yet I submit that the proposal is actually less radical politically, and possibly cheaper in economic cost, than the stampede for public ownership in which our most respectable conservatives have now joined.

Conservation Economics (1934); RMG 200

Our legal and economic structure was evolved on a terrain (central and western Europe) inherently more resistant to abuse than any other part of the earth's surface, and at a time when our engines for subjugating the soil were still too weak to ruin it. We have transplanted that structure to a new terrain, at least half of which is set on a hair-trigger of ecologic balance. We have invented engines of unprecedented coarseness and power, and placed them freely in the hands of ignorant men.

Conservation Economics (1934); RMG 202

When we invent a new machine, we usually assume that its use makes us immune to the ecological penalties which other flesh is heir to. This mechanistic arrogance is, to a conservationist, the keynote of the century.

Deer and Dauerwald in Germany: I. History (1936)

Is it sound economics to regard any plant as a separate entity, to proscribe or encourage it on the grounds of its individual performance? What will be the effect on animal life, on the soil, and on the health of the forest as an organism? Is there not an aesthetic as well as an economic issue? Is there, at bottom, any real distinction between aesthetics and economics?

Conservation (c. 1938); RR 152

I suspect that the forces inherent in unguided economic evolution are not all beneficent. Like the forces inside our own bodies, they may become malignant, pathogenic. I believe that many of the economic forces inside the modern body-politic are pathogenic in respect to harmony with land.

Conservation (c. 1938); RR 153

My own gropings come to a dead end when I try to appraise the profit motive. For a full generation the American conservation movement has been substituting the profit motive for the fear motive, yet it has failed to motivate. We can all see profit in conservation practice, but the profit accrues to society rather than to the individual. This, of course, explains the trend, at this moment, to wish the whole job on the government.

Conservation (c. 1938); RR 156

. . . We have excess plowland; our conviction of this is so unanimous that we spend a billion out of the public chest to retire the surplus from cultivation. In the face of such an excess, can any reasonable man claim that economics prevents us from getting a life, as well as a livelihood, from our acres?

The Farmer as a Conservationist (1939); RMG 259

Poor land may be rich country, and vice versa. Only economists mistake physical opulence for riches. Country may be rich despite a conspicuous poverty of physical endowment, and its quality may not be apparent at first glance, nor at all times.

Country (1941); RR 31

. . . Our credit-rating in the bank of nature is not what it used to be.

Of Mice and Men ms. (1941)

What we call economic laws are merely the impact of our changing wants on the land which supplies them. When that impact becomes destructive of our own tenure in the land, as is so conspicuously the case today, then the thing to examine is the validity of the wants themselves.

The Role of Wildlife in a Liberal Education (1942); RMG 303

Industries wince with pain when fixers and planners lay violent hands on their highly organized economic community, yet these same industries fix their forests to death with never a flicker of recognition that the same principle is involved. In neither case do we understand all the intricacies of internal adjustment. Communities are like clocks, they tick best while possessed of all their cogs and wheels.

The Last Stand (1942); RMG 293

One is apt to make the error of assuming that a corporation possesses the attributes of a prudent person. It may not. It is a new species of animal, created by mutation, with a morphology of its own and a behavior pattern which will unfold with time. One can only say that its behavior pattern as an owner of forests is so far not very prudent.

The Last Stand (1942); RMG 294

. . . It is cheaper to raise wheat by exploitation than by honest farming. It wouldn't be cheaper if exploitation wheat lacked a market. You are the market, but transportation has robbed you of all power to discriminate. If you want conservation wheat, you will have to raise it yourself.

Land-Use and Democracy (1942); RMG 297

. . . There is value in any experience that reminds us of our dependency on the soil-plant-animal-man food chain, and of the fundamental organization of the biota. Civilization has so cluttered this elemental man-earth relation with gadgets and middlemen that awareness of it is growing dim. We fancy that industry supports us, forgetting what supports industry.

Wildlife in American Culture (1943); ASCA 178

[The book's] title, to my way of thinking, is a very happy one. It implies clearly that there are natural and unnatural principles which may be applied to land, and that only those harmonious with the inner mechanisms of the land itself can succeed in the long run. It implies that ecology, and not economics, is the final arbiter of success in land management.

Review of *Natural Principles of Land Use* (1944)

The fallacious assumption that each separate act of conservation can or must be profitable before its practice can be recommended to farmers is possibly responsible for the meagre fruits of forty years of education, extension, and public demonstration in the conservation field. It is undoubtedly responsible for many dubious claims of profit which are commonly made, or implied, in presenting the subject to the public. It is presumably axiomatic that any "program" saddled with over-claims will backfire in the long run.

Conservation: In Whole or in Part? (1944); RMG 317

Sound conservation propaganda must present land health, as well as land products, as the objective of "good" land use.

Conservation: In Whole or in Part? (1944); RMG 317

Some components of land can be conserved profitably, but others not. All are profitable to the community in the long run. Unified conservation must therefore be activated primarily as an obligation to the community, rather than as an opportunity for profit.

Conservation: In Whole or in Part? (1944); RMG 319

Girdling the old oak to squeeze one last crop out of the barnyard has the same finality as burning the furniture to keep warm.

Deadening (c. 1946); RR 129

The Flambeau [River] case illustrates the dangers that lurk in the semi-honest doctrine that conservation is only good economics. The defenders of the Flambeau tried to prove that the river in its wild state would produce more fish and tourists than the impounded river would produce butterfat, but this is not true. We should have claimed that a little gain in butterfat is less important to the state than a large loss in opportunity for a distinctive form of outdoor recreation.

The Ecological Conscience (1947); RMG 344

. . . Our bigger-and-better society is now like a hypochondriac, so obsessed with its own economic health as to have lost the capacity to remain healthy. The whole world is so greedy for more bathtubs that it has lost the stability necessary to build them, or even to turn off the tap. Nothing could be more salutary at this stage than a little healthy contempt for a plethora of material blessings.

Perhaps such a shift of values can be achieved by reappraising things unnatural, tame, and confined in terms of things natural, wild, and free.

Foreword to *A Sand County Almanac* (1949); ASCA ix

Sometimes in June, when I see unearned dividends of dew hung on every lupine, I have doubts about the real poverty of the sands. On solvent farmlands lupines do not even grow, much less collect a daily rainbow of jewels. If they did, the weed-control officer, who seldom sees a dewy dawn, would doubtless insist that they be cut. Do economists know about lupines?

The Sand Counties (1949); ASCA 102

One basic weakness in a conservation system based wholly on economic motives is that most members of the land community have no economic value. Wildflowers and songbirds are examples. Of the 22,000 higher plants and animals native to Wisconsin, it is doubtful whether more than 5 per cent can be sold, fed, eaten, or otherwise put to economic use. Yet these creatures are members of the biotic community, and if (as I believe) its stability depends on its integrity, they are entitled to continuance.

The Land Ethic (1949); ASCA 210

Time was when biologists somewhat overworked the evidence that [predatory] creatures preserve the health of game by killing weaklings, or that they control rodents for the farmer, or that they prey only on "worthless" species. Here again, the evidence had to be economic in order to be valid. It is only in recent years that we hear the more honest argument that predators are members of the community, and that no special interest has the right to exterminate them for the sake of a benefit, real or fancied, to itself.

The Land Ethic (1949); ASCA 211–12

To sum up: a system of conservation based solely on economic self-interest is hopelessly lopsided. It tends to ignore, and thus eventually to eliminate, many elements in the land community that lack commercial value, but that are (as far as we know) essential to its healthy functioning. It assumes, falsely, I think, that the economic parts of the biotic clock will function without the uneconomic parts. It tends to relegate to government many functions eventually too large, too complex, or too widely dispersed to be performed by government.

The Land Ethic (1949); ASCA 214

It is inconceivable to me that an ethical relation to land can exist without love, respect, and admiration for land, and a high regard for its value. By value, I of course mean something far broader than mere economic value; I mean value in the philosophical sense.

The Land Ethic (1949); ASCA 223

It of course goes without saying that economic feasibility limits the tether of what can or cannot be done for land. It always has and it always will. The fallacy the economic determinists have tied around our collective neck, and which we now need to cast off, is the belief that economics determines *all* land-use. This is simply not true. An innumerable host of actions and attitudes, comprising perhaps the bulk of all land relations, is determined by the land-users' tastes and predilections, rather than by his purse. The bulk of all land relations hinges on investments of time, forethought, skill, and faith rather than on investments of cash.

The Land Ethic (1949); ASCA 225

14 ENVIRONMENTAL POLICY

Keeper

Leopold as Practical Moralist and Pragmatic Policy Analyst

Bryan G. Norton

Aldo Leopold's ideas and pronouncements on environmental policy, read fifty years after his death, establish how far Leopold was ahead of his—and our own—time. The ideas expressed in these quotations draw upon his experience with a broad spectrum of conservation issues. They demonstrate how Leopold's approach, if followed, would immensely improve the process and substance of environmental policy, even today. Although Leopold was not a philosopher, he developed a remarkably complex and subtle "philosophy" of environmental management. He loved to speculate on "big"—or as he often said "general"—ideas, but he was much more than a prophet of a future environmental consciousness. The ideas he lived by were the ideas that were forced upon him by years of thoughtful and painful experience. His discussions of policy often read like briefings he might like to have given to his first boss, the eminently practical Gifford Pinchot. In these discussions Leopold generally eschewed "intangible" ideas, accepting common philosophical and religious commitments as constraints on his speculations; yet he gave—or struggled valiantly to give—carefully articulated reasons and justifications for all of his management precepts.

It may be helpful to list some of the ideas, articulated between 1920 and his death in 1948, that establish Leopold's claim to prescience in the area of management theory and process. First, he insisted—contrary to his contemporaries and in opposition to most of today's congressional representatives—that ethics, not economics, ultimately validate environmental policies. Second, in anticipation of the current trend toward public and stakeholder participation in policy process, Leopold expressed his progressivist-populist faith that it must be farmers, sportsmen, and other citizens themselves who accomplish conservation. This second belief led to a third idea, one that is anathema to many environmental managers today, as it was to Leopold's own contemporaries in government resource agencies. He believed that public-servant environmentalists should be just that; that the highest calling of resource managers was education and public involvement, rather than what he derisively called the "ciphers" of management economics.[1] Fourth, Leopold recognized before others that management cannot simply be scientific in the sense of *applying* fixed principles of science; rather, and more important, we should be *managing* scientifically in the dynamic sense. Leopold thus insisted on policies designed to get results *and* reduce our ignorance through experiments with real controls.

Similarly, today's still-nascent but increasingly important ideas of ecosystem management were given shape by Leopold in his relentless attacks on atomistic management, which separated management of the land into "many separate field forces."[2] He advocated instead an integrated approach to the management of resources. To these innovations we could add mention of Leopold's extraordinary concerns for our resource legacy to future Americans and a coherent and reflective concept of "sustainable development."

Each of these ideas—and there are others—would have qualified Leopold as an important innovator. But the totality of them, and the way in which Leopold used his unparalleled powers of observation to illustrate, sharpen, and weave these points together, mark him as the premier genius in the field. We would do well to listen to him very carefully when we choose actions to alter or "improve" on nature and natural functioning of ecosystems.

I regard Leopold the policy analyst, the policy-maker, and the practical moralist as the originator and spiritual father of the flourishing tradition of "adaptive ecosystem management," so ably espoused today by C. S. Holling, Carl Walters, Kai Lee, and others.[3] Scientifically, Leopold anticipated the idea of ecological resilience, so prominent in the writings of Holling and the adaptive managers, when he described semiarid countries as "set in a hair-trigger equilibrium."[4] He clearly recognized that shortsighted management could render ecological systems and processes vulnerable to collapse. Leopold also anticipated a unifying theoretical idea, which later came to be called "general systems theory," or (in theoretical ecology) "hierarchy theory." Leopold's brilliant insight— that managers and agriculturalists must, to be successful, "think like a mountain"—was not (or at least was not only) a mystical vision.[5] It was hard-won wisdom, that: (a) the manager, who observes and manipulates, is a part of the system, and not only views it but changes it from within; and (b) we can understand observed nature more coherently if we see it as a nested hierarchy of subsystems, with larger, slower-moving systems forming the "environment" for the smaller systems that compose it.

This scalar analysis, which would be incorporated wholesale into adaptive management, was embodied in Leopold's brilliant simile. In "Thinking Like a Mountain" Leopold provided a case study. The policy of killing wolves to increase deer herds seemed, from a short-term, human perspective to be a good idea to Leopold and others. He learned, however, that good policy must pass not only the short-term test of human economic reasoning but also the test of the mountain, which requires an ecological and evolutionary perspective. In addition to anticipating the adaptive managers' ideas of multiscalar analysis, Leopold also foresaw their emphasis on the need to include citizens and stakeholders in an iterative process that, at its best, involves social learning and the development of locally effective and cooperative institutions.

Leopold was a "scientific" manager who eventually, and sometimes through painful experience, came to appreciate both the strengths and the weaknesses of science in the practice of management. Because he had the professional mentality of a manager before becoming a professor, Leopold developed a nose for relevant science. Management, for him, asked interesting questions of ecology, and ecology provided useful tools for potential application. Accordingly, Leopold was scornful of pure theory when unrelated to practice, complaining that we argue over our abstract and conflicting ideas as to what needs to be done; instead, he suggested, we should "go out and try them."[6] He enjoyed speculation, but was disdainful of it when it was cut loose from experience, and from pressing environmental problems.

Much has been written about Leopold's science and about his moral beliefs. Few authors and commentators, however, have acknowledged that Leopold expressed a quite sophisticated philosophy of science and epistemology, which was for him intertwined with his management philosophy. Because he functioned as a manager in both the political and scientific worlds simultaneously, he constantly faced both controversy and uncertainty. Consequently, he judged facts by their usefulness. In the 1923 manuscript "Some Fundamentals of Conservation in the Southwest" Leopold expressed a sophisticated version of Darwinian epistemology, using it to cut through uncertainty about broad theoretical principles. Ultimately, he reasoned, our scientific and managerial behavior must be adaptive or we will not survive as a culture; we will "be judged in 'the derisive silence of eternity.'"[7] However, his healthy respect for the uncertainties of management left him wary of general pronouncements that lacked tight connection to actual experimental test. His concluding discussion of conservation morality in "Some Fundamentals" includes no less than five cautionary statements about the limits of philosophical and speculative language.

Leopold implicitly practiced (even as it was being articulated by Herbert Simon and others) the decision method known as "satisficing."[8] In "Game and Wild Life Conservation" (1932) he concluded that the only way to protect any wildness is "to set up within the economic Juggernaut certain new cogs and wheels whereby the residual love of nature" may be fractionally protected.[9] For Leopold satisficing meant triangulating through waters made choppy by mindless devotion to "progress" and boosterism, while relying on nothing more than the experimental spirit of science, democratic involvement, and faith in the traditions of good sportsmanship and husbandry expressed as respect for self and land. Satisficing—even moralistic satisficing in the style of Leopold—recognizes that policy cannot be guided by grandiose prior plans or principles, but must seek, with an eye toward best alternatives and pilot projects, to gradually improve policies and keep track of what works.

Although Leopold was quite successful in articulating a practical *and integrated* philosophy of environmental policy, confusion may be avoided if one thinks of Leopold's theories of management as quite distinct from his environmental ethics. My point is not that Leopold's views on value and management were unconnected, but rather that he related them differently than most professional environmental ethicists do today. Leopold worked from observation toward theory, whereas most of today's environmental ethicists attempt to establish universal principles and then "apply" them to particular cases. Leopold's powers of observation were legendary. As illustrated in his first attempt to survey conservation ethics in "Some Fundamentals of Conservation," his discussions of morality were usually preceded by a careful empirical analysis of trends and problems in resource use. He spent the first two-thirds of that landmark paper explaining what he saw from horseback in the vast lands under his management as director of operations for the Forest Service in the Southwest. He concluded that simple observation revealed damage from human use and that the damage was having economic impact. Ethics, then, were layered onto Leopold's practical, day-to-day approach of experimentalism and his daily recognition of the importance of economic motives. Leopold waxes philosophic, then, in order to explain and make sense of the whole field of environmental management; but he takes this to include economic and other established values, as well as new and more speculative ideas that might guide us to a more complete understanding of values and policy.

In "Some Fundamentals of Conservation" Leopold reviews ethical and metaphysical ideas—including anthropocentrism, organicism (the view that the earth itself is a living organism), nonanthropocentrism, and the possibility that "God himself likes to hear birds sing and see flowers grow"—as possible moral bases for conservation.[10] But he treats these ideas not as a philosopher would, trying to ascertain their truth based on a priori reasoning. Instead, he "screens" ethical beliefs for their policy usefulness, weighing their interest, plausibility, and verifiability, as well as their political appeal. So Leopold, writing from the perspective of a policy-maker in 1923, was willing to speculate on many ideas (indeed, he did so with obvious delight), but he began and ended his speculation with an anthropocentric framework. In the end he emphasized that the nobility we humans claim requires, independently of any moral demands placed on us by nature itself, that we mend our ways and protect ecological communities as we develop our lands. Along the way he considered and specifically dismissed organicism *as a guide to management,* because most managers believe "this reason is too intangible to either accept or reject as a guide to human conduct." He also adopted an agnostic position on the anthropocentrism-nonanthropocentrism debate, resolving that he would "not dispute the point."[11]

Now we are in a better position to understand the relationship Leopold saw between ethics and policy. Most of the decisions he faced could, he thought, be guided by economic criteria, provided he took a long enough view of economics. He also knew, however, that there were other decisions that, if made on strictly individual, economic grounds, would irreversibly damage the things he loved most about the region—the trout streams, the wild vistas, and so forth. Leopold, most basically, believed in the "convergence hypothesis."[12] He believed that human interests and the "interests" of the natural world converge, and that if we were to protect humans—recognizing the full range of human values as projected into the indefinite future—one would also protect the natural world as an ongoing, dynamic biotic community. This leaves the hypothesis of intrinsic value in nature open, allowing Leopold to act in the long-term interests of humans as at least an approximation of what would be "good for nature." It also allows him, in policy contexts, to appeal to either human-oriented or nature-oriented explanations and justifications for the management goals he espoused, broadening the political base for conservation. He often speculated about values beyond the usual human-oriented values that dominated management in his day, but he carefully avoided resting controversial management proposals on these ideas. Leopold tried, whenever possible, to base real decisions on careful observation and experiment rather than speculation. This dualism, and this partial disengagement of Leopold's ethical thought from his management philosophy, explains how Leopold can both enjoy speculation and also wax disdainful of abstract thought.

Leopold saw, at least by 1933, that general philosophical solutions and "isms"—"Socialism, Communism, Fascism" and "Technocracy"—would fail, because they would not, or could not, adjust "men and machines to land."[13] Leopold knew long before the "isms" failed that "husbandry of somebody else's land is a contradiction in terms."[14] But he also knew—contra conservative privatizers of today—that many public interests must be protected on public lands. He appreciated that communities of users must, with the help of sympathetic agency managers acting as teachers, maintain control of those public lands, using their government to realize community-based values and goals that go far beyond economic ones.

Conservation . . . is an aspect of the national philosophy, not a group of governmental "projects."

Leopold (third from left) with other councillors of the Wilderness Society, 1946. (Courtesy Aldo Leopold Foundation)

Monopoly in sport is essentially repugnant to democratic principle. If it benefits the game supply, this compromise of democratic principle may be tolerated if not carried too far. But if it does not benefit the game supply, there is no valid excuse for its existence.

The Posting Problem (1922)

Philosophy . . . suggests one reason why we cannot destroy the earth with moral impunity; namely, that the "dead" earth is an organism possessing a certain kind and degree of life, which we intuitively respect as such. Possibly, to most men of affairs, this reason is too intangible to either accept or reject as a guide to human conduct. But philosophy also offers another and more easily debatable question: was the earth made for man's use, or has man merely the privilege of temporarily possessing an earth made for other and inscrutable purposes? The question of what he can properly do with it must necessarily be affected by this question.

Most religions, insofar as I know, are premised squarely on the assumption that man is the end and purpose of creation, and that not only the dead earth, but all creatures thereon, exist solely for his use. The mechanistic or scientific philosophy does not start with this as a premise, but ends with it as a conclusion, and hence may be placed in the same category for the purpose in hand. . . .

Since most of mankind today profess either one of the anthropomorphic religions or the scientific school of thought which is likewise anthropomorphic, I will not dispute the point. It just occurs to me, however, in answer to the scientists, that God started his show a good many million years before he had any men for audience—a sad waste of both actors and music—and in answer to both, that it is just barely possible that God himself likes to hear birds sing and see flowers grow.

> Some Fundamentals of Conservation in the Southwest (1923);
> RMG 95–96

. . . If there be, indeed, a special nobility inherent in the human race— a special cosmic value, distinctive from and superior to all other life— by what token shall it be manifest?

By a society decently respectful of its own and all other life, capable of inhabiting the earth without defiling it? Or by a society like that of John Burroughs' potato bug, which exterminated the potato, and thereby exterminated itself? As one or the other shall we be judged in "the derisive silence of history."

> Some Fundamentals of Conservation in the Southwest (1923);
> RMG 97

If conservation does not mean production, then it means nothing at all. I do not mean production merely in the limited industrial sense of boards, meat, dollars, or even tourists. I mean that attitude of mind which will not tolerate the existence of idle, lifeless land in America. I mean that attitude of mind which regards the existence of such land as a challenge to the technical skill and social foresight of the nation, and which feels the non-acceptance of that challenge as something unworthy of good citizenship.

> Wild Followers of the Forest (1923)

There must exist in the public mind that fundamental respect for living things and that fundamental aversion to unjustifiable killing and to unnecessary ugliness which in all lands and all times has been a necessary foundation for good morals and good taste.

> Wild Followers of the Forest (1923)

We will accomplish conservation when we, as a nation, scorn waste, pollution, and unproductiveness as something damaging, not only to the individual reputation of the waster, but to the self-respect of the craft and the society of which he is a member.

Wild Followers of the Forest (1923)

. . . Just why are we so much more intense about decoying newcomers to New Mexico than we are about securing better education, better recreational facilities, better public health service, and cleaner government for the citizens already here? . . .

Can anyone deny that the vast fund of time, brains, and money now devoted to making our city big would actually make it better if diverted to betterment instead of bigness?

Moreover are we sure that if we effected these internal betterments for our own citizens, that we would have to bribe, threaten and cajole new people and new institutions to come here? I am afraid we could not keep them away.

A Criticism of the Booster Spirit (1923); RMG 100

The boosters of Santa Fe and Las Vegas conceived a scenic highway across the Sangre de Cristo Range. To recreate and inspire their own citizens? No indeed, to fetch tourists. It was "the wonderland of the Americas," and like all wonderlands except that of the refreshing Alice, it far excelled Switzerland, with which the boosters are always entirely familiar. What would this scenic highway cost? "A mere detail, that—find out later—all we know is that it would cost too much for us to build. It's about time the government did something for northern New Mexico anyhow." Could the government, in justice to existing needs for roads elsewhere, afford to appropriate? "We are not representing 'elsewhere'—we are building up our city." Should the "wonderland" continue under the Agricultural Department as a National Forest? "It will continue under the department that helps us get the money. If your department won't, there are plenty of others that will."

Thus is the pork barrel filled—and emptied.

A Criticism of the Booster Spirit (1923); RMG 101

A hundred percenter in making the flag fly and the eagle scream, [the booster] is awkward in self-government. Worshipping commerce, he is slow to regulate its own abuses.

A Criticism of the Booster Spirit (1923); RMG 103

I once knew a doctor, who on the completion of his medical studies, returned to his home town to practice. He soon saw that the place was too small for him. "I realized," he says, "that I would either have to move to the kind of town I needed, or else make over my home town into that kind of a place. I decided to make over my home town."

A Criticism of the Booster Spirit (1923); RMG 104

Every day on my way to my office I pass a booster billboard which exhorts me as follows: "Cities do not happen—BE A BUILDER—Support your Chamber of Commerce." Splendid truths, the first two. I detest billboards, but this one interests me. Be a builder! There is a real ring in those words. . . .

. . . Is it too much to hope that this force, harnessed to a finer ideal, may some day accomplish good as well as big things? That our future standard of civic values may even exclude quantity, obtained at the expense of quality, as not worth while? When this is accomplished shall we vindicate the truth that "the virtue of a living democracy consists not in its ability to avoid mistakes, but in its ability to profit by them."

A Criticism of the Booster Spirit (1923); RMG 104–5

. . . Mark this well: the total possible acreage of tillable irrigable land, the total possible acre-feet of accessible water and the total storage capacity of dam-sites—these three things set the limits of the total possible future development of the Southwest. The virgin supply of each was limited; the subsequent losses, no matter with what "energy" we replace them, are steadily lowering the limits already set. To a degree we are facing the question of whether we are here to "skin" the Southwest and then get out, or whether we are here to found a permanent civilized community with room to grow and improve.

Pioneers and Gullies (1924); RMG 110, ALS 169–70

Natural resources are interdependent, and in semi-arid countries are often set in a hair-trigger equilibrium which is quickly upset by uncontrolled use. As a consequence, uncontrolled use of one local resource may menace the economic system of whole regions. Therefore, to protect the public interest, certain resources must remain in public ownership, and ultimately the use of all resources will have to be put under public regulation, regardless of ownership. . . . But while partial provision has been made, through the Forest Service and Reclamation Service, to conserve the forests and the water supply, no provision has been made to conserve that fundamental resource, land.

Pioneers and Gullies (1924); RMG 112–13, ALS 173–74

Regulated monopoly is the only possible future basis for game management on privately owned lands. Public shooting grounds are obviously the future basis for game management on publicly-owned or leased lands and water, and public ownership must be increased to the extent necessary to prevent monopoly on private lands from becoming undemocratic. There is the whole thing in a nutshell.

Ten New Developments in Game Management (1925); ALS 120

... Our tendency is not to call things resources until the supply runs short. When the end of the supply is in sight we "discover" that the thing is valuable.

This has been true of the latest natural resource to be "discovered," namely the group of things collectively called Outdoor Recreation. We had to develop tenements and tired-business-men before Outdoor Recreation was recognized as a category of human needs, though the use of the outdoors for recreational purposes is as old as the race itself. This "discovery" that we need a national policy on Outdoor Recreation is in fact so new that the ink has barely dried on its birth certificate. And, as usual, we are becoming conscious of thousands of wasteful errors in the past handling of recreational resources which an earlier discovery might have avoided.

I submit that this endless series of more or less post-mortem discoveries is getting rather tedious. I for one am piqued in my sense of national pride. Can not we for once foresee and provide? Must it always be hindsight, followed by hurried educational work, laborious legislative campaigns, and then only partially effective action at huge expense? Can not we for once use foresight, and provide for our needs in an orderly, ample, correlated, economical fashion?

The Last Stand of the Wilderness (1925)

To preserve any land in a wild condition is, of course, a reversal of economic tendency, but that fact alone should not condemn the proposal. A study of the history of land utilization shows that good use is largely a matter of good balance—of wise adjustment between opposing tendencies.

Wilderness as a Form of Land Use (1925); RMG 136

The very same reasons that necessitate the establishment of additional parks and forests in the East, North, and South necessitate the dedication of parts of those forests and parks to wilderness recreation.

Of course it will be difficult or impossible to establish in these regions wilderness areas as large or as absolute as in the West, and this brings up another probable error—the assumption that an area is either wild or not wild, that there is no place for intermediate degrees of wildness.

All land planning must deal in intermediate degrees and especially in the skillful dovetailing of many uses in a single area. If this were not true, even the generous proportions of America would be already outgrown as a container for this Nation. The wilderness idea is merely a proposition in good land planning.

Untitled address on wilderness conservation (1926)

We conservationists are the doctors of our game supply. We have many ideas as to what needs to be done, and these ideas quite naturally conflict. We are in danger of pounding the table about them, instead of going out on the land and giving them a trial. The only really new thing which this game policy suggests is that we quit arguing over abstract ideas, and instead go out and try them.

The American Game Policy in a Nutshell (1930)

. . . Mobile game must be protected by the whole community over which it ranges, and not left to the local units of that community.

Report on a Game Survey of the North Central States (1931), 216

I realize that every time I turn on an electric light, or ride on a Pullman, or pocket the unearned increment on a stock, or a bond, or a piece of real estate, I am "selling out" to the enemies of conservation. When I submit these thoughts to a printing press, I am helping cut down the woods. When I pour cream in my coffee, I am helping to drain a marsh for cows to graze, and to exterminate the birds of Brazil. When I go birding or hunting in my Ford, I am devastating an oil field, and re-electing an imperialist to get me rubber. Nay more: when I father more than two children I am creating an insatiable need for more printing presses, more cows, more coffee, more oil, and more rubber, to supply which more birds, more trees, and more flowers will either be killed, or what is just as destructive, evicted from their several environments.

What to do? I see only two courses open to the likes of us. One is to go live on locusts in the wilderness, if there is any wilderness left. The other is surreptitiously to set up within the economic Juggernaut certain new cogs and wheels whereby the residual love of nature, inherent even in Rotarians, may be made to recreate at least a fraction of those values which their love of "progress" is destroying. A briefer way to put it is: if we want Mr. Babbitt to rebuild outdoor America, we must let him use the same tools wherewith he destroyed it. He knows no other.

Game and Wild Life Conservation (1932); RMG 165–66

. . . In times of economic stress conservation services are in danger of being regarded by many citizens of full vote but scant understanding as a kind of altruistic luxury, to be curtailed to any requisite degree, or perhaps dispensed with altogether. The present economic depression has so far constricted the income but not the reasoning power of the average voter. At this time, however, there are evidences of a further change. In many quarters the attitude toward tax-reduction is coming to be not that of reasonable men confronted with the necessity of stringent cuts in the cost of government, but that of unreasonable men determined to slash anything and everything they can lay hands on, in a kind of blind vengeance for tax burdens which have become unbearable, but which may not have originated, to any considerable degree, in the items slashed.

Weatherproofing Conservation (1933)

In some states separate administrative overheads are maintained, and in many separate field forces, for game, forestry, fish and parks. The separate field forces sometimes coadminister the identical areas. We cannot change this by law or fiat alone, and there is certainly a limit to what one individual worker's mind can encompass. . . . The merging of administrative forces presents great technical and political difficulties, but may none the less be an economic necessity.

Weatherproofing Conservation (1933)

Land classifications and economic surveys have, of course, long recognized [the] diverse physical aptitudes of land, but is it not now time to recognize the administrative, financial, and educational adjustments which they entail?

Weatherproofing Conservation (1933)

Coordination may be preached and legislated from the top down, but must be built from the bottom up. . . .

I plead, in short, for tearing down some of the stone walls which now subdivide the conservation fort, and using the material to heighten the external defenses.

Weatherproofing Conservation (1933)

As nearly as I can see, all the new isms—Socialism, Communism, Fascism, and especially the late but not lamented Technocracy—outdo even Capitalism itself in their preoccupation with one thing: The distribution of more machine-made commodities to more people. They all proceed on the theory that if we can all keep warm and full, and all own a Ford and a radio, the good life will follow. Their programs differ only in ways to mobilize machines to this end. Though they despise each other, they are all, in respect of this objective, as identically alike as peas in a pod. They are competitive apostles of a single creed: *salvation by machinery.*

We are concerned here, not with their proposals for adjusting men and machinery to goods, but rather with their lack of any vital proposal for adjusting men and machines to land. To conservationists they offer only the old familiar palliatives: Public ownership and private compulsion.

The Conservation Ethic (1933); RMG 188

Man thinks of himself as not subject to any density limit. Industrialism, imperialism, and that whole array of population behaviors associated with the "bigger and better" ideology are direct ramifications of the Mosaic injunction for the species to go the limit of its potential, *i.e.,* to go and replenish the earth. But slums, wars, birth-controls, and depressions may be construed as ecological symptoms that our assumption about human density limits is unwarranted. . . .

Game Management (1933), 49

In the long run, no system [of hunting controls] is satisfactory which does not conserve the rich variety of our game fauna, as distinguished from merely its most resistant and "shootable" species. . . . Landowner initiative, left wholly to its own devices, would inevitably tend to sacrifice the unprofitable to the profitable forms of wild life. It would tend unduly to sacrifice migratory to resident, non-game to game, and predatory to game species. For these reasons, sound public policy must seek to encourage and develop private incentive *without relaxing* restrictive safeguards.

Game Management (1933), 211–12

. . . Conservation will ultimately boil down to rewarding the private landowner who conserves the public interest. It asserts the new premise that if he fails to do so, his neighbors must ultimately pay the bill. It pleads that our jurists and economists anticipate the need for workable vehicles to carry that reward. It challenges the efficacy of single-track land laws, and the economy of buying wrecks instead of preventing them. It advances all these things, not with any illusion that they are truth, but out of a profound conviction that the public is at last ready to do something about the land problem. . . .

Conservation Economics (1934); RMG 202

I am too keenly aware of the complexities of public land administration to attempt any allocation of blame, or any inventory of remedies [for overgrazing]. Underneath all the welter of superficial facts, however, lies the basic inference that the schools which trained the administrators of these public properties failed to impart to them that perception of dynamic ecological forces, without which damage to land remains invisible until after it has occurred. Let no layman crow over this statement as an indictment of technicians, until he himself learns how hard it is to foresee and prevent the abuse of land. It merely reflects something we have learned about human ecology. We know almost as little about the ecological mechanism of these United States as a hen knows about the cosmic chemistry which controls her life and her productivity.

Whither 1935?—A Review of the American Game Policy (1935)

Real coordination [of forestry and wildlife conservation] cannot be grafted upon pre-existing practices—it must be built into them. This implies a reorganization and synthesis of all land-relationships, including the professions which lead them, the schools which teach them, the research which guides them, and the laws which regulate and support them. Since the purpose of wildlife cropping is recreation rather than utility, there is implied a gradual recasting of the esthetic as well as the economic relation between land and people.

> Preliminary Report on Forestry and Game Management (1935)

Conservation is a protest against destructive land use. It seeks to preserve both the utility and beauty of the landscape. It now invokes the aid of science as a means to this end. Science has never before been asked to write a prescription for an esthetic ailment of the body politic. The effort may benefit scientists as well as laymen and land.

> Land Pathology (1935); RMG 212

Lack of mutual cooperation among conservation groups is reflected in laws and appropriations. Whoever gets there first writes the legislative ticket to his own particular destination. We have somehow forgotten that all this unorganized avalanche of laws and dollars must be put in order before it can permanently benefit the land, and that this onerous job, which is evidently too difficult for legislators and propagandists, is being wished upon the farmer and upon the administrator of public properties. The farmer is still trying to make out what it is that the many-voiced public wants him to do. The administrator, who is seldom trained in more than one of the dozen special fields of skill comprising conservation, is growing gray trying to shoulder his new and incredibly varied burdens. The stage, in short, is all set for somebody to show that each of the various public interests in land is better off when all cooperate than when all compete with each other.

> Coon Valley: An Adventure in Cooperative Conservation (1935); RMG 218–19

Even if it were geographically possible for public agencies to cover the needs of conservation, I am afraid it is humanly impossible to build a public organization equal to the task. I see in the history of the last 3 years much evidence that there is a maximum velocity for expansion of a bureau, beyond which more money ceases to deliver more results. There may also be a maximum size, i.e., mere bigness may in itself kill that inner something essential to effective work. I also suspect that cooperation between Federal and State agencies has often been inverse to their rate of growth. We must not forget the probability that there are intellectual saturation points, carrying capacities, vulnerability curves, and peck-orders in that aspect of human ecology which we call government.

> Remarks on Wildlife Management by Private Agencies (1936)

... There is an absentee public, including not only those who do not use public properties but also those yet unborn, whose tastes and preferences may differ from those of the user. This absentee public has a property right in natural resources equal to that of the user.

> Second Report of [the Society of American Foresters] Game Policy
> Committee (1937)

The Biological Survey is *the* research agency for bureaus, but who shows up at hearings to ask the wherewithal in its behalf? Is research, indeed, a mere job which can be delegated? Or is it an organic function—a kind of intellectual endocrine—which must be evolved in and by the organism which is to use it? I direct this question to the reorganizers who play chess with bureaus. I don't know the answer. I do know that in any enterprise except government it would be imprudent to spend so rapidly and learn so slowly.

> The Research Program (1937)

All the acts of government ... are of slight importance to conservation except as they affect the acts and thoughts of citizens. A bigger conservation bureau is not necessarily a better one. Perfect coordination among bureaus is not necessarily progress; citizens may learn more from bureau quarrels than bureau regimentation. In fact, bureaus do not matter except as they mobilize brains to influence people. It has happened again and again that the smallest bureau has the biggest thoughts. One of the plainest lessons from the New Deal boom in bureaus is that accomplishment is *not* proportional to size, appropriations, or authority, nor is it much affected by organization blueprints.

> Conservation Blueprints (1937)

Conservation ... is an aspect of the national philosophy, not a group of governmental "projects." I can see just one important thing that might be accomplished by the new plan [for reorganizing governmental conservation]: such an exaggeration of the bureaucratic concept of progress that the average citizen may come at last to realize that the "Secretary of Conservation" is not Mr. Ickes, but himself.

> Conservation Blueprints (1937)

Public policies for outdoor recreation are controversial. Equally conscientious citizens hold opposite views on what it is and what should be done to conserve its resource-base. Thus the Wilderness Society seeks to exclude roads from the hinterlands, and the Chamber of Commerce to extend them, both in the name of recreation. The game-farmer kills hawks and the bird-lover protects them in the name of shot-gun and field-glass hunting respectively. Such factions commonly label each other with short and ugly names, when, in fact, each is considering a different component of the recreational process. These components *differ widely in their characteristics or properties*. A given policy may be true for one but false for another.

Conservation Esthetic (1938); ASCA 168

There is a widespread rebellion against blanket predator control, but it centres in intellectuals who know nothing of administration, who are rarely offered administrative positions, and who usually shun them when offered as a wolf shuns a poisoned carcass. Natural resources, then, are one of many public interests which suffer from the current refusal of highly trained men to enter "politics."

Report on Huron Mountain Club (1938)

Foresters complain of periodic damage from too many rabbits. Why, then, continue the public policy of wolf-extermination? We debate such questions in terms of economics and biology. The mammalogists assert the wolf is a natural check on too many deer. The sportsmen reply they will take care of excess deer. Another decade of argument and there will be no wolves to argue about. One conservation inkpot cancels another until the resource is gone.

Conservation (c. 1938); RR 149–50

. . . Public aids to better private land use will accomplish their purpose only as the farmer matches them with this thing which I have called skill. . . . Subsidies and propaganda may evoke the farmer's acquiescence, but only enthusiasm and affection will evoke his skill. It takes something more than a little "bait" to succeed in conservation.

The Farmer as a Conservationist (1939); RMG 258

Government cannot own and operate small parcels of land, and it cannot own and operate good land at all.

The Farmer as a Conservationist (1939); RMG 260

Is it not just as illogical to confine wildlife research to a single bureau as it is to confine conservation to a single department?

The State of the Profession (1940); RMG 278

If cash profit be the only valid motive for decent land-use, then conservation is headed for catastrophic failure. Good land-use is a balance between utility and esthetics. It yields a highly variable mixture of individual and community profits, of cash and unponderable profits, and all accrue from investments which vary from borrowed cash on the one hand to mere loving care on the other. He is a brave man who can say in each case whether it pays, or it doesn't pay.

This being the case, conservation education should rest its argument on decency and social behavior, rather than on profits alone. There should be no ambiguity on this point.

The distinction between private cash profit and community benefit is being used to promote subsidy, or even compulsion, on the ground that government is the community, and is thus asserting its own interest. There is a degree of validity in this, but when we assert that the private landowner has an obligation to the community, the necessity for such governmental intervention decreases to a considerable degree.

Conservation and Politics ms. (c. 1941)

To analyze the problem of [conservation] action, the first thing to grasp is that government, no matter how good, can only do certain things. Government can't raise crops, maintain small scattered structures, administer small scattered areas, or bring to bear on small local matters that combination of solicitude, foresight, and skill which we call husbandry. Husbandry watches no clock, knows no season of cessation, and for the most part is paid for in love, not dollars. Husbandry of somebody else's land is a contradiction in terms. Husbandry is the heart of conservation.

The second thing to grasp is that when we lay conservation in the lap of the government, it will always do the things it can, even though they are not the things that most need doing.

The present over-emphasis on game farms, fish hatcheries, nurseries and artificial reforestation, importation of exotic species, predator control, and rodent control is here in point. These are things government can do. Each has an alternative, more or less developed, along naturalistic lines, i.e., management or guidance of natural processes. Research shows these alternatives to be, in general, superior. But they involve husbandry, which government can do only on its own lands. Government lands are a minor fraction of our land area. Therefore government neglects the superior things that need doing, and does the inferior things that it can do. It then imputes to these things an importance and an efficacy they do not merit, thus distorting the growth of public intelligence.

Land-Use and Democracy (1942); RMG 298

One of the curious evidences that "conservation programs" are losing their grip is that they have seldom resorted to self-government as a cure for land-abuse. "We who are about to die," unless democracy can mend its land-use, have not tried democracy as a possible answer to our problem.

Land-Use and Democracy (1942); RMG 299

This brings us to the real and indispensable functions of government in conservation. Government is the tester of fact vs. fiction, the umpire of bogus vs. genuine, the sponsor of research, the guardian of technical standards, and, I hasten to add, the proper custodian of land which, for one reason or another, is not suited to private husbandry. These functions will become real and important as soon as conservation begins to grow from the bottom up, instead of from the top down, as is now the case.

Land-Use and Democracy (1942); RMG 300

If America is here to stay, she must have healthy land to live on, for, and by. Hitler's taunt that no democracy uses its land decently, while true of our past, must be proven untrue in the years to come.

Armament for Conservation ms. (1942)

We now know that animal populations have behavior patterns of which the individual animal is unaware, but which he nevertheless helps to execute. Thus the rabbit is unaware of cycles, but he is the vehicle for cycles.

We cannot discern these behavior patterns in the individual, or in short periods of time. The most intense scrutiny of an individual rabbit tells us nothing of cycles. The cycle concept springs from a scrutiny of the mass through decades.

This raises the disquieting question: do human populations have behavior patterns of which we are unaware, but which we help to execute? Are mobs and wars, unrests and revolutions, cut of such cloth?

Many historians and philosophers persist in interpreting our mass behaviors as the collective result of individual acts of volition. The whole subject matter of diplomacy assumes that the political group has the properties of an honorable person. On the other hand, some economists see the whole of society as a plaything for processes, our knowledge of which is largely *ex post facto*.

It is reasonable to suppose that our social processes have a higher volitional content than those of the rabbit, but it is also reasonable to suppose that we, as a species, contain population behavior patterns of which nothing is known because circumstance has never evoked them. We may have others the meaning of which we have misread.

Wildlife in American Culture (1943); ASCA 186

Ecology is now teaching us to search in animal populations for analogies to our own problems. By learning how some small part of the biota ticks, we can guess how the whole mechanism ticks. The ability to perceive these deeper meanings, and to appraise them critically, is the woodcraft of the future.

Wildlife in American Culture (1943); ASCA 187

Lop-sided conservation is encouraged by the fact that most Bureaus and Departments are charged with the custody of a single resource, rather than with the custody of the land as a whole. Even when their official titles denote a broader mandate, their actual interests and skills are commonly much narrower. The term "land" now brackets a larger span of knowledge than one human mind can encompass.

Conservation: In Whole or in Part? (1944); RMG 316

If we grant the premise that an ecological conscience is possible and needed, then its first tenet must be this: economic provocation is no longer a satisfactory excuse for unsocial land-use, (or, to use somewhat stronger words, for ecological atrocities). This, however, is a negative statement. I would rather assert positively that decent land-use should be accorded social rewards proportionate to its social importance.

The Ecological Conscience (1947); RMG 345

The cowman who cleans his range of wolves does not realize that he is taking over the wolf's job of trimming the herd to fit the range. He has not learned to think like a mountain. Hence we have dustbowls, and rivers washing the future into the sea.

Thinking Like a Mountain (1949); ASCA 132

When the private landowner is asked to perform some unprofitable act for the good of the community, he today assents only with out-stretched palm. If the act costs him cash this is fair and proper, but when it costs only fore-thought, open-mindedness, or time, the issue is at least debatable. The overwhelming growth of land-use subsidies in recent years must be ascribed, in large part, to the government's own agencies for conservation education: the land bureaus, the agricultural colleges, and the extension services. As far as I can detect, no ethical obligation toward land is taught in these institutions.

The Land Ethic (1949); ASCA 213–14

PART III

Conservation and Culture

"That land yields a cultural harvest," Leopold wrote in his foreword to *A Sand County Almanac,* "is a fact long known, but latterly often forgotten."[1] Leopold never forgot. Throughout his career as a professional in conservation, he retained his ability to step back from immediate scientific, economic, and political concerns, and to gather in the cultural harvest. The quotations in this section are fruits of this labor.

Leopold was raised as a sportsman in the classic sense of the word and remained a hunter into his final years. In his enthusiasm for the hunt, and his commitment to fair chase, lay the basis of his intellectual innovations and his fully developed conservation philosophy. However, he also understood that changes in technology and in the landscape itself had altered the very nature of the hunt. He was unwilling to close his eyes to these changes. In this sense, hunting was for Leopold a proving ground in the relationship between nature and culture. The quotations in Chapter 15 address this vital part of Leopold's life.

The next three chapters—on history, education, and the arts and sciences—work together. They provide insight, we hope, into the integrated nature of Leopold's intellect. It is no exaggeration to say that everything Leopold wrote and thought was informed by history. In this way he became an early exemplar of what has now matured into the field of environmental history. For Leopold, reading the landscape, any landscape, was an exercise in both natural and human history. Such an approach was essential if increasingly landless moderns were to hold on to their bearings in time and space. Education, it followed, could not afford to neglect these connections; it had to equip citizens to think in new ways about the world we were (and are) so quickly altering.

In the chapter on "Arts and Sciences" we have placed passages of obvious importance that don't quite fit elsewhere. Although at first they may appear somewhat random, a vibrant thread does in fact bind them together. All address, in one way or another, the segregation of the sciences, arts, and humanities in the academy, in modern life, and in our appreciation of the natural world. Leopold rejected the "senseless barrier" that we have erected between these domains.[2]

Land esthetics and land ethics were profoundly connected in Leopold's view. He held strong notions and high standards in each of these arenas, but he was not inflexible. In response to a critic of his wilderness advocacy, Leopold once wrote, "I suspect there are two categories of judgement which *cannot* be delegated to experts, which every man *must* judge for himself, and on which the intuitive conclusion of the non-expert is perhaps as likely to be correct as that of the professional. One of these is what is right. The other is what is beautiful."[3] Granted the inherent diversity of human definitions of the right and the beautiful, Leopold over the course of his career put forward a radical notion: that whatever criteria may have sufficed to inform such judgments in the past, increased weight must in the future be given to the evolutionary and ecological context in which they are made.

The final chapter in this volume brings together quotations that illustrate the development and the many shades of Leopold's literary voice. The voice of Leopold that most readers know—that of the author of *A Sand County Almanac*—was rather late in its emergence. Leopold was already fifty years old before the first of the *Almanac* essays were written. But long before then he had shown the potential that flowered there. Aldo Leopold was always writing, and scattered throughout his earlier writings one may hear the many tones of his *magnum opus:* wit, lyricism, irony, bemusement, acuity, wonder, regret, awe. These selections are only samples from a much larger sea.

One of conservation's essential challenges, Leopold suggested, was "how to bring about a striving for harmony with land among a people many of whom have forgotten there is any such thing as land, among whom education and culture have become almost synonymous with landlessness."[4] Science could offer information; policies could offer guidance; but the will and desire to *conserve* could arise only from the rich medium of cultural encouragements and rewards.

15 HUNTING AND FISHING

☙

Hunting for Common Ground

Richard Nelson

Aldo Leopold, November 15, 1927: "Just short of the top I suddenly saw a large buck in a pine thicket about 50 yards up the hill, looking me over. I moved to avoid a bush, drew to the barb at point blank, and let fly. The unmistakable thud of the arrow striking flesh told me I had hit."[1]

In the milieu that has evolved since his death in 1948, it may be easy to overlook or minimize the fact that Leopold was an ardent, lifelong hunter and fisherman. Without question, these compelling interests affected the deepest currents in his life: his passion for nature and the outdoors, his perspectives on ecology and wildlife management, his vision for an emerging conservation movement, his thinking on environmental ethics, and his sense of humanity's place in the biotic community.

Though it is not always made explicit, many of the essays and sketches in *A Sand County Almanac* grew out of Leopold's hunting and fishing excursions. In "Red Legs Kicking," he declares that boyhood hunting pursuits still carry for him "a vivid sharpness of form, color, and atmosphere that half a century of professional wildlife experience has failed to obliterate or to improve upon."[2]

Hunting and fishing assume a more prominent role in the *Round River* journals, and in the accompanying meditations, where Leopold underscores his own "hunting fever." He asserts that for humans, hunting is "almost a physiological characteristic" and a wellspring for our sense of affiliation with the natural world. At one point he concludes, "the man who does not like to see, hunt, photograph, or otherwise outwit birds or animals is hardly normal. He is supercivilized, and I for one do not know how to deal with him."[3]

Those of us imbued with a modern environmental conscience are likely to find some of the hunting episodes in Leopold's *Round River* journals disconcerting. For example, during their travels through the Colorado River delta country in 1922, Aldo and his brother Carl killed coyotes and bobcats as eagerly as they hunted edible game. In those days no one questioned the virtues and benefits of eliminating predatory animals; nor did Leopold until some years later, when he reflected upon his role in killing a mother wolf in the Arizona mountains and watching the "fierce green fire" fade from her eyes.[4] This death transformed not only Leopold the hunter, but also Leopold the biologist and essayist, eventually carrying reverberations across the Western world. Leopold's recognition that four-legged predators have a useful and rightful place in the biotic community has gradually taken root, and this attitude is gaining acceptance today among hunters, as it is in American society as a whole.

Aldo Leopold was born at a turning point in American environmental history. Between 1850 and 1900, the unregulated pursuit of game for commercial markets and for subsistence precipitated what wildlife historians Richard McCabe and Thomas McCabe have called "the period of greatest hunting pressure on wildlife *ever.*"[5] The passenger pigeon and American bison became the symbols of this bleak era, but many other species of birds and mammals were devastated as well. Few people realize, for example, that by the early twentieth century white-tailed deer had become rare in many states, especially east of the Mississippi. In New York and adjacent New England, the mere sighting of deer tracks was enough to make local headlines. In Wisconsin a conservation commissioner predicted that his state's increasingly scarce whitetails were "destined sooner or later to cease to be a game animal."[6]

As a youthful hunter, Leopold witnessed the aftermath of this plundering and he reached maturity during the awakening that followed. It was the "sportsmen" hunters, faced with dwindling or vanished game, who lobbied most vigorously for strict hunting regulations, wildland protection, habitat restoration, and scientific game management. Early leadership came from a cadre of influential Eastern outdoorsmen, most importantly from publisher George Bird Grinnell, who originated the Audubon Society, and President Theodore Roosevelt, a cofounder (with Grinnell and others) of the Boone and Crockett Club—organizations dedicated to resurrecting wildlife populations. Out of his own hunting background Leopold would emerge to help lay the foundations of wildlife ecology and management.

Aldo Leopold wrote at a time when species like the white-tailed deer had begun their slow, tenuous recovery; when poaching of depleted game jeopardized this recovery; when over-cut forests and other damaged habitats badly needed restoration; when few people aside from hunters and fishermen cared seriously about wildlife populations. The ingrained national attitudes—that resources are limitless and destined to be exploited for human gain—persisted. On the other hand, America was far less urbanized then, and people had a clearer understanding than they do today of what it means to plant and harvest crops, to raise and butcher livestock, to hunt and process wild game as part of their lifeway. Consequently, they tended to know from direct experience where food comes from. They understood that death is essential in sustaining all life, human and otherwise. These are elemental facts that the supermarket has allowed us to forget.

In Leopold's time as now there were, of course, nonhunters who cared deeply about nature—the bird enthusiasts, for example, who fought for protection of species like egrets, which had been severely overhunted for the millinery trade. As both an avid sportsman and a professional biologist, Leopold could speak to everyone concerned about wildlife and the environment, and he urged that nonhunters and hunters create coalitions to strengthen their collective voice. After all, everyone who cares about the natural world—hunter and fisherman, birdwatcher and biologist, hiker and camper, canoeist and kayaker, country dweller and suburbanite—suffers a loss when the environment is degraded and wildlife disappears.

Today overhunting is rarely a significant problem, thanks in considerable measure to Leopold's applied principles of wildlife management. Poaching, while still a vexing issue, has subsided as a threat to game populations. Many species, such as bison, elk, pronghorn, and black bear, have made phenomenal recoveries. A few—notably white-tailed deer, Canada goose, and snow goose—are widely considered overabundant. Our great predators, the wolf and the mountain lion, have been reintroduced or have returned on their own to long-abandoned homelands. But human population growth and habitat destruction imperil literally thousands of wild species, and the coming era may be chillingly reminiscent of that dark half-century between 1850 and 1900.

This is why Leopold's call for a coalition between hunting and nonhunting outdoor enthusiasts is as vital today as during his lifetime. According to the latest national survey, there are fourteen million hunters and about thirty-five million fishermen (residents sixteen years of age or older) in the United States. These groups constitute an enormous, politically diverse, socially heterogeneous, strongly focused constituency for the environment. In addition, sixty-three million Americans spend some of their time watching, feeding, or photographing wildlife. Now, imagine the effect on our nation's environmental agencies, policies, and politics if these groups were to combine forces.

To achieve anything near this potential, hunters and nonhunters must be willing to overcome, or at least accept, their differences. Leopold recognized the importance of mutual understanding between these groups, and perhaps this is why he wrote so eloquently about hunters' experiences, their motivations, their love for nature, and their sense of connection with the environment. Repeatedly, sociological studies have shown that hunters are motivated, above all else, by their desire to be close to nature. Also high among their motivations are sharing the hunting experience with friends and getting away from "civilization"; interestingly, hunters give much lower priority to the actual taking of game. Says Leopold: "Poets sing and hunters scale the mountains primarily for one and the same reason—the thrill to beauty."[7]

Among the greatest strengths of Aldo Leopold's work is its ability to bring us together in our common desire to experience and to protect the beauty, richness, and sustenance provided by wild nature. It is important to keep in mind that this legacy comes to us from a man who loved to hunt and fish.

Every ground is a hunting ground, whether it lies between you and the curbstone, or in those illimitable woods where rolls the Oregon.

Leopold on Missouri hunt with Carl Leopold, 1938. (Courtesy Aldo Leopold Foundation)

It is hardly necessary to point out that [the] commercialization of hunting privileges will take place first on lands of high value—that is, agricultural lands. It is already foreshadowed by the wholesale posting of such lands throughout the country. It will take place last, if at all, on lands of low value—forest lands. It is also evident that it will take place first with upland game and last, if at all, with migratory game. But it will, in the not-far-distant future, result in *the end of free hunting* for a larger part of the five million sportsmen now dependent on wild game for outdoor recreation.

> The National Forests: The Last Free Hunting Grounds of the
> Nation (1919)

A wide-open market, almost universal game farming, commercialized shooting privileges, and some incidental overflow shooting for the poor man—is this not the sum and substance of the European system? It is. And the European system of game management is undemocratic, unsocial, and therefore dangerous. I assume that it is not necessary to argue that the development of any undemocratic system in this country is to be avoided at all costs.

> Wild Lifers vs. Game Farmers: A Plea for Democracy in Sport
> (1919); RMG 66, ALS 59

Shooting privileges in Europe have, of course, been commercialized for centuries. Robin Hood enjoyed about the last free hunting in Europe, and his privileges came nearer being *de facto* than *de jure*. Today European hunting is limited almost exclusively to the privileged classes. Do we want American sport to drift into the same kind of a predicament?

> A Plea for State-Owned Ducking Grounds (1919); ALS 63

Rounding the point of a little bench, I suddenly felt a shock that seemed to freeze my feet to the ground. (I'm sure I felt that turkey in my knees quite as soon as I saw him!) There he was, right over the point of the bench, a big hump-backed gobbler, clipping the seeds off a stalk of wild oats.

I knew there must be more behind the point. My plan was to slip forward a few steps to a little oak tree and get a rest for the first shot. But I couldn't make my knees behave! I freely confess it, they were wobbling— wobbling like a reed shaken in the wind. I can look the biggest blacktail buck in the face without a tremor, but turkey? Never!

> A Turkey Hunt in the Datil National Forest (1919); ALS 47

About two miles below camp the river began to break up and we soon encountered a complete log jam which stopped all further progress. I used to talk pretty bravely about wiggling through the Labyrinth of the Colorado, of which this is probably the head. But we learned something on the Rillito.

> The Delta Colorado (1922); RR 24

A man may not care for golf and still be human, but the man who does not like to see, hunt, photograph, or otherwise outwit birds or animals is hardly normal. He is supercivilized, and I for one do not know how to deal with him. Babes do not tremble when they are shown a golf ball, but I should not like to own the boy whose hair does not lift his hat when he sees his first deer. We are dealing, therefore, with something that lies pretty deep.

Goose Music (c. 1922); RR 167

Some can live without opportunity for the exercise and control of the hunting instinct, just as I suppose some can live without work, play, love, business, or other vital adventure. But in these days we regard such deprivations as unsocial. Opportunity for exercise of all the normal instincts has become to be regarded more and more as an inalienable right. The men who are destroying our wildlife are alienating one of these rights, and doing a terribly thorough job of it. More than that, they are doing a permanent job of it. When the last corner lot is covered with tenements we can still make a playground by tearing them down, but when the last antelope goes by the board, not all the playground associations in Christendom can do aught to replace the loss.

Goose Music (c. 1922); RR 167–68

If wild birds and animals are a social asset, how much of an asset are they? It is easy to say that some of us, afflicted with hereditary hunting fever, cannot live satisfactory lives without them.

Goose Music (c. 1922); RR 168

. . .What is a wild goose worth? As compared with other sources of health and pleasure, what is its value in the common denominator of dollars?

I have a ticket to the symphony. It stood me two iron men. They were well spent, but if I had to choose, I would forgo the experience for the sight of the big gander that sailed honking into my decoys at daybreak this morning. It was bitter cold and I was all thumbs, so I blithely missed him. But miss or no miss, I saw him, I heard the wind whistle through his set wings as he came honking out of the gray west, and I felt him so that even now I tingle at the recollection. I doubt not that this very gander has given ten other men two dollars' worth of thrills. Therefore I say he is worth at least twenty dollars to the human race.

Goose Music (c. 1922); RR 168–69

. . . The ethics of sportsmanship is not a fixed code, but must be formulated and practiced by the individual, with no referee but the Almighty.

Goose Music (c. 1922); RR 172

. . . I have congenital hunting fever and three sons. As little tots, they spent their time playing with my decoys and scouring vacant lots with wooden guns. I hope to leave them good health, an education, and possibly even a competence. But what are they going to do with these things if there be no more deer in the hills, and no more quail in the coverts? No more snipe whistling in the meadow, no more piping of widgeons and chattering of teal as darkness covers the marshes; no more whistling of swift wings when the morning star pales in the east! And when the dawn-wind stirs through the ancient cottonwoods, and the gray light steals down from the hills over the old river sliding softly past its wide brown sandbars—what if there be no more goose music?

Goose Music (c. 1922); RR 173

It has been a memorable trip—maybe the best we ever made—and we have made some that are hard to beat. It is the first trip we have made together since we went to Drummond Island with Dad about 1906 or 1907. How Dad would have loved it! I am reminded of Izaak Walton's terse but loving tribute—"an excellent angler, now with God."

Canada, 1924 (1924); RR 54

I am trying to make it clear that a wilderness hunting trip is by way of becoming a rich man's privilege, whereas it has always been a poor man's right. Are we prepared to accept the consequences of the change? Do we really realize its possible effect on the nation's character and happiness?

A Plea for Wilderness Hunting Grounds (1925); ALS 156

Returned via the Gila rim. Walking along this high prairie in the somber sunset with a howling wind tossing the old cedars along the rim, and a soaring raven croaking over the abyss below, was a solemn and impressive experience. Jumped three whitetails right out on the prairie but it was too late to see horns. They were very pretty bounding over the sea of yellow grama grass with the wind blowing them along like tufts of thistledown. Felt our way down the rocky dugway to camp.

The Gila, 1927 (1927); RR 100

When directly opposite me, and about 60 yards distant, [the deer] stopped, seemed to ponder the fate of nations, and then to my utter surprise, plunged squarely down the hill and directly at me, but still obscured by brush. As they filed across a very small opening I made out that the first two were does, while the last seemed to be a spiker. I drew on a clear opening under a juniper where I knew they would pass, about 30 yards to my left, and in a moment the two does filed by in that peculiar hesitating trot which makes it uncertain whether the next instant will bring a total stop or a terrified leap. Then came the spiker. I was not yet sure whether his horns were 6 inches (the legal minimum) and devoted the first instant of clear vision to verifying this fact, instead of to a final appraisal of distance and aim, as I should have. Then I shot. The arrow passed over his back and splintered harmlessly on the rocks. I had held only two feet under instead of three feet.

The spiker bounded up the hill. At 120 yards I shot a second arrow, just as a sort of good-bye.

More perfect chances to make a kill do not occur, except in deer hunters' dreams.

The Gila, 1929 (1929); RR 122

Environmental control, like every other really potent idea, is a two-edged sword. It is the only possible way of keeping alive the sport of hunting in the face of unregulated human population growth. This is one edge of the sword. The other is that overcontrol is open to many abuses. A case in point is the bitterness which European nature-lovers feel toward the excessive and indiscriminate predator control practiced on private hunting preserves. This should be a lesson to managers of both private and public hunting grounds in this country. Moreover, excessive manipulation of environment tends to artificialize sport, and thus destroy the very recreational values which the conservation movement seeks to retain.

Game Management in the National Forests (1930); ALS 126–27

If the cessation of legalized hunting offered a sure means of perpetuating all classes of game in abundance, it might be the part of wisdom to fall back on it as a last resort. The opportunity to see and study game is just as valuable as the opportunity to shoot it, and half a loaf is better than none.

It is a biological and economic certainty, however, that farm game tends to disappear, even under complete protection, without deliberate and purposeful provision of cover and feed.

It is also a biological and economic probability that migratory game would tend to be seriously reduced, even under complete protection, without artificial offsets to the drainage of marshlands.

It is furthermore probable that universal prohibition of hunting could not be enforced without large funds.

Report to the American Game Conference on an American Game Policy, Appendix (1930)

The recreational value of a head of game is inverse to the artificiality of its origin, and hence in a broad way to the intensiveness of the system of game management which produced it.

Game Methods: The American Way (1931); RMG 158

. . .The bag limit [has become] the minimum proof of prowess, rather than the maximum limit of respectability (for which it was originally intended).

> Game Methods: The American Way (1931); RMG 162

Most of our atavistic instincts, including hunting, find their exercise only through the frank acceptance of illusion. . . . To kill a mess of game "by strength of hound" or quickness of trigger, and bring it home to the family, is just about as necessary to most grown Americans as for their very young sons to go fishing in the family washtub. And that, in my opinion, is very necessary indeed.

> Game Methods: The American Way (1931); RMG 163

The cause of sport is injured by claiming for it benefits which may not exist. Sport needs no defense if it maintains the game supply. No unsound arguments will keep it alive if it does not.

> *Report on a Game Survey of the North Central States* (1931), 55

No prudent man would risk a dollar's worth of fly and leader pulling a trout upstream through the giant tooth-brush of alder stems comprising the bend of that creek. But, as I said, no prudent man is a fisherman. By and by, with much cautious unraveling, I got him into open water, and finally aboard the creel.

I shall now confess to you that none of those three trout had to be beheaded, or folded double, to fit their casket. What was big was not the trout, but the chance. What was full was not my creel, but my memory. Like the white-throats, I had forgotten it would ever again be aught but morning on the Fork.

> The Alder Fork—A Fishing Idyl (1932); ASCA 40

TO MY FATHER
CARL LEOPOLD
PIONEER IN SPORTSMANSHIP
Dedication of *Game Management* (1933)

Many sportsmen still habitually place the blame for game shortage on "vermin" or "politics" or even on "too many restrictive laws." Many non-shooting protectionists, with equal regularity, place the blame on "too many sportsmen." Such verdicts are hardly entitled to be called diagnoses. The wish is too obviously father to the thought. They represent merely the age-old insistence of the human mind to fix on some visible scapegoat the responsibility for invisible phenomena which they cannot or do not wish to understand.

> *Game Management* (1933), 212

We sportsmen are paying the piper for several decades of stagnation in the development of hunting controls. We have been fighting a rear-guard action for the very existence of sports afield. If we continue to regard the issue as a battle, we shall probably continue our retreat. But if we can see the issue as a mutual problem, confronting not only our-selves but also farmers, landowners, and protectionists, and soluble by their mutual cooperation, then a brighter outcome may be anticipated.

Game Management (1933), 228

The hope is sometimes expressed that [the hunting instinct] will be "outgrown." This attitude seems to overlook the fact that the resulting vacuum will fill up with something, and not necessarily with something better. It somehow overlooks the biological basis of human nature,—the difference between historical and evolutionary time-scales. We can re-fine our manner of exercising the hunting instinct, but we shall do well to persist as a species at the end of the time it would take to outgrow it.

Game Management (1933), 391

There is, in short, a fundamental unity of purpose and method be-tween bird-lovers and sportsmen. Their common task of teaching the public how to modify economic activities for conservation purposes is of infinitely greater importance, and difficulty, than their current differ-ences of opinion over details of legislative and administrative policy. Un-less and until the common task is accomplished, the detailed manipula-tion of laws is in the long run irrelevant.

Game Management (1933), 405

The relations of sportsmen and zoophiles continue bad. The game research group has, perhaps, gained some respect in both camps, and thus gained a position as possible mediator, but who can mediate when each monthly batch of sporting periodicals contains fresh offense against those who should be our natural allies?

There are two main sources of friction: Our refusal to face the conse-quences of past mistakes in waterfowl policy, and our refusal to learn anything new about predator-control.

Whither 1935?—A Review of the American Game Policy (1935)

The trophy-hunter is the caveman reborn. Trophy-hunting is the prerog-ative of youth, racial or individual, and nothing to apologize for.

The disquieting thing in the modern picture is the trophy-hunter who never grows up, in whom the capacity for isolation, perception, and hus-bandry is undeveloped, or perhaps lost. He is the motorized ant who swarms the continents before learning to see his own back yard, who consumes but never creates outdoor satisfactions.

Conservation Esthetic (1938); ASCA 176

As the buck bounded down the mountain with a goodbye wave of his snowy flag, I realized that he and I were actors in an allegory. Dust to dust, stone age to stone age, but always the eternal chase! It was appropriate that I missed, for when a great oak grows in what is now my garden, I hope there will be bucks to bed in its fallen leaves, and hunters to stalk, and miss, and wonder who built the garden wall.

Song of the Gavilan (1940); ASCA 150–51

The woodcock is a living refutation of the theory that the utility of a game bird is to serve as a target, or to pose gracefully on a slice of toast. No one would rather hunt woodcock in October than I, but since learning of the sky dance I find myself calling one or two birds enough. I must be sure that, come April, there be no dearth of dancers in the sunset sky.

Sky Dance of Spring (1941); ASCA 34

. . .The sportsman of the future must get his satisfactions by enlarging himself rather than by enlarging his bag. The homebound sportsman unable to name the ducks slung over his shoulder is an anachronism, a relic of that I-got-my-limit-era which nearly ruined the continent and its resources. Few sportsmen have ever tried the sport of learning something about the game they pursue, the wildlife they see, or the plants they tramp over. Why is this species here? Whence does it come, where go? What limits its abundance? What was its role in history? What are its prospects for survival? What peculiarities of habit and habitat comprise its "standard of living"? To always seek but never quite achieve a "bag-limit" of answers to such questions is the sport of the future.

Introduction to *The Ducks, Geese, and Swans of North America* (1943)

. . . There is value in any experience that exercises those ethical restraints collectively called "sportsmanship." Our tools for the pursuit of wildlife improve faster than we do, and sportsmanship is a voluntary limitation in the use of these armaments. It is aimed to augment the role of skill and shrink the role of gadgets in the pursuit of wild things.

A peculiar virtue in wildlife ethics is that the hunter ordinarily has no gallery to applaud or disapprove of his conduct. Whatever his acts, they are dictated by his own conscience, rather than by a mob of onlookers. It is difficult to exaggerate the importance of this fact.

Wildlife in American Culture (1943); ASCA 178

The sportsman has no leaders to tell him what is wrong. The sporting press no longer represents sport; it has turned billboard for the gadgeteer. Wildlife administrators are too busy producing something to shoot at to worry much about the cultural value of the shooting. Because everybody from Xenophon to Teddy Roosevelt said sport has value, it is assumed that this value must be indestructible.

> Wildlife in American Culture (1943); ASCA 181–82

Knowledge of the whereabouts of good hunting or fishing is a very personal form of property. It is like rod, dog, or gun: a thing to be loaned or given as a personal courtesy. But to hawk it in the marketplace of the sports column as an aid to circulation seems to me another matter.

> Wildlife in American Culture (1943); ASCA 182–83

. . . Two decades of experience show that sportsmen in most states lack the foresight and courage to forego easy hunting now for the sake of permanence and quality in the future big-game crop. Like the timber barons and the livestock kings of unhappy memory, deer hunters are quite content to clip coupons paid out of capital account. The present forage and the future forest are the capital from which coupons now too often are paid.

> Summarization of the Twelfth North American Wildlife Conference (1947)

The common denominator of all hunters is the realization that there is always something to hunt. The world teems with creatures, processes, and events that are trying to elude you. . . . Every ground is a hunting ground, whether it lies between you and the curbstone, or in those illimitable woods where rolls the Oregon. The final test of the hunter is whether he is keen to go hunting in a vacant lot.

> The Deer Swath (1948); RR 128

The dog knows what is grouseward better than you do. You will do well to follow him closely, reading from the cock of his ears the story the breeze is telling. When at last he stops stock-still, and says with a sideward glance, "Well, get ready," the question is, ready for what? A twittering woodcock, or the rising roar of a grouse, or perhaps only a rabbit? In this moment of uncertainty is condensed much of the virtue of grouse hunting. He who must know what to get ready for should go and hunt pheasants.

> Smoky Gold (1949); ASCA 55

Hunts differ in flavor, but the reasons are subtle. The sweetest hunts are stolen. To steal a hunt, either go far into the wilderness where no one has been, or else find some undiscovered place under everybody's nose.

> Smoky Gold (1949); ASCA 55

Here, come October, I sit in the solitude of my tamaracks and hear the hunters' cars roaring up the highway, hell-bent for the crowded counties to the north. I chuckle as I picture their dancing speedometers, their strained faces, their eager eyes glued on the northward horizon. At the noise of their passing, a cock grouse drums his defiance. My dog grins as we note his direction. That fellow, we agree, needs some exercise; we shall look him up presently.

Smoky Gold (1949); ASCA 56

. . . My earliest impressions of wildlife and its pursuit retain a vivid sharpness of form, color, and atmosphere that half a century of professional wildlife experience has failed to obliterate or to improve upon. . . .

I could draw a map today of each clump of red bunchberry and each blue aster that adorned the mossy spot where he lay, my first partridge on the wing. I suspect my present affection for bunchberries and asters dates from that moment.

Red Legs Kicking (1949); ASCA 120, 122

16 ENVIRONMENTAL HISTORY

Leopold and the Changing Landscape of History

Donald Worster

The landscape through which Aldo Leopold walked was deeply historical, filled with intimations of the past. In the Southwest, Wisconsin, or
Iowa, the places he knew best, he looked for evidence of change, usually
finding—though not always—a pattern of degradation. He was the historian of fauna, flora, soils, and ecological communities. The theory of
evolution, of course, taught him to think historically, and he was the first
of our conservation leaders who truly absorbed an evolutionary perspective on nature. But he went beyond biology to emphasize the long history of humans interacting with nature.

Leopold found in his outdoor surroundings a rich tapestry of human
meanings, human passions and interests, human follies and miscalcula-
tions. A board washed ashore told him a story about somebody's life,
and his woodpile became an archive of anonymous experience. A single
farm, if read closely, even a single tree on that farm, became the biography of a family struggling through the generations. Whole societies, he
realized, write their values onto the face of the land as surely as they
express themselves in books, paintings, or artifacts. Indeed, the whole
landscape is, to some extent, an artifact, the outcome of an endless dialogue between the human and the nonhuman.

Even wilderness, which is commonly defined as a place with very limited human history, was for Leopold a place rich in historical meaning.
The wild was significant in part because it had mattered to people, provided a context for their lives, a spiritual resource, and because it had
influenced American culture and character. He did not want to expunge
all human traces from the continent, or to erase history, but to preserve
the remaining wilderness as a symbol of the nation's past and a resource
for the future.

Among the great heroes of conservation only a few—Henry David
Thoreau or George Perkins Marsh—approach Leopold as persons
steeped in historical awareness. Commonly, conservation has focused on
the burning issues of the day, with little patience for digging through

the layers of time to gain perspective. Leopold, in contrast, feared that conservation was doomed to failure if it was too preoccupied with solving the problems of the moment. It would fail to uncover the roots of the brambles it was trying to clear away. America's environmental problems did not begin in 1945 or 1900; some of the roots go back to the nineteenth or eighteenth or seventeenth centuries, some back to Moses or before. Many environmentalists still have to learn that passing a new law or regulation, or improving the way we produce energy or drive automobiles, can be no substitute for understanding how we came to behave in nature as we do.

I share Leopold's conviction that most of our environmental problems—at least the ones we can have any hope of fixing—are caused by cultural beliefs and attitudes, often deeply seated. He speaks of civilization as "the successive dominance of a series of ideas" and identifies engineering as the dominant idea of the modern industrial society.[1] More accurately, it seems to me, the driving idea of modernity has been wealth—its expansion and accumulation. Engineering has only been a tool to express that idea. The modern history of pursuing a universal, unlimited wealth, for all its real achievements, has also been the history of ecological plunder and degradation. If we don't know that history well, then we lack an adequate sense of causality. We are also unlikely to find our way to an alternative idea.

In Leopold's day academic historians paid almost no attention to the landscape or its record of ecological patterns. They were largely concerned with past politics, and then only at the elite levels of presidents and kings; affairs of state, in their view, did not encompass soil erosion or biodiversity. Leopold's sometime neighbor in Madison, Wisconsin, the historian Frederick Jackson Turner, famous for his thesis that the frontier had spawned American democracy, was an exception—at least Turner acknowledged that the land may work important social change. The frontier historian, however, did not really think about history as embedded in complex ecological processes, specific to each place, and he ignored such darker environmental consequences of westward expansion as the dispossession of the native peoples, the slaughter of bison, the plowing up of fragile grasslands, and the pollution of rivers. Historians like Turner believed too uncritically in the ideology of progress, "the growth of the republic," the pageant of America.

When in "The Land Ethic" Leopold called for an ecological interpretation of history, he had something new in mind, something yet to be invented. The core assumption must be that humans are only one species in a biotic whole, and history must be about that whole, not humans isolated from their context. The culture-bearing animal must still be seen as an animal. A half century after he called for that more inclusive, dynamic history, open-eyed to the costs of progress, a new field of environmental history has emerged, and it is shifting the focus away from culture and society to culture, society, and the rest of nature. History in general has become a little more aware of evolution, ecology, land, water, and climate. We may hope that scientists, from their side, have likewise become more sensitive to the role of human culture and material creations in changing the face of the earth.

Leopold was on shakier ground when he moved from the past to the future, from history to prophecy. No one knows what the next dominant set of ideas will be, replacing wealth or engineering, nor when that transition will occur. That change is constant, in culture as well as in the biophysical environment, does not need be argued to our era, when change has become so dramatic, but the direction of change does need to be argued over. We don't have all the facts to make predictions, and we never will. Leopold wanted to see ecological thinking inform a new era in cultural history, for reasons both ethical and practical, and his sense of the past told him that era was possible, perhaps even imminent. He seems to have believed that he was living at one of those axial moments of history, when profoundly new religions, philosophies, and ethics are born. A few decades later we have to admit that such a transformation is very slow in coming, if it is coming at all, and industrial civilization looks as though it will persist for a while.

A history that is more alert to the landscape around us, looking for clues there about our past behavior and acknowledging the agency of nature in human life, is, however, a good place to begin the long, difficult process of change. It can help overcome one-generation thinking. It may even promote a wider idea of responsibility, which is all that conservation asks.

A sense of history should be the most precious gift of science and of the arts . . .

Skunk tracks in the snow. (Photo by Aldo Leopold. Courtesy Robert A. McCabe family and Aldo Leopold Foundation)

There are still millions of people whose opinions on wild life conservation, if they have any, are based in some degree on the assumption that the abundance of game must bear an inverse ratio to degree of settlement, and that the question of how long our game will hold out must be measured by the time it will take for man to completely occupy the land.

It is the writer's belief that this assumption is not only incorrect, but that it is exerting an incalculably mischievous influence against the progress of the movement for wild life conservation. To let the public think that economic progress spells the disappearance of wild life, is to let them believe that wild life conservation is ultimately hopeless.

> The Popular Wilderness Fallacy: An Idea That Is Fast Exploding (1918); RMG 49–50

The same tree rings which assure us that Southwestern climate has been stable for 3,000 years warn us plainly that it has been decidedly unstable from year to year, and that the drouth now so strongly impressed on every mind and pocketbook is not an isolated or an accidental bit of hard luck, but a periodic phenomenon the occurrence of which may be anticipated with almost the same certainty as we anticipate the days and the seasons. It is cause for astonishment that our attitude toward these drouths which wreck whole industries, cause huge wastes of wealth and resources, and even empty the treasures of commonwealths should still be that of the Arkansan toward his roof—in fair weather no need to worry, and in foul weather too wet to work.

> Some Fundamentals of Conservation in the Southwest (1923);
> RMG 90

[The] concept of a "balance of nature" compresses into three words an enormously complex chain of phenomena. But history bears out the law as given. [T. S.] Woolsey says that decadence has followed deforestation in Palestine, Assyria, Arabia, Greece, Tunisia, Algeria, Italy, Spain, Persia, Sardinia, and Dalmatia. Note that all of these are arid or semiarid. What well-watered country has ever suffered serious permanent damage to all its organic resources from human abuse? None that I know of except China. It might be reasonable to ascribe this one exception to the degree of abuse received. Sheer pressure of millions through uncounted centuries was simply too much.

> Some Fundamentals of Conservation in the Southwest (1923);
> RMG 91

Granting that the earth is for man—there is still a question: what man? Did not the cliff dwellers who tilled and irrigated these our valleys think that they were the pinnacle of creation—that these valleys were made for them? Undoubtedly. And then the Pueblos? Yes. And then the Spaniards? Not only thought so, but said so. And now we Americans? Ours beyond a doubt! (How happy a definition is that one of [A.T.] Hadley's which states, "Truth is that which prevails in the long run"!)

Five races—five cultures—have flourished here. We may truthfully say of our four predecessors that they left the earth alive, undamaged. Is it possibly a proper question for us to consider what the sixth shall say about us?

> Some Fundamentals of Conservation in the Southwest (1923);
> RMG 96

History and experience have shown . . . [that] to graze the range at all often means to overgraze the water-courses and bottom lands. Some concentration of stock at these points is difficult to avoid, even under careful management. When a bad flood encountered a virgin water-course full of vigorous trees, willows, vines, weeds and grass, it may have scoured it pretty severely, but the living roots remained to spring up and recover the land and cause the next more moderate flood to heal the scars instead of enlarging them. But when floods encounter a watercourse through bare fields, timber grazed clear of all undergrowth, and earthscars like roads, trails, and ditches built parallel with the stream, the gouges left by one flood are liable to be enlarged by the next flood; an unprotected channel is excavated; the trees merely act as levers to pry off the undermined banks; the process of oxbowing cuts first one side of the bottom and then the other, eating into the very base of the hills; side-gullies running back from the deepened creek-channel cut at right angles into the remaining bottoms and benches, draining the natural *cienegas* and hay meadows and changing the grasses to a less resistant forage type, and in the long run our "improved" valley becomes a desolation of sandbars, rockpiles and driftwood, a sad monument to the unintelligence and misspent energy of us, the pioneers.

> Pioneers and Gullies (1924); RMG 108–9, ALS 167–68

[Leopold explains his theory of ecological change in the Arizona brushfields]

Previous to the settlement of the country, fires started by lightning and Indians kept the brush thin, kept the juniper and other woodland species decimated, and gave the grass the upper hand with respect to possession of the soil. In spite of periodic fires, this grass prevented erosion. Then came the settlers with their great herds of livestock. These ranges had never been grazed and they grazed them to death, thus removing the grass and automatically checking the possibility of widespread fires. The removal of the grass relieved the brush species of root competition and of fire damage and thereby caused them to spread and "take the country." The removal of grass-root competition and of fire damage brought in the reproduction. In brief, the climax type is and always has been woodland. The thick grass and thin brush of presettlement days represented a temporary type. The substitution of grazing for fire brought on a transition of thin grass and thick brush. This transition type is now reverting to the climax type—woodland.

> Grass, Brush, Timber, and Fire in Southern Arizona (1924); RMG 115–16, ALS 182

How many of those whole-hearted conservationists who berate the past generation for its short-sightedness in the use of natural resources have stopped to ask themselves for what new evils the next generation will berate us?

> The Last Stand of the Wilderness (1925)

From the earliest times one of the principal criteria of civilization has been the ability to conquer the wilderness and convert it to economic use. To deny the validity of this criterion would be to deny history. But because the conquest of wilderness has produced beneficial reactions on social, political, and economic development, we have set up, more or less unconsciously, the converse assumption that the ultimate social, political, and economic development will be produced by conquering the wilderness entirely—that is, by eliminating it from our environment.

My purpose is to challenge the validity of such an assumption and to show how it is inconsistent with certain cultural ideas which we regard as most distinctly American.

Wilderness as a Form of Land Use (1925); RMG 134

There is little question that many of the attributes most distinctive of America and Americans are the impress of the wilderness and the life that accompanied it. If we have any such thing as an American culture (and I think we have), its distinguishing marks are a certain vigorous individualism combined with ability to organize, a certain intellectual curiosity bent to practical ends, a lack of subservience to stiff social forms, and an intolerance of drones, all of which are the distinctive characteristics of successful pioneers. These, if anything, are the indigenous part of our Americanism, the qualities that set it apart as a new rather than an imitative contribution to civilization. Many observers see these qualities not only bred into our people, but built into our institutions. Is it not a bit beside the point for us to be so solicitous about preserving those institutions without giving so much as a thought to preserving the environment which produced them and which may now be one of our effective means of keeping them alive?

Wilderness as a Form of Land Use (1925); RMG 138

In 1874 [A. H.] Bogardus wrote with pride, "Mr. Gillot . . . *being a man of great enterprise . . .* planted hedges all over his estate." In 1930 it is a sign of no enterprise at all if there remain even a single [osage orange] hedge on even the "back forty." Thus do fashions change. Thus also is game and wild life ever left out of account until after the change has been accomplished.

Report on a Game Survey of the North Central States (1931), 65

Came now the settler, bringing axe, plow, cow, rail fence, hedges, weeds, and grain. The axe converted shady woods into brushy stumplots. The plow flanked them with weedy stubbles, bearing bumper crops of strange but nourishing seeds with a regularity hitherto unknown to quaildom. Plow furrows further out on the prairie checked the sweep of fires and promptly the border shrubs romped outward up every draw and coulee, with bobwhite at their heels. Moreover the upland settlers planted thousands of miles of hedge around their new-broken grain-fields, converting vast reaches of the hitherto forbidden prairie into quail-heaven. All these simultaneous augmentations of both food and cover induced such an increase in quail as Iowa had never seen, nor will ever see again. This was the golden age for sports afield.

> Report of the Iowa Game Survey, Chapter Two: Iowa Quail (1932)

It is high time that the former distribution of [osage orange] hedges be recorded, for some day such historians as really understand the epic of Iowa will want to know.

> Report of the Iowa Game Survey, Chapter Two: Iowa Quail (1932)

How does a game survey resurrect the dates of such "trivial" events, now lost in the limbo of forgotten things?

This is how: Art Dotey was a farmer in Clear Creek township, Keokuk County. He was in arrears at the bank, and like many others in like case, harbored a secret ambition to retrieve his fortunes in the new wheat-lands of the Canadian prairie, then booming.

Art's father had taught him that the correct time to plant corn was when the bursting buds of osage "were as long as squirrel's ears."

One spring Art waited for the osage to tell him when to plant, but no buds came. Hence he was three weeks late in his seeding. Hence the frost caught his crop. Hence the bank foreclosed. Hence Art pulled up stakes for Canada.

Mrs. Jean Breitenbaugh, when questioned, remembered that it was 29 years ago when Art's family came to bid her goodbye, so it must have been the winter of 1901–2 which killed the hedges.

> Report of the Iowa Game Survey, Chapter Two: Iowa Quail (1932)

A harmonious relation to land is more intricate, and of more conse-quence to civilization, than the historians of its progress seem to realize. Civilization is not, as they often assume, the enslavement of a stable and constant earth. It is a state of *mutual and interdependent cooperation* between human animals, other animals, plants, and soils, which may be disrupted at any moment by the failure of any of them. Land-despoliation has evicted nations, and can on occasion do it again. As long as six virgin continents awaited the plow, this was perhaps no tragic matter—eviction from one piece of soil could be recouped by despoiling another. But there are now wars and rumors of wars which foretell the impending saturation of the earth's best soils and climates. It thus becomes a matter of some importance, at least to ourselves, that our dominion, once gained, be self-perpetuating rather than self-destructive.

> The Conservation Ethic (1933); RMG 183

Unforeseen ecological reactions not only make or break history in a few exceptional enterprises—they condition, circumscribe, delimit, and warp all enterprises, both economic and cultural, that pertain to land.

The Conservation Ethic (1933); RMG 185

In short, the reaction of land to occupancy determines the nature and duration of civilization. In arid climates the land may be destroyed. In all climates the plant succession determines what economic activities can be supported. Their nature and intensity in turn determine not only the domestic but also the wild plant and animal life, the scenery, and the whole face of nature. We inherit the earth, but within the limits of the soil and the plant succession we also *rebuild* the earth—without plan, without knowledge of its properties, and without understanding of the increasingly coarse and powerful tools which science has placed at our disposal.

The Conservation Ethic (1933); RMG 185

It is astonishing how few of those who have learned by rote rule or "nature study" the *statics* of the land's present inhabitants or condition, ever learn to read the *dynamics* of its past history and probable future. To see merely what a range is or has is to see nothing. To see *why* it is, how it *became,* and the direction and velocity of its changes—this is the great drama of the land, to which "educated" people too often turn an unseeing eye and a deaf ear. The stumps in a woodlot, the species age and form of fencerow trees, the plow-furrows in a reverted field, the location and age of an old orchard, the height of the bank of an irrigation ditch, the age of the trees or bushes in a gully, the fire-scars on a sawlog—these and a thousand other roadside objects spell out words of history, and of destiny, of game and of peoples. They are the final authority on the history of the recent past and the trend of the immediate future.

Game Management (1933), 387–88

It is not unthinkable that the present world-wide disturbances which we call revolution, depression, and real-politik are the preliminary rumblings of Nature over an unhealthy population-density. If the machines whereby we hope artificially to maintain or increase that density are really a contravention of ecological laws, nature is capable of sweeping them into the discard with all the nonchalance of an advancing glacier. What I am trying to say is that the study of cycles may ultimately throw light on sociology, as well as conservation.

The Game Cycle—A Challenge to Science (1934)

The two great cultural advances of the past century were the Darwinian theory and the development of geology. The one explained how and the other where we live. Compared with such ideas the whole gamut of mechanical and chemical invention pales into a mere matter of current ways and means.

Just as important, however, as the origin of plants, animals, and soil is the question of how they operate as a community. Darwin lacked time to unravel . . . more than the beginnings of an answer. That task has fallen to the new science of ecology, which is daily uncovering a web of interdependencies so intricate as to amaze—were he here—even Darwin himself, who, of all men, should have the least cause to tremble before the veil.

Wilderness ms. (c. 1935)

As in America, the [German] landscape is a human document written upon the page of geological history. In a truly mathematical sense, it is an integrated expression of all the virtues, foibles, and fallacies of its successive generations of human occupants.

Naturschutz in Germany (1936)

. . . We have traced through a period of nine centuries the slow but inexorable growth of a system of silviculture incompatible with a natural and healthy game stand, and of a system of game management incompatible with a natural and healthy silviculture.

Deer and Dauerwald in Germany: II. Ecology and Policy (1936)

The "wood factory" concept [in forestry] fell on friendly soil when transplanted to pre-war America. It would be foolish, of course, to infer that it contains no truth. It would be equally foolish to overlook the degree to which it has been amended and superseded in its place of origin by new and broader concepts of forest land use. The Germans now realize that increment bought at the expense of soil health, landscape beauty, and wildlife is poor economics as well as poor public policy.

Deer and Dauerwald in Germany: II. Ecology and Policy (1936)

. . . It is ironical that Chihuahua, with a history and a terrain so strikingly similar to southern New Mexico and Arizona should present so lovely a picture of ecological health, whereas our own states, plastered as they are with National Forests, National Parks and all the other trappings of conservation, are so badly damaged that only tourists and others ecologically color-blind, can look upon them without a feeling of sadness and regret. . . .

. . . So great was the fear of Indians that the Sierras were never settled, hence never grazed, hence never eroded. This holds true up to Pancho Villa's revolution of 1916. During the revolution bandits performed the same ecological function as Indians. Since then, depression and unstable land policies have served to keep the mountains green.

It is this chain of historical accidents which enables the American conservationist to go to Chihuahua today and feast his eyes on what his own mountains were like before the Juggernaut. To my mind these live oak-dotted hills fat with side oats grama, these pine-clad mesas spangled with flowers, these lazy trout streams burbling along under great sycamores and cottonwoods, come near to being the cream of creation. But on our side of the line the grama is mostly gone, the mesas are spangled with snakeweed, the trout streams are now cobble-bars.

Conservationist in Mexico (1937); RMG 239–40, ALS 201–3

The cranes stand, as it were, upon the sodden pages of their own history. These peats are the compressed remains of the mosses that clogged the pools, of the tamaracks that spread over the moss, of the cranes that bugled over the tamaracks since the retreat of the ice sheet. An endless caravan of generations has built of its own bones this bridge into the future, this habitat where the oncoming host again may live and breed and die.

To what end? Out on the bog a crane, gulping some luckless frog, springs his ungainly hulk into the air and flails the morning sun with mighty wings. The tamaracks re-echo with his bugled certitude. He seems to know.

Marshland Elegy (1937); ASCA 96

All history shows this: that civilization is not the progressive elaboration of a single idea, but the successive dominance of a series of ideas. Greece, Rome, the Renaissance, the industrial age, each had a new and largely distinct zone of awareness. The people of each lived not in a better, nor a worse, but in a new and different intellectual field. Progress, if there be any, is the slender hoard of fragments retained from the whole intellectual succession.

Engineering is clearly the dominant idea of the industrial age. What I have here called ecology is perhaps one of the contenders for a new order. In any case our problem boils down to increasing the overlap of awareness between the two.

Engineering and Conservation (1938); RMG 253

The "balance of nature" is a mental image for land and life which grew up before and during the transition to ecological thought. It is commonly employed in describing the biota to laymen, but ecologists among each other accept it only with reservations, and its acceptance by laymen seems to depend more on convenience than on conviction. . . .

To the ecological mind, balance of nature has merits and also defects. Its merits are that it conceives of a collective total, that it imputes some utility to all species, and that it implies oscillations when balance is dis-

turbed. Its defects are that there is only one point at which balance occurs, and that balance is normally static.

A Biotic View of Land (1939); RMG 267

Evolutionary changes . . . are usually slow and local. Man's invention of
tools has enabled him to make changes of unprecedented violence, ra-
pidity, and scope.

A Biotic View of Land (1939); ASCA 217, RMG 269

There once were men capable of inhabiting a river without disrupting
the harmony of its life. They must have lived in thousands on the Gavilan, for their works are everywhere. Ascend any draw debouching on any
canyon and you find yourself climbing little rock terraces or check dams,
the crest of one level with the base of the next. Behind each dam is a
little plot of soil that was once a field or garden, sub-irrigated by the
showers which fell on the steep adjoining slopes. On the crest of the
ridge you may find the stone foundations of a watch tower; here the
hillside farmer probably stood guard over his polka-dot acrelets. House-
hold water he must have carried from the river. Of domestic animals he
evidently had none. What crops did he raise? How long ago? The only
fragment of an answer lies in the 300-year-old pines, oaks, or junipers
that now find rootage in his little fields. Evidently it was longer ago than
the age of the oldest trees.

Song of the Gavilan (1940); ASCA 150

. . . The [wildlife] research program pays too little attention to the
history of wildlife, and our system of publications makes no provision for
historical monographs. We do not yet appreciate how much historical
evidence can be dug up, or how important it can be in the appraisal of
contemporary ecology.

The State of the Profession (1940); RMG 279

The history of wildlife is too often regarded as the domain of old-
timers indulging in nostalgic reflection, or of professors writing post-
mortems on the wild pigeon and the buffalo.

It has now become apparent that such history has other uses. Present-
day problems in conservation and land use, viewed in the light of
contemporary evidence alone, often baffle the investigator. The same
problem, viewed in the light of history, may often be deciphered as the
repetition of some historic pattern.

Wisconsin Wildlife Chronology (1940)

The Congressmen who voted money to clear the ranges of bears were
the sons of pioneers. They acclaimed the superior virtues of the fron-

tiersman, but they strove with might and main to make an end of the frontier.

We forest officers, who acquiesced in the extinguishment of the bear, knew a local rancher who had plowed up a dagger engraved with the name of one of Coronado's captains. We spoke harshly of the Spaniards who, in their zeal for gold and converts, had needlessly extinguished the native Indians. It did not occur to us that we, too, were the captains of an invasion too sure of its own righteousness.

Escudilla (1940); ASCA 137

In 1812 we find the hero of Cooper's novel "Oak Openings" gathering wild honey on a commercial scale in southern Michigan, a region as yet devoid of settlements, and like the rest of the continent, devoid of native honey bees. The European bees had arrived long enough in advance of 1812 to enable the bears to develop a honey-hunting technique.

No one mapped the spread of the bee, and probably no one but the bears possessed the necessary data.

Spread of the Hungarian Partridge in Wisconsin (1940)

... He who owns a veteran bur oak owns more than a tree. He owns a historical library, and a reserved seat in the theater of evolution. To the discerning eye, his farm is labeled with the badge and symbol of the prairie war.

Bur Oak Is Badge of Wisconsin (1941); ASCA 30

... There is value in any experience that reminds us of our distinctive national origins and evolution, i.e. that stimulates awareness of history. Such awareness is "nationalism" in its best sense. For lack of any other short name, I shall call this ... the "split-rail value." For example: a boy scout has tanned a coonskin cap, and goes Daniel-Booneing in the willow thicket below the tracks. He is re-enacting American history. He is, to that extent, culturally prepared to face the dark and bloody realities of the present.

Wildlife in American Culture (1943); ASCA 177

The parentage of ideas about egg-openers, iceboxes, and cigarette-lighters is recorded in the United States Patent Office. ... The parentage of ideas about men and land is seldom recorded at all. By the time they appear in print they are usually step-children whose parentage has been forgotten.

Obituary: P. S. Lovejoy (1943)

Everything taken together, this book has the faults and merits of its generation. It hurries toward nowhere in particular, but sees a lot on the way. It arises out of the clash of two opposing philosophies of land use, but it does not admit their opposition nor doubt that they can be reconciled; indeed the book itself is a contribution toward this end. It uses the findings of land technology without projecting its trends, or worrying about future systems. No thinking conservationist can afford to pass it up, yet it is in essence a milepost in the accomplishment of a job, rather than a guide to wisdom.

Review of *Wildlife Refuges* (1943)

The reader . . . is given no . . . vivid picture of the ecological and economic processes by which the land resource has been worn down. The results of land abuse are made clear, but the interplay of forces producing those results is seldom elucidated. This defect is, in my opinion, shared by all other books on conservation so far written, whether technical or popular.

Review of *The American Land* (1943)

Most of conservation is the manipulation of the plant succession, yet the term is seldom mentioned in conservation propaganda. Most laymen do not know its meaning. Here is a dramatic case history, offering a chance to explain how succession has upset an industry through failure to foresee the penalties of reckless land use.

Review of "Fighting the Mesquite and Cedar Invasion on Texas Ranges" (1944); ALS 215

In curious contrast to his deep understanding of dogs, [author] Montague Stevens saw only the surface of the land he hunted over. His active days afield coincided with the advent of erosion in the cow country, but he did not see it. The better to keep up with his hounds, he practiced riding his horse across the cavernous arroyos which were then invading the fertile valleys, but he did not recognize the invasion as something new in history, nor did he perceive its cause: the terrific overgrazing practiced by the early cowmen. Small wonder, then, that less intelligent men still fail to perceive that something more important than bears is departing from the western range. New Mexico's grizzlies succumbed visibly to trap, gun, and poisoned bait, but New Mexico's fertile valleys slipped down the Rio Grande in the night. Neither will return.

The University of New Mexico has done well to preserve this saga of how the state was made safe for cows. How the state is to be made safe from cows is a saga yet to be written.

Review of *Meet Mr. Grizzly* (1944); ALS 220

Nostalgia for the good old days when everything was abundant is almost universal among conservationists. Comparison between the then and the now furnishes the pattern for most of our books, talks, and dreams. We lament the lost thunder of galloping buffalo, the sky-darkening clouds of pigeons and waterfowl, the flowery seas of prairie, the velvet silence of the virgin woods. Yet nothing is clearer than this: our grandfathers, who had the opportunity to see these things, did not value them, as personal experience, as highly as we think we would have.

There are two possible explanations. Appreciation may have been enhanced by the intervening gains in education, or we may be incapable of appreciating anything until it has grown scarce.

The first explanation flatters us, the second does not, so we usually admit the one and ignore the other.

Scarcity Values in Conservation ms. (c. 1946)

Men still live who, in their youth, remember [passenger] pigeons. Trees still live who, in their youth, were shaken by a living wind. But a decade hence only the oldest oaks will remember, and at long last only the hills will know.

On a Monument to the Passenger Pigeon (1947); ASCA 109

To love what *was* is a new thing under the sun, unknown to most people and to all pigeons. To see America as history, to conceive of destiny as a becoming, to smell a hickory tree through the still lapse of ages—all these things are possible for us, and to achieve them takes only the free sky, and the will to ply our wings.

On a Monument to the Passenger Pigeon (1947); ASCA 112

Our saw now cuts the 1860's, when thousands died to settle the question: Is the man-man community lightly to be dismembered? They settled it, but they did not see, nor do we yet see, that the same question applies to the man-land community.

Good Oak (1949); ASCA 15

There is an allegory for historians in the diverse functions of saw, wedge, and axe.

The saw works only across the years, which it must deal with one by one, in sequence. From each year the raker teeth pull little chips of fact, which accumulate in little piles, called sawdust by woodsmen and archives by historians; both judge the character of what lies within by the character of the samples thus made visible without. It is not until the transect is completed that the tree falls, and the stump yields a collective view of a century. By its fall the tree attests the unity of the hodge-podge called history.

The wedge, on the other hand, works only in radial splits; such a split yields a collective view of all the years at once, or no view at all, depending on the skill with which the plane of the split is chosen. (If in doubt, let the section season for a year until a crack develops. Many a hastily driven wedge lies rusting in the woods, embedded in unsplittable cross-grain.)

The axe functions only at an angle diagonal to the years, and this only for the peripheral rings of the recent past. Its special function is to lop limbs, for which both saw and wedge are useless.

The three tools are requisite to good oak, and to good history.

Good Oak (1949); ASCA 16–17

The spring flood brings us more than high adventure; it brings likewise an unpredictable miscellany of floatable objects pilfered from upriver farms. An old board stranded on our meadow has, to us, twice the value of the same piece new from the lumberyard. Each old board has its own individual history, always unknown, but always to some degree guessable from the kind of wood, its dimensions, its nails, screws, or paint, its finish or the lack of it, its wear or decay. One can even guess, from the abrasion of its edges and ends on sandbars, how many floods have carried it in years past.

Our lumber pile, recruited entirely from the river, is thus not only a collection of personalities, but an anthology of human strivings in upriver farms and forests. The autobiography of an old board is a kind of literature not yet taught on campuses, but any riverbank farm is a library where he who hammers or saws may read at will. Come high water, there is always an accession of new books.

Come High Water (1949); ASCA 24–25

The Highway Department says that 100,000 cars pass yearly over this route during the three summer months when the Silphium is in bloom. In them must ride at least 100,000 people who have "taken" what is called history, and perhaps 25,000 who have "taken" what is called botany. Yet I doubt whether a dozen have seen the Silphium, and of these hardly one will notice its demise. If I were to tell a preacher of the adjoining church that the road crew has been burning history books in his cemetery, under the guise of mowing weeds, he would be amazed and uncomprehending. How could a weed be a book?

This is one little episode in the funeral of the native flora, which in turn is one episode in the funeral of the floras of the world. Mechanized man, oblivious of floras, is proud of his progress in cleaning up the landscape on which, willy-nilly, he must live out his days. It might be wise to prohibit at once all teaching of real botany and real history, lest some future citizen suffer qualms about the floristic price of his good life.

Prairie Birthday (1949); ASCA 46

It is a kind providence that has withheld a sense of history from the thousands of species of plants and animals that have exterminated each other to build the present world. The same kind providence now withholds it from us. Few grieved when the last buffalo left Wisconsin, and few will grieve when the last Silphium follows him to the lush prairies of the never-never land.

Prairie Birthday (1949); ASCA 50

I try to read, from the age of the young jackpines marching across an old field, how long ago the luckless farmer found out that sand plains were meant to grow solitude, not corn. Jackpines tell tall tales to the unwary, for they put on several whorls of branches each year, instead of only one. I find a better chronometer in an elm seedling that now blocks the barn door. Its rings date back to the drouth of 1930. Since that year no man has carried milk out of this barn.

Smoky Gold (1949); ASCA 57

A sense of history should be the most precious gift of science and of the arts, but I suspect that the grebe, who has neither, knows more history than we do. His dim primordial brain knows nothing of who won the Battle of Hastings, but it seems to sense who won the battle of time. If the race of men were as old as the race of grebes, we might better grasp the import of his call. Think what traditions, prides, disdains, and wisdoms even a few self-conscious generations bring to us! What pride of continuity, then, impels this bird, who was a grebe eons before there was a man.

Clandeboye (1949); ASCA 161

To the laborer in the sweat of his labor, the raw stuff on his anvil is an adversary to be conquered. So was wilderness an adversary to the pioneer.

But to the laborer in repose, able for the moment to cast a philosophical eye on his world, that same raw stuff is something to be loved and cherished, because it gives definition and meaning to his life. This is a plea for the preservation of some tag-ends of wilderness, as museum pieces, for the edification of those who may one day wish to see, feel, or study the origins of their cultural inheritance.

Many of the diverse wildernesses out of which we have hammered America are already gone; hence in any practical program the unit areas to be preserved must vary greatly in size and in degree of wildness.

Wilderness (1949); ASCA 188–89

That man is . . . only a member of a biotic team is shown by an ecological interpretation of history. Many historical events, hitherto explained

solely in terms of human enterprise, were actually biotic interactions between people and land. The characteristics of the land determined the
facts quite as potently as the characteristics of the men who lived on it.

The Land Ethic (1949); ASCA 205

In short, the plant succession steered the course of history; the pioneer simply demonstrated, for good or ill, what successions inhered in
the land. Is history taught in this spirit? It will be, once the concept of
land as a community really penetrates our intellectual life.

The Land Ethic (1949); ASCA 207

I have purposely presented the land ethic as a product of social evolution because nothing so important as an ethic is ever "written." Only
the most superficial student of history supposes that Moses "wrote" the
Decalogue; it evolved in the minds of a thinking community, and Moses
wrote a tentative summary of it for a "seminar." I say tentative because
evolution never stops.

The Land Ethic (1949); ASCA 225

17 EDUCATION

᪥

What Is Education For?

David W. Orr

Aldo Leopold was a man for all seasons: naturalist, scientist, philosopher, public citizen, conservationist, family man, and writer, but in his later years he earned his keep as a professor. By all accounts Leopold was an extraordinarily effective teacher, but he is not commonly regarded as an educational philosopher. As the passages in this chapter reveal, however, Leopold thought deeply and critically about the role of education relative to problems of land. Consider, for example, the following quotation from "Song of the Gavilan": "There are men charged with the duty of examining the construction of the plants, animals and soils which are the instruments of the great orchestra. These men are called professors. Each selects one instrument and spends his life taking it apart and describing its strings and sounding boards. This process of dismemberment is called research. The place for dismemberment is called a university."[1] In this and other passages written over three decades, Aldo Leopold challenged the bedrock assumptions of formal education while the professional educators of his time were mostly content to dabble with lesser things. His critique of both the substance and the process of formal education is scathing and, I think, more relevant now than then.

At a time when education and research were becoming more and more specialized, Leopold proposed a "reversal of specialization," so that "instead of learning more and more about less and less," we might "learn more and more about the whole biotic landscape."[2] Instead of glorifying human cultural accomplishments, Leopold proposed that teachers also cultivate in their students "a refined taste in natural objects."[3] While others were advancing the study of economics as a way to extend human domination over the natural world, Leopold proposed the study of "land economics" in order to promote a "universal curiosity to understand the land mechanism."[4] As professors were focusing increasingly on preparing students for careers, Leopold proposed "education as a means of building citizens" who understand "how the land is

255

put together."[5] While educators were cozying up to those offering one technological panacea or another, Leopold asked, "Does the educated citizen know he is only a cog in an ecological mechanism?"[6] And if it did not teach such things, he did not think that it had much value. In contrast with those who were creating an education calibrated for a fossil-fuel dependent world, Leopold was saying that education ought to promote "experience that reminds us of our dependency on the soil-plant-animal-man food chain."[7] Not content with a utilitarian curriculum, Leopold instead was teaching his students "to see the land, to understand what he sees, and enjoy what he understands."[8] While others were proposing to increase the volume of education, Leopold inconveniently noticed that "we have more education but less soil [and] fewer healthy woods."[9] As educators became more and more enamored of technology in the curriculum as a solution to nearly everything, Leopold called for the establishment of experimental areas "on which conservation problems and techniques can be shown."[10]

More forcefully than any other member of the educational establishment of his time, Aldo Leopold argued that education ought to help build a civilization that was, as he put it, more than a trial balloon. But toward the end of his life Leopold was pessimistic about the directions of education relative to issues of land and the transition to what is now called "sustainability." The educational system, he wrote, "is headed away from, rather than toward, an intense consciousness of land . . . seem[ing] deliberately to avoid ecological concepts."[11] Relative to the magnitude of the challenges ahead, the direction of education has not changed much since *A Sand County Almanac* was first published. Leopold's influence, however, is increasingly evident. Environmental education, for example, is now an established part of the curriculum in many schools, colleges, and universities.

In his emphasis on practical experience outside the classroom, Leopold's views on education bear a family resemblance to those of John Dewey and Alfred North Whitehead. But more clearly than they or anyone before him Leopold saw the critical relationship between the life of the mind and the prospects for life. Conservation education, for Leopold, was rooted in one's affections for particular places and grew by cultivation of the powers of close observation. Theory followed. But Leopold is most interesting to us as an educator not because he wrote long complex tomes on educational theory, but rather because he was a consummate student of the land who could change his mind as the evidence warranted. The Aldo Leopold writing in his years of "trigger-itch" is far less interesting than the man who wrote "The Land Ethic." But the two were joined in fact by the unstinting honesty and passion for land that characterized Leopold's life. We continue to read him, not just because of his considerable felicity with words and images, but because of the unity between the man and his words and between the words and our larger ecological prospects. And if education does not connect thought, words, and deeds with our obligations as citizens of the land community, then, as Leopold once asked, what is education for?

Once you learn to read the land, I have no fear of what you will do to it, or with it. And I know many pleasant things it will do to you.

Leopold with students on a winter field trip at the University of Wisconsin Arboretum in Madison, 1945. (Photo by Robert A. McCabe. Courtesy University of Wisconsin–Madison Memorial Library, Department of Special Collections)

. . . A good healthy curiosity is better equipment with which to venture forth than any amount of learning or education. Education is attained by and not for these things. And schooling, which I hold to be an entirely separate thing, is only a period of leisure whose object is to show us where an education is to be found.

A Man's Leisure Time ms. (1920)

The conservationist must look to the agricultural college for both thought and action. If it be true that modern agriculture essays to teach not only how to fatten a hog, but how people may live on land, then the agricultural colleges are confronted by a challenge, and an opportunity. They have the chance to give physical and economic meaning to those aspirations which we designate as conservation.

Vegetation and Birds (1931)

The business of a University has heretofore been conceived to be the preparation of citizens to cope with their environment. The University must now take on the additional function of preserving an environment fit to support citizens.

What Is the University of Wisconsin Arboretum? ms. (c. 1934)

Few public movements display a wider gap between aspiration and achievement than conservation.

To the end of narrowing this gap, we are embarked on two large-scale experiments. One is premised on the notion that conservation is something a nation buys. The other is premised on the notion that conservation is something a nation *learns.*

Review of *Our Natural Resources and Their Conservation* (1937)

Paradox is the earmark of valid truth, and to the extent that any textbook fails to point this out, it fails of attaining University stature.

Review of *Our Natural Resources and Their Conservation* (1937)

There is . . . reason for believing that rural people with abundant opportunity for wildlife avocations are inhibited from developing them by the sheer momentum of the stampede toward the mechanical and the synthetic. Agricultural colleges, in equipping the farmer with power machinery and an industrial concept of his vocation, have inadvertently equipped him with urbanized recreations and hobbies. Whatever may be the merits of the rural golf course, the rural movie, and other purchased rural recreations, it may fairly be questioned whether they should displace the enjoyment of wild things available to any farmer on his own land without cost.

The University and Conservation of Wisconsin Wildlife (1937)

It is important . . . that the budding layman-ornithologist be taught to grasp the principles of biological science, but it is also important to show him the personal satisfaction to be derived from the scholarly development of his hobby. These are two jobs, of which the University has so far performed only the first.

The University and Conservation of Wisconsin Wildlife (1937)

The love of nature is a matter of affection and esthetics. The understanding of nature is science. The use of natural resources is economics.

The conservation movement is composed of people in whom these three elements are mixed in widely varying proportions. It follows that there must be internal controversy. History abundantly fulfills this expectation.

The controversial nature of this field simply sets up this specification: All three elements must be represented in a sound university program. A university may be defined as a place where controversies are conducted at such close range that they have a superior chance of smelting out usable truth.

The University and Conservation of Wisconsin Wildlife (1937)

... There is a dangerous tendency for laymen to conceive of teaching as a process of indoctrination with pre-determined truth. Only those charged with the discovery of facts through research can appreciate the tentative nature of the conclusions on which many conservation policies are now based.

It follows that in organizing the primary university conservation structure, teaching and research should never be divorced. Teaching should be entrusted only to productive research workers. University teaching without research soon becomes sterile.

The University and Conservation of Wisconsin Wildlife (1937)

Universities pretend to measure their success by the light they throw on the world's problems, but the yardstick actually used is the number of graduates they can get jobs for.

The Research Program (1937)

Selling professional training without a research base is like selling securities without a property base. The right to teach must be earned, not seized. The ultimate danger lies in an over-supply of mediocre half-trained wildlife managers, an under-supply of highly trained wildlife ecologists, an under-supply of vocational field workers, and an under-supply of non-professional education for future citizens.

The Research Program (1937)

... The forces which threaten wildlife emanate from its environment, and their operation cannot be understood by a public versed only in names and habits of species. Such a public, as a critic of conservation policies, is equivalent to a person having a wide personal acquaintance, but no knowledge of business, as a critic of politics or economics. Both lack an "inside" picture of the struggle for existence. Ecology is the politics and economics of animals and plants.

The citizen-conservationist needs an understanding of wildlife ecology not only to enable him to function as a critic of sound policy, but to enable him to derive maximum enjoyment from his contacts with the land. The jig-saw puzzle of competitions and cooperations which constitute the wildlife community are inherently more interesting than mere acquaintance with its constituent species, for the same reason that a newspaper is inherently more interesting than a telephone directory.

Teaching Wildlife Conservation in Public Schools (1937)

Of 30 students in the 1936 farmers' short course in game management at the University [of Wisconsin], 4 professed, in personal interview, a special interest in natural history derived from their teachers. Four others had derived such an interest from family or friends. Twelve had read natural history books from school libraries. This may be a valid sample of the spread and effectiveness of conservation teaching to date.

It was very noticeable that the teachers who had awakened such interests had done so by the contagion of their enthusiasm, rather than by merely transmitting information.

Teaching Wildlife Conservation in Public Schools (1937)

There seems to be little realization of the fact that to write a really competent non-technical conservation text, which shall fairly cover the component fields and be at once sound science, sound policy, and sound pedagogy, is a task calling for very uncommon mental powers, not to mention time and funds. It is a task at least as exacting as the scientific fact-finding which underlies it.

Teaching Wildlife Conservation in Public Schools (1937)

The end-objective of conservation teaching must be, I think, to show the prospective citizen that conservation is impossible so long as land-utility is given blanket priority over land-beauty. In short, it is his personal philosophy of land use, as well as his vote and his dollar, which will ultimately determine the degree to which the conservation idea is converted from preachment into practice.

Teaching Wildlife Conservation in Public Schools (1937)

The most serious defect in the whole collection of teaching materials is the absence of the phrase "we don't know." Just why are we so undemocratic in professing ignorance? It seems a special privilege of scientists.

Teaching Wildlife Conservation in Public Schools (1937)

Schools and universities need nearby pieces of land on which conservation problems and techniques can be shown, and researches performed. School forests are a move in this direction, but why not also school refuges, management areas, and floral preserves?

Teaching Wildlife Conservation in Public Schools (1937)

What is our educational system doing to encourage personal amateur scholarship in the natural-history field? We can perhaps seek an answer to this question by dropping in on a typical class in a typical zoology department. We find there students memorizing the names of the bumps on the bones of a cat. It is important, of course, to study bones; otherwise we should never comprehend the evolutionary process by which animals came into existence. But why memorize the bumps? We are told that this is part of biological discipline. I ask, though, whether a comprehension of the living animal and how it holds its place in the sun is not an equally important part. Unfortunately the living animal is virtually omitted from the present system of zoological education.

Natural History—The Forgotten Science (1938); RR 60–61

To visualize more clearly the lopsidedness and sterility of biological education as a means of building citizens, let's go afield with some typical Phi Beta Kappa student and ask him some questions. We can safely assume he knows how angiosperms and cats are put together, but let us test his comprehension of how the land is put together.

We are driving down a country road in northern Missouri. Here is a farmstead. Look at the trees in the yard and the soil in the field and tell us whether the original settler carved his farm out of prairie or woods. Did he eat prairie chicken or wild turkey for his Thanksgiving? What plants grew here originally which do not grow here now? Why did they disappear? What did the prairie plants have to do with creating the corn-yielding capacity of this soil? Why does this soil erode now but not then?

Again, suppose we are touring the Ozarks. Here is an abandoned field in which the ragweed is sparse and short. Does this tell us anything about why the mortgage was foreclosed? About how long ago? Would this field be a good place to look for quail? Does short ragweed have any connection with the human story behind yonder graveyard? If all the ragweed in this watershed were short, would that tell us anything about the future of floods in the stream? About the future prospects for bass or trout?

I fear that our Phi Beta Kappa biologist would consider these questions insane, but they are not. Any amateur naturalist with a seeing eye should be able to speculate intelligently on all of them, and have a lot of fun doing it. You will see, too, that modern natural history deals only incidentally with the identity of plants and animals, and only incidentally with their habits and behaviors. It deals principally with their relations to each other, their relation to the soil and water in which they grow, and their relations to the human beings who sing about "my country" but see little or nothing of its inner workings. This new science of relationships is called ecology, but what we call it matters nothing. The question is, does the educated citizen know he is only a cog in an ecological mechanism? That if he will work with that mechanism his mental wealth and his material wealth can expand indefinitely? But that if he refuses to work with it, it will ultimately grind him to dust? If education does not teach us these things, then what is education for?

Natural History—The Forgotten Science (1938); RR 62–64

We need knowledge—public awareness—of the small cogs and wheels, but sometimes I think there is something we need even more. It is the thing that *Forest and Stream,* on its editorial masthead, once called "a refined taste in natural objects." Have we made any headway in developing a "refined taste in natural objects"?

Conservation (c. 1938); RR 149

We shall never achieve harmony with land, any more than we shall achieve justice or liberty for people. In these higher aspirations the important thing is not to achieve, but to strive. It is only in mechanical enterprises that we can expect that early or complete fruition of effort which we call "success."

The problem, then, is how to bring about a striving for harmony with land among a people many of whom have forgotten there is any such thing as land, among whom education and culture have become almost synonymous with landlessness. This is the problem of "conservation education."

When we say "striving," we admit at the outset that the thing we need must grow from within. No striving for an idea was ever injected wholly from without.

Conservation (c. 1938); RR 155–56

What conservation education must build is an ethical underpinning for land economics and a universal curiosity to understand the land mechanism. Conservation may then follow.

Conservation (c. 1938); RR 157

In selecting his major for undergraduate work, the [wildlife] student will encounter the question: What biological field offers the best "gateway" to professional training? There is no "best" that can be laid down for all individuals. It is desirable that the profession be recruited from majors in a wide variety of sciences and in the arts of land use. In general, some biological science is the best gateway to a career in research; some agricultural art (including forestry) to a career in policy or administration. It is a conspicuous fact, however, that men who are narrowly specialized, either by training or temperament, seldom occupy any large professional niche for very long.

Academic and Professional Training in Wildlife Work (1939)

In addition to academic preparation, the student should have attained, by his own efforts, considerable knowledge and field skill in some branch of natural history (such as ornithology, mammalogy, ichthyology, or botany). Animals, plants, and soils are the alphabet of wildlife management; in five years a good school can teach a student to spell words with it, but he must in some degree know his alphabet at the start.

Academic and Professional Training in Wildlife Work (1939)

The student who feels drawn to the outdoors but has never been impelled to undertake some systematic study of outdoor subjects *on his own account* should not expect a wildlife school to do it for him. That is to say, no wildlife school can make a professional man out of absolutely raw material in five years. Habitual self-teaching is a necessity.

Academic and Professional Training in Wildlife Work (1939)

. . . No institution can teach wildlife management of professional grade without land or water on which ecological experiments are being made, or on which the techniques of management are being tested. That is to say, a school must be practicing management and critically appraising its success before it can teach students to do likewise.

Academic and Professional Training in Wildlife Work (1939)

The student will do well, in selecting a school, to ask about the character of its faculty, its research output, its management areas, its library, and its reference collections, rather than about its buildings, its curricula, and its appropriations. These are the trappings of scholarship; they mean little without the scholarship itself.

Academic and Professional Training in Wildlife Work (1939)

Prudence never kindled a fire in the human mind; I have no hope for conservation born of fear. The 4-H boy who becomes curious about why red pines need more acid than white is closer to conservation than he who writes a prize essay on the dangers of timber famine.

The Farmer as a Conservationist (1939); RMG 258

What the student (and teacher!) now needs is a text which cuts at right angles to [the] arbitrary divisions of the land problem; a text which describes the common mechanism of soils, waters, plants and animals as one integral whole; a text which treats of farms, forests, ranges and parks not as different resources, but as different uses of a single resource, the properties of which are first described as a single system, and then traced in their various land-use manifestations.

Review of *Conservation in the United States* (1940)

A March morning is only as drab as he who walks in it without a glance skyward, ear cocked for geese. I once knew an educated lady, banded by Phi Beta Kappa, who told me that she had never heard or seen the geese that twice a year proclaim the revolving seasons to her well-insulated roof. Is education possibly a process of trading awareness for things of lesser worth? The goose who trades his is soon a pile of feathers.

When Geese Return Spring Is Here (1940); ASCA 18

Our educational system is such that white fringed orchis means as little to the modern citizen of Wisconsin as it means to a cow. Indeed it means less, for the cow at least sees something to eat, whereas the citizen sees only three meaningless words.

Exit Orchis (1940)

The salient characteristic of this book is a simple, lucid dignity of expression, free of "scientific" ambiguity, and devoid of ballyhoo. It lacks that listen-my-children-and-you-shall-hear note of patronage so objectionable in most sermons from on high.

Review of *This Is Our Land: The Story of Conservation in the United States* (1941)

A wildlife restoration plan is . . . a plan for educating landowners, private and public, to want wildlife, and to understand how their wants may be fulfilled. This may sound like propaganda, but the shoe is on the other foot. We must *undo* the propaganda, brought to bear on landowners for the last century, which teaches that the land is a factory to be operated solely for profit. The land is a factory, but it is also a place to live, and wildlife helps make it a good place.

What took a century to do cannot be undone in a decade. Education must begin at the bottom and work upward. The land-philosophy of agricultural schools and extension agencies must be turned inside out. Wildlife education is no separate thing; it is part and parcel of land-education, and of social philosophy.

Planning for Wildlife ms. (1941)

Botany, geography, geology, zoology, and even history can be understood only if the plant succession is understood. Yet how many "educated" persons, or even teachers, know the plant succession of their own back yards?

Planning for Wildlife ms. (1941)

Columbus surmised that it might be only a few days' walk across the continent to the richness of the China seas. His successors, the pioneers, took 350 years to break through to the Pacific. When they got there they found that the riches were not in the China seas at all, but on the continent they had explored en route.

Just so do we, the forerunners of ecological exploration, surmise that a few classes in "nature study" will lead us across to the riches of perception. Our successors, I hope, may find it a longer task. When they at least break through they may find that the riches lie not at their destination, but en route.

Wilderness Values (1941)

To learn the hydrology of the biotic stream we must think at right angles to evolution and examine the collective behavior of biotic materials. This calls for a reversal of specialization; instead of learning more and more about less and less, we must learn more and more about the whole biotic landscape.

The Round River—A Parable (c. 1941); RR 159

One of the penalties of an ecological education is that one lives alone in a world of wounds. Much of the damage inflicted on land is quite invisible to laymen. An ecologist must either harden his shell and make believe that the consequences of science are none of his business, or he must be the doctor who sees the marks of death in a community that believes itself well and does not want to be told otherwise.

The Round River—A Parable (c. 1941); RR 165

The bulk of our funds and brains are invested in professional education. In my opinion it is time to "swap ends" to curtail sharply the output of professionals, and to throw the manpower and dollars thus released into a serious attempt to tell the whole campus, and thus eventually the whole community, what wildlife conservation is all about.

The Role of Wildlife in a Liberal Education (1942); RMG 301

Liberal education in wildlife is not merely a dilute dosage of technical education. It calls for somewhat different teaching materials and sometimes even different teachers. The objective is to teach the student to see the land, to understand what he sees, and enjoy what he understands. I say land rather than wildlife, because wildlife cannot be understood without understanding the landscape as a whole. Such teaching could well be called land ecology rather than wildlife, and could serve very broad educational purposes.

Perhaps the most important of these purposes is to teach the student how to put the sciences together in order to use them. All the sciences and arts are taught as if they were separate. They are separate only in the classroom. Step out on the campus and they are immediately fused. Land ecology is putting the sciences and arts together for the purpose of understanding our environment. . . .

With such a synthesis as a starting point, the tenets of conservation formulate themselves almost before the teacher can suggest them.

The Role of Wildlife in a Liberal Education (1942); RMG 302–3

There is a prevalent assumption that conservation education is making headway, albeit slowly. It is assumed that if we reach good people with good educational materials, that good results will follow. I wonder if this does not over-simplify the problem.

Post-war Prospects (1944)

Acts of conservation without the requisite desires and skills are futile. To create these desires and skills, and the community motive, is the task of education.

Conservation: In Whole or in Part? (1944); RMG 319

Herein lies the tragedy of modern land-use education. We have spent several generations teaching the farmer that he is not obligated to do anything on or to his land that is not profitable to him as an individual. We can thank his neglect and inertia, and perhaps the hollow sound of our own voice, for the survival of such useless plants and animals, and such natural soils and waters, as remain alive today.

The Land-Health Concept and Conservation ms. (1946)

I am trying to teach you that this alphabet of "natural objects" (soils and rivers, birds and beasts) spells out a story, which he who runs may read— if he knows how. Once you learn to read the land, I have no fear of what you will do to it, or with it. And I know many pleasant things it will do to you.

Wherefore Wildlife Ecology? (1947); RMG 337

Despite nearly a century of propaganda, conservation still proceeds at a snail's pace; progress still consists largely of letterhead pieties and convention oratory. On the back forty we still slip two steps backward for each forward stride.

The usual answer to this dilemma is "more conservation education." No one will debate this, but is it certain that only the *volume* of education needs stepping up? Is something lacking in the *content* as well?

It is difficult to give a fair summary of its content in brief form, but, as I understand it, the content is substantially this: obey the law, vote right, join some organizations, and practice what conservation is profitable on your own land; the government will do the rest.

Is not this formula too easy to accomplish anything worth-while? It defines no right or wrong, assigns no obligation, calls for no sacrifice, implies no change in the current philosophy of values. In respect of land-use, it urges only enlightened self-interest. Just how far will such education take us?

The Ecological Conscience (1947); ASCA 207–8; cf. RMG 338

We speak glibly of conservation education, but what do we mean by it? If we mean indoctrination, then let us be reminded that it is just as easy to indoctrinate with fallacies as with facts. If we mean to teach the capacity for independent judgment, then I am appalled by the magnitude of the task.

The Ecological Conscience (1947); RMG 343

The ecological conscience . . . is an affair of the mind as well as the heart. It implies a capacity to study and learn, as well as to emote about the problems of conservation.

The Ecological Conscience (1947); RMG 343

Tell me of what plant-birthday a man takes notice, and I shall tell you a good deal about his vocation, his hobbies, his hay fever, and the general level of his ecological education.

Prairie Birthday (1949); ASCA 44

My dog . . . thinks I have much to learn about partridges, and, being a professional naturalist, I agree. He persists in tutoring me, with the calm patience of a professor of logic, in the art of drawing deductions from an educated nose. I delight in seeing him deduce a conclusion, in the form of a point, from data that are obvious to him, but speculative to my unaided eye. Perhaps he hopes his dull pupil will one day learn to smell.

Like other dull pupils, I know when the professor is right, even though I do not know why. . . . Like any good professor, the dog never laughs when I miss, which is often. He gives me just one look, and proceeds up the stream in quest of another grouse.

Red Lanterns (1949); ASCA 63–64

When I call to mind my earliest impressions, I wonder whether the process ordinarily referred to as growing up is not actually a process of growing down; whether experience, so much touted among adults as the thing children lack, is not actually a progressive dilution of the essentials by the trivialities of living.

Red Legs Kicking (1949); ASCA 120

Education, I fear, is learning to see one thing by going blind to another.

Clandeboye (1949); ASCA 158

... The education actually in progress makes no mention of obligations to land over and above those dictated by self-interest. The net result is that we have more education but less soil, fewer healthy woods, and as many floods as in 1937.

The Land Ethic (1949); ASCA 209

One of the requisites for an ecological comprehension of land is an understanding of ecology, and this is by no means co-extensive with "education"; in fact, much higher education seems deliberately to avoid ecological concepts. An understanding of ecology does not necessarily originate in courses bearing ecological labels; it is quite as likely to be labeled geography, botany, agronomy, history, or economics. This is as it should be, but whatever the label, ecological training is scarce.

The Land Ethic (1949); ASCA 224

The evolution of a land ethic is an intellectual as well as an emotional process. Conservation is paved with good intentions which prove to be futile, or even dangerous, because they are devoid of critical understanding either of the land, or of economic land-use. I think it is a truism that as the ethical frontier advances from the individual to the community, its intellectual content increases.

The Land Ethic (1949); ASCA 225

18   ARTS AND SCIENCES

᭝

Between Imagination and Observation

Gary Paul Nabhan

Within an hour of watching the mating "sky dance" of the woodcock for the very first time, I leaned back against an oak trunk near the Illinois-Wisconsin border and read Leopold's essay about this very same avian ritual.[1] And I was astonished.

Like many readers before and since, I was astonished not merely by the scientific precision of his phenomenological descriptions, but by their artfulness as well. Could it be, I wondered, that both good field science and fine art are rooted in the same medium, the ecotone between the cultivated skill of careful observation and the wilds of the human imagination?

Leopold spent his life in such ecotones, roaming between Iowa's croplands and its remnant prairies; between Wisconsin's dairy farms and their sandy, untended margins; between the Southwest's yellow pine forests and its ancient agricultural terraces. He somehow came to feel as comfortable at Yale as he did hunting quail, and to read deer tracks with as much interest as he did the classic literature of the Western world.

A century before Leopold, Henry David Thoreau was often frustrated in his attempts at understanding nineteenth-century natural science while maintaining a transcendentalist poet's world view: "What sort of science," he asked, "is that which enriches the understanding but robs the imagination?" He worried that his own detailed scientific observations of plant dispersal and animal behavior made for dull reading. One critic agreed, claiming that Thoreau's "views as wide as heaven" had been "narrowed down to the microscope," as he had feared.[2]

Leopold, on the other hand, seldom doubted that artistic prose was compatible with astute scientific observation. He was delighted whenever he found such dovetailing in the works of his colleagues. Rigorously trained in the scientific method, but having always read widely in other fields, he gradually integrated more and more imaginative elements into his natural history writing. Leopold's narrative prose fully blossomed late in his life, after he had fully established his credibility as a scientist with countless data-laden, expository articles. Perhaps for that reason, he could say that science was not enough if it stood alone—that to approach a full understanding of the world, its ethical, poetic, and spiritual dimensions must be fully integrated. Long-practiced in writing expressively to his mother, other family members, friends, and colleagues, Leopold then turned his skills as a storyteller toward reaching a larger audience.

Leopold was not the only scientist-writer of his era to do so: Donald Culross Peattie, Edwin Way Teale, Paul Errington, Ed Ricketts, John Steinbeck, Loren Eiseley, G. Evelyn Hutchinson, Archie Carr, Vladimir Nabokov, Rachael Carson, Edgar Anderson, and Carl Sauer were also adept at finding in the natural sciences metaphors which illuminated the human condition. They too were eloquent spokespersons for the wild world around them. But perhaps none grounded his or her personal philosophy in such a profound understanding of the structure and function of natural communities.

It is because of his eminence as a scientist-philosopher as well as his grace as a writer that Leopold, more than any of these other literary scientists, enabled the next generation of scientists to explore their poetic voices without apology. Leopold's prose legitimized the position that a competent scientist should be sanctioned to write persuasively and gracefully in many styles, for many audiences, if indeed his or her subject matter really "matters." In this sense Leopold's heirs are many, from David Ehrenfeld, E. O. Wilson, Stephen Jay Gould, and Jared Diamond to Wes Jackson, Richard Nelson, and David Quammen.

Recent studies confirm what Leopold intuitively understood and exemplified: that narrative stories are not only more interesting to students than didactic, expository texts covering the same topics, but that stories have greater staying power and evoke more activism. Story is one of the most effective means we have for keeping the complexity of the natural world in our heads. If the biophilia hypothesis is ever rigorously tested, will cognitive scientists confirm that we are hard-wired to understand more natural history as story than as baldly posited facts in computer-generated graphic models or as mathematical theory? Read Leopold's tales from *Sand County*, then juxtapose them with any quantitatively oriented text on wildlife management, then write me in a year to tell me what you remember of both.

All this said, it would be inaccurate to summarize Leopold's legacy as having merely "paved the way" for other scientists to write more evocative narratives from the field, for in a sense he did the exact opposite. Instead, he invited them to get off the well-traveled roads of scientific discourse and to explore uncharted territory, where an animal's lingering scent might clue us into the presence of significant lives hidden nearby.

If science cannot lead us to wisdom as well as power, it is surely no science at all.

Leopold in his office at the University of Wisconsin, c. 1940. (Photo by Robert A. McCabe. Courtesy Aldo Leopold Foundation)

A man may make a splendid start in life by knowing his business, but before he climbs the ladder very far it becomes even more important that he know men—all kinds of men. But in general he can really know only as many kinds of men as he himself is. Hence the thousands of single-track minds that climb a rung or two and stop, because they know too much business and too little humanity.

A Man's Leisure Time ms. (1920)

Supposing there were no longer any painting, or poetry, or goose music? It is a black thought to dwell upon, but it must be answered. In dire necessity somebody might write another *Iliad*, or paint an "Angelus," but fashion a goose?. . .

. . . If . . . we can live without goose music, we may as well do away with stars, or sunsets, or *Iliads*. But the point is that we would be fools to do away with any of them.

Goose Music (c. 1922); RR 170–71

. . . It is the essence of both sportsmanship and science habitually to doubt our own ability to truly understand all that we see in nature.

The American Game Policy on Predators ms. (1932)

. . . The biological mechanism of population increase . . . is one of those "scientific" subjects which cannot be concisely described except by means of tables and graphs, but the lay reader should not allow his unfamiliarity with these seemingly dry forms of expression to becloud his realization of the music inherent in their columns and curves. These are, in fact, the code symbols wherewith we may reconstruct the score of a great symphony. Education may be considered a success, and conservation an assured fact, when both layman and scientist can shift their attention from the symbol to the music—can hear with John Muir "every cell in a swirl of enjoyment, humming like a hive, singing the old new song of creation."

Game Management (1933), 38

Does the lay reader, perchance, regard these "properties" [of wild populations] as dry science, of small consequence to one who simply loves the living bird or beast? Let him pause before so deciding. "Love," if we mean by that word something more than mere reaction to hormones and instincts, implies an effort to understand. Can we understand wild things without understanding their properties? The blind personification of animals, commonly known as nature-faking, arises from failure to face this question.

Game Management (1933), 48–49

One of the anomalies of modern ecology is that it is the creation of two groups, each of which seems barely aware of the existence of each other. The one studies the human community almost as if it were a separate entity, and calls its findings sociology, economics, and history. The other studies the plant and animal community [and] comfortably relegates the hodge-podge of politics to "the liberal arts." The inevitable fusion of these two lines of thought will, perhaps, constitute the outstanding advance of the present century.

Wilderness ms. (c. 1935)

I do not know whether the nesting pairs [of thick-billed parrots] are as noisy as these roistering flocks that greeted me in September. I do know that in September, if there are parrots on the mountain, you will soon know it. As a proper ornithologist, I should doubtless try to describe the call. It superficially resembles that of the piñon jay, but the music of the pinoneros is as soft and nostalgic as the haze hanging in their native canyons, while that of the Guacamaja is louder and full of the salty enthusiasm of high comedy.

The Thick-billed Parrot in Chihuahua (1937); ASCA 139–40

One of the unmistakable trends of the last decade has been the recognition of complex interactions among soils, waters, plants and animals, with a corresponding interdependence among the earth sciences and the agricultural arts.

Review of *Our Natural Resources and Their Conservation* (1937)

. . . To own an otter range carries (to my mind) the same public responsibility as to own a piece by Phidias or Michael Angelo. . . .

The otter has been a rarity for so long that neither science nor art has touched him. His life history, his evolution as a species, his psychology, his physiology, are virgin fields for scientific inquiry, and the interpretation of his remarkable "personality" is a virgin field for literature and art. [Henry] Williamson in his "Tarka the Otter" has made a start toward literary interpretation. Only the beaver and the buffalo outrank the otter as "personifications" of American history.

Report on Huron Mountain Club (1938)

One of the self-imposed yokes we are casting off is the false idea that farm life is dull. What is the meaning of John Steuart Curry, Grant Wood, Thomas Benton? They are showing us drama in the red barn, the stark silo, the team heaving over the hill, the country store, black against the sunset. All I am saying is that there is also drama in every bush, if you can see it. When enough men know this, we need fear no indifference to the welfare of bushes, or birds, or soil, or trees. We shall then have no need of the word conservation, for we shall have the thing itself.

The Farmer as a Conservationist (1939); RMG 263

There are men charged with the duty of examining the construction of the plants, animals, and soils which are the instruments of the great orchestra. These men are called professors. Each selects one instrument and spends his life taking it apart and describing its strings and sounding boards. This process of dismemberment is called research. The place for dismemberment is called a university.

A professor may pluck the strings of his own instrument, but never that of another, and if he listens for music he must never admit it to his fellows or to his students. For all are restrained by an ironbound taboo which decrees that the construction of instruments is the domain of science, while the detection of harmony is the domain of poets.

Professors serve science and science serves progress. It serves progress so well that many of the more intricate instruments are stepped upon and broken in the rush to spread progress to all backward lands. One by one the parts are thus stricken from the songs of songs. If the professor is able to classify each instrument before it is broken, he is well content.

Science contributes moral as well as material blessings to the world. Its great moral contribution is objectivity, or the scientific point of view. This means doubting everything except facts; it means hewing to the facts, let the chips fall where they may. One of the facts hewn to by science is that every river needs more people, and all people need more inventions, and hence more science; the good life depends on the indefinite extension of this chain of logic. That the good life on any river may likewise depend on the perception of its music, and the preservation of some music to perceive, is a form of doubt not yet entertained by science.

Song of the Gavilan (1940); ASCA 153–54

We are attempting to manage wildlife, but it is by no means certain that we shall succeed, or that this will be our most important contribution to the design for living.

For example, we may, without knowing it, be helping to write a new definition of what science is for.

We are not scientists. We disqualify ourselves at the outset by professing loyalty to and affection for a thing: wildlife. A scientist in the old sense may have no loyalties except to abstractions, no affections except for his own kind.

The State of the Profession (1940); RMG 276

The definitions of science written by, let us say, the National Academy, deal almost exclusively with the creation and exercise of power. But what about the creation and exercise of wonder, of respect for workmanship in nature? I see hints of such dissent, even in the writings of the scientifically elect—Fraser Darling, for example. Of course, we have always had such writers (David, Isaiah, John Muir) but they were not scientifically elect; they were only poets.

The State of the Profession (1940); RMG 276

I daresay few wildlife managers have any intent or desire to contribute to art and literature, yet the ecological dramas which we must discover if we are to manage wildlife are inferior only to the human drama as subject matter for the fine arts. . . .

There are straws which indicate that this senseless barrier between science and art may one day blow away, and that wildlife ecology, if not wildlife management, may help do the blowing. . . . In our profession, and on its fringes, are a growing number of painters and photographers who are also researchers. These intergrades in human taxonomy are perhaps more important than those which so perplex the mammalogists and ornithologists. Their skulls are not yet available to the museums, but even a layman can see that their brains are distinctive.

The State of the Profession (1940); RMG 277

Not the least merit of [this] volume is its simplicity and clarity. The reader is never befuddled, nor is he forced to swallow any needless ecological jargon. (One might even conclude that the absence of such jargon is becoming an earmark of ecological competence. The works of Charles Elton, Fraser Darling, and Margaret Nice would likewise support such a view.)

Review of *The Birds of Buckeye Lake, Ohio* (1940)

No "language" adequate for portraying the land mechanism exists in any science or art, save only ecology. A language is imperative, for if we are to guide land-use we must talk sense to farmer and economist, pioneer and poet, stockman and philosopher, lumberjack and geographer, engineer and historian.

Biotic Land Use ms. (c. 1940)

If science cannot lead us to wisdom as well as power, it is surely no science at all.

Ecology and Politics (1941); RMG 284

The most convincing proof that ecological perception has not yet spread beyond the self-erected walls of science lies in the fact that there is as yet no expression of ecological drama in art or literature. [Donald Culross] Peattie's novel, A Prairie Grove, is proof that ecology may, some day, escape into the common life of common people.

Wilderness Values (1941)

Who is the land? We are, but no less the meanest flower that blows. Land ecology discards at the outset the fallacious notion that the wild community is one thing, the human community another.

What are the sciences? Only categories for thinking. Sciences can be taught separately, but they can't be used separately, either for seeing land or doing anything with it. It was a surprise to me to find this was "news" to many well-trained but highly specialized graduate students.

What is art? Only the drama of the land's workings.

> The Role of Wildlife in a Liberal Education (1942); RMG 303

Every farm woodland, in addition to yielding lumber, fuel, and posts, should provide its owner a liberal education. This crop of wisdom never fails, but it is not always harvested.

> A Lesson from the Woodlands (1943); ASCA 73

. . .We are now confronted by the fact, known at least to a few, that wars are no longer won; the concept of top dog is now a myth; all wars are lost by all who wage them; the only difference between participants is the degree and kind of losses they sustain. The reason for this change is obvious: science has so sharpened the fighter's sword that it is impossible for him to cut his enemy without cutting himself.

My central thesis is that a parallel situation exists in our war with nature.

> The Biotic War ms. (c. 1944)

Reading [*One Day on*] *Beetle Rock* reminds me, as a forester, that our profession has not yet produced a respectable biography of a tree or a stand. I hope some day to see both. Certainly the ecology of a forest is drama of the first water. Certainly there are many foresters who know this, even though they do not admit it in public. The false partition between science and art is being breached in other professions; why not in ours? *Beetle Rock* is one of these breaches; it is good ecology and good literature.

> Review of *One Day on Beetle Rock* (1945)

This is no popularized account of the fox squirrel in the obnoxious sense, but rather a forthright exposition of a forthright piece of thinking. Perhaps an honest ham does not need to be tenderized to be palatable.

> Review of *Michigan Fox Squirrel Management* (1945)

The divorcement of things practical from things beautiful, and the relegation of either to specialized groups or institutions, has always been lethal to social progress, and now it threatens the land-base on which the social structure rests. The fallacy has its roots in an imperfect view of growth. All sciences, arts, and philosophies are converging lines; what seems separate today is fused tomorrow. Tomorrow we shall find out that no land unnecessarily mutilated is useful. . . .

> The Land-Health Concept and Conservation ms. (1946)

Art and science are separate pigeonholes of God's desk. Men achieve greatness by guessing the contents of one or the other, but never of both. What would be achieved by guessing the contents of both to be identical? I don't know. I'd like to see someone try it.

Ecology and the Arts ms. (c. 1946)

Many of the events of the annual cycle recur year after year in a regular order. A year-to-year record of this order is a record of the rates at which solar energy flows to and through living things. They are the arteries of the land. By tracing their responses to the sun, phenology may eventually shed some light on that ultimate enigma, the land's inner workings.

Yet it must be confessed that with all its weighty subject-matter, phenology is a very personal sort of science. Once he learns the sequence of events, the phenologist falls easily into the not-very-objective role of successful seer and prophet. He may even fall in love with the plants and animals which so regularly fulfil his predictions, and he may harbor the pleasant illusion that he is "calling shots" for the biota, rather than vice versa.

A Phenological Record for Sauk and Dane Counties, Wisconsin, 1935–1945 (1947)

Among contemporary phenologists are botanists, foresters, game managers, ornithologists, range managers, and zoologists. Phenology . . . is a "horizontal science" which transects all ordinary biological professions. Whoever sees the land as a whole is likely to have an interest in it.

A Phenological Record for Sauk and Dane Counties, Wisconsin, 1935–1945 (1947)

Modern technology has much to answer for in the ruthless destruction of natural beauty, but even the most jaundiced observer of technical "progress" must admit that in such photography as Mr. [Edgar M.] Queeny's, beauty becomes immortal. Bird motions so rapid that they are not even visible to the unaided eye are here portrayed for leisurely enjoyment throughout the year. I cannot avoid the conclusion that perhaps the only vicious thing in modern technology is the kind of people who wield its gadgets, and think they are civilized for this reason.

Review of *Prairie Wings: Pen and Camera Flight Studies* (1947)

Time was when the aim of science was to understand the world, and to learn how man may live in harmony with it. If I read Darwin right, he was more concerned with understanding than with power. But science, as now decanted for public consumption, is mainly a race for power.

Science has no respect for the land as a community of organisms, no concept of man as a fellow passenger in the odyssey of evolution.

On a Monument to the Passenger Pigeon (1947)

That land is a community is the basic concept of ecology, but that land is to be loved and respected is an extension of ethics. That land yields a cultural harvest is a fact long known, but latterly often forgotten.

These essays attempt to weld these three concepts.

Foreword to *A Sand County Almanac* (1949); ASCA viii–ix

19 LAND ESTHETICS

≉

Through Successive Stages
of the Beautiful

Joni L. Kinsey

The land ethic was, in many ways, Aldo Leopold's crowning achievement. Although it proposes a radical reconception of traditional relationships, the ethic is based on a remarkably simple premise: that humans are members of the land community who must respect the existence of their "fellow-members"[1]—other living things—and the common environment upon which all depend for sustenance and survival. Leopold's genius lay not only in the formulation of the idea, but in its vehicle: an exceptionally engaging and accessible book that charms as it instructs, inspires even as it sobers. As the quotations in this volume illustrate, the same quality was evident in much of Leopold's other writing as well.

For all of its simplicity in form and fundamental message, Leopold's writing was remarkably complex. Just as Leopold could find within a single crane, flower, or tree, a world of telling nuance and significance, so too do his proposals and his writing reveal within their concise precision a web of understanding, both of human action and perception and of the natural world and its workings.

Leopold's writing, in *Sand County* and elsewhere, drew upon his broad experience in many aspects of land management, both personal and professional. It is informed prominently of course by the natural sciences. No less integral, however, to its persuasive power and compelling elegance is Leopold's ability to draw on psychology, philosophy, and esthetics—all interrelated humanistic disciplines—allowing him to convey to his readers the importance of his ideas and observations in their own lives. Of these, esthetics may be at once the most and least appreciated, for it lies at both the surface of his writing and at the heart of his message.

The most commonly recognized aspect of esthetics—the visual—especially marks the essays of *A Sand County Almanac*. In the book's first part, the "almanac" itself, Leopold overtly observes his surroundings over the course of a year. Every element is seen and many described with a wealth of visual detail. Every page conjures pictures of great variety, color, texture, and shape, from the smallest leaf to the most panoramic scene. Leopold also employs motifs from the esthetic world. He sees a river, for example, as an artist painting the landscape as it provides successive layers of colors, textures, and shapes of plants and animal tracks: "It is a river who wields the brush, and it is the same river who, before I can bring my friends to view his work, erases it forever from human view. After that it exists only in my mind's eye."[2]

Sound is another esthetic which both fascinates and preoccupies Leopold. Although he often appreciates the "music" of nature for its own sake, in other instances he characterizes it in strikingly visual terms: "What one remembers is the invisible hermit thrush pouring silver chords from impenetrable shadows; the soaring crane trumpeting from behind a cloud; the prairie chicken booming from the mists of nowhere; the quail's Ave Maria in the hush of dawn."[3] Here Leopold describes sounds as coloristic effects, "silver chords from impenetrable shadows," but even more intriguing is the intangibility of their presence. The observed is, ironically, unseen, but all the more memorable for its invisibility.

Leopold does not neglect other esthetic creations in his observations, finding poetry, for example, in the smallest aspects of natural life: "whereas I *write* a poem by dint of mighty cerebration, the yellow-leg *walks* a better one just by lifting his foot."[4] Such eloquent articulations of common events in the natural world are the most easily appreciated aspects of Leopold's work. He knew that he had to engage his audience, walking with them from their first observations to their fullest recognitions: "Our ability to perceive quality in nature begins, as in art, with the pretty. It expands through successive stages of the beautiful to values as yet uncaptured by language."[5]

But beauty is not only in details or even in sweeping vistas. Leopold's most important contribution to esthetics may be in his appreciation of landscapes usually considered ordinary or even worthless. His own worn-out plot in central Wisconsin offers him endless encounters with the extraordinary, and he consistently affirms the special qualities of bogs, marshes, and prairies, seeing the mysteries of life even in backyard weeds. In this, as Roderick Nash has argued, he is the heir to Thoreau, who found at Walden Pond a lifetime of instruction.[6] Leopold's landscapes are varied, as he takes us through the sand counties, the Southwest, the forests, and the mountains, but he never values one landscape more than another. He even suggests that humble sites are more rewarding than the conventionally beautiful, if only because they require more effort to see fully: "In country, as in people, a plain exterior often conceals hidden riches, to perceive which requires much living in and with."[7] It is an object lesson for anyone who deals in the esthetics of landscape.

Perception, the fundamental act of esthetics, is of great concern to Leopold, for only through the development of this faculty can the truth and imperative of the land ethic be realized and acted upon. Relating it to the growth of parkland sightseeing he wrote, "It is the expansion of transport without a corresponding growth of perception that threatens us with qualitative bankruptcy of the recreational process. Recreational development is a job not of building roads into lovely country, but of building receptivity into the still unlovely human mind."[8] In this deceptively pragmatic statement Leopold is obviously referring to recreation not only in the sense of nature tourism, but also as re-creation, the act of restoring and rejuvenating the fullness of life to both the seer and the seen.

Perceptive insight is not always, or even usually, the purview of the well educated. Leopold notes that "the Ph.D. [in ecology] may become as callous as an undertaker to the mysteries at which he officiates"; that "the weeds in a city lot convey the same lesson as the redwoods"; that "the farmer may see in his cow-pasture what may not be vouchsafed to the scientist adventuring in the South Seas"; that "perception . . . cannot be purchased with either learned degrees or dollars."[9] Both a gentle reminder to his better educated readers that they still had things to learn and a reassurance to those less well-read, this humbling passage also reinforces a central theme of the land ethic: that as a mystery and a treasure, the biota is infinitely fine from its smallest element to its fullest totality.

For all of his emphasis on the role of beauty in perceiving the natural world, Leopold recognized that relying on this alone to convey the importance and universality of the land ethic would limit the effect of its message. Scientists, economists, land developers, government officials— those who most need the idea (and many of whom still haven't gotten it)—would especially dismiss such a book as sentimental musing. To speak to them Leopold drew upon his extensive expertise as a forester, wildlife manager, and professor. He balanced personal reflections with more prosaic observations and facts to help his less esthetically inclined readers recognize the "values yet uncaptured" by language, economics, and science.

These values are, it seems, recognition of the elegant interrelationship of each and every element within the biota, and awe at the workings of that integrated whole and our role within it. In order to more fully envision this, Leopold recognized in "The Land Ethic," the reader needed "some mental image of land as a biotic mechanism."[10] He adopted here the ecological notion of land as a pyramidal structure comprised of layers of interdependent elements and species, webs of food chains, "a tangle . . . so complex as to seem disorderly, yet the stability of the system proves it to be a highly organized structure. Its functioning depends on the co-operation and competition of its diverse parts."[11] Nothing so much as a *great design,* Leopold's image of the biota could be equally appreciated by artists, scientists, economists, and mechanics.

Removing one of the parts or altering the power dynamic within the community of life begins the slow deterioration of the whole. In his essay "Guacamaja" Leopold explained this through the concept of beauty: "Everybody knows . . . that the autumn landscape in the north woods is the land, plus a red maple, plus a ruffed grouse. In terms of conventional physics, the grouse represents only a millionth of either the mass or the energy of an acre. Yet subtract the grouse and the whole thing is dead. An enormous amount of some kind of motive power has been lost."[12] Thus the beauty of the living world lies not only in the particular loveliness of the grouse itself, but in the unity of the life force of which it is an essential part. This is quite obviously a higher level in Leopold's "successive stages" of beauty than the merely pretty.

The culmination of these stages, the Whole, is only glimpsed through sustained contemplation, but that fleeting glance captures the essence of the land ethic. Leopold caught such a glance in the mountains of Mexico: "on a still night, when the campfire is low and the Pleiades have climbed over rimrocks, sit quietly and listen for a wolf to howl, and think hard of everything you have seen and tried to understand. Then you may hear it—a vast pulsing harmony—its score inscribed on a thousand hills, its notes the lives and deaths of plants and animals, its rhythms spanning the seconds and the centuries."[13] Although such epiphanies are subtle and rare, Leopold believed that they are available to even average seekers. In fact, it is to these individuals that he ascribes the most power in their relationships with the land: "it is hard for us to visualize a creative art of land-beauty which is the prerogative, not of esthetic priests but of dirt farmers, which deals not with plants but with biota, and which wields not only spade and pruning shears, but also draws rein on those invisible forces which determine the presence or absence of plants and animals."[14]

The culminating expression of Leopold's esthetic came in the closing pages of the *Almanac:* "We can be ethical only in relation to something we can see, feel, understand, love, or otherwise have faith in."[15] All of these responses, with the possible exception of faith (although that too can be argued), are basically esthetic. Sight and touch are obviously sensory. Understanding is a consequence of thoughtful perception and insight. And love, as a passion, is one of the fundamental consequences of esthetic contemplation, as philosophers since Plato have recognized. Esthetic tools provide the means by which we perceive the object of our affection and arouse our response to it.

For Leopold esthetics were as important to understanding nature and our role in it as science. His oft-cited criteria for an ethical relationship with land are especially telling: "Examine each question in terms of what is ethically and *esthetically* right, as well as what is economically expedient.

A thing is right when it tends to preserve the integrity, stability, and *beauty* of the biotic community. It is wrong when it tends otherwise."[16] This was not a soft-headed sentiment but a statement of respect for the great design of which we are a part.

Our ability to perceive quality in nature begins, as in art, with the pretty. It expands through successive stages of the beautiful to values as yet uncaptured by language.

Leopold taking a photograph at the University of Missouri, 1938. (Photo by Charles W. Schwartz. Courtesy University of Wisconsin–Madison Archives)

⊯

. . . Some people persist in the odd notion that recreation is derived only from motor roads and scenery. They don't know that for some of us there can be more scenery in a flock of teal than in a flock of Yosemites, or at any rate that the scenery alone is a pretty sad affair unless it contains some fur, fins or feathers.

The Posting Problem (1922)

Poets sing and hunters scale the mountains primarily for one and the same reason—the thrill to beauty. Critics write and hunters outwit their game primarily for one and the same reason—to reduce that beauty to possession.

Goose Music (c. 1922); RR 170–71

What value has wildlife from the standpoint of morals and religion? I heard of a boy once who was brought up an atheist. He changed his mind when he saw that there were a hundred-odd species of warblers, each bedecked like to the rainbow, and each performing yearly sundry thousands of miles of migration about which scientists wrote wisely but did not understand. No "fortuitous concourse of elements" working blindly through any number of millions of years could quite account for why warblers are so beautiful. No mechanistic theory, even bolstered by mutations, has ever quite answered for the colors of the cerulean warbler, or the vespers of the woodthrush, or the swansong, or—goose music. I dare say this boy's convictions would be harder to shake than those of many inductive theologians.

Goose Music (c. 1922); RR 171

A few months ago somebody discovered that the Bursum Bill raised the question of possible disintegration of the Pueblo Indian communes. A booster editor, commenting on the situation, coolly pointed out that the tourist-getting value of the Indians depended on their distinctive culture, which should therefore be preserved until our industrial development made it no longer possible to do so. This was, I hope, the ultimate impertinence of boosterism in the Southwest. That the Indian culture and ours should have been placed in competition for the possession of this country was inevitable, but the cool assumption that this last little fragment must necessarily disappear in order that an infinitesimal percentage of soot, bricks, and dollars may be added to our own, betrays a fundamental disrespect for the Creator, who made not only boosters, but mankind, in his image.

A Criticism of the Booster Spirit (1923); RMG 102

. . . The measure of civilization is in its contrasts. A modern city is a national asset, not because the citizen has planted his iron heel on the breast of nature, but because of the different kinds of man his control over nature has enabled him to be. . . . If, once in a while, he has the opportunity to flee the city, throw a diamond hitch upon a packmule, and disappear into the wilderness of the Covered Wagon Days, he is just that much more civilized than he would be without the opportunity. It makes him one more kind of a man—a pioneer.

Conserving the Covered Wagon (1925); RMG 129

In all the category of outdoor vocations and outdoor sports there is not one, save only the tilling of the soil, that bends and molds the human character like wilderness travel. Shall this fundamental instrument for building citizens be allowed to disappear from America, simply because we lack the vision to see its value? Would we rather have the few paltry dollars that could be extracted from our remaining wild places than the human values they can render in their wild condition?

The Last Stand of the Wilderness (1925)

Wild nature is only one generation behind us here—in Europe centuries have elapsed. Aesthetic standards of living are, I suppose, more or less delimited in their range by the actualities of experience.

Game Methods: The American Way (1931); RMG 158

. . . There is hardly an acre [of the Rio Grande watershed] that does not tell its own story to those who understand the speech of hills and rivers.

The Virgin Southwest (1933); RMG 175

. . . It is hard for us to visualize a creative art of land-beauty which is the prerogative, not of esthetic priests but of dirt farmers, which deals not with plants but with biota, and which wields not only spade and pruning shears, but also draws rein on those invisible forces which determine the presence or absence of plants and animals.

The Conservation Ethic (1933); RMG 191

We of the industrial age boast of our control over nature. Plant or animal, star or atom, wind or river—there is no force in earth or sky which we will not shortly harness to build "the good life" for ourselves.

But what is the good life? Is all this glut of power to be used for only bread-and-butter ends? Man cannot live by bread, or Fords, alone. Are we too poor in purse or spirit to apply some of it to keep the land pleasant to see, and good to live in?

Preface to *Game Management* (1933), xxxi

Biological science, if it had no economic import at all, would nevertheless be justified by its enrichment of the human faculty for observation. Jason, Eric, Magellan, Daniel Boone, saw only the cover of the Great Book. Its free translation is the unique privilege of post-Darwinian explorers.

Game Management (1933), 388

We might, if we chose to spend the money, release each year millions of artificially reared birds, and thus "maintain" a supply of game in the quantitative sense. But would we thus maintain value? I think not.

Game Management (1933), 392

The economic determinist regards the land as a food-factory. Though he sings "America" with patriotic gusto, he concedes any factory the right to be as ugly as need be, provided only it be efficient.

There is another faction which regards economic productivity as an unpleasant necessity, to be kept, like a kitchen, out of sight. Any encroachment on the "parlor" of scenic beauty is quickly resented, sometimes in the name of conservation.

There is a third, and still smaller, minority with which game management, by its very essence, is inevitably aligned. It denies that kitchens or factories need be ugly, or farms lifeless, in order to be efficient.

That ugliness which the first faction welcomes as the inevitable concomitant of progress, and which the second regretfully accepts as a necessary compromise, the third rejects as the clumsy result of poor technique, bunglingly applied by a human community which is morally and intellectually unequal to the consequences of its own success.

These are simply three differing conceptions of man's proper relation to the fruitfulness of the earth: three different ideas of productivity. Any practical citizen can understand the first conception, and any esthete the second, but the third demands a combination of economic, esthetic, and biological competence which is somehow still scarce.

It would, of course, be absurd to say that the first two attitudes are devoid of truth. It seems to be an historical fact, however, that such few "adjustments" as they have accomplished have not kept pace with the accelerating disharmony between material progress and natural beauty. Even the noble indignation of the second school has been largely barren of any positive progress toward a worthier land-use.

Quite evidently we are confronted with a conflict of priorities—a philosophical problem of "what it is all about." Our moral leaders are so far not concerned with this issue. . . .

. . . Examples of harmonious land-use are the need of the hour.

Game Management (1933), 420–22

Is it a rosy dream to envisage the ultimate emergence of an American system [of conservation], founded upon ecological science, unencumbered by too much history, utilizing to the utmost our basic advantage of elbow-room, and so integrated with our sociology and economics as to perpetuate indefinitely the opportunity for contact with natural beauty? It seems to me not a dream, but a challenge.

Review of *Notes on German Game Management* (1934)

When some old rattletrap of a building catches fire we all rush to the rescue, but when the compound interest of 10,000 years of plants catches fire, our officials sit by with folded hands while the average citizen's depth of understanding is reflected by the observation that he dislikes the smell of peat smoke.

What Is the University of Wisconsin Arboretum? ms. (c. 1934)

The unprecedented velocity of land-subjugation in America involved much hardship, which in turn created traditions which ignore esthetic land uses. The subsequent growth of cities has permitted a re-birth of esthetic culture, but in landless people who have no opportunity to apply it to the soil. The large volume and low utility of conservation legislation may be attributed largely to this maladjustment; also the dissentious character of the conservation movement.

Land Pathology (1935); RMG 214

Parks are over-crowded hospitals trying to cope with an epidemic of esthetic rickets; the remedy lies not in hospitals, but in daily dietaries. The vast bulk of land beauty and land life, dispersed as it is over a thousand hills, continues to waste away under the same forces as are undermining land utility. The private owner who today undertakes to conserve beauty on his land does so in defiance of all man-made economic forces from taxes down—or up. There is much beauty left—animate and inanimate—but its existence, and hence its continuity, is almost wholly a matter of accident.

Land Pathology (1935); RMG 216

The physics of beauty is one department of natural science still in the Dark Ages. Not even the manipulators of bent space have tried to solve its equations. Everybody knows, for example, that the autumn landscape in the north woods is the land, plus a red maple, plus a ruffed grouse. In terms of conventional physics, the grouse represents only a millionth of either the mass or the energy of an acre. Yet subtract the grouse and the whole thing is dead. An enormous amount of some kind of motive power has been lost.

It is easy to say that the loss is all in our mind's eye, but is there any sober ecologist who will agree? He knows full well that there has been an ecological death, the significance of which is inexpressible in terms of contemporary science. A philosopher has called this imponderable essence the *numenon* of material things. It stands in contradistinction to *phenomenon,* which is ponderable and predictable, even to the tossings and turnings of the remotest star.

The Thick-billed Parrot in Chihuahua (1937); ASCA 137–38

Our ability to perceive quality in nature begins, as in art, with the pretty. It expands through successive stages of the beautiful to values as yet uncaptured by language. The quality of cranes lies, I think, in this higher gamut, as yet beyond the reach of words.

This much, though, can be said: our appreciation of the crane grows with the slow unraveling of earthly history. His tribe, we now know, stems out of the remote Eocene. The other members of the fauna in which he originated are long since entombed within the hills. When we hear his call we hear no mere bird. We hear the trumpet in the orchestra of evolution. He is the symbol of our untamable past, of that incredible sweep of millennia which underlies and conditions the daily affairs of birds and men.

And so they live and have their being—these cranes—not in the constricted present, but in the wider reaches of evolutionary time. Their annual return is the ticking of the geologic clock. Upon the place of their return they confer a peculiar distinction. Amid the endless mediocrity of the commonplace, a crane marsh holds a paleontological patent of nobility, won in the march of aeons, and revocable only by shotgun. The sadness discernible in some marshes arises, perhaps, from their once having harbored cranes. Now they stand humbled, adrift in history.

Marshland Elegy (1937); ASCA 96–97

Recreation is commonly spoken of as an economic resource. Senate committees tell us, in reverent ciphers, how many millions the public spends in its pursuit. It has indeed an economic aspect—a cottage on a fishing-lake, or even a duck-point on a marsh, may cost as much as the entire adjacent farm.

It has also an ethical aspect. In the scramble for unspoiled places, codes and decalogues evolve. We hear of "outdoor manners." We indoctrinate youth. We print definitions of "What is a sportsman?" and hang a copy on the wall of whosoever will pay a dollar for the propagation of the faith.

It is clear, though, that these economic and ethical manifestations are results, not causes, of the motive force. We seek contacts with nature because we derive pleasure from them. As in opera, economic machin-

ery is employed to create and maintain facilities. As in opera, professionals make a living out of creating and maintaining them, but it would be
false to say of either that the basic motive, the *raison d'être*, is economic.
The duck-hunter in his blind and the operatic singer on the stage, despite the disparity of their accoutrements, are doing the same thing.
Each is reviving, in play, a drama formerly inherent in daily life. Both
are, in the last analysis, esthetic exercises.

Conservation Esthetic (1938); ASCA 167–68

We come now to another component [of outdoor recreation]: the
perception of the natural processes by which the land and the living
things upon it have achieved their characteristic forms (evolution) and
by which they maintain their existence (ecology). That thing called "nature study," despite the shiver it brings to the spines of the elect, constitutes the first embryonic groping of the mass-mind toward perception.

The outstanding characteristic of perception is that it entails no consumption and no dilution of any resource.

Conservation Esthetic (1938); ASCA 173

Let no man jump to the conclusion that Babbitt must take his Ph.D.
in ecology before he can "see" his country. On the contrary, the Ph.D.
may become as callous as an undertaker to the mysteries at which he
officiates. Like all real treasures of the mind, perception can be split into
infinitely small fractions without losing its quality. The weeds in a city lot
convey the same lesson as the redwoods; the farmer may see in his cow-
pasture what may not be vouchsafed to the scientist adventuring in the
South Seas. Perception, in short, cannot be purchased with either
learned degrees or dollars; it grows at home as well as abroad, and he
who has a little may use it to as good advantage as he who has much.
As a search for perception, the recreational stampede is footless and
unnecessary.

Conservation Esthetic (1938); ASCA 174

Our grandfathers did not, could not, know the origin of their prairie
empire. They killed off the prairie fauna and they drove the flora to a
last refuge on railroad embankments and roadsides. To our engineers
this flora is merely weeds and brush; they ply it with grader and mower.
Through processes of plant succession predictable by any botanist, the
prairie garden becomes a refuge for quack grass. After the garden is
gone, the highway department employs landscapers to dot the quack
with elms, and with artistic clumps of Scotch pine, Japanese barberry,
and Spiraea. Conservation Committees, en route to some important
convention, whiz by and applaud this zeal for roadside beauty.

Conservation (c. 1938); RR 148

The mere propagation of biological facts, however interesting, is sterile unless those facts are woven into the cultural pattern of the community. There are other new "threads" which must be woven in at the same time, else the wildlife threads lose much of their significance. Some of these are

1. A sense of history
2. A sense of art

These are dangerous words because, in the sterile educational system of today, they convey the idea that the farmer should be *reading* history and should be *taught* esthetics. The exact opposite is truth. Every farmer, willy-nilly, is *writing* history, and *painting* a new landscape for Wisconsin. The only question is whether he is aware of it, and whether he is critical of the result.

> Improving the Wildlife Program of the Soil Conservation Service ms. (1940)

The song of a river ordinarily means the tune that waters play on rock, root, and rapid. . . .

This song of the waters is audible to every ear, but there is other music in these hills, by no means audible to all. To hear even a few notes of it you must first live here for a long time, and you must know the speech of hills and rivers. Then on a still night, when the campfire is low and the Pleiades have climbed over rimrocks, sit quietly and listen for a wolf to howl, and think hard of everything you have seen and tried to understand. Then you may hear it—a vast pulsing harmony—its score inscribed on a thousand hills, its notes the lives and deaths of plants and animals, its rhythms spanning the seconds and the centuries.

> Song of the Gavilan (1940); ASCA 149

John Muir, who grew up amid the prairie flowers in Columbia County, foresaw their impending disappearance from the Wisconsin landscape. In about 1865 he offered to buy from his brother a small part of the meadow of the family homestead, to be fenced and set aside as a floral sanctuary or reservation. His offer was refused. I imagine that his brother feared not so much the loss of a few square rods of pasture as he feared the ridicule of his neighbors.

> Exit Orchis (1940)

That wildlife is merely something to shoot at or to look at is the grossest of fallacies. It often represents the difference between rich country and mere land.

> Country (1941); RR 32

The taste for country displays the same diversity in aesthetic competence among individuals as the taste for opera, or oils. There are those who are willing to be herded in droves through "scenic" places; who find mountains grand if they be proper mountains, with waterfalls, cliffs, and lakes. To such the Kansas plains are tedious. They see the endless corn, but not the heave and the grunt of ox teams breaking the prairie. History, for them, grows on campuses. They look at the low horizon, but they cannot see it, as de Vaca did, under the bellies of the buffalo.

In country, as in people, a plain exterior often conceals hidden riches, to perceive which requires much living in and with.

Country (1941); RR 32–33

Gadgets . . . are of slight consequence. What matters is our ability to see the land as an organism. Most civilized men do not realize that science, in enabling us to see land as an organism, has given us something far more valuable than motors, radios, and television. It is the intellectual exploration of land, including aboriginal land or wilderness, that constitutes the frontier of the present century. Unless we can see the full gamut of landscapes from wild to tame, we lose a part of our explorer's birthright.

Wilderness Values (1941)

One dead weight which depresses perception is the false belief that higher perception means studies rather than sports. We administrators do our best to perpetuate this fallacy by delegating educational functions to nonsporting people. As a matter of fact there is no higher or more exciting sport than that of ecological observation. If anyone doubts this, let him read Fraser Darling's Wild Country, Naturalist on Rona, or A Herd of Red Deer.

This same false cleavage between studies and sports explains why the Natural Area Committee of the Ecological Society does not cooperate with the Wilderness Society, though both are asking for the perpetuation of wilderness. "Serious" ecological studies of a professional nature are, of course, important, and they of course have a place in wilderness areas. The fallacy lies in the assumption that all ecology must be professional, and that wilderness sports and wilderness perception are two things rather than one. Good professional research in wilderness ecology is destined to become more and more a matter of perception; good wilderness sports are destined to converge on the same point. A sportsman is one who has the propensity for perception in his bones. Trigger itch, wanderlust, and buck fever are simply the genetical raw materials out of which perception is built.

Wilderness Values (1941)

. . . Just watch the fence posts. Soon a flash of silver will tell you on which post the plover has alighted and folded his long wings. Whoever invented the word "grace" must have seen the wing-folding of the [up-land] plover.

The Plover Is Back from Argentine (1942); ASCA 34

The other day I noticed, on the front lawn of a successful doctor, a mountain ash tree in process of strangulation by a wire which had been wrapped around it years ago. The doctor passes within three feet of this tree four times a day. He either has not seen the wire, or he has no concept of a tree as a living thing, or he attaches no value to the tree, or he fears that a rusty wire might soil his gloves. This doctor would instantly detect, and act upon, any human body similarly threatened, nor would he spare gloves in doing so. My guess is that he, as an "economic man," has outgrown any consciousness of land, plants, or animals, except perhaps during the hunting season, when he shows brief interest in game birds.

Post-war Prospects (1944)

From the beginnings of history, people have searched for order and meaning in [the sequence of natural] events, but only a few have discovered that keeping records enhances the pleasure of the search, and also the chance of finding order and meaning.

A Phenological Record for Sauk and Dane Counties, Wisconsin, 1935–1945 (1947)

That there is some basic fallacy in present-day conservation is shown by our response to it. Instead of living it, we turn it over to bureaus. Even the landowner, who has the best opportunity to practice it, thinks of it as something for government to worry about.

I think I know what the fallacy is. It is the assumption, clearly borrowed from modern science, that the human relation to land is only economic. It is, or should be, esthetic as well. In this respect our present culture, and especially our science, is false, ignoble, and self-destructive.

If the individual has a warm personal understanding of land, he will perceive of his own accord that it is something more than a breadbasket. He will see land as a community of which he is only a member, albeit now the dominant one. He will see the beauty, as well as the utility, of the whole, and know the two cannot be separated. We love (and make intelligent use of) what we have learned to understand.

Wherefore Wildlife Ecology? (1947); RMG 337

For one species to mourn the death of another is a new thing under the sun. The Cro-Magnon who slew the last mammoth thought only of steaks. The sportsman who shot the last pigeon thought only of his prowess. The sailor who clubbed the last auk thought of nothing at all. But we, who have lost our pigeons, mourn the loss. Had the funeral been ours, the pigeons would hardly have mourned us. In this fact, rather than in Mr. DuPont's nylons or Mr. Vannevar Bush's bombs, lies objective evidence of our superiority over the beasts.

On a Monument to the Passenger Pigeon (1947); ASCA 110

Daniel Boone had a stand of game to make any hunter's mouth water. Let us assume he had ten times as good a one as you or I have. Did he therefore have ten times as good a return from his day afield? I say no, because he had only a meagre understanding of wildlife. He had superlative skill in hunting, but the existence of wild things he accepted with as little thought as you or I accept the existence of a cloud, a breeze, or a sunset.

The wildlife crop, since Daniel Boone's day, has gone down, but the same scientific progress that brought about the decline has also added constantly to our understanding of wildlife, and hence to its value to us. Wildlife, to Boone, had only meat or trophy value.

Boone knew what a species was, but science itself did not then know where species came from. He had no inkling of distribution except within Virginia and Kentucky.

Boone knew migration, but he did not know that the April plover piping among his buffalo had just arrived from the pampas, and would next week pipe among the muskoxen on the tundra.

Boone knew predation, but he never guessed that it benefited the prey as well as the predator; he had no concept of the intricate interdependence of wild things. To him, as to other pioneers, the only good varmint was a dead one.

Boone, like others of his time, construed all animal behaviors as acts of volition; this is proved by his imputation of guilt or innocence to animals. Innate behavior patterns, as presently understood, were then still a century in the offing.

Lastly, Boone had no inkling that the trillium he stepped upon had an evolutionary history as long as his own, and a *modus vivendi* as dramatic, and perhaps as important, as that of any buffalo, or Indian, or pioneer.

In short, Daniel Boone had little of that understanding of wild things which we possess, or are free to possess, today. It has grown on us so gradually that we are not conscious of it, or aware of how much it has added to the value of a day afield. Still less are we aware that its growth has only begun.

The primary purpose of wildlife research is, in my view, to develop and expand this understanding of the biotic drama. It must, of course, contrive also to keep wildlife on the map, in good quantity, and in as much diversity as possible.

Why and How Research? (1948)

It is the sole remnant of this plant along this highway, and perhaps the sole remnant in the western half of our county. What a thousand acres of Silphiums looked like when they tickled the bellies of the buffalo is a question never again to be answered, and perhaps not even asked.

Prairie Birthday (1949); ASCA 45

I know a painting so evanescent that it is seldom viewed at all, except by some wandering deer. It is a river who wields the brush, and it is the same river who, before I can bring my friends to view his work, erases it forever from human view. After that it exists only in my mind's eye.

Like other artists, my river is temperamental; there is no predicting when the mood to paint will come upon him, or how long it will last. But in midsummer, when the great white fleets cruise the sky for day after flawless day, it is worth strolling down to the sandbars just to see whether he has been at work.

The Green Pasture (1949); ASCA 51

There is a peculiar virtue in the music of elusive birds. Songsters that sing from top-most boughs are easily seen and as easily forgotten; they have the mediocrity of the obvious. What one remembers is the invisible hermit thrush pouring silver chords from impenetrable shadows; the soaring crane trumpeting from behind a cloud; the prairie chicken booming from the mists of nowhere; the quail's Ave Maria in the hush of dawn.

The Choral Copse (1949); ASCA 53

To arrive too early in the marsh is an adventure in pure listening; the ear roams at will among the noises of the night, without let or hindrance from hand or eye. When you hear a mallard being audibly enthusiastic about his soup, you are free to picture a score guzzling among the duck-weeds. When one widgeon squeals, you may postulate a squadron without fear of visual contradiction. And when a flock of bluebills, pitching pondward, tears the dark silk of heaven in one long rending nose-dive, you catch your breath at the sound, but there is nothing to see except stars.

Too Early (1949); ASCA 61

One day I buried myself, prone, in the muck of a muskrat house. While my clothes absorbed local color, my eyes absorbed the lore of the marsh. A hen redhead cruised by with her convoy of ducklings, pink-billed fluffs of greenish-golden down. A Virginia rail nearly brushed my nose. The shadow of a pelican sailed over a pool in which a yellow-leg alighted with warbling whistle; it occurred to me that whereas I *write* a poem by dint of mighty cerebration, the yellow-leg *walks* a better one just by lifting his foot.

Clandeboye (1949); ASCA 160

We can be ethical only in relation to something we can see, feel, understand, love, or otherwise have faith in.

The Land Ethic (1949); ASCA 214

Your true modern is separated from the land by many middlemen, and by innumerable physical gadgets. He has no vital relation to it; to him it is the space between cities on which crops grow. Turn him loose for a day on the land, and if the spot does not happen to be a golf links or a "scenic" area, he is bored stiff. If crops could be raised by hydroponics instead of farming, it would suit him very well. Synthetic substitutes for wood, leather, wool, and other natural land products suit him better than the originals. In short, land is something he has "outgrown."

The Land Ethic (1949); ASCA 223–24

By and large, our present problem is one of attitudes and implements. We are remodeling the Alhambra with a steam-shovel, and we are proud of our yardage. We shall hardly relinquish the shovel, which after all has many good points, but we are in need of gentler and more objective criteria for its successful use.

The Land Ethic (1949); ASCA 225–26; cf. The Conservation Ethic (1933); RMG 185

20 LAND ETHICS

☙

Into Terra Incognita
J. Baird Callicott

A new subdiscipline in philosophy called "environmental ethics" made its debut in the early 1970s in response to the realization, dawning over us in the previous decade, that the natural environment was in a state of crisis. I seem to have offered the first course in the subject at the University of Wisconsin–Stevens Point in 1971. *A Sand County Almanac* was then practically the only text available for such a course (and a quarter century later it remains at the core of the syllabus for my current offering in the field). The first sentence of the first academic paper in the field, "Is There a Need for a New, an Environmental Ethic?," cited "The Land Ethic."[1] If that paper had been written by me, the fact would not be noteworthy. But it was written by Australian philosopher Richard Sylvan (then Routley) and presented to the Fifteenth World Congress of Philosophy in Varna, Bulgaria, in 1973. Aldo Leopold's ideas were steadily making their way into formal philosophical discourse in North America, Australia, and Europe.

In retrospect, other amateur (I use this word not condescendingly, but more literally to indicate a nonprofessional labor of love) philosophers were also seminal in the eventual flowering forth of academic environmental ethics, most notably Henry David Thoreau and John Muir. But Aldo Leopold stands out even in this august company as steering environmental ethics into uncharted waters, or, to shift metaphors apropos the land ethic, into terra incognita. As Sylvan noted, Leopold envisioned an "ethic dealing with man's relation to land and to the animals and plants which grow upon it."[2] This was, as Sylvan explained, virtually unprecedented in the annals of Western moral philosophy (and Sylvan had to extend his own expository powers to the utmost just to articulate it). Heretofore all Western ethics had dealt exclusively with man's relation to his fellow man. If the land and the animals and plants that grow upon it had figured into such traditional ethics at all, it was as property or as the stage upon which the human morality play was acted out. Aldo Leopold made it possible for academic philosophers to imagine the possibility of a *nonanthropocentric* environmental ethic.

Another feature of Leopold's vision of a land ethic was also foreign, if not to all previous Western ethics, at least to all the modern versions thereof. Modern moral philosophy is not only anthropocentric; it is concerned exclusively with human individuals—their rights, interests, happiness, and welfare—not with wholes. A society, community, state, or nation is a mere aggregate of individual human beings, the welfare or happiness of which is the sum total of that of the constituent persons. This is why many people steeped in the radical individualism of modern Western ethics can view Leopold as a hypocrite, since he was an unregenerate hunter. But Leopold, viewing land through the lens of ecology, thought of the integrity, stability, and beauty of a biotic community as something transcending the aggregate of the rights, interests, happiness, and welfare of the plants, animals, soils, and waters that compose it. The land ethic is, in a word, *holistic* as well as nonanthropocentric. According to the land ethic, the right of the individual member of the biotic community to life, liberty, and the pursuit of happiness is subordinate to the integrity, stability, and beauty of the community as such. The land ethic, as Leopold sketched it, grants species the "right to continued existence," whereas a specimen warrants only respect. The lot of individual creatures is to "suck hard, live fast, and die often."[3]

To say, then, that Leopold has set an agenda for research in environmental ethics for decades, perhaps even centuries, to come would be no exaggeration. For centuries past, philosophers have been searching for reasons why we should morally enfranchise other human beings. Human beings are created in the image of God, we are uniquely rational, we are uniquely autonomous, we are presumptive signatories to an implicit social contract . . . By what parity of reasoning should we morally enfranchise fellow members of the biotic community and the community as such? Leopold appears to advocate such an extension of ethics, and hints at how it might be justified, but the complete brief for a nonanthropocentric environmental ethic has yet to be filed.

And when conflicts arise, why should the integrity, stability, and beauty of the biotic community trump the life, liberty, and pursuit of happiness of one of its members? Why should innocent deer, for example, be killed to protect the integrity of a forest? Leopold appears to advocate giving priority to the integrity of the whole over the welfare of the part, and hints at how it may be justified, but the complete brief for a holistic environmental ethic has yet to be filed.

Supposing that a holistic nonanthropocentric environmental ethic can be convincingly developed, how can we make an exception of ourselves, as, certainly, Leopold would? We too are "plain member[s] and citizen[s]" of the biotic community;[4] why then should we tolerate, any more than we would an overpopulation of deer, a human overpopulation that threatens the integrity of the biotic community, or deal with the problem any differently? Leopold seems to champion the superiority of human interests, rights, and welfare when they conflict with the integrity, stability, and beauty of the biotic community, but the relationship between holistic nonanthropocentric environmental ethics and individualistic anthropocentric social ethics has not been fully explored or adequately explained.

There are other problems that Leopold has put on the research agenda of environmental philosophy. "The Land Ethic" is the culmination of a larger work devoted to a single overarching goal: bringing its reader around to an evolutionary-ecological view of the world. Part I of *A Sand County Almanac* presents that world view personally, experientially, descriptively, locally, concretely, and immediately. Part II presents it conceptually, abstractly, universally, and impersonally. Part III, "The Upshot," explores the axiological implications of such a worldview—its esthetic and ethical implications. But modern philosophy divorces "fact" and "value." In light of this shibboleth how can science inform, or indeed, as Leopold suggests, *transform* our ways of valuing the world? And even assuming that this philosophical obstacle to Leopold's project in the *Almanac* can be avoided, science, like the world it describes, is dynamic. Today's science is tomorrow's myth. Leopold based his land ethic on the latest developments in ecology . . . fifty years ago. Have changes in ecology over the last half century undermined the land ethic?

The land ethic is an enduring source of wisdom for structuring our human relationship with land and the animals and plants that grow upon it. The reader who consults this section of this volume will find answers to many of his or her land ethical questions in these quotations. But more important, I think—and what really makes these words so enduring and beguiling—is not the answers they give but the questions they evoke.

We abuse land because we regard it as a commodity belonging to us. When we see land as a community to which we belong, we may begin to use it with love and respect.

Leopold indicating growth in planted red pine, c. 1947. (Photo by Robert A. McCabe. Courtesy University of Wisconsin–Madison Archives)

Many of the world's most penetrating minds have regarded our so-called "inanimate nature" as a living thing, and probably many of us who have neither the time nor the ability to reason out conclusions on such matters by logical processes have felt intuitively that there existed between man and the earth a closer and deeper relation than would necessarily follow the mechanistic conception of the earth as our physical provider and abiding place.

Of course, in discussing such matters we are beset on all sides with the pitfalls of language. The very words *living thing* have an inherited and arbitrary meaning derived not from reality, but from human perceptions of human affairs. But we must use them for better or for worse.

Some Fundamentals of Conservation in the Southwest (1923); RMG 94

[The Russian philosopher Piotr Ouspensky] states that it is at least not impossible to regard the earth's parts—soil, mountains, rivers, atmosphere, etc.—as organs, or parts of organs, of a coordinated whole, each part with a definite function. And, if we could see this whole, as a whole, through a great period of time, we might perceive not only organs with coordinated functions, but possibly also that process of consumption and replacement which in biology we call the metabolism, or growth. In such a case we would have all the visible attributes of a living thing, which we do not now realize to be such because it is too big, and its life processes too slow. And there would also follow that invisible attribute—a soul, or consciousness—which not only Ouspensky, but many philosophers of all ages, ascribe to all living things and aggregations thereof, including the "dead" earth.

There is not much discrepancy, except in language, between this conception of a living earth, and the conception of a dead earth, with enormously slow, intricate, and interrelated functions among its parts, as given us by physics, chemistry, and geology. The essential thing for present purposes is that both admit the interdependent functions of the elements.

> Some Fundamentals of Conservation in the Southwest (1923); RMG 95

. . . Conservation is not merely a thing to be enshrined in outdoor museums, but a *way of living on land;* . . . it must ultimately prevail on all lands, public and private, or go down in history as a pleasant but futile pipe-dream.

> Game Cropping in Southern Wisconsin (1927)

We can say this: That what we call "development" is not a unidirectional process, especially in a semi-arid country. To develop this land we have used engines that we could not control, and have started actions and reactions far different from those intended. Some of these are proving beneficial; most of them harmful. This land is too complex for the simple processes of "the mass-mind" armed with modern tools. To live in real harmony with such a country seems to require either a degree of public regulation we will not tolerate, or a degree of private enlightenment we do not possess.

But of course we must continue to live with it according to our lights. Two things hold promise of improving those lights. One is to apply science to land-use. The other is to cultivate a love of country a little less spangled with stars, and a little more imbued with that respect for mother-earth—the lack of which is, to me, the outstanding attribute of the machine-age.

> The Virgin Southwest (1933); RMG 179–80

Some scientists will dismiss this matter [of conservation ethics] forth-with, on the ground that ecology has no relation to right and wrong. To such I reply that science, if not philosophy, should by now have made us cautious about dismissals. An ethic may be regarded as a mode of guid-ance for meeting ecological situations so new or intricate, or involving such deferred reactions, that the path of social expediency is not dis-cernible to the average individual. Animal instincts are just this. Ethics are possibly a kind of advanced social instinct in-the-making.

Whatever the merits of this analogy, no ecologist can deny that our land-relation involves penalties and rewards which the individual does not see, and needs modes of guidance which do not yet exist. Call these what you will, science cannot escape its part in forming them.

The Conservation Ethic (1933); RMG 182

We of the machine age admire ourselves for our mechanical ingenu-ity; we harness cars to the solar energy impounded in carboniferous for-ests; we fly in mechanical birds; we make the ether carry our words or even our pictures. But are these not in one sense mere parlor tricks com-pared with our utter ineptitude in keeping land fit to live upon?

The Conservation Ethic (1933); RMG 184

[Some regard] conservation as a kind of sacrificial offering, made for us vicariously by bureaus, on lands nobody wants for other purposes, in propitiation for the atrocities which still prevail everywhere else. We have made a real start on this kind of conservation, and we can carry it as far as the tax-string on our leg will reach. Obviously, though, it con-serves our self-respect better than our land. Many excellent people ac-cept it, either because they despair of anything better, or because they fail to see the *universality of the reactions needing control.* That is to say their ecological education is not yet sufficient.

The Conservation Ethic (1933); RMG 187–88

We can, it seems, stomach the burning or plowing-under of over-produced cotton, coffee, or corn, but the destruction of mother-earth, however "sub-marginal," touches something deeper, some sub-economic stratum of the human intelligence wherein lies that something—per-haps the essence of civilization—which [Woodrow] Wilson called "the decent opinion of mankind."

The Conservation Ethic (1933); RMG 189

To build a better motor we tap the uttermost powers of the human brain; to build a better countryside we throw dice. Political systems take no cognizance of this disparity, offer no sufficient remedy. There is, how-ever, a dormant but widespread consciousness that the destruction of land, and of the living things upon it, is wrong. A new minority have espoused an idea called conservation which tends to assert this as a positive principle. Does it contain seeds which are likely to grow?

The Conservation Ethic (1933); RMG 189

Every countryside proclaims the fact that we have, today, less control in the field of conservation than in any other contact with surrounding nature. We patrol the air and the ether, but we do not keep filth out of our creeks and rivers. We stand guard over works of art, but species representing the work of aeons are stolen from under our noses. We stamp out the diseases of crops and livestock, but we do not know what ails the grouse, or the ducks, or the antelope. In a certain sense we are learning more rapidly about the fires that burn in the spiral nebulae than those that burn in our forests. We aspire to build a mechanical cow before we know how to build a fishway, or control a flood, or handle a woodlot so it will produce a cover of grouse.

Game Management (1933), xxxi

The game manager manipulates animals and vegetation to produce a game crop. This, however, is only a superficial indication of his social significance. What he really labors for is to bring about a new attitude toward the land.

Game Management (1933), 420

Herein lies the social significance of game management. It promulgates no doctrine, it simply asks for land and the chance to show that farm, forest, and wild life products can be grown on it, to the mutual advantage of each other, of the landowner, and of the public. It proposes a motivation—the love of sport—narrow enough actually to get action from human beings as now constituted, but nevertheless capable of expanding with time into that new social concept toward which conservation is groping.

In short, twenty centuries of "progress" have brought the average citizen a vote, a national anthem, a Ford, a bank account, and a high opinion of himself, but not the capacity to live in high density without befouling and denuding his environment, nor a conviction that such capacity, rather than such density, is the true test of whether he is civilized. The practice of game management may be one of the means of developing a culture which will meet this test.

Game Management (1933), 422–23

There must be born in the public mind a certain fundamental respect for living things, and for the epic grandeur of the processes which created them. Society must see itself not as the terrestrial end-result of a completed evolution, but as the custodian of an incompleted one. In its ultimate analysis, the conservation movement may prove to be a denial of anthropocentric philosophies.

The real threat to the future of "Outdoor America" lies not in the agencies which destroy it, but in the multiplication of people who think they can live without it.

The Social Consequences of Conservation ms. (c. 1933)

For twenty centuries and longer, all civilized thought has rested upon one basic premise: that it is the destiny of man to exploit and enslave the earth.

The biblical injunction to "go forth and multiply" is merely one of many dogmas which imply this attitude of philosophical imperialism.

During the past few decades, however, a new science called ecology has been unobtrusively spreading a film of doubt over this heretofore unchallenged "world view." Ecology tells us that no animal—not even man—can be regarded as independent of his environment.

The Arboretum and the University (1934); RMG 209

What can the social and physical sciences . . . do toward hastening the needed adjustment between society as now equipped, and land-use as now practiced? . . .

In my opinion, there are two possible forces which might operate *de novo,* and which universities might possibly create by research. One is the formulation of mechanisms for protecting the public interest in private land. The other is the revival of land esthetics in rural culture.

The further refinement of remedial practices is equally important, but need not here be emphasized because it already has some momentum.

Out of these three forces may eventually emerge a land ethic more potent than the sum of the three, but the breeding of ethics is as yet beyond our powers. All science can do is safeguard the environment in which ethical mutations might take place.

Land Pathology (1935); RMG 214–15

Every American has tattooed on his left breast the basic premise that manifestations of economic energy are inherently beneficent. Yet there is one which to me seems malignant, not inherently, but because a good thing has outrun its limits of goodness. We learn, in ecology at least, that all truths hold only within limits. Here is a good thing—the improvement in economic tools. It has exceeded the speed, or degree, within which it was good. Equipped with this excess of tools, society has developed an unstable adjustment to its environment, from which both must eventually suffer damage or even ruin. Regarding society and land collectively as an organism, that organism has suddenly developed pathological symptoms, i.e. self-accelerating rather than self-compensating departures from normal functioning. The tools cannot be dropped, hence the brains which created them, and which are now mostly dedicated to creating still more, must be at least in part diverted to controlling those already in hand. Granted that science can invent more and more tools, which might be capable of squeezing a living even out of a ruined countryside, yet who wants to be a cell in that kind of a body politic? I for one do not.

Land Pathology (1935); RMG 217

. . . We seem ultimately always thrown back on individual ethics as the basis of conservation policy. It is hard to make a man, by pressure of law or money, do a thing which does not spring naturally from his own personal sense of right or wrong.

Conservationist in Mexico (1937); RMG 243–44, ALS 207

The real substance of conservation lies not in the physical projects of government, but in the mental processes of citizens. The road in park or forest is not the thing; what matters is where and for what the park-visitor or forest-user wants roads. The acreage bought for public parks or forests is not the thing; what matters is whether private landowners regard their forests and their landscapes as a public trust. The fire put out by a CCC crew is not the thing; what matters is whether people are careless with fire in the woods. The can of fish dumped is not the thing; what matters is the attitude of the fisherman toward the public resource he is privileged to harvest. The sheep grazing permit is not the thing; what matters is whether the sheepman knows or cares that he is helping to build the Great American Desert. The sawlog sold is not the thing; what matters is whether the citizen who buys a board or a newspaper knows or cares where it comes from, knows or cares whether it is the product of exploitation or land-cropping. The regulation on ducks is not the thing; what matters is whether the duck hunter is ashamed or proud to bequeath to his sons a duckless, marshless continent, and if ashamed, whether this in any wise affects his trigger-finger. Lastly and most important, the check-dam in a farmer's gully is not the thing; what matters is whether a social stigma attaches to the ownership of a gullied farm; whether the farmer realizes that to leave behind a fertile, stable, and beautiful farmstead is in these days a greater and more difficult achievement than to endow a hospital or found an industry.

Conservation Blueprints (1937)

The engineer has respect for mechanical wisdom because he created it. He has disrespect for ecological wisdom, not because he is contemptu-

ous of it, but because he is unaware of it. We have, in short, two professions whose responsibilities for land use overlap much, but whose respective zones of awareness overlap only a little.

Engineering and Conservation (1938); RMG 253

We end, I think, at what might be called the standard paradox of the
twentieth century: our tools are better than we are, and grow better
faster than we do. They suffice to crack the atom, to command the tides.
But they do not suffice for the oldest task in human history: to live on a
piece of land without spoiling it.

Engineering and Conservation (1938); RMG 254

Conservationists have, I fear, adopted the pedagogical method of the
prophets: we mutter darkly about impending doom if people don't
mend their ways. The doom is impending, all right; no one can be an
ecologist, even an amateur one, without seeing it. But do people mend
their ways for fear of calamity? I doubt it. They are more likely to do it
out of pure curiosity and interest.

Natural History—The Forgotten Science (1938); RR 64

Conservation is a state of harmony between men and land. By land is
meant all of the things on, over, or in the earth. Harmony with land is
like harmony with a friend; you cannot cherish his right hand and chop
off his left. That is to say, you cannot love game and hate predators; you
cannot conserve the waters and waste the ranges; you cannot build the
forest and mine the farm. The land is one organism. Its parts, like our
own parts, compete with each other and co-operate with each other.
The competitions are as much a part of the inner workings as the co-
operations. You can regulate them—cautiously—but not abolish them.

Conservation (c. 1938); RR 145–46

When one considers the prodigious achievements of the profit motive
in wrecking land, one hesitates to reject it as a vehicle for restoring land.
I incline to believe we have overestimated the scope of the profit motive.
Is it profitable for the individual to build a beautiful home? To give his
children a higher education? No, it is seldom profitable, yet we do both.
These are, in fact, ethical and aesthetic premises which underlie the economic system. Once accepted, economic forces tend to align the smaller
details of social organization into harmony with them.

No such ethical and aesthetic premise yet exists for the condition of
the land these children must live in. Our children are our signature to
the roster of history; our land is merely the place our money was made.
There is as yet no social stigma in the possession of a gullied farm, a

wrecked forest, or a polluted stream, provided the dividends suffice to send the youngsters to college. Whatever ails the land, the government will fix it.

Conservation (c. 1938); RR 156–57

Sometimes I think that ideas, like men, can become dictators. We Americans have so far escaped regimentation by our rulers, but have we escaped regimentation by our own ideas? I doubt if there exists today a more complete regimentation of the human mind than that accomplished by our self-imposed doctrine of ruthless utilitarianism. The saving grace of democracy is that we fastened this yoke on our own necks, and we can cast it off when we want to, without severing the neck. Conservation is perhaps one of the many squirmings which foreshadow this act of self-liberation.

The Farmer as a Conservationist (1939); RMG 259

With a truer picture of the biota, the scientist might take his tongue out of his cheek, the layman might be less insistent on utility as a prerequisite for conservation, more hospitable to the "useless" cohabitants of the earth, more tolerant of values over and above profit, food, sport, or tourist-bait. Moreover, we might get better advice from economists and philosophers if we gave them a truer picture of the biotic mechanism.

A Biotic View of Land (1939); RMG 267

The combined evidence of history and ecology seems to support one general deduction: the less violent the man-made changes [in the land], the greater the probability of successful readjustment in the [biotic] pyramid. Violence, in turn, varies with human population density; a dense population requires a more violent conversion. . . .

This deduction runs counter to our current philosophy, which assumes that because a small increase in density enriched human life, that an indefinite increase will enrich it indefinitely. Ecology knows of no density relationship that holds for indefinitely wide limits. All gains from density are subject to a law of diminishing returns.

A Biotic View of Land (1939); ASCA 220; cf. RMG 270–71

Our profession began with the job of producing something to shoot. However important this may seem to us, it is not very important to the emancipated moderns who no longer feel soil between their toes.

We find that we cannot produce much to shoot until the landowner changes his ways of using land, and he in turn cannot change his ways until his teachers, bankers, customers, editors, governors, and trespassers change their ideas about what land is for. To change ideas about what land is for is to change ideas about what anything is for.

Thus we started to move a straw, and end up with the job of moving a mountain.

The State of the Profession (1940); RMG 280

Conservation, viewed in its entirety, is the slow and laborious unfolding of a new relationship between people and land.

Wisconsin Wildlife Chronology (1940)

Ecology is a science that attempts [the] feat of thinking in a plane perpendicular to Darwin. Ecology is an infant just learning to talk, and, like other infants, is engrossed with its own coinage of big words. Its working days lie in the future. Ecology is . . . a belated attempt to convert our collective knowledge of biotic materials into a collective wisdom of biotic navigation. This, in the last analysis, is conservation.

The Round River—A Parable (c. 1941); RR 159

Conservation is our attempt to put human ecology on a permanent footing.

Land-Use and Democracy (1942); RMG 298

Conservation is a state of health in the land-organism. Health expresses the cooperation of the interdependent parts: soil, water, plants, animals, and people. It implies collective self-renewal and collective self-maintenance.

When any one part lives by depleting another, the state of health is gone. As far as we know, the state of health depends on the retention in each part of the full gamut of species and materials comprising its evolutionary equipment.

Culture is a state of awareness of the land's collective functioning. A culture premised on the destructive dominance of a single species can have but short duration.

Land-Use and Democracy (1942); RMG 300

It seems to me unlikely that land-abuses will be stopped by any conceivable extension of present conservation policies. They are good as far as they go, but in most cases they go only far enough to retard, rather than to reverse, the retrogression of the land. Something more fundamental is needed; something which offers everybody a chance to think, judge, work, and sacrifice.

Armament for Conservation ms. (1942)

The tortuous evolution of international wildlife law shows again and again that faulty premises, used to rationalize a good move, often eventually rise to smite the user. . . . Just so has "archaic utilitarianism" undermined many otherwise praiseworthy moves for faunal conservation. Mr. [Sherman Strong] Hayden concludes, I think rightly, that the only sure foundation for wildlife conservation is "the right of things to exist for their own sake."

Review of The International Protection of Wild Life (1943)

The circumstantial evidence is that stability and diversity in the native community were associated for 20,000 years, and presumably depended on each other. Both are now partly lost, presumably because the original community has been partly lost and greatly altered. Presumably the greater the losses and alterations, the greater the risk of impairments and disorganizations.

This leads to the "rule of thumb" which is the basic premise of ecological conservation: the land should retain as much of its original membership as is compatible with human land-use. The land must of course be modified, but it should be modified as gently and as little as possible.

Conservation: In Whole or in Part? (1944); RMG 315

If the components of land have a collective as well as a separate welfare, then conservation must deal with them collectively as well as separately. Land-use cannot be good if it conserves one component and injures another. Thus a farmer who conserves his soil but drains his marsh, grazes his woodlot, and extinguishes the native fauna and flora is not practicing conservation in the ecological sense. He is merely conserving one component of land at the expense of another.

Conservation: In Whole or in Part? (1944); RMG 316

Land-use is good only when it considers all the components of land, but its human organization often tends to conserve one at the expense of others.

Conservation: In Whole or in Part? (1944); RMG 319

What will happen to wild values after the war when the fruits of military chemistry and military engineering fall into the eager lap of modern man? DDT, capable of eradicating everything from mosquitoes up and down? Family airplanes, ready to eradicate solitude from the face of the map? Power machinery capable of rebuilding the earth on a scale almost comparable to the ice-age? If such tools are to fall short of achieving our ecological suicide, it is time for us to learn caution and restraint in our power to eradicate wild things.

Ticks and Deer: A Lesson in Conservation ms. (1944)

The citizen who aspires to something more than milk-and-water conservation must first of all be aware of land and all its parts. He must feel for soil, water, plants, and animals the same affectionate solicitude as he feels for family and friends. Family and friends are often useful, but affection based on utility alone leads to the same pitfalls and contradictions in land as in people.

The Biotic War ms. (c. 1944)

... Our power to disorganize the land is growing faster than our understanding of it, or our affection for it.

Review of *Our Heritage of Wild Nature* (1946)

Why is it that the land we die for in time of war is freely looted of its fertility, forests, water, and wildlife in times of peace?

The answer, I think, is quite simple. Land, to the average citizen, means the people on the land. There is no affection for or loyalty to the land as such, or to its non-human cohabitants. The concept of land as a community, of which we are only members, is limited to a few ecologists. Ninety-nine percent of the world's brains and votes have never heard of it. . . .

If and when the ecological idea takes root, it is likely to alter things. We need not be prophets to sense this. Every ecologist feels discomfort in trying to adjust the world in which he works to that in which he lives. This discomfort reflects a nonconformity. It may be a serious one.

The Role of Wildlife in Education ms. (c. 1946)

There must be some force behind conservation, more universal than profit, less awkward than government, less ephemeral than sport, something that reaches into all times and places where men live on land, something that brackets everything from rivers to raindrops, from whales to hummingbirds, from land-estates to window-boxes.

I can see only one such force: a respect for land as an organism; a voluntary decency in land-use exercised by every citizen and every land-owner out of a sense of love for and obligation to that great biota we call America.

This is the meaning of conservation, and this is the task of conservation education.

The Meaning of Conservation ms. (c. 1946)

Self-interest . . . requires any society to alter and manage the biota on the areas needed for habitation. The motivation for such alterations and management is referable to economics; the technique to agriculture; but the obligation to restrain these alterations and to respect biotic values underlies both, and is referable to ethics. The basic motivation for conservation is therefore not economic, but ethical.

Ecology and Economics in Land Use ms. (c. 1946)

It is a century now since Darwin gave us the first glimpse of the origin of species. We know now what was unknown to all the preceding caravan of generations: that men are only fellow-voyagers with other creatures in the odyssey of evolution. This new knowledge should have given us, by this time, a sense of kinship with fellow-creatures; a wish to live and let live; a sense of wonder over the magnitude and duration of the biotic enterprise.

Above all we should, in the century since Darwin, have come to know that man, while now captain of the adventuring ship, is hardly the sole object of its quest, and that his prior assumptions to this effect arose from the simple necessity of whistling in the dark.

On a Monument to the Passenger Pigeon (1947); ASCA 109–10

There is a basic distinction between the fact that land yields us a living, and the inference that it exists for this purpose. The latter is about as true as to infer that I fathered three sons in order to replenish the woodpile.

Draft foreword to *A Sand County Almanac* (1947)

These essays are one man's striving to live by and with, rather than on, the American land.

I do not imply that this philosophy of land was always clear to me. It is rather the end-result of a life-journey, in the course of which I have felt sorrow, anger, puzzlement, or confusion over the inability of conservation to halt the juggernaut of land-abuse.

Draft foreword to *A Sand County Almanac* (1947)

I need a short name for what is lacking; I call it the ecological conscience. Ecology is the science of communities, and the ecological conscience is therefore the ethics of community life.

The Ecological Conscience (1947); RMG 340

A new idea is, of course, never created by one individual alone. A prophet is one who recognizes the birth of an idea in the collective mind, and who defines and clarifies, with his life, its meanings and its implications.

Charles Knesal Cooperrider, 1889–1944 (1948); ALS 229

We abuse land because we regard it as a commodity belonging to us. When we see land as a community to which we belong, we may begin to use it with love and respect. There is no other way for land to survive the impact of mechanized man, nor for us to reap from it the esthetic harvest it is capable, under science, of contributing to culture.

Foreword to *A Sand County Almanac* (1949); ASCA viii

We classify ourselves into vocations, each of which either wields some particular tool, or sells it, or repairs it, or sharpens it, or dispenses advice on how to do so; by such division of labors we avoid responsibility for the misuse of any tool save our own. But there is one vocation—philosophy—which knows that all men, by what they think about and wish for, in effect wield all tools. It knows that men thus determine, by their manner of thinking and wishing, whether it is worth while to wield any.

Axe-in-Hand (1949); ASCA 68

An ethic, ecologically, is a limitation on freedom of action in the struggle for existence. An ethic, philosophically, is a differentiation of social from anti-social conduct. These are two definitions of one thing. The thing has its origin in the tendency of interdependent individuals or groups to evolve modes of co-operation. The ecologist calls these symbioses. Politics and economics are advanced symbioses in which the original free-for-all competition has been replaced, in part, by co-operative mechanisms with an ethical content.

The Land Ethic (1949); ASCA 202; cf. The Conservation Ethic (1933); RMG 181

The first ethics dealt with the relation between individuals; the Mosaic Decalogue is an example. Later accretions dealt with the relation between the individual and society. The Golden Rule tries to integrate the individual to society; democracy to integrate social organization to the individual.

There is as yet no ethic dealing with man's relation to land and to the animals and plants which grow upon it. . . . The land-relation is still strictly economic, entailing privileges but not obligations.

The extension of ethics to this third element in human environment is, if I read the evidence correctly, an evolutionary possibility and an ecological necessity.

The Land Ethic (1949); ASCA 202–3; cf. The Conservation Ethic (1933); RMG 182

Individual thinkers since the days of Ezekiel and Isaiah have asserted that the despoliation of land is not only inexpedient but wrong. Society, however, has not yet affirmed their belief. I regard the present conservation movement as the embryo of such an affirmation.

The Land Ethic (1949); ASCA 203; The Conservation Ethic (1933); RMG 182

All ethics so far evolved rest upon a single premise: that the individual is a member of a community of interdependent parts. His instincts prompt him to compete for his place in that community, but his ethics prompt him also to co-operate (perhaps in order that there may be a place to compete for).

The land ethic simply enlarges the boundaries of the community to include soils, waters, plants, and animals, or collectively: the land.

> The Land Ethic (1949); ASCA 203–4

A land ethic of course cannot prevent the alteration, management, and use of these "resources," but it does affirm their right to continued existence, and, at least in spots, their continued existence in a natural state.

In short, a land ethic changes the role of *Homo sapiens* from conqueror of the land-community to plain member and citizen of it. It implies respect for his fellow-members, and also respect for the community as such.

In human history, we have learned (I hope) that the conqueror role is eventually self-defeating. Why? Because it is implicit in such a role that the conqueror knows, *ex cathedra,* just what makes the community clock tick, and just what and who is valuable, and what and who is worthless, in community life. It always turns out that he knows neither, and this is why his conquests eventually defeat themselves.

> The Land Ethic (1949); ASCA 204

. . . The existence of obligations over and above self-interest is taken for granted in such rural community enterprises as the betterment of roads, schools, churches, and baseball teams. Their existence is not taken for granted, nor as yet seriously discussed, in bettering the behavior of the water that falls on the land, or in the preserving of the beauty or diversity of the farm landscape. Land-use ethics are still governed wholly by economic self-interest, just as social ethics were a century ago.

> The Land Ethic (1949); ASCA 209; cf. The Ecological Conscience (1947); RMG 340

Obligations have no meaning without conscience, and the problem we face is the extension of the social conscience from people to land.

No important change in ethics was ever accomplished without an internal change in our intellectual emphasis, loyalties, affections, and convictions. The proof that conservation has not yet touched these foundations of conduct lies in the fact that philosophy and religion have not yet heard of it. In our attempt to make conservation easy, we have made it trivial.

> The Land Ethic (1949); ASCA 209–10; cf. The Ecological Conscience (1947); RMG 341, 338

A land ethic . . . reflects the existence of an ecological conscience, and this in turn reflects a conviction of individual responsibility for the

health of the land. Health is the capacity of the land for self-renewal.
Conservation is our effort to understand and preserve this capacity.

The Land Ethic (1949); ASCA 221

Perhaps the most serious obstacle impeding the evolution of a land
ethic is the fact that our educational and economic system is headed
away from, rather than toward, an intense consciousness of land.

The Land Ethic (1949); ASCA 223

The "key-log" which must be moved to release the evolutionary process for an ethic is simply this: quit thinking about decent land-use as
solely an economic problem. Examine each question in terms of what is
ethically and esthetically right, as well as what is economically expedient.
A thing is right when it tends to preserve the integrity, stability, and
beauty of the biotic community. It is wrong when it tends otherwise.

The Land Ethic (1949); ASCA 224–25; cf. The Ecological
Conscience (1947); RMG 345

21   LEOPOLD'S VOICE

☙

The Reach of Words

Curt Meine

In September 1936 Aldo Leopold and a friend, Ray Roark, journeyed from Wisconsin to the Mexican state of Chihuahua for a two-week bow hunt in the Sierra Madre Occidental. This was, for Leopold, a return to the semiarid mountain landscapes where as a young forester he first gained his professional footing as well as his ecological acumen. It was, however, his first experience of the Sierra Madre, and the comparison with forests on the American side of the border startled him.

Accustomed as Leopold was to southwestern forests marked by intensive grazing, loss of grass cover, accelerated rates of erosion, and other effects of recently intensified human use, he was struck by the beauty and integrity of the Sierra Madre. The hills, "live oak-dotted" and "fat with side oats grama," retained their soils and their associated biological diversity. Clear streams ran through streamside *bosques* of willow, cottonwood, and sycamore. Predator and prey populations seemed to interact in a normal fashion. Fires occasionally swept through the mountains with "no ill effects," maintaining the forests in a more open state than in neighboring Arizona or New Mexico. For Leopold the Sierra Madre came "near to being the cream of creation."[1] He would later write that in these hills he "first clearly realized . . . that all my life I had seen only sick land, whereas here was a biota still in perfect aboriginal health."[2]

Shortly after his return to Wisconsin, Leopold composed a brief but spirited essay in which he celebrated the distinctive voice of the Mexican mountains—the thick-billed parrot. "As a proper ornithologist," he felt obliged to describe the voice of the parrots: loud, chattering, riotous, "full of the salty enthusiasm of high comedy."[3] Leopold submitted the piece to a "proper" ornithological journal, *The Condor,* which immediately published it in its first issue of 1937.

Leopold, at fifty years old, was already well established as a leader in the conservation world. He had been among the nation's first trained foresters and served for twenty highly productive years in the U.S. Forest Service. Beginning in the mid-1920s he had broken trail for the emerging profession of wildlife management. He was nationally recognized as a leading advocate for more effective wildlife conservation policies and for protection of the wild remnants of the nation's public domain. He gained an academic foothold when he joined the faculty of the University of Wisconsin in 1933. Yet, in 1937, Aldo Leopold had not yet even begun to think about the collection of essays through which millions of readers would come to know him, *A Sand County Almanac.*

Leopold had a strong reputation as one of the conservation movement's most effective writers. His output of professional essays, technical reports, policy statements, editorials, and position papers had begun in earnest in the late 1910s and had never slackened. In 1933 he published his classic textbook *Game Management,* which provided not only technical definition but a conceptual foundation for the new field. Leopold's paper trail had crossed all the realms of his interest, from the protection of wilderness to the ecology of grouse, from the sociology of hunters to the economics of farming. And there was hardly an item in his body of published work that did not contain its share of ironic images, playful commentaries, and unexpected turns of phrase. For all of his output, however, Leopold had not yet fully developed the voice that would characterize the writer of *Sand County* fame.

Perhaps the "roistering flocks" of parrots inspired and liberated the proper scientist in Leopold. Perhaps Leopold had arrived at a secure stage in his career and felt free to perform, like the parrots, "a sort of morning drill in the high reaches of the dawn."[4] Perhaps he had begun to sense a growing need to communicate not only with fellow professionals, but with the lay audience in whose hands, hearts, and minds he knew that conservation's success ultimately rested. In any event, with the publication of "The Thick-billed Parrot in Chihuahua"—later revised and published in the *Almanac* as "Guacamaja" ("as the natives euphoniously call the parrot")—Leopold went public with this new and still tentative voice.[5] He would try it out later that same year when he published "Marshland Elegy," his powerful essay on cranes and wetlands, in *American Forests.*[6] And by the end of 1938 he had begun to produce regular short essays on wildlife topics for the *Wisconsin Agriculturist and Farmer,* a biweekly publication that went out to the state's farmers. These writings were the seeds of the manuscript that, many stages of growth later, became *A Sand County Almanac.*[7]

Leopold's literary voice developed along with that manuscript. Its inflections would reflect ten years of further professional growth, experience, frustration, and accomplishment; a world war and the first rumbles of the postwar economic boom; the opinions of close friends and colleagues; seasoning in his professorial and public roles; and many a weekend, field excursion, and planting trip at the Leopold family's "shack" near Madison. Writing in the quiet predawn of his campus office, Leopold turned over and over and over again the phrases that would inform conservation novices, inspire fellow professionals, penetrate glazed eyes, challenge entrenched critics, and build political bridges—but, above all, that would record his own personal impressions and increasing self-awareness. Leopold was in fact a writer, and had been since his schoolboy days. As the essay collection grew, he began to think of himself more self-consciously in this role. And especially in the last several years of his life he achieved the fullness of his voice.

As the quotations in this section show, that voice was not entirely new, and it was not simple. Many of the tones had long been present in Leopold's prose. Leopold wrote in varied modes over his lifetime, always with distinction and flair. He experimented, within the bounds of his professional outlets, throughout his career. With the more nuanced and evocative writing of his later years he was able to draw those qualities together, to mix them, to play them off one another. In these quotations Leopold is sarcastic, ironic, wry, richly allusive, sober, bemused, intensely aural, wise, pithy, balanced, detached, biting, warm, rhythmic, metaphoric, measured, engaged, respectful. As in a well-aged wine, the component flavors came from the sun and soil and fruit; they seasoned within the vessel; they blended in the vintage prose of *A Sand County Almanac*.

Leopold's voice has endured remarkably well, given the accelerating pace at which knowledge has accumulated and prose styles have changed over the intervening decades. Occasionally his allusions sound more distant, his stances seem more awkward, a fact has become dated, edges of a thought have been frayed by time. But perhaps because he was dealing with universals—sky, rocks, soils, waters, plants, and animals; history's deep foundations; the poetry of place names and the irony of progress; human hubris and orneriness; our self-delusion and self-awareness; our capacity for plunder and for wonder, almost in the same moment—Leopold remains a steadfast reference. We sense a solid base here, in a writer who knew the workings of the natural world around him, and who made allowances for the behavior of his own complicated species within it.

And one more thing. Leopold was dealing with serious matters, literally of life and death—matters of contemporary ecological change whose profundity lies, like the sandhill crane's ineffable beauty, "beyond the reach of words."[8] And yet, Leopold's writing is suffused with understated humor and a plain joy. Just as Leopold did not like to think of being young "without wild country to be young in," perhaps he did not like to discuss even the darkest conservation dilemmas without offering a bit of the wild delight that wells from within.[9] It is that quality of Leopold's voice that may be the most enduring, and the most necessary, of all.

There are some who can live without wild things, and some who cannot.

Leopold entering notes into field journal at the Shack, 1946. (Photo by Carl Leopold. Courtesy Aldo Leopold Foundation)

❧

Isaiah was the Roosevelt of the Holy Land. He knew a whole lot about everything, including forests, and told what he knew in no uncertain terms. . . .

. . . Isaiah (44–14) also tells how a man plants a fir tree, and after the rain has nourished it, he cuts it down and uses a part to warm himself, a part to bake bread, a part to make utensils, and a part to fashion a graven image. Graven images, if one is to believe the prophets, must have been an important product of the wood using industries of that day.

> The Forestry of the Prophets (1920); RMG 71, 75

I confess my own leisure to be spent entirely in search of adventure, without regard to prudence, profit, self improvement, learning, or any other serious thing. I find that these serious things are a good deal like heaven; when they are too closely pursued as conscious objectives, they are never attained and seldom even understood.

> A Man's Leisure Time ms. (1920)

I reined up, not sure whether the old cow was dead, or just dying. She had come down out of the drouth-stricken hills to drink, I guess. And now she lay there, quite still, on the hot sandbar. A swarm of brilliant green flies buzzed about her head, and plagued her mouth and eyes. She had craned her neck—the mark was there in the sand—as if for one last look up into the cruel cliffs of Blue River.

I was reflecting on this—especially the ghoulish flies—when it happened. A flash of vermilion—a soft bubbling warble—and a little red bird hovered over the old cow's head, snapping up flies right and left, one after another, for each a cry of ecstasy, in very joy of living. And then with one quick crimson sweep of wing, it disappeared into the green depths of a cottonwood.

Did the old cow see the bird? No. Her dead eyes stared up into the cliffs. Her calf was somewhere up there.

For a while I looked at the old cow, and thought about the little red bird. Then I rode on down Blue River.

> Blue River (1922); RR 108–9

Possibly, in our intuitive perceptions, which may be truer than our science and less impeded by words than our philosophies, we realize the indivisibility of the earth—its soil, mountains, rivers, forests, climate, plants, and animals, and respect it collectively not only as a useful servant but as a living being, vastly less alive than ourselves in degree, but vastly greater than ourselves in time and space—a being that was old when the morning stars sang together, and, when the last of us has been gathered unto his fathers, will still be young.

> Some Fundamentals of Conservation in the Southwest (1923);
> RMG 95

And if there be, indeed, a special nobility inherent in the human race— a special cosmic value, distinctive from and superior to all other life— by what token shall it be manifest?

By a society decently respectful of its own and all other life, capable of inhabiting the earth without defiling it? Or by a society like that of John Burroughs' potato bug, which exterminated the potato, and thereby exterminated itself? As one or the other shall we be judged in "the derisive silence of eternity."

Some Fundamentals of Conservation in the Southwest (1923);
RMG 97

The booster's yardstick is the dollar, and if he recognizes any other standard of value, or any other agency of accomplishment, he makes it a point of pride not to admit it. Even works of charity are bought and sold, like cabbages or gasoline. Do we want to do something for the Boy Scouts? We levy a subscription, hire an architect, and build them a cabin in the mountains (which the Scouts ought to have built themselves), and proceed to forget the Scout movement. We can not see that what we should give toward such causes is usually not much money, but a little human interest.

A Criticism of the Booster Spirit (1923); RMG 102

The Lord did well when he put the loon and his music into this lonesome land.

Canada, 1924 (1924); RR 41

I am conscious of a considerable personal debt to the continent of South America.

It has given me, for instance, rubber for motor tires, which have carried me to lonely places on the face of Mother Earth where all her ways are pleasantness, and all her paths are peace.

It has given me coffee, and to brew it, many a memorable campfire with the dawn-wind rustling in autumnal trees.

It has given me rare woods, pleasant fruits, leather, medicines, nitrates to make my garden bloom, and books about strange beasts and ancient peoples. I am not unmindful of my obligation for these things. But more than all of these, it has given me the River of the Mother of God. . . .

. . . Its name, resonant of the clank of silver armor and the cruel progress of the Cross, yet carrying a hush of reverence and a murmur of the prows of galleons on the seven seas, has always seemed the symbol of Conquest, the Conquest that has reduced those Unknown Places, one by one, until now there are none left.

The River of the Mother of God (1924); RMG 123–24

The Lily chooses her birds well. In the cool dawn a hundred white-throats lament in minor chorus that as yet undiscovered tragedy that broke the heart of "poor Canada." An occasional winter wren breaks in upon them with so jovial a whistle that one is led to think perhaps Canada after all has outgrown her secret sorrow. During the day's fishing, anxious mother grouse cluck to their hidden broods and red-wings extoll the lush greenness of the little marshes along the Lily's banks. Not until the last evening light is upon the aspens do the thrushes begin. This is also the hour when fishermen go to sleep. The ringing cadences are clear at first, then dimmer with the waning sunset, until at last the windings and unwindings of thrushes' song merge with the windings and unwindings of the Lily and the long lines that fall unerringly upon her trouty pools in fishermen's dreams.

The Lily (1927); RR 95

The basic trouble [in game management] is that the great majority of both our sportsmen and protectionists are people who push a pen, not a plow. To him who reads fencerows, thickets, and fields as the letters of a great and tragic history, the direction to go is clear.

Game Methods: The American Way (1931); RMG 162

... To expect closed seasons alone to bring back the prairie chicken is about like petting a starving dog, instead of feeding him. It makes the petter feel virtuous, but it hardly helps the dog.

The Prairie Chicken: A Lost Hope, or an Opportunity? (1931)

How like fish we are: ready, nay eager, to seize upon whatever new thing some wind of circumstance shakes down upon the river of time! And how we rue our haste, finding the gilded morsel to contain a hook. Even so, I think there is some virtue in eagerness, whether its object prove true or false. How utterly dull would be a wholly prudent man, or trout, or world!

The Alder Fork—A Fishing Idyl (1932); ASCA 39

Year by year and foot by foot [shrubs and vines] crept outward over the sod, a leafy vanguard for the forest in age-long battle with the prairie. In wet years the massed oaks entrenched themselves behind their fireproof greenery, smothering the grasses under sodden leaves and shade. In dry years the grasses countercharged, withering the oaken ramparts with blasts of flame.

Back and forth through the centuries the tree-line advanced and retreated, and in the scars of this perpetual conflict grew those native seeds and fruits which gave sustenance to the quail.

Report of the Iowa Game Survey, Chapter Two: Iowa Quail (1932)

All through history tyrannical majorities have condoned their acts of violence on the grounds of punishing "wickedness." The hawk which kills my pheasant is wicked and cruel, and hence must die. Some hawks in some situations doubtless should die, but let us at least admit that we kill the hawk out of self-interest, and in so doing we act on exactly the same motives as the hawk did.

> The American Game Policy on Predators ms. (1932)

Oil pollution is theoretically entirely controllable, and Congress in 1924 passed an "Oil Pollution Act." However, ships are so mobile, and the discharge of oil from sewers is determined by so many thousands of people, that it may be doubted whether any force but inherent decency can do more than mitigate the evil. The main hope is that oil hurts resort properties as well as birds. For property values we have a real respect.

> *Game Management* (1933), 351

Our research has been lopsided,—for not one of our twenty waterfowl species have we even half the life-history facts now available for quail, or ruffed grouse, or pheasants. . . . This is said looking directly at the Committees of Congress, at the Survey, at the big Foundations, the big Associations, the sporting industries, and the waterfowl states, each of whom has spent enough in the last decade printing their clashing opinions to pay for a complete study of a waterfowl species. If only waterfowl could swim in ink! If only they could feed on the broad acres of paper we have dedicated to guesses about their welfare!

> Necessity for Game Research (1934)

It may flatter our ego to be called the sons of man, but it would be nearer the truth to call ourselves the brothers of our fields and forests.

> The Arboretum and the University (1934); RMG 209

. . . Sportsmen and zoophiles have a common enemy of vastly greater importance to both than any real conflict of interest over hawks, ducks, or the legitimate uses of gunpowder. That enemy is public indifference. The basic issue in wildlife conservation is whether machine-made man, who outnumbers us five to one, really cares enough about wild things to steer the industrial juggernaut around our interests. We and the zoophiles are like two small boys quarreling in the street over marbles, unmindful of what is coming down the hill. Unless we make common cause, we bid fair to make only a common grease-spot on the broad highway of progress.

> Whither 1935?—A Review of the American Game Policy (1935)

[The] effect of too many deer on the ground flora of the [German] forest deserves special mention because it is an illusive burglary of esthetic wealth, the more dangerous because unintentional and unseen. . . . The forest landscape is deprived of a certain exuberance which arises from a rich variety of plants fighting with each other for a place in the sun. It is almost as if the geological clock had been set back to those dim ages when there were only pines and ferns. I never realized before that the melodies of nature are music only when played against the undertones of evolutionary history. In the German forest—that forest which inspired the *Erlkonig*—one now hears only a dismal fugue out of the timeless reaches of the carboniferous.

Wilderness (1935); RMG 228–29

[In Germany], as with us, the shiftless sportsman on unmanaged range blames the game shortage on "vermin," which, we are soberly informed, hunt year-around. (I wonder when this profound deduction was first made, and in what century it will cease to be regarded as news.)

Farm Game Management in Silesia (1936)

[The thick-billed parrot] is a discovery only because so few have visited his haunts. Once there, only the deaf and blind could fail to perceive his role in the mountain life and landscape. Indeed you have hardly finished breakfast before the chattering flocks leave their roost on the rimrocks and perform a sort of morning drill in the high reaches of the dawn. Like squadrons of cranes they wheel and spiral, loudly debating with each other the question (which also puzzles you) whether this new day which creeps slowly over the canyons is bluer or golder than its predecessors, or less so. The vote being a draw, they repair by separate companies to the high mesas, for their breakfast of pine-seed-on-the-half-shell.

The Thick-billed Parrot in Chihuahua (1937); ASCA 138

A dawn wind stirs on the great marsh. With almost imperceptible slowness it rolls a bank of fog across the wide morass. Like the white ghost of a glacier the mists advance, riding over phalanxes of tamarack, sliding across bog-meadows heavy with dew. A single silence hangs from horizon to horizon.

Out of some far recess of the sky a tinkling of little bells falls soft upon the listening land. Then again silence. Now comes a baying of some sweet-throated hound, soon the clamor of a responding pack. Then a far clear blast of hunting horns, out of the sky into the fog.

High horns, low horns, silence, and finally a pandemonium of trumpets, rattles, croaks, and cries that almost shakes the bog with its nearness, but without yet disclosing whence it comes. At last a glint of sun reveals the approach of a great echelon of birds. On motionless wing they emerge from the lifting mists, sweep a final arc of the sky, and settle in clangorous descending spirals to their feeding grounds. A new day has begun on the crane marsh.

Marshland Elegy (1937); ASCA 95

Some day, perhaps in the very process of our benefactions, perhaps in the fullness of geologic time, the last crane will trumpet his farewell and spiral skyward from the great marsh. High out of the clouds will fall the sound of hunting horns, the baying of the phantom pack, the tinkle of little bells, and then a silence never to be broken, unless perchance in some far pasture of the Milky Way.

Marshland Elegy (1937); ASCA 101

Like medieval theology, [conservation literature] expresses its discontent in the pattern of a personal devil, who stands in urgent need of demolition by the writer. The protectionist's devil is usually the sportsman. The sportsman's devil is usually "vermin," or the "game hog," or some other visible malefactor. The invisible deterioration of habitat which causes the real damage, and to which both kinds of crusaders are at least indirectly a party, is commonly ignored or dismissed as incidental.

Teaching Wildlife Conservation in Public Schools (1937)

In some cases [wildlife] research has created brand-new concepts hitherto non-existent. For example, there was, previous to a decade ago, no concept of widely differing values and functions as among things animals eat. The presence of a substance in a stomach was *prima facie* evidence of its food value. Thus if we opened the stomach of an arctic explorer and found he had been eating his boots, it was concluded that leather was a food for *homo sapiens,* and in case of a hard winter it should be hung on the bushes to keep the race alive. We now have the greatly superior concept of a *palatability sequence,* which supposes that the best food is eaten until it is gone, after which the next best is taken, and so on. Toward the end of the sequence the birds "eat their boots," and die.

Wildlife Research—Is It a Practical and Necessary Basis for Management? (1938)

No discussion of the utility of research would be complete without mentioning its contributions to the human comedy. The privilege of pulling the curtain strings on The Unknown always engenders priestcraft. We who divine the future for snipe and woodchuck mystify our congregations by the same devices as those who propound the law for sect and synagogue. It is an amusing coincidence that both enhance the stage effects by generous use of Latin.

Is there danger in these scientific struttings and boomings? I think not, so long as we have the grace to laugh when some wag sticks a cockleburr in our professional robes and vestments.

Wildlife Research—Is It a Practical and Necessary Basis for Management? (1938)

Perhaps one of the most unexpected discoveries of the decade is that some [wildlife] populations are internally rather than externally controlled. [Paul] Errington's muskrats trim their own numbers by fighting, without much help from predators, starvation, or disease. There is no place for this in the 1930 scheme of things. It's almost human.

Farmer-Sportsman, A Partnership for Wildlife Restoration (1939)

He is a reminiscent fellow, this farmer. Get him wound up and you will hear many a curious tidbit of rural history. He will tell you of the mad decade when they taught economics in the local kindergarten, but the college president couldn't tell a bluebird from a blue cohosh. Everybody worried about getting his share; nobody worried about doing his bit.

The Farmer as a Conservationist (1939); RMG 265

Most Wisconsin rivers are now otterless; monotonous ribbons of mud and water. A single otter will travel 20 miles of river, and to the mind of the initiated convert that long stretch of mud and water into a personality.

New Year's Inventory Checks Missing Game (1940); RMG 275

[C. H.] Guise's section on forests includes a new resource category, "wildflowers and other non-commercial plants." Such explicit recognition for this bureauless, lobbyless waif as a legitimate member of the conservation family is encouraging, but one could wish for a less apologetic tone in presenting him to polite society.

Review of *Conservation in the United States* (1940)

Food is the continuum in the Song of the Gavilan. I mean, of course, not only your food, but food for the oak which feeds the buck who feeds the cougar who dies under an oak and goes back into acorns for his erstwhile prey. This is one of many food cycles starting from and returning to oaks, for the oak also feeds the jay who feeds the goshawk who named your river, the bear whose grease made your gravy, the quail who taught you a lesson in botany, and the turkey who daily gives you the slip. And the common end of all is to help the headwater trickles of the Gavilan split one more grain of soil off the broad hulk of the Sierra Madre to make another oak.

Song of the Gavilan (1940); ASCA 152–53

Since the beginning, time had gnawed at the basaltic hulk of Escudilla, wasting, waiting, and building. Time built three things on the old mountain, a venerable aspect, a community of minor animals and plants, and a grizzly.

The government trapper who took the grizzly knew he had made Escudilla safe for cows. He did not know he had toppled the spire off an edifice a-building since the morning stars sang together.

Escudilla (1940); ASCA 136

Ecology tries to understand the interactions between living things and their environment. Every living thing represents an equation of give and take. Man or mouse, oak or orchid, we take a livelihood from our land and our fellows, and give in return an endless succession of acts and thoughts, each of which changes us, our fellows, our land, and its capacity to yield us a further living. Ultimately we give ourselves.

Ecology and Politics (1941); RMG 281

The county records may allege that you own this pasture, but the plover airily rules out such trivial legalities. He has just flown 4000 miles to reassert the title he got from the Indians, and until the young plovers are a-wing, this pasture is his, and none may trespass without his protest.

The Plover Is Back from Argentine (1942); ASCA 35

The sugar maple is as American as the rail fence or the Kentucky rifle. Generations have been rocked in maple cradles, clothed from maple spinning wheels, and fed with maple-sweetened cakes served on maple tables before maple fires. Yet the demise of the maple forest brings us less regret than the demise of an old tire. Like the shrew who burrows in maple woods, we take our environment for granted while it lasts.

The Last Stand (1942); RMG 292

An atom at large in the biota is too free to know freedom; an atom back in the sea has forgotten it. For every atom lost to the sea, the prairie pulls another out of the decaying rocks. The only certain truth is that its creatures must suck hard, live fast, and die often, lest its losses exceed its gains.

Odyssey (1942); ASCA 107

. . . I have seen few verbal machine-gunnings . . . which so convincingly portray the fact that our whole cultural structure is built of non-durable materials which will sag as the land weakens. Particularly does [the author] make mincemeat of the isolationist view that land abuses elsewhere do not matter here. . . .

After this promising introduction, the reader's hopes are deflated by a very ordinary series of resource outlines in Part II. . . .

My advice to the reader is this: by all means get this book. Close Part II with scotch tape, and then read.

Half-excellent [Review of *Conservation of Natural Resources*] (1942)

Why is the shovel regarded as a symbol of drudgery? Perhaps because most shovels are dull. Certainly all drudges have dull shovels, but I am uncertain which of these two facts is cause and which effect. I only know that a good file, vigorously wielded, makes my shovel sing as it slices the mellow loam. I am told there is music in the sharp plane, the sharp chisel, and the sharp scalpel, but I hear it best in my shovel; it hums in my wrists as I plant a pine. I suspect that the fellow who tried so hard to strike one clear note upon the harp of time chose too difficult an instrument.

Pines above the Snow (1943); ASCA 82

After this war, engineers are going to dam the Milky Way if we let them.

Review of *Wildlife Refuges* (1943)

The wild things that live on my farm are reluctant to tell me, in so many words, how much of my township is included within their daily or nightly beat. I am curious about this, for it gives me the ratio between the size of their universe and the size of mine, and it conveniently begs the much more important question, who is the more thoroughly acquainted with the world in which he lives?

Home Range (1943); ASCA 78

It is the part of wisdom never to revisit a wilderness, for the more golden the lily, the more certain that someone has gilded it. To return not only spoils a trip, but tarnishes a memory. It is only in the mind that shining adventure remains forever bright.

The Green Lagoons (1945); ASCA 141

Objectivity is possible only in matters too small to be important, or in matters too large to do anything about.

The Land-Health Concept and Conservation ms. (1946)

Each year, after the midwinter blizzards, there comes a night of thaw when the tinkle of dripping water is heard in the land. It brings strange stirrings, not only to creatures abed for the night, but to some who have been asleep for the winter. The hibernating skunk, curled up in his deep den, uncurls himself and ventures forth to prowl the wet world, dragging his belly in the snow. His track marks one of the earliest datable events in that cycle of beginnings and ceasings which we call a year.

A Phenological Record for Sauk and Dane Counties, Wisconsin, 1935–1945 (1947); ASCA 3

The pigeon was a biological storm. He was the lightning that played between two opposing potentials of intolerable intensity: the fat of the land and the oxygen of the air. Yearly the feathered tempest roared up, down, and across the continent, sucking up the laden fruits of forest and prairie, burning them in a traveling blast of life. Like any other chain reaction, the pigeon could survive no diminution of his own furious intensity. When the pigeoners subtracted from his numbers, and the pioneers chopped gaps in the continuity of his fuel, his flame guttered out with hardly a sputter or even a wisp of smoke.

On a Monument to the Passenger Pigeon (1947); ASCA 111

These essays were written for myself and my close friends, but I suspect that we are not alone in our discontent with the ecological *status quo*. If the reader finds here some echo of his own affections and of his own anxieties, they will have accomplished more than was originally intended.

Draft foreword to *A Sand County Almanac* (1947)

It is one of the ironies of human ecology that if there be a spark of divinity in an individual it is invisible at birth, is mistaken for less important things during his life, and becomes completely visible only after his death.

Charles Knesal Cooperrider, 1889–1944 (1948); ALS 229

There are some who can live without wild things, and some who cannot. These essays are the delights and dilemmas of one who cannot.

Like winds and sunsets, wild things were taken for granted until progress began to do away with them. Now we face the question whether a still higher "standard of living" is worth its cost in things natural, wild, and free. For us of the minority, the opportunity to see geese is more important than television, and the chance to find a pasque-flower is a right as inalienable as free speech.

These wild things, I admit, had little human value until mechanization assured us of a good breakfast, and until science disclosed the drama of where they come from and how they live. The whole conflict thus boils down to a question of degree. We of the minority see a law of diminishing returns in progress; our opponents do not.

Foreword to *A Sand County Almanac* (1949); ASCA vii

There are two spiritual dangers in not owning a farm. One is the danger of supposing that breakfast comes from the grocery, and the other that heat comes from the furnace.

Good Oak (1949); ASCA 6

In the beginning there was only the unity of the Ice Sheet. Then followed the unity of the March thaw, and the northward hegira of the international geese. Every March since the Pleistocene, the geese have honked unity from China Sea to Siberian Steppe, from Euphrates to

Volga, from Nile to Murmansk, from Lincolnshire to Spitsbergen. Every March since the Pleistocene, the geese have honked unity from Currituck to Labrador, Matamuskeet to Ungava, Horseshoe Lake to Hudson's Bay, Avery Island to Baffin Land, Panhandle to Mackenzie, Sacramento to Yukon.

By this international commerce of geese, the waste corn of Illinois is carried through the clouds to the Arctic tundras, there to combine with the waste sunlight of a nightless June to grow goslings for all the lands between. And in this annual barter of food for light, and winter warmth for summer solitude, the whole continent receives as net profit a wild poem dropped from the murky skies upon the muds of March.

The Geese Return (1949); ASCA 23

Draba plucks no heartstrings. Its perfume, if there is any, is lost in the gusty winds. Its color is plain white. Its leaves wear a sensible woolly coat. Nothing eats it; it is too small. No poets sing of it. Some botanist once gave it a Latin name, and then forgot it. Altogether it is of no importance—just a small creature that does a small job quickly and well.

Draba (1949); ASCA 26

. . . It is a fact, patent both to my dog and myself, that at daybreak I am the sole owner of all the acres I can walk over. It is not only boundaries that disappear, but also the thought of being bounded. Expanses unknown to deed or map are known to every dawn, and solitude, supposed no longer to exist in my county, extends on every hand as far as the dew can reach.

Great Possessions (1949); ASCA 41

My own farm was selected for its lack of goodness and its lack of highway; indeed my whole neighborhood lies in a backwash of the River Progress.

Prairie Birthday (1949); ASCA 46–47

In June it is completely predictable that the robin will give voice when the light intensity reaches 0.01 candle power, and that the bedlam of other singers will follow in predictable sequence. In autumn, on the other hand, the robin is silent, and it is quite unpredictable whether the covey-chorus will occur at all. The disappointment I feel on these mornings of silence perhaps shows that things hoped for have a higher value than things assured.

The Choral Copse (1949); ASCA 53–54

Early risers feel at ease with each other, perhaps because, unlike those who sleep late, they are given to understatement of their own achievements. Orion, the most widely traveled, says literally nothing. The coffee pot, from its first soft gurgle, underclaims the virtues of what simmers within. The owl, in his trisyllabic commentary, plays down the story of the night's murders. The goose on the bar, rising briefly to a point of order in some inaudible anserine debate, lets fall no hint that he speaks with the authority of all the far hills and the sea.

Too Early (1949); ASCA 59–61

At sunset on the last day of the grouse season, every blackberry blows out his light. I do not understand how a mere bush can thus be infallibly informed about the Wisconsin statutes, nor have I ever gone back next day to find out. For the ensuing eleven months the lanterns glow only in recollection. I sometimes think that the other months were constituted mainly as a fitting interlude between Octobers, and I suspect that dogs, and perhaps grouse, share the same view.

Red Lanterns (1949); ASCA 65–66

Out of the clouds I hear a faint bark, as of a far-away dog. It is strange how the world cocks its ears at that sound, wondering. Soon it is louder: the honk of geese, invisible, but coming on.

The flock emerges from the low clouds, a tattered banner of birds, dipping and rising, blown up and blown down, blown together and blown apart, but advancing, the wind wrestling lovingly with each winnowing wing. When the flock is a blur in the far sky I hear the last honk, sounding taps for summer.

It is warm behind the driftwood now, for the wind has gone with the geese. So would I—if I were the wind.

If I Were the Wind (1949); ASCA 66–67

To me an ancient cottonwood is the greatest of trees because in his youth he shaded the buffalo and wore a halo of pigeons, and I like a young cottonwood because he may some day become ancient. But the farmer's wife (and hence the farmer) despises all cottonwoods because in June the female tree clogs the screens with cotton. The modern dogma is comfort at any cost.

Axe-in-Hand (1949); ASCA 71

Perhaps our grandsons, having never seen a wild river, will never miss the chance to set a canoe in singing waters.

Flambeau (1949); ASCA 116

It must be poor life that achieves freedom from fear.

On Top (1949); ASCA 126

We reached the old wolf in time to watch a fierce green fire dying in her eyes. I realized then, and have known ever since, that there was something new to me in those eyes—something known only to her and to the mountain. I was young then, and full of trigger-itch; I thought that because fewer wolves meant more deer, that no wolves would mean hunters' paradise. But after seeing the green fire die, I sensed that neither the wolf nor the mountain agreed with such a view.

Thinking Like a Mountain (1949); ASCA 130

Notes
Quotation Sources
Contributors

Notes

In the notes below, citations of Aldo Leopold's writings are abbreviated as follows:

ASCA   Aldo Leopold, *A Sand County Almanac and Sketches Here and There* (New York: Oxford University Press, 1949)

ALS   David E. Brown and Neil B. Carmony, *Aldo Leopold's Southwest* (Albuquerque: University of New Mexico Press, 1995; originally published as *Aldo Leopold's Wilderness: Selected Early Writings by the Author of "A Sand County Almanac,"* Harrisburg, Penn.: Stackpole Books, 1990)

GM   Aldo Leopold, *Game Management* (New York: Charles Scribner's Sons, 1933; reprinted, Madison: University of Wisconsin Press, 1986)

RMG   Susan L. Flader and J. Baird Callicott, eds., *The River of the Mother of God and Other Essays by Aldo Leopold* (Madison: University of Wisconsin Press, 1991)

RR   Luna B. Leopold, ed., *Round River: From the Journals of Aldo Leopold* (New York: Oxford University Press, 1953)

A bracketed number in a note indicates the chapter within this volume where the quotation can be found.

FOREWORD

1. Leopold, "Marshland Elegy" (1937), ASCA, 95. [21]
2. Leopold, "Wherefore Wildlife Ecology" (1947), RMG, 337. [17]
3. Leopold, "Illinois Bus Ride" (1949), ASCA, 119. [5]
4. Leopold, "Thinking Like a Mountain" (1949), ASCA, 132. [4]
5. Leopold, "Marshland Elegy" (1937), ASCA, 101. [7]
6. Leopold, GM (1933), 388. [16]
7. Leopold, "Marshland Elegy" (1937), ASCA, 97. [19]
8. Leopold, "Wilderness" (1935), RMG, 229. [21]
9. Leopold, "The Farmer as a Conservationist" (1939), RMG, 263. [6]
10. Leopold, "Wherefore Wildlife Ecology" (1947), RMG, 337. [19]

INTRODUCTION

1. Leopold, Foreword (1949), ASCA, vii, ix. [21]

2. Luna B. Leopold, ed., *Round River: From the Journals of Aldo Leopold* (New York: Oxford University Press, 1953); David E. Brown and Neil B. Carmony, eds., *Aldo Leopold's Southwest* (Albuquerque: University of New Mexico Press, 1995; originally published as *Aldo Leopold's Wilderness: Selected Early Writings by the Author of "A Sand County Almanac"* [Harrisburg, Penn.: Stackpole Books, 1990]); Susan L. Flader and J. Baird Callicott, eds., *The River of the Mother of God and Other Essays by Aldo Leopold* (Madison: University of Wisconsin Press, 1991).

3. Leopold, "Good Oak" (1949), ASCA, 7.

4. Leopold, "The Land Ethic" (1949), ASCA, 224–25. [20]

5. J. Baird Callicott, *In Defense of the Land Ethic: Essays in Environmental Philosophy* (Albany: State University of New York Press, 1989), 84.

6. Leopold, "Conservation" (c. 1938), RR, 146–47. [9]

7. Leopold, "The Round River—A Parable" (c. 1941), RR, 165. [17]

8. Leopold, Review of A. F. Gustafson, H. Ries, C. H. Guise, and W. J. Hamilton, Jr., *Conservation in the United States, Ecology* 21:1 (January 1940), 92–93. [9]

9. Leopold, "Conservation Esthetic" (1938), ASCA, 165. [3]

10. N. Scott Momaday, *The Man Made of Words* (New York: St. Martin's Press, 1997), 9–11.

11. Leopold, "Song of the Gavilan" (1940), ASCA, 149. [19]

PART I. CONSERVATION SCIENCE AND PRACTICE

1. Leopold, "Conservation Economics" (1934), RMG, 197. [9]

2. Leopold, "The Role of Wildlife in a Liberal Education" (1942), RMG, 302–3. [17]

3. Leopold, "The Round River—A Parable" (c. 1941), RR, 159. [17]

1. AXE-IN-HAND

1. Susan Flader, "Aldo Leopold and the Evolution of Ecosystem Management," in *Sustainable Ecological Systems: Implementing an Ecological Approach to Land Management* (USDA Forest Service General Technical Report RM-247, May 1994), 15–19.

2. Leopold, "To the Forest Officers of the Carson" (1913), RMG, 43. [1]

3. Leopold, ibid., RMG, 44. [1]

4. Leopold, "Grass, Brush, Timber, and Fire in Southern Arizona" (1924), RMG, 119, ALS, 186. [1]

5. Quoted in Curt Meine, *Aldo Leopold: His Life and Work* (Madison: University of Wisconsin Press, 1988), 192.

6. Leopold, "Mr. Thompson's Wilderness," *USFS Service Bulletin* 12:26 (June 25, 1928), 1–2. [1]

7. See Leopold, "Notes on Wild Life Conservation in Germany," *Game Re-*

search News Letter 7 (October 21, 1935), 1–3; "Deer and Dauerwald in Germany: I. History," *Journal of Forestry* 34:4 (April 1936), 366–75.

8. Leopold, "The Last Stand" (1942), RMG, 294. [1]

9. Leopold to Clara Leopold, November 17, 1909, Aldo Leopold Papers, University of Wisconsin–Madison Archives.

10. Leopold, "Conservation Esthetic" (1938), ASCA, 175. [8]

11. Leopold, "Axe-in-Hand" (1949), ASCA, 68. [1]

2. OPEN THINKING ON THE RANGE

1. Leopold, "Pioneers and Gullies" (1924), RMG, 110, ALS, 170. [2]

2. Leopold, "Conservationist in Mexico" (1937), RMG, 243, ALS, 206–7. [2]

3. Leopold, "Preliminary Report on Forestry and Game Management," *Journal of Forestry* 33:3 (March 1935), 273–75. [2]

4. Leopold, "Pioneers and Gullies" (1924), RMG, 110, ALS, 170. [2]

5. Leopold, "Conservation" (c. 1938), RR, 147. [9]

6. This language is from Section 2 of the 1973 Endangered Species Act.

7. Leopold, "A Plea for Recognition of Artificial Works in Forest Erosion Control Policy," *Journal of Forestry* 19:3 (March 1921), 267–73. [2]

3. LEOPOLD AND THE "STILL UNLOVELY MIND"

1. Leopold, "Conservation Esthetic" (1938), ASCA, 166. [3]

2. Leopold, ibid., ASCA, 166. [3]

3. Leopold, "The Wilderness and Its Place in Forest Recreational Policy" (1921), RMG, 79, ALS, 148. [3]

4. E. Losos, J. Hayes, A. Phillips, D. Wilcove, and C. Alkire, "Taxpayer Subsidized Resource Extraction Harms Species," *Bioscience* 45 (1995), 446–55.

5. Leopold, "Conservation Economics" (1934), RMG, 196. [3]

6. Leopold, "Conservation Esthetic" (1938), ASCA, 166. [3]

7. Leopold, "Wilderness" (1949), ASCA, 194. [3]

8. Leopold, "Conservation Economics" (1934), RMG, 196. [3]

9. Leopold, "Wilderness Values," *1941 Yearbook, Park and Recreation Progress* (Washington, D.C.: National Park Service, 1941), 27–29. [19]

10. Leopold, "Conservation Esthetic" (1938), ASCA, 176–77. [3]

11. Leopold, "Wildlife in American Culture" (1943), ASCA, 184. [3]

4. BUILDING THE FOUNDATIONS OF WILDLIFE CONSERVATION

1. Leopold, "Necessity for Game Research," *Transactions of the Twentieth American Game Conference* (January 22–24, 1934), 92–95. [4]

2. Leopold, "The Research Program," *Transactions of the Second North American Wildlife Conference* (March 1–4, 1937), 104–7. [4]

3. Leopold, "Wildlife Research—Is It a Practical and Necessary Basis for Man-

agement?" *Transactions of the Third North American Wildlife Conference* (February 14–17, 1938), 42–45, 55. [4]

4. Leopold, "Ten New Developments in Game Management" (1925), ALS, 113. [4]

5. Leopold, GM (1933), 3. [4]

6. Leopold, with L. J. Cole, N. C. Fassett, C. A. Herrick, C. Juday, and G. Wagner, *The University and Conservation of Wisconsin Wildlife,* Bulletin of the University of Wisconsin, ser. no. 2211, general ser. no. 1995, Science Inquiry Publication no. 3, February 1937. [4]

7. Ibid. [4]

8. Leopold, "Academic and Professional Training in Wildlife Work," *Journal of Wildlife Management* 3:2 (April 1939), 156–61. [4]

9. Leopold, "Wild Followers of the Forest," *American Forestry* 29:357 (September 1923), 515–19, 568. [4]

10. Leopold, "Conservationist in Mexico" (1937), RMG, 242, ALS, 205. [4]

11. Leopold, GM (1933), 26. [4]

12. Leopold, "Whither 1935?—A Review of the American Game Policy," *Transactions of the Twenty-first American Game Conference* (January 21–23, 1935), 49–55. [4]

13. Leopold, "Game and Wild Life Conservation" (1932), RMG, 167. [4]

14. Leopold, "Game Methods: The American Way" (1931), RMG, 159. [4]

15. Leopold, "Game Cropping in Southern Wisconsin," *Our Native Landscape* 1 (1927). [8]

16. Leopold, GM (1933), 21. [4]

17. Leopold, Review of *The Status of Wildlife in the United States, Journal of Forestry* 38:10 (October 1940), 823. [4]

5. TRAVELING IN THE RIGHT DIRECTION

1. George Perkins Marsh, *Man and Nature: Or, Physical Geography as Modified by Human Action,* ed. Devaid Lowenthal (Cambridge, Mass.: Belknap Press of Harvard University Press, 1965; originally published 1864), 35.

2. Leopold to Clara Leopold, May 15, 1920, Aldo Leopold Papers, University of Wisconsin–Madison Archives.

3. Leopold, "Coon Valley: An Adventure in Cooperative Conservation" (1935), RMG, 219. [10]

4. Leopold, "Land-Use and Democracy" (1942), RMG, 300. [20]

5. Leopold, "The Farmer as a Conservationist," stencil circular 210, University of Wisconsin College of Agriculture, Extension Service (February 1939), 1–8.

6. Wendell Berry, *The Unsettling of America: Culture and Agriculture* (San Francisco: Sierra Club Books, 1977), 86; Leopold, "Erosion and Prosperity" ms., 1921, Aldo Leopold Papers, University of Wisconsin–Madison Archives. [5]

7. Leopold, "Conservation: In Whole or in Part?" (1944), RMG, 310. [9]

8. U.S. Natural Resources Conservation Service, U.S. Department of Agriculture, *America's Private Land: A Geography of Hope* (Washington, D.C.: Government Printing Office, 1996), 80.

9. Leopold, "The Ecological Conscience" (1947), RMG, 345–46. [12]

6. PREPARING FOR A SUSTAINABLE AGRICULTURE

1. Leopold, "The Land Ethic" (1949), ASCA, 222. [6]
2. Leopold, "Odyssey" (1942), ASCA, 108.

7. A PLACE OF HUMILITY

1. Leopold, "Wilderness" (1949), ASCA, 188. [7]
2. Leopold, ibid., ASCA, 200. [7]
3. Leopold, "The Land Ethic" (1949), ASCA, 203. [20]
4. Leopold, ibid., ASCA, 204. [20]
5. Leopold, ibid., ASCA, 204.
6. Leopold, "Wilderness" (1949), ASCA, 199. [7]
7. Leopold, "Wilderness as a Form of Land Use" (1925), RMG, 137. [7]
8. Leopold, "A Plea for Wilderness Hunting Grounds" (1925), ALS, 161. [7]
9. William Cronon, "The Trouble with Wilderness, or Getting Back to the Wrong Nature," in J. Baird Callicott and Michael P. Nelson, eds., *The Great New Wilderness Debate* (Athens: University of Georgia Press, 1998), 471–99, at 491–92.
10. Introduction, in Callicott and Nelson, eds., *The Great New Wilderness Debate*, 2.
11. Leopold, "The River of the Mother of God" (1924), RMG, 127. [7]

8. THE CONTINUING CHALLENGE OF RESTORATION

1. Leopold, "Wilderness as a Land Laboratory" (1941), ASCA, 196; cf. RMG, 288. [8]
2. Leopold, ibid., ASCA, 195; cf. RMG, 288. [8]

9. STANDING ON SOLID SHOULDERS

1. Raymond F. Dasmann, *Environmental Conservation* (New York: Wiley and Sons, 1959); David W. Ehrenfeld, *Biological Conservation* (New York: Holt, Rinehart, and Winston, 1970).
2. Leopold, "A Biotic View of Land" (1939), RMG, 267 [9]; Leopold, "Second Report of [the Society of American Foresters] Game Policy Committee," *Journal of Forestry* 35:2 (February 1937), 228–32. [9]
3. Leopold, "A Biotic View of Land" (1939), ASCA, 216; cf. RMG, 269. [9]
4. Leopold, "Conservation" (c. 1938), RR, 147–48. [9]
5. Leopold, "Wilderness as a Land Laboratory" (1941), ASCA, 194; cf. RMG, 287. [8]
6. Leopold, "Conservation" (c. 1938), RR, 148. [9]

PART II. CONSERVATION POLICY

1. Leopold, GM (1933), 423. [20]

10. ALDO LEOPOLD ON PRIVATE LAND

1. Leopold, "The Farmer as a Conservationist" (1939), RMG, 257. [8]
2. Leopold, "Whither 1935?—A Review of the American Game Policy," *Transactions of the Twenty-first American Game Conference* (January 21–23, 1935), 49–55. [6]
3. Leopold, "The Land Ethic" (1949), ASCA, 214. [13]
4. Leopold, ibid., ASCA, 214.
5. Leopold, "The Farm Wildlife Program: A Self-Scrutiny," ms. (c. 1937), Aldo Leopold Papers, University of Wisconsin–Madison Archives. [10]
6. Leopold, "A Biotic View of Land" (1939), RMG, 273. [10]

11. ALDO LEOPOLD ON PUBLIC LAND

1. Leopold to Clara Leopold, January 20, 1909, Aldo Leopold Papers, University of Wisconsin–Madison Archives.
2. Leopold, "On Top" (1949), ASCA, 126. [21]
3. Leopold, "Escudilla" (1940), ASCA, 133.
4. Leopold to Carl A. Leopold, May 20, 1911, Aldo Leopold Papers, University of Wisconsin–Madison Archives.
5. Leopold, "Conservation Economics" (1934), RMG, 196. [5]
6. Leopold, GM (1933), 274. [11]
7. Leopold, "Conservation Economics" (1934), RMG, 197. [11]
8. Leopold, "Summarization of the Twelfth North American Wildlife Conference," *Transactions of the Twelfth North American Wildlife Conference* (February 3–5, 1947), 529–36. [11]

12. THROWING YOUR WEIGHT AROUND

1. Leopold, "The Land Ethic" (1949), ASCA, 224–25. [20]
2. Leopold, "The Ecological Conscience" (1947), RMG, 345–46. [12]
3. Leopold, "A Man's Leisure Time" (1920), RR, 8. [12]
4. Leopold, "The Round River—A Parable" (c. 1941), RR, 165. [17]
5. Leopold, "The Land Ethic" (1949), ASCA, 221. [12]
6. Leopold, GM (1933), 405. [15]

13. DO ECONOMISTS KNOW ABOUT LUPINES?

1. Leopold, "The Sand Counties" (1949), ASCA, 102. [13]
2. Leopold, "A Biotic View of Land" (1939), RMG, 267.

3. Leopold, "The Game Situation in the Southwest," *Bulletin of the American Game Protective Association* 9:2 (April 1920), 3–5. [4]

4. Leopold, "Some Fundamentals of Conservation in the Southwest" (1923), RMG, 94. [13]

5. Leopold, Foreword (1949), ASCA, ix. [13]

6. Leopold, "The Ecological Conscience" (1947), RMG, 344. [13]

7. Leopold, "The Land Ethic" (1949), ASCA, 210. [13]

8. Leopold, ibid., ASCA, 213. [10]

9. Paul Hawken, *The Ecology of Commerce* (New York: HarperCollins, 1993), p. 3; Michael Rothschild, *Bionomics: The Inevitability of Capitalism* (New York: Henry Holt, 1990), xiii.

10. Quoted in Bryan G. Norton, "The Constancy of Leopold's Land Ethic," in Andrew Light and Eric Katz, eds., *Environmental Pragmatism* (London: Routledge Publishers, 1996), 86.

14. LEOPOLD AS PRACTICAL MORALIST AND PRAGMATIC POLICY ANALYST

1. Leopold, "The River of the Mother of God" (1924), RMG, 126–27. [7]

2. Leopold, "Weatherproofing Conservation," *American Forests* 39:1 (January 1933), 10–11, 48. [14]

3. See Bryan G. Norton, "Integration or Reduction: Two Approaches to Environmental Values," in Andrew Light and Eric Katz, eds., *Environmental Pragmatism* (London: Routledge Publishers, 1996), 105–38.

4. Leopold, "Pioneers and Gullies" (1924), RMG, 112, ALS 173. [14]. See C. S. Holling, "What Barriers? What Bridges?" in L. H. Gunderson, C. S. Holling, and S. S. Light, eds., *Barriers and Bridges to the Renewal of Ecosystems and Institutions* (New York: Columbia University Press, 1995), 3–34.

5. Leopold, "Thinking Like a Mountain" (1949), ASCA, 132. [14]. See Bryan G. Norton, "Context and Hierarchy in Aldo Leopold's Theory of Environmental Management," *Ecological Economics* 2 (1990), 119–27.

6. Leopold, "The American Game Policy in a Nutshell," *Transactions of the Seventeenth American Game Conference* (December 1–2, 1930), 281–83. [14]

7. Leopold, "Some Fundamentals of Conservation in the Southwest" (1923), RMG, 97. [14]

8. Herbert Simon, *Administrative Behavior* (New York: Free Press, 1945).

9. Leopold, "Game and Wildlife Conservation" (1932), RMG, 166. [14]

10. Leopold, "Some Fundamentals of Conservation in the Southwest" (1923), RMG, 96. [14]

11. Leopold, ibid., RMG, 95, 96. [14]

12. Bryan G. Norton, *Toward Unity among Environmentalists* (New York: Oxford University Press, 1991).

13. Leopold, "The Conservation Ethic" (1933), RMG, 188. [14]

14. Leopold, "Land-Use and Democracy" (1942), RMG, 298. [14]

PART III. CONSERVATION AND CULTURE

1. Leopold, Foreword (1949), ASCA, ix. [18]
2. Leopold, "The State of the Profession" (1940), RMG, 277. [18]
3. Leopold to H. A. Smith, December 20, 1935, Aldo Leopold Papers, University of Wisconsin–Madison Archives.
4. Leopold, "Conservation" (c. 1938), RR, 155–56. [17]

15. HUNTING FOR COMMON GROUND

1. Leopold, "The Gila, 1927" (1927), RR, 101.
2. Leopold, "Red Legs Kicking" (1949), ASCA, 120. [15]
3. Leopold, "Goose Music" (c. 1922), RR, 173, 167. [15]
4. Leopold, "Thinking Like a Mountain" (1949), ASCA, 130. [21]
5. Richard McCabe and Thomas McCabe, "Of Slings and Arrows: A Historical Retrospection," in *White-tailed Deer: Ecology and Management* (Harrisburg, Penn.: Stackpole Books, 1984), 19–72.
6. Richard Nelson, *Heart and Blood: Living with Deer in America* (New York: Vintage Books, 1998), 234; original source: Ernest Swift, *A History of Wisconsin Deer* (Madison: Wisconsin Conservation Department, 1946), 31.
7. Leopold, "Goose Music" (c. 1922), RR, 170. [19]

16. LEOPOLD AND THE CHANGING LANDSCAPE OF HISTORY

1. Leopold, "Engineering and Conservation" (1938), RMG, 253. [16]

17. WHAT IS EDUCATION FOR?

1. Leopold, "Song of the Gavilan" (1940), ASCA, 153. [18]
2. Leopold, "The Round River—A Parable" (c. 1941), RR, 159. [17]
3. Leopold, "Conservation" (c. 1938), RR, 149. [17]
4. Leopold, ibid., RR, 157. [17]
5. Leopold, "Natural History—The Forgotten Science" (1938), RR, 62. [17]
6. Leopold, ibid., RR, 64. [17]
7. Leopold, "Wildlife in American Culture" (1943), ASCA, 178. [13]
8. Leopold, "The Role of Wildlife in a Liberal Education" (1942), RMG, 302. [17]
9. Leopold, "The Land Ethic" (1949), ASCA, 209. [17]
10. Leopold, "Teaching Wildlife Conservation in Public Schools," *Transactions of the Wisconsin Academy of Sciences, Arts and Letters* 30 (1937), 77–86. [17]
11. Leopold, "The Land Ethic" (1949), ASCA, 223 [20], 224 [17].

18. BETWEEN IMAGINATION AND OBSERVATION

1. See Leopold, "Sky Dance" (1941), ASCA, 30–34.
2. Quoted in Gary Paul Nabhan, foreword to Bradley P. Dean, ed., *Faith in a Seed* (Washington, D.C., and Covelo, Calif.: Island Press, 1993), xiii.

19. THROUGH SUCCESSIVE STAGES OF THE BEAUTIFUL

1. Leopold, "The Land Ethic" (1949), ASCA, 204. [20]
2. Leopold, "The Green Pasture" (1949), ASCA, 51. [19]
3. Leopold, "The Choral Copse" (1949), ASCA, 53. [19]
4. Leopold, "Clandeboye" (1949), ASCA, 160. [19]
5. Leopold, "Marshland Elegy" (1937), ASCA, 96. [19]
6. See Roderick Nash, "Aldo Leopold: Prophet," ch. 11 in *Wilderness and the American Mind,* 3rd ed. (New Haven: Yale University Press, 1982), 182–99.
7. Leopold, "Country" (1941), RR, 33. [19]
8. Leopold, "Conservation Esthetic" (1938), ASCA, 176–77. [3]
9. Leopold, ibid., ASCA, 174. [19]
10. Leopold, "The Land Ethic" (1949), ASCA, 214.
11. Leopold, "A Biotic View of Land" (1939), ASCA, 215; cf. RMG, 268. [9]
12. Leopold, "The Thick-billed Parrot in Chihuahua" (1937), ASCA, 137. [19]
13. Leopold, "Song of the Gavilan" (1940), ASCA, 149. [19]
14. Leopold, "The Conservation Ethic" (1933), RMG, 191. [19]
15. Leopold, "The Land Ethic" (1949), ASCA, 214. [19]
16. Leopold, ibid., ASCA, 224–25; emphasis added. [20]

20. INTO TERRA INCOGNITA

1. Richard Routley, "Is There a Need for a New, an Environmental Ethic?" in Michael E. Zimmerman, J. Baird Callicott, George Sessions, Karen J. Warren, and John Clark, eds., *Environmental Philosophy: From Animal Rights to Radical Ecology,* 2nd ed. (Upper Saddle River, N.J.: Prentice Hall, 1998), 17–25.
2. Leopold, "The Land Ethic" (1949), ASCA, 203. [20]
3. Leopold, "The Land Ethic" (1949), ASCA, 204 [20]; "Odyssey" (1942), ASCA, 107. [21]
4. Leopold, "The Land Ethic" (1949), ASCA, 204. [20]

21. THE REACH OF WORDS

1. Leopold, "Conservationist in Mexico" (1937), RMG, 240, ALS, 203. [16]
2. Leopold, "Draft Foreword to *A Sand Country Almanac*" (1947), in J. Baird Callicott, ed., *Companion to "A Sand County Almanac": Interpretive & Critical Essays* (Madison: University of Wisconsin Press, 1987), 281–88. [7]
3. Leopold, "The Thick-billed Parrot in Chihuahua" (1937), ASCA, 139–40. [18]

4. Leopold, ibid., ASCA, 139, 138. [21]

5. See Leopold, "Guacamaja" (1949), ASCA, 137–41.

6. Leopold, "Marshland Elegy," *American Forests* 43:10 (October 1937), 472–74. Reprinted in ASCA, 95–101.

7. See Dennis Ribbens, "The Making of *A Sand County Almanac*," in Callicott, ed., *Companion to "A Sand County Almanac,"* 91–109; Curt Meine, "Moving Mountains: Aldo Leopold & *A Sand County Almanac*," *Wildlife Society Bulletin* 26:4 (1998), 697–706.

8. Leopold, "Marshland Elegy" (1937), ASCA, 96. [19]

9. Leopold, "The Green Lagoons" (1945), ASCA, 149. [7]

Quotation Sources

PUBLISHED SOURCES

Quotations for this volume were selected primarily from Aldo Leopold's published writings, which amount to some five hundred items. Susan L. Flader and
J. Baird Callicott's collection, *The River of the Mother of God and Other Essays by Aldo
Leopold* (1991), contains a comprehensive bibliography, which is recommended
to readers who wish to consult the original sources. This list includes only those
publications from which quotations have been excerpted for this volume. Unless
otherwise noted, Aldo Leopold was sole author.

Leopold's work was often reprinted; in most cases we have cited only the initial
publication. All items are presented in chronological order, although the exact
dates of first publication or composition for some items are difficult to determine. Items that remained unpublished at the time of Leopold's death but that
were later published in *Round River: From the Journals of Aldo Leopold* or in *The
River of the Mother of God* are included under the date of composition. Essays that
first appeared in print in *A Sand County Almanac and Sketches Here and There* are
listed by title only under the date 1949.

Abbreviations in brackets after the citation indicate that the item was republished in *A Sand County Almanac* [ASCA]; first published in *Round River* [RR];
republished in *Aldo Leopold's Southwest* [ALS]; or first published or republished
in *The River of the Mother of God* [RMG]. Numbers in bold type after the citation
are the page numbers of this volume indicating where quotations from that
source can be found.

To 1918

To the forest officers of the Carson. Burlington, Iowa, July 15, 1913. *Carson Pine
Cone* (July 1913). [RMG]   **7, 171**
Game conservation—A warning, also an opportunity. *Arizona* 7:1–2 (1916), 6.
[ALS]   **182**

1918

The popular wilderness fallacy: An idea that is fast exploding. *Outer's Book—
Recreation* 58:1 (January 1918), 43–46. [RMG]   **7, 8, 50, 240**
Make Stinking Lake a game refuge. *Bulletin of the American Game Protective Associa-
tion* 7:1 (January 1918), 16. Also published in *Outer's Book—Recreation* 58:4
(April 1918), 291. [ALS]   **182**
Forestry and game conservation. *Journal of Forestry* 16:4 (April 1918), 404–11.
[ALS, RMG]   **8, 24, 50, 51, 130**

Restocking the national forests with elk: Where and how it may be done. *Outer's Book—Recreation* 58:5 (May 1918), 412–15. [ALS]   **120–21**

Mixing trout in western waters. *Transactions of the American Fisheries Society* 47:3 (June 1918), 101–2.   **130–31**

Putting the "AM" in game warden: The story of how the New Mexico Game Protective Association substituted *Push for Politics* in their state game department. *Sportsmen's Review* 54:9 (August 31, 1918), 173–74.   **182–83, 183**

1919

The national forests: The last free hunting grounds of the nation. *Journal of Forestry* 17:2 (February 1919), 150–53.   **51, 171, 171–72, 227–28**

Wild lifers vs. game farmers: A plea for democracy in sport. *Bulletin of the American Game Protective Association* 8:2 (April 1919), 6–7. [ALS, RMG]   **51, 172, 193–94, 228**

A plea for state-owned ducking grounds. *Wild Life* (October 1919), 9. [ALS]   **172, 194, 228**

A turkey hunt in the Datil National Forest. *Wild Life* (December 1919), 4–5, 16. [ALS]   **52, 228**

1920

Wanted—national forest game refuges. *Bulletin of the American Game Protective Association* 9:1 (January 1920), 8–10, 22.   **52, 131**

Determining the kill factor for blacktail deer in the Southwest. *Journal of Forestry* 18:2 (February 1920), 131–34. [ALS]   **52**

"Piute forestry" vs. forest fire prevention. *Southwestern Magazine* 2:3 (March 1920), 12–13. [ALS, RMG]   **8**

The game situation in the Southwest. *Bulletin of the American Game Protective Association* 9:2 (April 1920), 3–5.   **52–53, 53**

The forestry of the prophets. *Journal of Forestry* 18:4 (April 1920), 412–19. [RMG]   **8–9, 317–18**

A Man's Leisure Time. Manuscript dated 10-15-20. [Revised partial version published in RR]   **36, 183**

1921

The essentials of a game refuge. *Literary Digest* 68:3 (January 15, 1921), 54.   **53**

A plea for recognition of artificial works in forest erosion control policy. *Journal of Forestry* 19:3 (March 1921), 267–73.   **24–25, 25, 77**

The wilderness and its place in forest recreational policy. *Journal of Forestry* 19:7 (November 1921), 718–21. [ALS, RMG]   **9, 36, 37, 104, 104–5**

1922

The posting problem. *Outdoor Life* 49:3 (March 1922), 186–88.   **206, 284**

Blue River. Manuscript dated 6-11-22. [RR]   **318**

The Delta Colorado. Journal entries dated October 25–November 14, 1922. [RR]   **228**

Erosion as a menace to the social and economic future of the Southwest. *Journal of Forestry* 44:9 (September 1946), 627–33. [Original manuscript prepared 1922] **77, 78, 228**

Goose Music. Undated manuscript, c. 1922. [RR]   **228–29, 229, 229–30, 271–72, 284**

1923

Some fundamentals of conservation in the Southwest. *Environmental Ethics* 1 (summer 1979), 131–41. Manuscript dated 1923 (probably March). [RMG] **26, 78, 131, 194, 206–7, 207, 241, 299, 300, 318, 318–19**

Wild followers of the forest: The effect of forest fires on game and fish—The relation of forests to game conservation. *American Forestry* 29:357 (September 1923), 515–19, 568.   **53, 131, 207, 207–8**

A Criticism of the Booster Spirit. Manuscript of address delivered 11-6-23. [RMG]   **37, 90, 208, 209, 284, 319**

Watershed Handbook. U.S. Forest Service, Southwestern District, December 1923. **26, 26–27, 27, 78, 79**

1924

Pioneers and gullies. *Sunset Magazine* 52:5 (May 1924), 15–16, 91–95. [ALS, RMG]   **27, 27–28, 28, 79, 80, 91, 158, 209, 241–42**

Canada, 1924. Journal entries dated June 11–25, 1924. [RR]   **230, 319**

Grass, brush, timber, and fire in southern Arizona. *Journal of Forestry* 22:6 (October 1924), 1–10. [ALS, RMG]   **9–10, 10, 28, 242**

The River of the Mother of God. Manuscript dated c. December 1924. [RMG]   **105, 105–6, 183, 319**

1925

Conserving the covered wagon. *Sunset Magazine* 54:3 (March 1925), 21, 56. [RMG]   **91, 106, 183, 285**

Natural reproduction of forests. *Parks and Recreation* 9:2 (April 1925), 366–72. **10, 10–11, 131**

The pig in the parlor. *USFS Service Bulletin* 9:23 (June 8, 1925), 1–2. [RMG]   **106–7**

Ten new developments in game management. *American Game* 14:3 (July 1925), 7–8, 20. [ALS]   **53, 209**

The last stand of the wilderness. *American Forests and Forest Life* 31:382 (October 1925), 599–604.   **11, 37, 38, 107, 210, 242, 285**

Wilderness as a form of land use. *The Journal of Land & Public Utility Economics* 1:4 (October 1925), 398–404. [RMG]   **38, 107, 172, 183, 194, 210, 243**

A plea for wilderness hunting grounds. *Outdoor Life* 56:5 (November 1925), 348–50. [ALS]   **38, 107–8, 108, 173, 194, 230**

Forestry and game management. *Colorado Forester* (Ft. Collins: Colorado Agricultural College, 1925), 29–30.   **54**

1926

[Untitled address on wilderness conservation]. *Proceedings of the Second National Conference on Outdoor Recreation, January 20–21, 1926* (69th Cong., 1st sess., 1926, S. Doc. 117), 61–65. **38, 108, 184, 194–95, 210**

The way of the waterfowl: How the Anthony Bill will help ducks and duck hunting; an example of New Mexico's refuge system in actual operation. *American Forests and Forest Life* 32:389 (May 1926), 287–91. **54, 121**

The next move: A size-up of the migratory bird situation. *Outdoor Life* 58:5 (November 1926), 363. **121**

1927

The Lily. Journal entry, c. June 28, 1927. [RR] **319–20**

Game cropping in southern Wisconsin. *Our Native Landscape* 1 (October 1927). **91, 121, 159, 300**

The Gila, 1927. Journal entries dated November 9–20, 1927. [RR] **230**

1928

The home builder conserves. *American Forests and Forest Life* 34:413 (May 1928), 276–78, 297. [RMG] **11, 184**

Mr. Thompson's wilderness. *USFS Service Bulletin* 12:26 (June 25, 1928), 1–2. **11–12, 12, 108**

The game survey and its work. *Transactions of the Fifteenth National Game Conference* (December 3–4, 1928), 128–32. **54**

1929

The Gila, 1929. Journal entries dated November 6–20, 1929. [RR] **230–31**

Progress of the game survey. *Transactions of the Sixteenth American Game Conference* (December 2–3, 1929), 64–71. **80**

Report of the Committee on American Wild Life Policy [Aldo Leopold, chairman]. *Transactions of the Sixteenth American Game Conference* (December 2–3, 1929), 196–210. **38, 54, 109, 121, 132**

Environmental controls: The forester's contribution to game conservation. *Ames Forester* 17 (1929), 25–26. **54**

1930

Wild game as a farm crop. *Game Breeder* 34:2 (February 1930), 39. **55, 91**

Environmental controls for game through modified silviculture. *Journal of Forestry* 28:3 (March 1930), 321–26. **12**

Game management in the national forests. *American Forests* 36:7 (July 1930), 412–14. [ALS] **55, 173, 231**

The decline of the jacksnipe in southern Wisconsin. *Wilson Bulletin* 42:3 (September 1930), 183–90. **195**

The American game policy in a nutshell. *Transactions of the Seventeenth American Game Conference* (December 1–2, 1930), 281–83. **55, 210–11**

Report to the American Game Conference on an American game policy. *Transac-*

tions of the Seventeenth American Game Conference (December 1–2, 1930), 284–309. [RMG]   **28, 28–29, 55, 132, 231**

1931

The forester's role in game management. *Journal of Forestry* 29:1 (January 1931), 25–31.   **132, 173**

Game methods: The American way. *American Game* 20:2 (March–April 1931), 20, 29–31. [RMG]   **55, 56, 132–33, 231, 232, 285, 320**

Game range. *Journal of Forestry* 29:6 (October 1931), 932–38.   **56**

Vegetation and birds. *Report of the Iowa State Horticultural Society, 66th Annual Convention, Nov. 12–14, 1931,* 66 (1931), 204–6.   **91, 257–58**

The prairie chicken: A lost hope, or an opportunity? *American Field* 116:50 (December 12, 1931), 1.   **320**

Report on a Game Survey of the North Central States. Madison: Sporting Arms and Ammunition Manufacturers' Institute, 1931.   **29, 38–39, 56, 56–57, 57, 80, 92, 109, 122, 133, 133–34, 134, 159, 211, 232, 243**

1932

Game and wild life conservation. *Condor* 34:2 (March–April 1932), 103–6. [RMG]   **57, 57–58, 184, 195, 211**

The alder fork: A fishing idyl. *Outdoor America* 10:10 (May 1932), 11. [ASCA]   **232, 320**

Grand-Opera Game. Manuscript dated c. summer 1932. [RMG]   **58**

Report of the Iowa game survey, chapter one: The fall of the Iowa game range. *Outdoor America* 11:1 (August–September 1932), 7–9.   **92**

Report of the Iowa game survey, chapter two: Iowa quail. *Outdoor America* 11:2 (October–November 1932), 11–13, 30–31.   **243–44, 244, 320**

1933

Weatherproofing conservation. *American Forests* 39:1 (January 1933), 10–11, 48.   **58, 184, 211, 212**

How research and game surveys help the sportsman and farmer. [Proceedings of the] *New England Game Conference (Feb. 11, 1933).* Cambridge: Samuel Marcus Press, for the Massachusetts Fish and Game Association, 51–56.   **134**

The Virgin Southwest. Manuscript dated 5-6-33. [RMG]   **29, 81, 285, 300**

The conservation ethic. *Journal of Forestry* 31:6 (October 1933), 634–43. [Presented as an address on 5-1-33. Portions revised and included in "The Land Ethic" in ASCA; RMG]   **58, 81, 134–35, 159, 159–60, 173, 173–74, 185, 195, 212, 244, 245, 285, 301, 301–2**

Game Management. New York: Charles Scribner's Sons, 1933.   **12, 29, 39, 58, 59, 59–60, 60, 60–61, 61, 81, 92, 109, 122, 135, 135–36, 174, 185, 212–13, 213, 232, 233, 245, 272, 285, 286, 302, 321**

1934

Necessity for game research. *Transactions of the Twentieth American Game Conference* (January 22–24, 1934), 92–95.   **61, 321**

Conservation economics. *Journal of Forestry* 32:5 (May 1934), 537–44. [RMG]
39, 81, 136–37, 160, 174, 174–75, 196, 213

Helping ourselves: Being the adventures of a farmer and a sportsman who produced their own shooting ground. (With Reuben Paulson.) *Field and Stream* 39:4 (August 1934), 32–33, 56. [RMG]   **62**

The arboretum and the university. *Parks and Recreation* 18:2 (October 1934), 59–60. [RMG]   **123, 303, 321**

Review of Ward Shepard, *Notes on German Game Management, Chiefly in Bavaria and Baden* (Senate Committee on Wild Life Resources, 1934). *Journal of Forestry* 32:7 (October 1934), 774–75.   **12, 62, 287**

The game cycle—A challenge to science. *Outdoor Nebraska* 9:4 (autumn 1934), 4, 14.   **137, 245**

Some thoughts on recreational planning. *Parks and Recreation* 18:4 (December 1934), 136–37.   **39, 39–40, 109, 160–61**

1935

Whither 1935?—A review of the American game policy. *Transactions of the Twenty-first American Game Conference* (January 21–23, 1935), 49–55.   **62, 92–93, 213, 233, 321**

Wildlife research rapidly growing. *American Game* 24:1 (January–February 1935), 5, 13.   **62**

Preliminary report on forestry and game management. *Journal of Forestry* 33:3 (March 1935), 273–75.   **13, 29–30, 213–14**

Land Pathology. Manuscript of address delivered 4-15-35. [RMG]   **161, 185, 214, 287, 303, 303–4**

Coon Valley: An adventure in cooperative conservation. *American Forests* 41:5 (May 1935), 205–8. [RMG]   **81–82, 82, 161, 214**

Wilderness. Undated manuscript, c. fall 1935. [RMG]   **13, 110, 321–22**

Why the Wilderness Society? *Living Wilderness* 1 (September 1935), 6.   **109, 123, 137**

Notes on wild life conservation in Germany. *Game Research News Letter* 6 (September 16, 1935), 1–3; and 7 (October 21, 1935), 1–3.   **13, 123, 137**

Forerunners of game management. *Colorado Forester* (Colorado State College, 1935), 12.   **137**

Wild life research in Wisconsin. *Transactions of the Wisconsin Academy of Sciences, Arts and Letters* 29 (1935), 203–8.   **62–63**

1936

Remarks on wildlife management by private agencies. *Proceedings of the North American Wildlife Conference,* February 3–7, 1936 (Senate Committee Print, 74th Cong., 2nd sess., 1936), 156–58.   **162, 175, 214**

Threatened species: A proposal to the Wildlife Conference for an inventory of the needs of near-extinct birds and animals. *American Forests* 42:3 (March 1936), 116–19. [ALS, RMG]   **63, 137, 138, 186**

Naturschutz in Germany. *Bird-Lore* 38:2 (March–April 1936), 102–11.   **13, 138, 186, 246**

Wildlife conference. *Journal of Forestry* 34:4 (April 1936), 430–31.   **63**

Deer and Dauerwald in Germany: I. History. *Journal of Forestry* 34:4 (April 1936), 366–75. **14, 196**

Deer and Dauerwald in Germany: II. Ecology and policy. *Journal of Forestry* 34:5 (May 1936), 460–66. **14, 64, 138, 246**

Means and Ends in Wild Life Management. Undated manuscript, c. May 1936. [RMG] **64, 93**

Farm game management in Silesia. *American Wildlife* 25:5 (September–October 1936), 67–68, 74–76. **322**

Review of *Upland Game Restoration* (Western Cartridge Co. and Winchester Repeating Arms Co., 1936). *Outdoor America* 2:2 (December 1936), 11. **64–65**

Wildlife Crops: Finding Out How to Grow Them. (With Gardiner Bump, George C. Embody, Carl L. Hubbs, and Herbert L. Stoddard.) Washington, D.C.: American Wildlife Institute, 1936. **93, 139**

1937

The thick-billed parrot in Chihuahua. *Condor* 39:1 (January–February 1937), 9–10. [Reprinted in ASCA as "Guacamaja"] **273, 287–88, 322**

Review of A. E. Parkins and J. R. Whitaker, *Our Natural Resources and Their Conservation* (New York, 1936). *Bird-Lore* 39:1 (January–February 1937), 74–75. **139, 186, 258, 273**

Second report of [the Society of American Foresters] Game Policy Committee. *Journal of Forestry* 35:2 (February 1937), 228–32. **14–15, 30, 139, 215**

The University and Conservation of Wisconsin Wildlife. (With L. J. Cole, N. C. Fassett, C. A. Herrick, Chancey Juday, and George Wagner.) Bulletin of the University of Wisconsin, ser. no. 2211, general ser. no. 1995, Science Inquiry Publication no. 3, February 1937. **65, 140, 186, 258, 258–59, 259**

The research program. *Transactions of the Second North American Wildlife Conference* (March 1–4, 1937), 104–7. **65, 140, 186, 215, 259**

Conservationist in Mexico. *American Forests* 43:3 (March 1937), 118–20, 146. [ALS, RMG] **15, 30, 65–66, 110, 246–47, 304**

Review of A. Vietinghoff-Reisch, "Forstlicher Naturschutz und Naturschutz im nationalen Lebensraume Deutschlands," *Zeitschr. f. Weltforstwirtschaft* 3 (1936), 868–85. *Journal of Forestry* 35:8 (August 1937), 794–95. **140**

Marshland elegy. *American Forests* 43:10 (October 1937), 472–74. [ASCA] **110, 140, 247, 288, 322, 323**

Conservation blueprints. *American Forests* 43:12 (December 1937), 596, 608. **215, 304**

Teaching wildlife conservation in public schools. *Transactions of the Wisconsin Academy of Sciences, Arts and Letters* 30 (1937), 77–86. **259–60, 260, 260–61, 323**

1938

Chukaremia. *Outdoor America* 3:3 (January 1938), 3. [RMG] **66**

Wildlife research—Is it a practical and necessary basis for management? *Transactions of the Third North American Wildlife Conference* (February 14–17, 1938), 42–45, 55. **66–67, 67, 140–41, 323**

Conservation esthetic. *Bird-Lore* 40:2 (March–April 1938), 101–9. [ASCA] **40–41, 41, 41–42, 42, 67, 110, 123, 215–16, 233, 288–89, 289**

Engineering and Conservation. Manuscript dated 4-11-38. [RMG] **82, 141, 186–87, 247, 304–5, 305**

Natural History—The Forgotten Science. Manuscript dated 4-26-38. [RR] **261, 261–62, 305**

Whither Missouri? *Missouri Conservationist* 1:1 (July 1938), 6. **93, 163**

Game Research News Letter 16 (November 1, 1938). **67**

Woodlot wildlife aids. *Wisconsin Agriculturist and Farmer* 65:27 (December 31, 1938), 4. **15**

Report on Huron Mountain Club. Huron Mountain Club, Michigan, 1938. **67, 68, 141, 163, 216, 273**

Conservation. From "A Survey of Conservation" manuscript, c. 1938. [RR; revised and combined with materials from "The Round River—A Parable" in expanded 1966 edition of ASCA] **141–42, 142, 163–64, 196, 197, 216, 262, 289, 305, 305–6**

1939

Farmer-sportsman, a partnership for wildlife restoration. *Transactions of the Fourth North American Wildlife Conference* (February 13–15, 1939), 145–49, 167–68. **68, 164, 324**

Academic and professional training in wildlife work. *Journal of Wildlife Management* 3:2 (April 1939), 156–61. **68–69, 262–63, 263**

The farmer as a conservationist. *American Forests* 45:6 (June 1939), 294–99, 316, 323. [RMG] **82, 93, 93–94, 94, 124, 142, 164, 197, 216, 263, 273, 306, 324**

A biotic view of land. *Journal of Forestry* 37:9 (September 1939), 727–30. [Portions revised and included in "The Land Ethic" in ASCA; RMG] **15, 69, 83, 94, 124, 142–43, 143, 164, 247–48, 248, 306**

1940

New Year's inventory checks missing game. *Wisconsin Agriculturist and Farmer* 67:3 (January 27, 1940), 10. [RMG] **143, 324**

Review of A. F. Gustafson, H. Ries, C. H. Guise, and W. J. Hamilton, Jr., *Conservation in the United States* (Ithaca, 1939). *Ecology* 21:1 (January 1940), 92–93. **143, 263–64, 324**

Windbreaks aid wildlife. *Wisconsin Agriculturist and Farmer* 67:5 (March 9, 1940), 15. **95**

When geese return spring is here. *Wisconsin Agriculturist and Farmer* 67:7 (April 6, 1940), 18. **264**

Report of the [American Ornithologists' Union] Committee on Bird Protection, 1939. (With Victor H. Cahalane, chairman, William L. Finley, and Clarence Cottam.) *Auk* 57:2 (April 1940), 279–91. **143–44**

Origin and ideals of wilderness areas. *Living Wilderness* 5 (July 1940), 7. **110–11**

Song of the Gavilan. *Journal of Wildlife Management* 4:3 (July 1940), 329–32. [ASCA] **234, 248, 273–74, 290, 324**

The state of the profession. *Journal of Wildlife Management* 4:3 (July 1940), 343–46. [RMG] **69, 144, 216, 248, 274, 274–75, 306–7**

Review of Milton B. Trautman, *The Birds of Buckeye Lake, Ohio* (University of Michigan Museum of Zoology Miscellaneous Publications no. 44 [May 7, 1940]). *Wilson Bulletin* 52:3 (September 1940), 217–18. **275**

Exit orchis: A little action now would save our fast disappearing wildlife. (Wisconsin) *Wildlife* 2:2 (August 1940), 17; reprinted in *American Wildlife* 29:5 (September–October 1940), 207. **164–65, 264, 290**

Review of *The Status of Wildlife in the United States* (Report of the Special [Senate] Committee on the Conservation of Wildlife Resources. S. Rprt. 1203, 76th Cong., 3rd sess., 1940). *Journal of Forestry* 38:10 (October 1940), 823. **69**

Birds earn their keep on Wisconsin farms. *Wisconsin Agriculturist and Farmer* 67:24 (November 30, 1940), 18. **95**

Wisconsin wildlife chronology. *Wisconsin Conservation Bulletin* 5:11 (November 1940), 8–20. **144, 248, 307**

Escudilla. *American Forests* 46:12 (December 1940), 539–40. [ASCA] **175, 248–49, 324–25**

Spread of the Hungarian partridge in Wisconsin. *Transactions of the Wisconsin Academy of Sciences, Arts and Letters* 32 (1940), 5–28. **249**

1941

Review of E. G. Cheyney and T. Shantz-Hansen, *This Is Our Land: The Story of Conservation in the United States* (St. Paul, 1940). *Journal of Forestry* 19:1 (January 1941), 72. **264**

Ecology and Politics. Undated manuscript, c. February 1941. [RMG] **275, 325**

John S. Main. (With F. N. Hamerstrom, Jr.) *Wilson Bulletin* 53:1 (March 1941), 31–32. **187**

Bur oak is badge of Wisconsin. *Wisconsin Agriculturist and Farmer* 68:7 (April 5, 1941), 10. [Revised and reprinted as "Bur Oak" in ASCA] **15, 249**

Pest-hunts. *Passenger Pigeon* 3:5 (May 1941), 42–43. **70**

Wilderness as a land laboratory. *Living Wilderness* 6 (July 1941), 3. [Portions revised and included in "Wilderness" in ASCA; RMG] **16, 42, 83, 111, 124, 124–25**

Sky dance of spring. Included in *Wildlife Conservation on the Farm* (collection of Leopold's short essays published by *Wisconsin Agriculturist and Farmer*, Racine, Wis., c. September 1941). [Rewritten as "Sky Dance" for ASCA] **234**

Cheat takes over. *Land* 1:4 (autumn 1941), 310–13. [Revised and reprinted in ASCA] **30, 83, 125**

Country. Early manuscript version dated 12-23-41. [RR] **197, 290, 290–91**

Lakes in relation to terrestrial life patterns. In James G. Needham et al., *A Symposium on Hydrobiology* (Madison: University of Wisconsin Press, 1941), 17–22. **83, 84**

Wilderness values. *1941 Yearbook, Park and Recreation Progress* (Washington, D.C.: National Park Service, 1941), 27–29; reprinted in *Living Wilderness* 7 (March 1942), 24–25. **42, 42–43, 43, 111–12, 175, 175–76, 265, 275, 291**

The Round River—A Parable. Undated manuscript, c. late 1941, early 1942. [RR; revised and combined with materials from "Conservation" in expanded 1966 edition of ASCA] **95, 146, 265, 307**

1942

The role of wildlife in a liberal education. *Transactions of the Seventh North American Wildlife Conference* (April 8–10, 1942), 485–89. [RMG] **146, 197, 265, 265–66, 275–76**

The grizzly—A problem in land planning. *Outdoor America* 7:6 (April 1942), 11–12. [Portions revised and included in "Wilderness" in ASCA]   **146, 176**

The plover is back from Argentine. *Wisconsin Agriculturist and Farmer* 69:10 (May 16, 1942), 10. [Reprinted as "Back from the Argentine" in ASCA]   **291–92, 325**

The last stand. *Outdoor America* 7:7 (May–June 1942), 8–9; reprinted in *Living Wilderness* 8 (December 1942), 25–26. [RMG]   **16, 16–17, 17, 176, 197, 198, 325**

Odyssey. *Audubon Magazine* 44:3 (May–June 1942), 133–35. [ASCA]   **95, 95–96, 146, 325**

Half-excellent (review of George T. Renner, *Conservation of Natural Resources*. New York: John Wiley & Sons, 1942). *Land* 2:2 (July 1942), 111–12.   **325**

Land-use and democracy. *Audubon Magazine* 44:5 (September–October 1942), 259–65. [RMG]   **165, 176–77, 187, 188, 198, 217, 218, 307**

1943

Flambeau: The story of a wild river. *American Forests* 49:1 (January 1943), 12–14, 47. Reprinted as "The Flambeau" in *Wisconsin Conservation Bulletin* 8:3 (March 1943), 13–17. [Portions revised and included in "Flambeau" in ASCA]   **17, 112**

Wildlife in American culture. *Journal of Wildlife Management* 7:1 (January 1943), 1–6. [ASCA]   **43, 198, 218, 234, 234–35, 235, 249**

Obituary: P. S. Lovejoy. *Journal of Wildlife Management* 7:1 (January 1943), 125–28.   **249**

A lesson from the woodlands. *Wisconsin Conservation Bulletin* 8:2 (February 1943), 25–27. [Reprinted as "A Mighty Fortress" in ASCA]   **276**

Pines above the snow. *Wisconsin Conservation Bulletin* 8:3 (March 1943), 27–29. [ASCA]   **17, 17–18, 18, 325**

Review of Sherman Strong Hayden, *The International Protection of Wild Life* (Columbia University Studies in History, Economics, and Public Law no. 491. New York, 1942). *Geographical Review* 33:2 (April 1943), 340–41.   **307–8**

The excess deer problem. *Audubon Magazine* 45:3 (May–June 1943), 156–57.   **70**

Review of Ira N. Gabrielson, *Wildlife Refuges* (New York, 1943). *Journal of Forestry* 41:7 (July 1943), 529–31.   **146–47, 249–50, 326**

What Is a Weed? Manuscript dated 8-2-43. [RMG]   **31, 96, 147**

Home range. *Wisconsin Conservation Bulletin* 8:9 (September 1943), 23–24. [ASCA]   **70, 326**

Review of William R. Van Dersal, *The American Land* (New York, 1943). *Journal of Forestry* 41:12 (December 1943), 928.   **250**

Introduction to *The Ducks, Geese, and Swans of North America: A* Vade Mecum *for the Naturalist and the Sportsman* by Francis H. Kortright (Washington, D.C.: American Wildlife Institute, 1943), v.   **234**

1944

Review of H. M. Bell and E. J. Dyksterhuis, Fighting the mesquite and cedar invasion on Texas ranges (*Soil Conservation* 9:5 [November 1943], 111–14). *Journal of Forestry* 42:1 (January 1944), 63. [ALS]   **31, 250**

Post-war prospects. *Audubon Magazine* 46:1 (January–February 1944), 27–29.
96, 147, 266, 292

Review of Montague Stevens, *Meet Mr. Grizzly* (Albuquerque, 1943). *Journal of Forestry* 42:3 (March 1944), 222. [ALS]   **250**

Review of Edward H. Graham, *Natural Principles of Land Use* (New York, 1944). *Soil Conservation* 10:2 (August 1944), 38–39.   **198**

Conservation: In Whole or in Part? Manuscript dated 11-1-44. [RMG]   **84, 147–48, 165–66, 188, 198, 198–99, 219, 266, 308**

1945

Review of Stanley P. Young and Edward H. Goldman, *The Wolves of North America* (Washington, D.C.: American Wildlife Institute, 1944). *Journal of Forestry* 43:1 (January 1945), 928–29. [ALS, RMG]   **125, 148–49**

The outlook for farm wildlife. *Transactions of the Tenth North American Wildlife Conference* (February 26–28, 1945), 165–68. [RMG]   **18, 70–71, 96–97, 97, 149**

Deer, wolves, foxes and pheasants. *Wisconsin Conservation Bulletin* 10:4 (April 1945), 3–5.   **18, 149, 149–50**

Review of Sally Carrighar, *One Day on Beetle Rock* (New York, 1944). *Journal of Forestry* 43:4 (April 1945), 301–2.   **276**

Review of Durward L. Allen, *Michigan Fox Squirrel Management* (Michigan Department of Conservation, Game Div., pub. no. 100, 1943). *Journal of Forestry* 43:6 (June 1945), 462.   **276**

The green lagoons. *American Forests* 51:8 (August 1945), 376–77, 414. [ASCA].   **112, 326**

1946

Review of A. G. Tansley, *Our Heritage of Wild Nature* (Cambridge University Press, 1945). *Journal of Forestry* 44:3 (March 1946), 215–16.   **309**

Review of S. Kip Farrington, Jr., *The Ducks Came Back: The Story of Ducks Unlimited* (New York: Coward-McCann, 1945). *Journal of Wildlife Management* 10:3 (July 1946), 281–83. [RMG]   **125, 188**

The deer dilemma. *Wisconsin Conservation Bulletin* 11:8–9 (August–September 1946), 3–5.   **18, 188**

Adventures of a Conservation Commissioner. Manuscript of address presented at the Midwest Wildlife Conference, December 1946. [RMG]   **71, 188–89**

Deadening. Undated manuscript, c. 1946. [RR]   **97, 199**

1947

A phenological record for Sauk and Dane counties, Wisconsin, 1935–1945. (With Sara Elizabeth Jones.) *Ecological Monographs* 17:1 (January 1947), 81–122.   **277, 292, 326**

Summarization of the Twelfth North American Wildlife Conference. *Transactions of the Twelfth North American Wildlife Conference* (February 3–5, 1947), 529–36.   **112–13, 177, 235**

Wherefore Wildlife Ecology? Undated lecture notes, c. spring 1947. [RMG]   **189, 266, 292**

Review of E. M. Queeny, *Prairie Wings: Pen and Camera Flight Studies* (New York: Ducks Unlimited, 1946). *Journal of Wildlife Management* 11:2 (April 1947), 190–91. **277**

On a monument to the passenger pigeon. In *Silent Wings*. Madison: Wisconsin Society for Ornithology, May 11, 1947, 3–5. [Revised and reprinted as "On a Monument to the Pigeon" in ASCA] **150, 251, 277–78, 292–93, 310, 326–27**

Draft foreword to *A Sand County Almanac* ["Great Possessions" manuscript], 7-31-47. In J. Baird Callicott, ed., *Companion to "A Sand County Almanac": Interpretive & Critical Essays* (Madison: University of Wisconsin Press, 1987), 281–88. **113, 310, 327**

The ecological conscience. *Bulletin of the Garden Club of America* (September 1947), 45–53. [Portions revised and included in "The Land Ethic" in ASCA; RMG] **71, 85, 166, 189, 199, 219, 266–67, 267, 310**

1948

Why and how research? *Transactions of the Thirteenth North American Wildlife Conference* (March 8–10, 1948), 44–48. **71, 293–94**

Charles Knesal Cooperrider, 1889–1994. *Journal of Wildlife Management* 12:3 (July 1948), 337–39. [ALS] **310, 327**

The Deer Swath. Undated manuscript, c. 1948. [RR] **235**

1949

The following essays were first published in ASCA.

Foreword. **125–26, 199, 278, 310, 327**
Good Oak. **251, 251–52, 327**
The Geese Return. **327–28**
Come High Water. **113, 252**
Draba. **328**
Great Possessions. **328**
Prairie Birthday. **126, 150, 252, 253, 267, 294, 328**
The Green Pasture. **294**
The Choral Copse. **294, 328**
Smoky Gold. **235, 236, 253**
Too Early. **294, 328–29**
Red Lanterns. **267, 329**
If I Were the Wind. **329**
Axe-in-Hand. **18–19, 19, 126, 311, 329**
The Sand Counties. **199**
Flambeau. **329**
Illinois Bus Ride. **85–86**
Red Legs Kicking. **236, 267**
On Top. **31, 329**
Thinking Like a Mountain. **71, 113, 177, 219, 329–30**
Clandeboye. **253, 268, 294–95**

UNPUBLISHED SOURCES

Quotations in this volume have been excerpted from the substantial body of unpublished materials located in the Aldo Leopold Papers at the University of Wisconsin Archives in Madison, Wisconsin. Items cited below include completed manuscripts, addresses, reports, notes, fragmentary manuscripts, and working drafts. The editors thank the University of Wisconsin Archives and the Aldo Leopold Foundation for permission to present these materials.

1920   A Man's Leisure Time. Typewritten draft dated 10-15-20; presented as an address at the University of New Mexico. Revised partial version published in RR.   **257, 271, 318**

1921   Erosion and Prosperity. Typewritten draft dated 1-18-21; presented as an address at the University of Arizona.   **76–77**

c. 1922   Skill in Forestry. Typewritten draft, undated; filed with correspondence dated 1922.   **9, 25**

1925   Memorandum for District Forester Kelly. Typewritten report dated 11-22-25; prepared following inspection report of Wichita National Forest, November 18–21, 1922.   **131–32**

1927   The Conservation of Wilderness Recreation Areas. Typewritten draft dated 2-19-27; presented at the meeting of the Getaway Club in Madison, Wisconsin.   **173**

1928   Science and Game Conservation. Typewritten draft dated 4-19-28; presented as an address at the convention of the Izaak Walton League of America.   **54, 132**

1931   Outline for Game Survey of Iowa. Typewritten notes dated 7-21-31.   **122**

1932   The American Game Policy on Predators. Typewritten draft dated 11-28-32.   **272, 320–21**

c. 1933   The Social Consequences of Conservation. Various handwritten materials, undated.   **302–3**

c. 1934   What Is the University of Wisconsin Arboretum, Wild Life Refuge, and Forest Experiment Preserve? Typewritten manuscript, undated.   **123, 258, 287**

c. 1935   Wilderness. Handwritten fragment, undated.   **245–46, 272**
         Untitled typewritten fragment, undated.   **161–62**
         Lecture notes. Typewritten and handwritten notes, undated.   **162**

c. 1937   The Farm Wildlife Program: A Self-Scrutiny. Handwritten and typewritten materials, undated.   **162, 162–63**

1939   [Report of the] Chair of Wildlife Management. Typewritten report dated 3-16-39, Department of Wildlife Ecology Papers, University of Wisconsin Archives.   **68**

1940   Improving the Wildlife Program of the Soil Conservation Service. Typewritten draft dated 5-3-40. **144, 290**

c. 1940   The Conservation League. Typewritten draft, undated. **187**

  Biotic Land Use. Typewritten draft with revisions, undated. **144–45, 145, 275**

1941   Planning for Wildlife. Typewritten manuscript dated 9-26-41. **95, 111, 165, 264**

c. 1941   Of Mice and Men. Handwritten and typewritten drafts, undated. **197**

  Untitled notes on biotic diversity. Typewritten notes, undated. **145, 146**

  Conservation and Politics. Typewritten manuscript, undated. **216–17**

1942   Armament for Conservation. Typewritten draft dated 11-23-42; prepared for seminar presentation. **218, 307**

1943   Mistakes I Have Made in Wildlife Research. Typewritten draft dated 2-9-43; prepared for presentation at the North American Wildlife Conference. **70**

1944   Ticks and Deer: A Lesson in Conservation. Typewritten draft dated 12-5-44. **308**

c. 1944   The Biotic War. Handwritten notes, undated. **276, 308–9**

1946   The Land-Health Concept and Conservation. Handwritten draft dated 12-21-46. **84–85, 97, 150, 266, 276, 326**

c. 1946   Conservation. Typewritten draft, filed with correspondence dated 8-8-46. **166**

  Ecology and the Arts. Handwritten notes, undated. **277**

  The Role of Wildlife in Education. Handwritten notes, undated. **309**

  The Meaning of Conservation. Handwritten notes, undated. **309**

  Scarcity Values in Conservation. Handwritten notes, undated. **189, 250–51**

  Ecology and Economics in Land Use. Handwritten notes, undated. **309**

c. 1947   Notes on Proposed Centennial Symposium on Ecological Conservation. Handwritten and typewritten draft, undated. **166**

Contributors

J. Baird Callicott is professor of philosophy and religion studies at the University of North Texas. He is author of *In Defense of the Land Ethic* (1989), *Earth's Insights* (1994), *Beyond the Land Ethic* (1999), and more than a hundred book chapters, journal articles, and book reviews in environmental philosophy. He is editor or coeditor of *Companion to "A Sand County Almanac"* (1987), *The River of the Mother of God and Other Essays by Aldo Leopold* (1991), *The Great New Wilderness Debate* (1998), and several other anthologies. In 1971, at the University of Wisconsin–Stevens Point, he designed and taught the first philosophy course in environmental ethics. He has served as president of the International Society of Environmental Ethics since 1997.

David Ehrenfeld is professor of biology at Rutgers University, where he teaches courses in ecology and conservation. He is the author of *The Arrogance of Humanism* (1981) and *Beginning Again: People and Nature in the New Millennium* (1993), and was the founding editor of the international journal *Conservation Biology*. He lectures widely and has written numerous articles for magazines and scientific publications.

Susan L. Flader is professor of United States western and environmental history at the University of Missouri–Columbia. In addition to her many articles, she has written or edited six books, including *Thinking Like a Mountain: Aldo Leopold and the Evolution of an Ecological Attitude Toward Deer, Wolves, and Forests* (1974; 1994), *The Great Lakes Forest: An Environmental and Social History* (1983), *The River of the Mother of God and Other Essays by Aldo Leopold* (1991), and *Exploring Missouri's Legacy: State Parks and Historic Sites* (1992). She has served as president of the American Society for Environmental History (1995–97) and the Missouri Parks Association (1982–86 and 1998–present), and as a director of the National Audubon Society, the American Forestry Association, and the Forest History Society.

Eric T. Freyfogle teaches property, natural resources, and environmental law at the University of Illinois College of Law, where he is the Max L. Rowe Professor. He is the author of *Justice and the Earth* (1993) and *Bounded People, Boundless Lands* (1998), as well as many scholarly and popular articles on property ownership and environmental policy. A native of central Illinois, he has long been active in many state and local environmental causes.

Wes Jackson is president of the Land Institute in Salina, Kansas. He served as professor of biology at Kansas Wesleyan University and later established the Environmental Studies Department at California State University, Sacramento. Jackson outlined the basis for agricultural research at the Land Institute in *New Roots for Agriculture* (1980). *Altars of Unhewn Stone* appeared in 1987 and *Meeting the Expectations of the Land,* edited with Wendell Berry and Bruce Colman, in 1984. *Becoming Native to This Place* (1994) sketches his vision for the resettlement of America's rural communities. His most recent work, *Rooted in the Land: Essays on Community and Place,* coedited with William Vitek, appeared in 1996. He is a recipient of the Pew Conservation Scholars award (1990) and a MacArthur Fellowship (1992).

Paul W. Johnson served from 1994 to 1997 as chief of the Natural Resources Conservation Service in the U.S. Department of Agriculture. As a representative in the Iowa General Assembly from 1984 to 1990, he was a major architect of the state's landmark Groundwater Protection Act and other legislation involving sustainable agriculture and the environment. He holds degrees in forestry from the University of Michigan, and has taught forestry in Ghana and worked with the USDA Forest Service in the Pacific Northwest. He served on the board on agriculture of the U.S. National Academy of Sciences from 1988 to 1994, contributing to major studies in forestry, agriculture, and conservation. After leaving the NRCS, Johnson returned to his family's farm in Iowa. In 1999 he was appointed director of Iowa's Department of Natural Resources.

Joni L. Kinsey is associate professor at the University of Iowa's School of Art and Art History with a specialty in American art. Among other topics, she has published on American architecture, women painters in the West, and polyptychs (multipaneled images) in American art. Her research has focused especially on landscape and regional issues within the visual culture of the United States, and she has written a number of articles and exhibition catalogue essays on these subjects. She is the author of *Thomas Moran: Surveying the American West* (1992) and *Plain Pictures: Images of the American Prairie* (1996).

Richard L. Knight is professor of wildlife conservation at Colorado State University. As a Ph.D. candidate at the University of Wisconsin–Madison, he conducted his dissertation research at the Leopold farm, where he lived in the Leopold "shack." He is on the board of governors of the Society for Conservation Biology and sits on the boards of the Center for the American West and the Natural Resources Law Center, both at the University of Colorado. He has coedited *A New Century for Natural Resources Management* (1995), *Wildlife and Recreationists* (1995), *Stewardship across Boundaries* (1998), and the forthcoming *Forest Fragmentation in the Southern Rocky Mountains*. With his wife he practices community-based conservation in the Livermore Valley, Colorado.

Gary K. Meffe is adjunct professor and conservation biologist in the Department of Wildlife Ecology and Conservation at the University of Florida. He has published more than seventy-five scientific papers on a wide variety of topics, including desert fishes of the Southwest and their conservation, fish community and evolutionary ecology, and the incorporation of conservation biology into land management. He is coeditor of *Ecology and Evolution of Livebearing Fishes* (1989), coauthor of *Biodiversity on Military Lands: A Handbook* (1996), and senior author of *Principles of Conservation Biology* (1994; 1997). He presently serves as editor of the journal *Conservation Biology*.

Curt Meine is a conservation biologist, writer, and historian based at the International Crane Foundation in Baraboo, Wisconsin. He has served as a consultant to many local, national, and international conservation agencies and organizations, lectured at universities throughout the United States, and taught at the University of Wisconsin–Madison. He is author of the biography *Aldo Leopold: His Life and Work* (1988), editor of the collection *Wallace Stegner and the Continental Vision: Essays on Literature, History, and Landscape* (1997), and has also contributed to a wide variety of journals and books. He serves on the editorial boards of *Conservation Biology* and *Environmental Ethics* and on the board of governors of the Society for Conservation Biology.

Gary Paul Nabhan has lived in and roamed the ancient cactus forests, mesquite grasslands, and hidden oases of the Sonoran Desert straddling the U.S.-Mexican border since 1975. Nabhan's original scholarship, based on more than two hundred articles he has authored or coauthored, integrates conservation biology, agroecology, ethnonutrition, and applied anthropology in unique ways. A cofounder of Native Seeds/SEARCH—a grassroots, multicultural conservation group—he now serves as Director of Conservation Biology at the Arizona–Sonora Desert Museum. He is a recipient of a MacArthur Fellowship, a Pew Scholarship on Conservation and the Environment, the Premio Gaia, and the John Burroughs Medal for natural history writing. His latest book, *Cultures of Habitat* (1997), features an essay on Leopold's views of culture and environmental health.

Richard Nelson is a cultural anthropologist who has authored *Hunters of the Northern Ice* (1969), *Hunters of the Northern Forest* (1973), *Shadow of the Hunter* (1980), *Make Prayers to the Raven* (1983), *The Island Within* (1989), and *Heart and Blood: Living with Deer in America* (1997). He is a recipient of the John Burroughs Medal for outstanding nature writing and has also received a Lannan Literary Award for nonfiction.

Bryan G. Norton writes on intergenerational equity, sustainability theory, biodiversity policy, and valuation methods. He is author of *Why Preserve Natural Variety?* (1987) and *Toward Unity among Environmentalists* (1991), editor of *The Preservation of Species* (1986), and coeditor of *Ecosystem Health: New Goals for Environmental Management* (1992) and *Ethics on the Ark* (1996). He has served on numerous advisory panels, including the Ecosystem Valuation Forum and the Risk Assessment Forum of the U.S. Environmental Protection Agency, and he was a charter member of the EPA's Environmental Economics Advisory Committee. He teaches at the Georgia Institute of Technology in Atlanta, Georgia.

David W. Orr is professor and chair of the Environmental Studies Program at Oberlin College. He is widely recognized for his pioneering work on environmental education, ecological literacy, and campus ecology. His awards include a National Conservation Achievement Award from the National Wildlife Federation in 1993, the Lyndhurst Prize in 1992, the Benton Box Award from Clemson University for his work in environmental education, and an Honorary Doctorate in Humane Letters from Arkansas College. He is author of *Ecological Literacy* (1992), *Earth in Mind* (1994), and more than ninety published articles. He is also coeditor of *The Global Predicament* (1979) and *The Campus and Environmental Responsibility* (1992). Orr serves as the education editor for *Conservation Biology* and as a member of the editorial advisory board of *Orion Nature Quarterly*.

Edwin P. (Phil) Pister retired in 1990 following thirty-eight years as a fishery biologist with the California Department of Fish and Game. He studied wildlife conservation and zoology under A. Starker Leopold at the University of California–Berkeley and spent his career supervising aquatic management and research within a ten-million-acre area encompassing approximately a thousand waters of the eastern Sierra–desert regions of California. He founded and serves as executive secretary of the Desert Fishes Council and is involved in desert ecosystem preservation throughout the American Southwest and adjoining areas of Mexico. He has served on the board of governors of the American Society of Ichthyologists and Herpetologists and the Society for Conservation Biology. He has lectured at more than seventy universities in North America and the United Kingdom and has authored more than seventy papers and book chapters.

Donald Snow is executive director of Northern Lights Research and Education Institute in Missoula, Montana. Under his leadership since 1984, Northern Lights has become a regional center for policy research and practice in the arena of alternative environmental dispute resolution and the use of collaborative processes to help citizens reach agreements in natural resource issues. Snow's essays, addresses, and poems have been widely published. In collaboration with other authors and editors he has produced four books, including *Northern Lights: A Selection of New Writing from the American West* (1994) and *The Next West: Public Lands, Community and Economy in the American West* (1997). His forthcoming book *The Book of the Tongass* is a compilation of essays and Native stories about Alaska's Tongass National Forest.

Stanley A. Temple is the Beers–Bascom Professor in Conservation in the Department of Wildlife Ecology at the University of Wisconsin–Madison. There he keeps Aldo Leopold's academic legacy alive by teaching the courses in wildlife ecology and management initiated by Leopold more than sixty years ago. His many contributions to conservation include service as president of the Society for Conservation Biology and chairman of the Wisconsin chapter of the Nature Conservancy. He and his students have worked on wildlife conservation problems around the world, with a focus on endangered species and biodiversity issues. Following Leopold's lead, he is restoring the "integrity, stability, and beauty of the biotic community" on the retired farm where he lives.

Jack Ward Thomas is the Boone and Crockett Professor of Wildlife Conservation, School of Forestry, the University of Montana, and Chief Emeritus, U.S. Forest Service. Thomas began his career as a wildlife researcher with the Texas Game and Fish Commission, joined the Forest Service in 1966, and held a variety of positions in wildlife biology research. In 1974 he led research at the Blue Mountains Research Lab in La Grande, Oregon, where he became well known for studies of elk and the spotted owl. In 1993 he was named to head the Forest Service Ecosystem Management Assessment Team, in response to President Clinton's Forest Conference in Portland, Oregon. He served as Chief of the USDA Forest Service from 1993 to 1996. He has published extensively in the fields of forestry, range management, philosophy, wildlife ecology, planning, and natural resources management.

Charles Wilkinson is the Moses Lasky Professor of Law and Distinguished Professor at the University of Colorado, Boulder. He is author or coauthor of eleven books on law, history, and society in the American West, including *Crossing the Next Meridian* (1992), *The Eagle Bird* (1992), and *Fire on the Plateau* (1999). A recipient of the National Wildlife Federation's National Conservation Award, he also serves on the Governing Council of the Wilderness Society.

Terry Tempest Williams was born in 1955 and grew up within sight of the Great Salt Lake. She is the author of several books, including *Pieces of White Shell: A Journey to Navajoland* (1984), *Coyote's Canyon* (1989), *Refuge: An Unnatural History of Family and Place* (1991), *An Unspoken Hunger: Stories from the Field* (1994), and *Desert Quartet: An Erotic Landscape* (1995). Collaborations include *Great and Peculiar Beauty: A Utah Reader* (1995), coedited with Thomas J. Lyon (1995); *Testimony: Writers of the West Speak on Behalf of Utah Wilderness* (1996), coedited with Stephen Trimble; and the anthology *New Genesis: A Mormon Reader on Land and Community* (1998), coedited with William B. Smith and Gibbs B. Smith. She has served as naturalist-in-residence at the Utah Museum of Natural History and is currently the Shirley Sutton Thomas Visiting Professor of English at the University of Utah. She has received a Lannan Literary Fellowship in creative nonfiction, along with a Guggenheim Fellowship. She lives with her husband, Brooke, in southern Utah.

Donald Worster grew up in Kansas and studied at the University of Kansas and Yale University. He is presently the Hall Distinguished Professor of American History at the University of Kansas. His primary interests are environmental history and the history of the American West, with secondary interests in agriculture and rural life. His books include *Nature's Economy: A History of Ecological Ideas* (1977, 1994) and *Rivers of Empire: Water, Aridity, and the Growth of the American West* (1992). He is currently working on a study of John Wesley Powell.

Joy B. Zedler is the first Aldo Leopold Professor of Restoration Ecology at the University of Wisconsin–Madison Arboretum and Botany Department. Zedler's research interests include restoration and wetland ecology, invasive plants, adaptive management, the role of biodiversity in ecosystem function, and the use of mesocosms in experimentation. She helps edit three peer-reviewed journals (*Wetlands Ecology and Management, Ecological Engineering,* and *Ecosystems*) and is a recipient of the National Wetlands Award for Science Research (Environmental Law Institute and Environmental Protection Agency). She is a member of the Nature Conservancy Governing Board; the Environmental Defense Fund Board of Trustees, Wisconsin Natural Areas Preservation Council, and several professional societies (including the Ecological Society of America, the American Society of Limnology and Oceanography, and the Society for Ecological Restoration). As director of research for the Arboretum, she is developing a Center for Restoration Ecology that seeks to improve restoration effectiveness nationwide.